Yearbook of International Humanitarian Law

Volume 18

More information about this series at http://www.springer.com/series/8912

Terry D. Gill
Editor-in-Chief

Yearbook of International Humanitarian Law Volume 18, 2015

ASSER PRESS

Springer

Editor-in-Chief
Terry D. Gill
University of Amsterdam and
Netherlands Defence Academy
Amsterdam/Breda
The Netherlands

Cover picture: Musa, a 25-year-old Kurdish marksman, stands atop a building as he looks at the destroyed Syrian town of Kobane on the Turkish frontier on 30 January 2015, after Kurdish forces recaptured the town from the jihadists on 26 January of that year.
Photo: Bulent Kilic. Reproduced with permission: www.anpfoto.nl Collection AFP

ISSN 1389-1359 ISSN 1574-096X (electronic)
Yearbook of International Humanitarian Law
ISBN 978-94-6265-140-1 ISBN 978-94-6265-141-8 (eBook)
DOI 10.1007/978-94-6265-141-8

Library of Congress Control Number: 2015950975

Published by T.M.C. ASSER PRESS, The Hague, The Netherlands www.asserpress.nl
Produced and distributed for T.M.C. ASSER PRESS by Springer-Verlag Berlin Heidelberg

Printed on acid-free paper

This Springer imprint is published by Springer Nature
The registered company is Springer-Verlag GmbH Berlin Heidelberg

Contents

In order to make the *Correspondents' Reports* immediately and widely available, they can be accessed online at

www.asser.nl/YIHL/correspondentsreports.

This has the added benefit of the reports being fully searchable, thereby better serving the needs of scholars and practitioners.

Part I
Contemporary Armed Conflicts and Their Implications for International Humanitarian Law

Chapter 1
Government Recognition and International Humanitarian Law Applicability in Post-Gaddafi Libya

Jose Serralvo

Abstract This article explores the relationship between the issue of government recognition and the applicability of international humanitarian law. Using the existence of competing governments in post-Gaddafi Libya as a case study, the article re-examines the meaning of the term "government" under public international law and proposes a distinct reading of what it means to be an effective government. It then considers how effectiveness can be used to differentiate between a *de jure* and a *de facto* government, and the international legal obligations of these two types of entities. Finally, the article applies this framework to the realm of the laws of war. In particular, it analyses how the existence of competing governments affects the scope of application of Additional Protocol II to the Geneva Conventions and the possible existence of an international armed conflict.

Keywords Government recognition · *De facto* government · *De jure* government · Effectiveness · Legitimacy · International humanitarian law · Scope of application · Additional Protocol II to the Geneva Conventions · Third state intervention · Government consent · International armed conflict

Contents

The views expressed in this article reflect the author's opinions only.

J. Serralvo (✉)
Visiting Practitioner, Columbia University's Human Rights Institute, New York, USA
e-mail: jose.serralvo@gmail.com

T.D. Gill et al. (eds.), *Yearbook of International Humanitarian Law 2015*,
Yearbook of International Humanitarian Law 18,
DOI 10.1007/978-94-6265-141-8_1

"La république française ne veut point être reconnue;
elle est en Europe ce que le soleil est sur l'horizon:
tant pis pour qui ne veut pas la voir et ne veut pas en profiter".
Napoléon Bonaparte[1]

"What does recognition mean?
One can recognize a man as an emperor or as a grocer.
Recognition is meaningless without a defining formula".
Winston Churchill[2]

1.1 Introduction: The Deceitful Death of Recognition

For over half a century, ever since Lauterpacht and Chen published their seminal monographs on recognition under international law,[3] scholars have paid little consistent attention to this issue, "with more recent work tending merely to integrate some more contemporary examples into old conceptual frameworks".[4] This trend arguably reached its peak in the late 1980s, when a renowned publicist solemnly declared "the death of recognition".[5] According to Henkin, the figure had "created havoc in the world of fact" and—although lingering in diplomatic jargon—it did not "belong in the language of law".[6] In his view, long academic debates on who could be recognized, and by whom, and as what, made little or no sense. The argument was simple: "An entity that is in fact a State is a State"[7]; "A *régime* that governs in fact is a Government and must be treated as such".[8]

---

[1] "The French Republic no more needs recognition in Europe than the sun requires to be recognized in the horizon: too bad for those who do not want to see it and do not want to take advantage of it". Thibaudeau 1828, p. 291.

[2] Kimball 1987, p. 334.

[3] Lauterpacht 1947; Chen 1951.

[4] Roth 2001, p. 121.

[5] Henkin 1990, p. 30.

[6] Ibid., pp. 30–31.

[7] Ibid., p. 31.

[8] Ibid., p. 32.

And if recognition of States was an expendable corpse, recognition of governments was little more than an irritating phantom. In the second half of the twentieth century, with a view to avoiding this cumbersome *ignis fatuus*, more and more States kept pledging that they would stop recognizing governments as part of their foreign policy.[9] For instance, in April 1980, the British government made the following announcement to the House of Lords:

> […] we have decided that we shall no longer accord recognition to Governments. We have […] concluded that there are practical advantages in following the policy of many other countries in not according recognition to Governments.[10]

The USA, France or Australia was just some of the dozens of countries that decided to go down the same road.[11] In fact, the approach kept gaining momentum in the following couple of decades, to the point of prompting the European Union to make a similar declaration in 1999:

> The Union recalls that it does not recognise governments, and even less political personalities, but States, according to the most common international practice.[12]

The main reason for this policy was always straightforward. The public has generally seen recognition of a particular government as a synonym for approval of the entity in question. Every time a change of *régime* came about after a bloody insurgence or had a doubtful human rights record, the recognizing government inevitably saw itself in an embarrassing situation.[13] Needless to say, States also saw a policy of non-recognition of governments as a cautious way to avoid hasty decisions and the risk of positioning themselves on the side of the wrong contender.

Despite its much-anticipated advantages, the policy was never implemented. Talmon has convincingly demonstrated that all this rhetoric "signifie[d] only a change in the method of according recognition, not the abolition of the recognition as such".[14] States adopting this view simply resorted, as a rule, to the so-called implicit recognition of the new authorities in power, i.e. they started dealing with such authorities as though they were indeed the government.

The alleged (and deceitful) death of recognition—and all the gibberish surrounding it—has resulted in at least two major conundrums. First, nobody seems

---

[9] Talmon 1998, pp. 3–6; Doswald-Beck 1984, p. 371: "it is no longer the habit of States to officially recognize governments".

[10] Cited in Warbrick 1981, pp. 574–575.

[11] Charlesworth 1991; Galloway 1978, pp. 124–125. Galloway (rightly) concludes that the US policy on abandoning recognition has been only partially respected: "In cases in which the United States does not perceive major policy interests at stake, it will […] deemphasize the entire recognition process. In the few instances in which the United States perceived major political interests at issue, the United States has shown a tendency to revive the use of recognition to pursue policy goals".

[12] European Commission 1999, p. 60.

[13] Shaw 2014, p. 331.

[14] Talmon 1998, p. 3.

to be paying attention to the fact that the very same States who (voluntarily) pledged to stop recognizing governments have kept doing it not only implicitly, as shown by Talmon, but also *explicitly*. To give one recent example, in March 2016, the Ministers of Foreign Affairs of France, Germany, Italy, UK and USA and the High Representative of the European Union for Foreign Affairs and Security Policy "express[ed their] full support to [Libya's] Government of National Accord" and recognized it "as the sole legitimate government in Libya".[15]

Second, and more importantly, the meaningful influence of recognition upon certain branches of international law, and above all upon international humanitarian law (IHL), has gone largely unnoticed. This is both surprising and incomprehensible. Difficulties in the domain of government recognition usually arise either during or in the immediate aftermath of an armed conflict—a domain mostly governed by IHL.[16] It is therefore difficult to understand why so little has been written on the way in which recognizing a particular government (or not), as well as the mere existence of competing claims to represent the State, may affect the scope of application of the laws of war. Arguably, this gap is partly due to the failure of IHL scholars to address international law as a coherent and holistic corpus—or to the failure of publicists to see IHL beyond a final, self-reliant chapter at the end of their manuals. In reality, since IHL is but a branch of international law, clearly defining pivotal concepts, such as what it means to be a government, should be a precondition for conducting an accurate IHL analysis. The situation in post-Gaddafi Libya is just one among many recent examples in which this type of cross-fertilization is needed.

The purpose of this article is to shed some light on the question of how—in view of the existence of competing governments claiming to represent the State—certain IHL rules apply to the different armed conflicts in Libya. In particular, it aims at clarifying whether any of the non-international armed conflicts in Libya is governed by Additional Protocol II to the Geneva Conventions[17] and whether any of the multiple instances of foreign intervention in the country, e.g. by Egypt or the USA, amounts to an international armed conflict. Before that, Sect. 1.2 will present an overview of the current factual situation in Libya. It will provide some key information to understand the fracture between its two main governments: the House of Representatives and the General National Council. In addition, the role of two other key actors, the Government of National Accord—the *third* entity

[15] Ministers of Foreign Affairs of France, Germany, UK, Italy, USA and EU 2016.

[16] Although other branches of international law also apply in armed conflict, IHL is considered *lex specialis*. See ICJ, *Legal Consequences of the Construction of a Wall in the Occupied Palestinian Territory*, Advisory Opinion, 9 July 2004, (2004) ICJ Rep 136, para 106.

[17] As it will be shown later, the Protocol Additional to the Geneva Conventions of 12 August 1949, and relating to the Protection of Victims of Non-International Armed Conflicts, opened for signature 8 June 1977, 1125 UNTS 609 (entered into force 7 December 1978) (Additional Protocol II) only applies when governmental armed forces fight with an organized armed group. Hence, elucidating who is the government becomes a question of paramount importance.

currently claiming to represent the State of Libya—and the Islamic State Group, will be briefly outlined. Section 1.3 will focus on the meaning of the word "government", as well as on the main criterion to understand who the government of a State is at a given moment, namely the level of effectiveness of the body in question. Although effectiveness is also the cornerstone of one of the many doctrines on recognition, it is submitted that seeing effectiveness as the main constitutive element of a government—and not just as one among many doctrines on recognition—will contribute to clarify the current situation in Libya. Then, Sect. 1.4 will address the main aspects of recognition under public international law, including its legal implications and the difference between *de jure* and *de facto* government recognition. In this sense, the article will put forward an innovative approach that should help IHL practitioners and scholars when it comes to dealing with the existence of competing governments. Finally, the last part of this study will analyse the issue of IHL applicability to the clashes taking place in Libya, paying particular attention to the two questions mentioned above: the scope of application of Additional Protocol II and the possibility to trigger an international armed conflict through foreign involvement.

1.2 A Tale of Two (or Three) Governments

1.2.1 House of Representatives v. General National Congress

Since the death of Colonel Gaddafi in August 2011, Libya's instability has been increasing steadily. The proliferation of a myriad of militias, with either conflicting or overlapping agendas, has often been paraded as both cause and consequence of the absence of a central authority in the country.[18] Be it as it may, the truth is that lack of a strong political and security environment led not only to successive failures in all transitional governance arrangements, but also to a multilayered armed confrontation.[19] Clashes reached a new peak in May 2014, when General Haftar's self-proclaimed Libyan National Army launched Operation Dignity, a military campaign against Islamist militias in Benghazi.[20] According to Haftar, his objective was to "eliminate extremist terrorist groups".[21] However, and although a

---

[18] UN High Commissioner for Refugees (2015) Position on Returns to Libya: Update I. http://www.refworld.org/docid/561cd8804.html. Accessed 21 March 2016, paras 2–3.

[19] Ibid.

[20] El Gomati A (2016) Khalifa Haftar: Fighting terrorism or pursuing political power? http://www.aljazeera.com/indepth/opinion/2014/06/khalifa-hifter-operation-dignity-20146108259233889.html. Accessed 21 March 2016.

[21] Anderson J (2015) The Unravelling. http://www.newyorker.com/magazine/2015/02/23/unravelling. Accessed 21 March 2016.

detailed account of all the motives underlying today's violence in Libya goes well beyond the scope of this article, it should be noted that the reasons are much more complex than the Islamist *v.* Anti-Islamist oversimplified dichotomy offered by the media. General Haftar's coalition includes, *inter alia*, ex-Gaddafi officials that participated in the 2011 uprising but mistrust the revolutionary leadership and Gaddafi loyalists who blame Islamist groups for the rampant disorder and bad governance.[22] Their main common feature is not so much their Anti-Islamism, but rather their strong opposition to the marginalization of civil servants from the former *régime*, as proposed by the Political Isolation Law.[23] On the other hand, the Islamist faction—which includes the Muslim Brothers and the Salafis—also comprises entrepreneurs and other minority groups. This bloc has two unifying threads: the fact of having fought together in 2011 and their desire to transform the State inherited from Gaddafi.[24] Only some of the groups within the Islamist faction actively advocate for the imposition of Islamic law across Libya—among them is Ansar-al Sharia.

In June 2014, legislative elections led to the creation of a new parliament in Libya, the House of Representatives (HoR), which was set to replace the previous General National Congress (GNC). Nationalist and liberal factions won the majority of seats, while the Islamist groups were reduced to approximately 30 seats (out of a total of 200).[25] However, only 18% of the electorate turned out to the polls.[26] This result fuelled on-going clashes between Islamist groups and the so-called pro-secular militias. Prime Minister al-Thani and his cabinet moved to Tobruk in August 2014, after Islamist militias took control of Tripoli.[27] Despite the turmoil, the HoR, i.e. the new parliament, was inaugurated that very same month in Tobruk. Together, the HoR and the cabinet of Prime Minister al-Thani constitute the bulk of the eastern (or Tobruk-based) government. From mid-2014 until late 2015, al-Thani's administration was often referred to as "the internationally recognized government". Indeed, at least for a (hard to circumscribe) period of time, it enjoyed recognition by a majority of States, including the USA, most European countries and the members of the Organization of Petroleum Exporting Countries (OPEC).[28] It was also the entity representing Libya at the United Nations (UN).

---

22 International Crisis Group 2016, pp. 7–8.

23 Ibid.

24 Ibid.

25 Xinhua (2014) Libya publishes parliamentary election results. http://www.turkishweekly.net/news/169449/-libya-publishes-parliamentary-election-results.html. Accessed 21 March 2016.

26 Al-Jazeera (2014) Libyans mourn rights activists amid turmoil. http://www.aljazeera.com/news/middleeast/2014/06/libyans-mourn-rights-activist amid-turmoil-201462616143674 0827.html. Accessed 21 March 2016.

27 Jackson L (2014) Sudanese minister meets rival Libyan factions in mediation bid. http://www.reuters.com/article/2014/11/10/us-libya-security-sudan-idUSKCN0IU1I820141110. Accessed 21 March 2016.

28 Fox S (2014) OPEC picks a side in Libya's Battle of the Governments. http://www.middleeasteye.net/news/opec-picks-side-libya-s-battle-governments-1012742004. Accessed 21 March 2016.

Since October 2014, General Haftar, as well as the like-minded Zintani Brigades (operating in the West of the country), began referring to themselves as Libya's official army.[29] In January 2015, the Tobruk-based government publicly recalled General Haftar for army duty, thus recognizing his "Libyan National Army" as the official armed forces of Libya.[30] However, some analysts continued to see Haftar's forces as just "another militia, rather than the official security forces loyal to the State".[31]

Dismissing the results of the June 2014 elections, a coalition of Islamist militias, dominated by the Misrati Brigades and regrouped under the name of Libya Dawn, launched a successful attack against Tripoli. Political figures linked to the Misrati Brigades reconvened the GNC, the predecessor to the HoR, which appointed Omar al-Hassi as Prime Minister of a new government, based in Tripoli.[32] Turkey, Qatar and Sudan recognized al-Hassi's government as the legitimate representative of the State of Libya.[33] At least four other countries, namely Jordan, Kuwait, Belarus and Serbia, also expressed at some point their support for the GNC.[34] During the period examined in this article, i.e. June 2014 to March 2016, neither of the two governments exercised effective control over the whole of the territory. That said, some analysts seem to believe that "the theoretically 'illegitimate' government of the GNC control[led] far more territory, money and arms than its partially 'legitimate' opponents in the HoR".[35]

---

[29] Pack J (2014) Situation Report: Libya. http://tonyblairfaithfoundation.org/religion-geopolitics/country-profiles/libya/situation-report. Accessed 21 March 2016.

[30] Laessing U (2015) Libya recalls former general Haftar for army duty. http://www.reuters.com/article/2015/01/19/us-libya-security-idUSKBN0KS1SH20150119. Accessed 21 March 2016. The government of Tobruk went a step further in its endorsement when it officially named General Haftar head of the Libyan army: BBC News (2015) Libya names anti-Islamist General Haftar as army chief. http://www.bbc.com/news/world-africa-31698755. Accessed 21 March 2016.

[31] Oxford Analytica Daily Brief (2015) Libya beheadings strengthen anti-Islamist agenda. https://dailybrief.oxan.com/Analysis/DB197699/Libya-beheadings-strengthen-anti-Islamist-agenda. Accessed 21 March 2016.

[32] The Economist (2015) Libya's civil war: That it should come to this. http://www.economist.com/news/briefing/21638123-four-year-descent-arab-spring-factional-chaos-it-should-come. Accessed 21 March 2016. In March 2015, Khalifa al-Ghawi replaced al-Hassi as acting Prime Minister of the GNC.

[33] The Economist (2015) Libya: The next failed State. http://www.economist.com/news/leaders/21638122-another-font-global-mayhem-emergingnot-helped-regional-meddling-and-western. Accessed 21 March 2016.

[34] Middle East Eye (2014) Libya recalls 7 ambassadors for recognizing Islamist government. http://www.middleeasteye.net/news/libya-recalls-7-ambassadors-recognising-islamist-government-1969719678#sthash.3zIOmpNC.dpuf. Accessed 21 March 2016.

[35] Pack, above n 29. Nevertheless, at least some of the abundant cartography that has proliferated to try to circumscribe the areas of influence of each of the two governments has given the upper hand to the Tobruk administration. See, e.g., BBC News (2015) Libya urges UN to lift arms embargo to tackle IS. http://www.bbc.com/news/world-middle-east-31523944. Accessed 21 March 2016.

To complicate matters even further, the Supreme Court ruled in November 2014 that an amendment made in March 2014 to Libya's transitional constitution was illegal. The amendment had paved the way for the June 2014 elections, which were consequently declared void by the Supreme Court.[36] In other words, the Supreme Court, located in Tripoli, stripped the Tobruk-based HoR of its main claim to constitutional legitimacy.

The internal political outlook has also been encumbered by foreign involvement in the country. Egypt and the United Arab Emirates reportedly launched air strikes against weapon depots in Tripoli in August 2014.[37] Moreover, Egypt's air force attacked Islamist positions in Benghazi in October 2014.[38] None of those attacks were openly admitted by either of the involved authorities. Nonetheless, in February 2015, after the Islamic State Group (ISG) beheaded 21 Egyptian Coptic Christians, Egypt publicly acknowledged that it had launched air strikes against this group both in Derna and in Sirte. Egyptian warplanes hit ISG's training bases and weapons stockpiles, killing over 60 ISG fighters.[39] Although the Tobruk-based government gave its consent to this foreign intervention, the Tripoli-based GNC "strongly condemn[ed] the Egyptian aggression", considering it "an assault against Libyan sovereignty".[40] The USA has also launched a series of air strikes inside Libya, including one against an Al-Qaeda-affiliated target in June 2015[41] and at least two against the ISG (one in November 2015 and one in February 2016).[42]

And just when it seemed that things could not get more convoluted, a new actor emerged and an old one started gaining importance.

---

[36] The Guardian (2015) Libya Supreme Court rules anti-Islamist parliament unlawful. http://www.theguardian.com/world/2014/nov/06/libya-court-tripoli-rules-anti-islamist-parliament-unlawful. Accessed 21 March 2016.

[37] Pack, above n 29.

[38] Ibid.

[39] Malsin J and Stephen C (2015) Egyptian Air strikes in Libya Kill Dozens of Isis militants. http://www.theguardian.com/world/2015/feb/16/egypt-air-strikes-target-isis-weapons-stockpiles-libya. Accessed 21 March 2016.

[40] LBC Group (2015) Tripoli-based parliament says Egyptian strike assault on sovereignty. http://www.lbcgroup.tv/news/201401/libyan-air-force-commander-says-at-least-40-milita. Accessed 21 March 2016.

[41] Schmitt E (2015) U.S. Airstrike in Libya Targets Planner of 2013 Algeria Attack. http://www.nytimes.com/2015/06/15/world/middleeast/us-airstrike-targets-qaeda-operative-in-libya.html?_r=0. Accessed 21 March 2016.

[42] Stewart P (2015) U.S. Wage Air Strike on Islamic State Leader in Libya. http://www.reuters.com/article/us-usa-libya-strike-idUSKCN0T315920151114. Accessed 21 March 2016; Raghavan S, Ryan M and Murphy B (2016) U.S. Strike on Libya Camp Escalates Campaign Against Islamic State. https://www.washingtonpost.com/world/reports-airstrikes-target-suspected-islamic-state-base-in-libya/2016/02/19/e622c12a-d6f7-11e5-be55-2cc3c1e4b76b_story.html. Accessed 21 March 2016.

1.2.2 *Government of National Unity and the Rise of the Islamic State Group*

In November 2014, the black flags of the ISG started waving over public buildings in the Libyan city of Derna—barely 160 kilometres away from Tobruk. At that time, it was estimated that the group had approximately 800 fighters in Libya.[43] Many of them had arrived directly from Syria and Iraq, but the majority belonged to former jihadist networks that were present in the area and had decided to pledge allegiance to the ISG.[44] Since then, the group has made steady gains in the country. At the time of writing, in March 2016, it is believed to be in control of a stretch of territory to the east of Sirte of more than 250 kilometres and to possess training camps, storage areas, fortifications and operational cells all around the country, including in its two largest cities—Tripoli and Benghazi.[45] Moreover, the ISG now commands an estimated 5000 fighters[46] and has launched hit-and-run operations against forces and infrastructure associated with both the HoR and the GNC governments—including some of Libya's major oil ports.[47]

The threat of the ISG, in turn, led Western leaders and the United Nations Support Mission in Libya (UNSMIL) to push ardently for the creation of a government of national unity reassembling the executives of Tripoli and Tobruk.[48] A political solution to the governance crisis seemed suddenly as the only viable alternative to put an end to the resolute expansion of the ISG. This logic was based on a two-prong assumption. First, a unified government would be able to devote its military capabilities to fighting the jihadists, instead of focusing on fighting each other. Second, a unified government would also facilitate any future foreign intervention. Although—as mentioned above—some countries have already carried out air strikes inside the country, the European Union has repeatedly stated that it

---

[43] Cruickshank P, Robertson N, Lister L and Karadsheh J (2014) ISIS Comes to Libya. http://www.cnn.com/2014/11/18/world/isis-libya/. Accessed 21 March 2016.

[44] Ibid.; Banco E (2015) ISIS Establishes Stronghold in Derna. http://www.ibtimes.com/isis-establishes-stronghold-derna-libya-1721425. Accessed 21 March 2016.

[45] El Amrani I (2016) How Much of Libya Does the Islamic State Control? http://foreignpolicy.com/2016/02/18/how-much-of-libya-does-the-islamic-state-control/. Accessed 21 March 2016; UN Security Council (2016) Report of the Secretary-General on the United Nations Support Mission in Libya, UN Doc. S/2016/182, paras 24–29.

[46] The Economist (2016) The Next Front Against the Islamic State. http://www.economist.com/news/middle-east-and-africa/21690057-libyas-civil-war-has-given-caliphate-fresh-opportunities-western-military. Accessed 21 March 2016.

[47] Ibid. See also El Amrani, above n 45.

[48] BBC News (2015) Libya UN Envoy Leon Urges Unity Government Within Weeks. http://www.bbc.com/news/world-africa-33872355. Accessed 21 March 2016; Reuters (2015) France, Italy See Need to Stop Islamic State in Libya. http://www.reuters.com/article/us-libya-security-italy-france-idUSKBN0TF13820151126. Accessed 21 March 2016; Stephen C (2015) Western Leaders Urge Libyan Factions to Allow Bombing of ISIS Fighters. http://www.theguardian.com/world/2015/dec/19/libya-urged-unity-airstrikes-against-islamic-state-isis. Accessed 21 March 2016.

would not intervene on Libyan soil until it obtained the consent of a government of national unity.[49]

Against this backdrop, it is easy to understand why in September 2015, after more than a year of failed negotiations, the United Nations Security Council (UNSC) called for "the immediate formation of a Government of National Accord".[50] Three months later, on December 17, an agreement was signed in Morocco between "representatives" of the HoR and the GNC. The so-called Government of National Accord was formed as a result of this agreement. Nevertheless, both of the rival parliaments in Tripoli and Tobruk have subsequently rejected the outcome of the negotiations and "insisted that the signatories represented only themselves".[51] This did not prevent the UN from appointing a Presidential Council which took upon itself the task of naming a third government, led by Prime Minister Sarraj and based in Tunis.[52] Hence, Libya has now three governments: the Tobruk-based government linked to the HoR that came out of the June 2014 elections, the Tripoli-based government linked to the GNC that contested the June 2014 elections and the Tunis-based Government of National Accord that came out of a controversial deal brokered by the UN. Unlike the latter, both the HoR and the GNC control a substantive part of the national territory. They both have their own parliament, their own set of ministries and their own courts and exercise a certain degree of law enforcement within their respective spheres of influence. Not only is the Government of National Accord an ineffective entity in a foreign territory, but the latest developments seem to indicate that their ambitions to establish their headquarters in Tripoli will not be fulfilled anytime soon. Khalifa al-Ghawi, the new Prime Minister of the Tripoli-based government, has threatened to arrest the members of the Government of National Accord if they set foot in the Western part of the country.[53] And yet, despite having been born in exile and enjoying zero effectiveness at the domestic level, the European Union and the USA have opted for recognizing the Government of National Accord as the "sole legitimate government" of Libya.[54]

[49] Middle East Eye (2015) Western Nations Plot Fresh Military Intervention in Libya. http://www.middleeasteye.net/news/western-nations-plot-fresh-military-intervention-libya-say-military-sources-619439313#sthash.OAOIBMPG.dpuf. Accessed 21 March 2016; Zampano G (2016) Italy Wary of Libyan Intervention. http://www.wsj.com/articles/italy-wary-of-libyan-intervention-1457530385. Accessed 21 March 2016.

[50] UN Security Council (2015) Resolution 2238 (2015), UN Doc. S/RES/2238, para 2.

[51] The Economist, above n 46.

[52] Ibid.

[53] Ibid.

[54] Ministers of Foreign Affairs of France, Germany, United Kingdom, Italy, USA and EU 2016.

Interestingly, the UN not only pushed for the creation of the Government of National Accord, but it also backed its recognition in a rather unprecedented manner.[55] Needless to say, throughout the last few decades, the organization has endlessly striven to bring civil wars to an end by bolstering one of the contenders.[56] However, it is arguably the first time in which the UN has initially acknowledged the legitimacy of one of two parties to a dispute, in this case the Tobruk-based HoR,[57] it has then moved to "artificially impos[ing]"[58] the creation of a third party, i.e. the Government of National Accord, and has finally ended up disregarding the alleged legitimacy of the entity it had initially endorsed. A UNSC resolution approved on 23 December 2015 can be mentioned as an example of the latter. The resolution only uses the word "government" when referring to the Government of National Accord. The HoR, which until September 2015 had been considered the effective government of Libya by that same organ, was suddenly

[55] The UN has traditionally held the view that the organization itself "does not possess any authority to recognize either a new State or a new government of an existing State" and that "the linkage of representation in an international organization and recognition of a government is a confusion of two institutions which have superficial similarities but are essentially different", see UN Security Council (1950) Letter Dated 8 March 1950 from the Secretary-General to the President of the Security Council Transmitting a Memorandum on the Legal Aspects of the Problem of Representation in the United Nations, UN Doc. S/1466, pp. 2–3. There is no systematic study of the practice of the UN with regard to the recognition of governments. In fact, the only scholar who has conducted any in-depth research into the link between the UN and the notion of recognition decided to focus on recognition of States only, consciously avoiding the issue of recognition of governments (see Dugard 1987, pp. 2–6). Nevertheless, in the case of Libya, the UN has arguably gone beyond its usual policy and acted as assertively as—and in some cases even more assertively than—its Member States. Suffice to recall that the Special Representative of the Secretary-General and head of UNSMIL, Martin Kobler, has himself called "on the international community to work with the Government of National Accord as the sole legitimate authority and to support the GNA in assuming its responsibilities to exercise sole and effective oversight over Libyan financial institutions", see UN Support Mission in Libya (2016) Martin Kobler Welcomes Libyan Political Dialogue Statement: Libyans Eager to Have Strong Accord Government. https://unsmil.unmissions.org/Default.aspx?ctl=Details&tabid=3543&mid=6187&ItemID=2099517. Accessed 21 March 2016.

[56] For recent examples thereof, see the UNSC "support for the legitimacy of the President of Yemen, Abdo Rabbo Mansour Hadi"—UN Security Council (2015) Resolution 2216 (2015), UN Doc. S/RES/2216, Preamble; or its recognition of President Ouattara in Ivory Coast—UN Security Council (2011) Resolution 1975 (2011), UN Doc. S/RES/1975, para 1.

[57] See, e.g., UN Security Council (2015) Resolution 2213 (2015), UN Doc. S/RES/2213—apart from the explicit reference to the Tobruk-based HoR in the preamble, all calls to cooperate with the Libyan government univocally refer to the eastern administration in Tobruk.

[58] Pack J (2016) Forging a Libyan Anti-IS Coalition Should Trump a Unity Government. http://www.middleeasteye.net/columns/forging-libyan-anti-coalition-should-trump-unity-government-1330204379. Accessed 21 March 2016.

out of the picture and demoted to being a petty component of a generic "all parties in Libya".[59]

At the time of writing, it is simply impossible to foresee how the political (and military) situation will evolve. Whatever the future might bring, it will hardly leave external observers more bewildered than the current state of affairs. Plenty of questions surround the ill-matched triumvirate. Is Libya a three-government State with no effective representative? Or are all the three entities simultaneously representing the State? And who was in charge in 2015, before the creation of the Government of National Accord? To answer these questions, it is first necessary to delve into the ordinary and legal meanings of the word "government".

1.3 Effectiveness and the Question of Being (or not Being) a Government

Any attempt to define the notion of government would be incomplete if it did not start by setting it apart from the notion of State. According to the most widely accepted definition, a State is a person of international law which "possess[es] the following qualifications: (a) a permanent population; (b) a defined territory; (c) government; and (d) capacity to enter into relations with other States".[60] Thus, a government is a prerequisite for statehood.[61] In other words, a government is one of the constitutive elements of a State. But once a State is established, it continues to have international legal personality even if one of these elements, and in particular the existence of a government, is temporarily absent.[62] A civil war, a foreign occupation or a natural disaster might all disrupt the effectiveness of the government, but this does not by itself indicate the extinction of the State under international law. On the contrary, there is "a strong presumption"[63] that these changes do not put an end to statehood, not even when the country undergoes

---

[59] UN Security Council (2015) Resolution 2259 (2015), UN Doc. S/RES/2259, paras 5 and 18. It is true that in October 2015, the mandate of the HoR came to an end, see, e.g., Pack J and Klass B (2015) Talking With the Wrong Libyans. http://www.nytimes.com/2015/06/15/opinion/talking-with-the-wrong-libyans.html?_r=0. Accessed 21 March 2016. But in view of the fact that this mandate had been contested since the very beginning, not least of all by the Libyan Supreme Court, it is hard to believe that the October deadline had anything to do with this change of policy.

[60] Montevideo Convention on the Rights and Duties of States, opened for signature 26 December 1933, 164 LNTS 19 (entered into force 26 December 1934), Article 1.

[61] Crawford 2006, p. 33.

[62] Jennings and Watts 1992, pp. 122–123; Crawford 2006, p. 33; Evans 2010, p. 222; Brownlie 1999, p. 71.

[63] Crawford 2006, p. 33.

extended periods of internal turmoil, as it happened, for example, in Lebanon during the 1970s.[64] In the same vein, there have been certain cases in which a State has come into being despite the absence of a government *ab initio*. Both Crawford and Evans cite, by way of illustration, the case of the Democratic Republic of the Congo, which became an independent State in 1960 despite the absence of anything resembling an effective government.[65] When Belgium granted its independence to the former Belgian Congo (now known as the Democratic Republic of the Congo), the country was in turmoil and lacked an effective administration. However, the international community had no doubt as to its statehood. Crawford concludes therefrom that "the requirement of 'government' is less stringent than has been thought, at least in particular contexts".[66]

Scholars unanimously mention independence as another of the basic prerequisites of statehood. However, the way in which they incorporate the idea of independence varies in each case. Brownlie and Shaw portray independence as the essence of—or an equivalent to—being able to enter into relations with other States.[67] If a State really possesses the capacity to engage with other States, it is presumed to also have a sufficient level of independence to make its own decisions without unduly succumbing to external pressures. Oppenheim and Evans, on the other hand, see independence as an essential appendix to normal governmental attributes; a government is not really a government if it is not independent.[68] Both interpretations are analogous. In the first case, independence is seen as a hallmark of statehood and in the second one as one of the distinguishing marks of a government. What seems clear is that it is not enough that a government exists. It must also be able to exercise autonomous authority and make its own decisions without the interference of foreign actors.

The other key element of a government is its level of effectiveness. Being an "effective" entity is seen as a *condition sine qua non* to be considered the government of a State.[69] Although authors also differ on the exact meaning of effectiveness, it is generally believed that a government is effective when it enjoys the habitual obedience of the bulk of the population and is able to maintain law and order and establish basic institutions.[70] Paraphrasing Weber, some authors under-

[64] Evans 2010, p. 222.

[65] Ibid., pp. 221–222; Crawford 2006, pp. 56–57.

[66] Crawford 2006, p. 57.

[67] Brownlie 1999, pp. 71–72; Shaw 2014, p. 147.

[68] Jennings and Watts 1992, p. 122 (emphasis in the original): "be a *sovereign* government […] independence all around, within and without the borders of the country"; Evans 2010, p. 221: "independent government".

[69] Shaw 2014, pp. 328–332; Evans 2010, pp. 221–223; Brownlie 1999, pp. 90–91; Kaczorowska 2010, p. 222; Ferraro and Cameron 2016, para 234: "Under international law, the key condition for the existence of a government is its effectiveness".

[70] Jennings and Watts 1992, p. 150; Ferraro and Cameron 2016, para 234; Crawford 2006, p. 59; Lauterpacht 1970, p. 324. Lauterpacht adds that this obedience is "not necessarily willing".

stand effectiveness as having the "power to assert a monopoly over the exercise of legitimate physical violence within the territory".[71] The latter is obviously not strictly met in many situations, including in the event of an internal armed conflict, where at least one of the parties will be an organized armed group interfering with the State's monopoly on physical violence. International law does not establish specific requirements as to the nature and extent of governmental control over the territory.[72] As mentioned above, a government might remain a government even if it is unable to impose law and order in *certain* regions and—logically—even if it does not enjoy the habitual obedience of the *whole* of the population.

It is impossible to provide a closed list of archetypical governmental activities. As referred to by the International Law Commission, "what is regarded as 'governmental' depends on the particular society, its history and traditions".[73] That said, it is important to note that—even though some authors tend to overlook it—whatever the functions of a government, they cannot be circumscribed to the national territory. On the contrary, "[e]ffectiveness is the ability to exert State functions internally and externally, i.e. in relations with other States".[74] Keeping this in mind is of paramount importance in understanding the issue of government recognition. As a general rule, States participate in the benefits of international law through the medium of its government.[75] One could even say that a government is the main and "for most purposes the only" organ by which the State acts in international relations.[76] Representing the State outside its borders is thus a governmental function *par excellence*. It is possible to imagine a *Grundnorm* attributing the ordinary administration of the country to well-defined territorial entities. In such a State, the daily tasks of a central government might have little to do with ensuring law and order, or running basic institutions throughout the land, or asserting a monopoly over violence. And yet, the central government would always retain a major role—and often an exclusive one—in dealing with other States. Governmental effectiveness must always be seen from both an internal and an external perspective. These two aspects constitute the basic binomial of sovereignty. At the same time, the existence of external sovereignty presupposes—and is based upon—the presence of internal one. If a central government does not have

[71] Evans 2010, p. 221.

[72] Crawford 2006, p. 59.

[73] UN General Assembly (2001) Draft Articles on Responsibility of States for Internationally Wrongful Acts with Commentaries, UN Doc. A/56/10, p. 43.

[74] Ferraro and Cameron 2016, para 234. See also Quoc Dinh 2002, p. 416 (emphasis in the original): "Exigence de l'effectivité gouvernementale.—L'effectivité signifie ici la capacité réelle d'exercer toutes les fonctions étatiques, y compris le maintien de l'ordre et de la sécurité à l'intérieur, et l'exécution des engagements extérieurs".

[75] Lauterpacht 1970, p. 309.

[76] Crawford 2006, pp. 33 and 60.

any authority over the population it claims to represent, it cannot speak on behalf of the State in the international scene.[77]

In conclusion, a government is the representative of a State. It must be independent and effective. Effectiveness includes not only the possibility to operate inside the territory, but also the capacity to represent the State outside its own borders *vis-à-vis* other States. Unfortunately, things are not always that clear. Problems immediately arise when two or more entities claim to represent the same State, or when a partially ineffective entity claims to be a government. It is in this context that the notion of government recognition reveals all its significance.

1.4 Government Recognition in International Law

1.4.1 Recognition: Meaning, Nature and Theories

Recognition simply means the acceptance by the recognizing State of the existence of a particular entity or situation.[78] A State can recognize another State, or a government, or a belligerent, or an insurgent group.[79] In principle, a government should be recognized as the representative of a State when it is effective—in the way it has been described in the previous section. However, when it comes to the recognition of governments, the first thing to keep in mind is that it is often a conspicuously political act, based on political considerations.[80] Many States have not even pretended to hide the political nature of the act. When in 1948 Syria questioned the recognition of Israel by the USA, the US representative to the UN answered as follows:

> I should regard it as highly improper for me to admit that any country on earth can question the sovereignty of the United States of America in the exercise of that highly political act of recognition […] Moreover, I would not admit here, by implication or by direct

[77] Fauchille 1923, p. 225 (emphasis in the original): "L'autonomie ou souveraineté intérieure est la base, le support de la souveraineté extérieure. Le deuxième ne saurait exister sans le première […] L'une est la condition *sine qua non* de l'autre. Une association d'hommes qui ne jouerait pas dans son sein du pouvoir souverain, qui n'exercerait pas sur elle-même la souveraineté intérieure, l'*imperium* et la *jurisdictio*, manquerait de l'individualité nécessaire pour posséder et exercer la souveraineté extérieure".

[78] Shaw 2014, p. 329; Peterson 1997, p. 1.

[79] Peterson 1997, p. 1.

[80] Shaw 2014, p. 329: "Political considerations have usually played a large role in the decision whether or not to grant recognition"; Evans 2010, pp. 238–240; Verhoeven 1975, p. 65: "D'un examen sommaire de la pratique internationale, se dégagent d'emblée deux constatations élémentaires concernant les reconnaissances de gouvernement: d'abord qu'elles sont statistiquement les plus nombreuses, ensuite qu'elles sont *a priori* extrêmement politisées".

> answer, that there exists a tribunal of justice or of any other kind, anywhere, that can pass judgement upon the legality or the validity of that act of my country.[81]

The political nature of recognition might open the door to lack of transparency, uncertainty and arbitrariness. That is one of the reasons why scholars like Henkin have questioned the alleged legality of recognition and argued instead that if a *régime* actually governs, it must simply be treated as a government.[82] Authors have also held that States cannot claim "unlimited discretion" when it comes to making recognition decisions. If a government does not exercise effective control, the assumption goes, and recognition should not be granted.[83] But there are examples galore to the contrary.[84] One does not need to look back at the decade-long recognition of Chiang Kai-Shek's administration as the government of mainland China to understand that the effectiveness rule—i.e. granting recognition merely on the basis of effectiveness—is loaded with exceptions. The initial recognition of President Ouattara in Côte d'Ivoire in 2011, the continuous endorsement of President Hadi in Yemen in 2015 or the recent recognition of the Tunis-based Government of National Accord as the "legitimate government" of Libya in 2016 clearly demonstrate that the effectiveness criterion is not always heeded—and sometimes even glaringly disregarded. And whether one likes it or not, this seemingly discretionary act has substantive legal consequences. It affects, for instance, the diplomatic and consular status of the agents of the recognized government, its access to foreign courts, the possibility to benefit from existing treaty arrangements, the respect of immunities from foreign prosecution, the establishment of trade relations or the right to claim State funds on deposit in the recognizing State.[85]

The Libyan Investment Authority (LIA) provides a good example of the latter. With assets valued at an estimated $67 billion, the LIA was created in 2006 to manage the income from Libya's oil wealth.[86] In January 2014, the chairman of

---

[81] Cited in UN Security Council, above n 55, p. 3. The US refers here to the discretionary nature of the act of recognizing a State and not a government. Interestingly, although both acts are opened to a great margin of interpretation, scholars have usually considered that the recognition of States is subjected to more objective criteria—and it is hence less political—than the recognition of governments (see Shaw 2014, p. 328; Gamboa and Fernández 2006, p. 119): "Así como en el reconocimiento de los Estados nuevos la cuestión política tiene gran importancia y mueve esencialmente a los demás Estados que reconocen, en el reconocimiento de Gobiernos influye en mayor medida el interés político".

[82] Henkin 1990, pp. 31–33.

[83] Peterson 1997, p. 35.

[84] Note that the following examples refer to instances in which more or less ineffective entities have been recognized as the government of a State. This does not necessarily mean that they were the real government. As it will be reiterated later, being recognized as the government is not always a synonym for being the actual government.

[85] Menon 1990, p. 157.

[86] Delaney J (2016) Libya's Sovereign Fund May Hold Key to Country's Civil War. http://www.institutionalinvestor.com/article/3518495/investors-sovereign-wealth-funds/libyas-sovereign-fund-may-hold-key-to-countrys-civil-war.html. Accessed 21 March 2016.

this wealth fund filed a suit in the UK against Goldman Sachs and Société Générale, claiming that both banks were selling complex instruments that had resulted in the LIA losing billions of dollars.[87] In October 2014, the Tobruk-based HoR appointed a new chairman to preside over the fund. Throughout 2015, two different chairmen—one backed by the government of Tobruk and the other one backed by its rival in Tripoli—fought for control of the LIA. Finally, in March 2016, a justice at the High Court in London adjourned the question saying it would be "premature" for him to make a decision.[88] According to Justice William Blair, he received a letter from the British government claiming that it expected Libyan authorities to clarify the leadership of the fund in a matter of weeks.[89] Regardless of the final result of this case, it is interesting to note that the Foreign and Commonwealth Office claimed in its letter that it had not recognized either the government of Tobruk or that of Tripoli. Instead, British authorities claimed that its "highest priority" was to support the UN-backed Government of National Accord.[90] The lawyer of the chairman appointed by Tobruk, in turn, argued that "the unity government does not yet exist and so the Tobruk government is the rightful government for now". Without entering (yet) into the details of who is the effective government, it is important to emphasize at this stage that even if/when recognition is primarily based on political considerations, it can—and does—give rise to concrete legal consequences.

However, the fact that the discretionary act of recognition triggers a series of legal consequences does not necessarily mean that the whole fate of the government in question is subjected to the whim of a third State. The nature of recognition is key in understanding this. Indeed, it is the nature of recognition that will allow us to propose a basic theory thereof—one that will hopefully elude the obscurity of most of the existing doctrines.[91]

---

[87] Ibid.

[88] Clark S and Coker M (2016) U.K. Judge Adjourns Tug-of-War Case Over Libyan Sovereign Wealth Fund. http://www.wsj.com/articles/u-k-judge-adjourns-tug-of-war-case-over-libyan-sovereign-wealth-fund-1457366498. Accessed 21 March 2016.

[89] Ibid.

[90] Ibid.

[91] Brownlie 1986, pp. 627–628: "In the case of 'recognition', theory has not only failed to enhance the subject but has created a *tertium quid* which stands, like a bank of fog on a still day, between the observer and the contours of the ground which calls for investigation. With rare exceptions, the theories on recognition have not only failed to improve the quality of thought but have deflected lawyers from the application of ordinary methods of legal analysis"; Verhoeven 1975, p. 65: "[I]l n'empêche que la fréquence et la politisation des reconnaissances de gouvernement ont alimenté les incessantes controverses doctrinales qui se nourrissent de leurs ambiguïtés". This author agrees with the previous statements. It is submitted that if we focus on the different theories of recognition, we will not be able to see the forest for the trees. As it can be deduced from Sect. 1.3 and as will be further clarified later on, this article simply adheres to the doctrine of effectiveness. For an analysis of the main doctrines, from Tobar to Estrada, from effectiveness to legitimism, from the new democratic legitimism to *de factoism*, see, e.g., Menon 1990, pp. 164–176; Roth 2001, pp. 124–199; Peterson 1997, pp. 51–85.

Scholars have discussed in length whether recognition is constitutive or declaratory. The constitutive theory dates back to Hegel. Its proponents argue that it is the act of recognition by other States that actually creates a new State or a new government.[92] According to this theory, a new government would not become a new government once it is effective, but rather when others consider that it is effective and decide to endorse it.[93] The declaratory view, on the other hand, holds that States and governments exist as soon as they become a reality, i.e. as soon as they fulfil the conditions of statehood or become an effective government.[94] Both theories are partially true—and partially false. Shaw best summarizes this in his analysis of the *Tinoco* arbitration case:

> [W]here the degree of authority asserted by the new administration is uncertain, recognition by other States will be a vital factor. But where the new government is firmly established, non-recognition will not affect the legal character of the new government [...] Taft's view of the nature of recognition is an interesting amalgam of the declaratory and constitutive theories, in that recognition can become constitutive where the factual conditions (i.e. the presence or absence of effective control) are in dispute, but otherwise is purely declaratory or evidential.[95]

Neither Shaw nor the arbitrator of the *Tinoco* case seems to provide a straightforward legal explanation for the "amalgam of the declaratory and constitutive theories". The author of this article would like to put forth a simple argument in favour of this mixed theory. Under international law, a government becomes a government once it is effective[96]—all other theories of recognition do not seem to

[92] Lauterpacht 1947, pp. 38–41.

[93] Ibid. See also Shaw 2014, pp. 322–333.

[94] As mentioned in the introduction and earlier in this section, Louis Henkin is one of the supporters of this theory (see Henkin 1990, pp. 31–32).

[95] Shaw 2014, pp. 329–330. See also UN 2006, p. 381: "The non-recognition by other nations of a government claiming to be a national personality, is usually appropriate evidence that it has not attained the independence and control entitling it by international law to be classed as such. But when recognition *vel non* of a government is by such nations determined by inquiry, not into its *de facto* sovereignty and complete governmental control, but into its illegitimacy or irregularity of origin, their non-recognition loses something of evidential weight on the issue with which those applying the rules of international law are alone concerned [...] Such non-recognition for any reason, however, cannot outweigh the evidence disclosed by this record before me as to the *de facto* character of Tinoco's government, according to the standard set by international law".

[96] Kelsen 1941, p. 615. See also Menon 1990, p. 159: "The principle of effectiveness of control is a fundamental concept and uncontroverted. Recognition of a government which is not in effective control of the territory would constitute premature recognition and would be considered intervention with the domestic affairs of the State".

hold ground.[97] As mentioned in the previous section, being effective means having the ability to exert State functions both internally and externally. For the most part, a government can only operate as a government outside its borders if other States have recognized it. But if a government is fully effective internally, then it is a government no matter what. (Henkin is right, and the declaratory theory becomes unobjectionable.) Lack of recognition might affect the relationship between the non-recognizing State A and the effective government of the State B, but it will not affect the status of the latter under international law. On the other hand, if a government is only partially effective internally, or if there are two or more entities claiming to be the government, then the act of recognition could become constitutive. This is so because by receiving the support of a critical mass of States, a government that is not fully effective internally gains in much needed external effectiveness. In such a scenario, recognizing the partially ineffective government (or one of the competing entities claiming to be a government) can help to tip the

[97] Current State practice seems to indicate that the legality of a government or its constitutional continuity (the so-called legitimacy doctrine) is not decisive criteria when it comes to recognition (see, e.g., Lauterpacht 1947, pp. 102–106, and in particular p. 105): "Its application is clearly illogical in a world in which all governments owe their origin to a revolutionary event in a more or less distant pass". There are simply too many instances of recognition of unconstitutional governments as to pretend that legitimacy is anything else but a tool to underpin the State's own discretion. Furthermore, there are good reasons to repudiate the legitimacy doctrine. First, it can lead to the interference of foreign powers in the internal affairs of the State. Second, foreign powers will not always have the means to pass judgement upon the constitutional order of another State. The case of Libya shows this in a very clear manner: Who was the legitimate government in 2015? The Tobruk-based HoR stemmed from democratic elections, but the Supreme Court declared the elections void. Foreign powers would hardly have the means, nor the legal expertise, to ascertain whether the Supreme Court of Libya is right or wrong—in which case, basing the act of recognition of either the government of Tobruk or that of Tripoli on their respective levels of legitimacy becomes simply impossible. Third, the doctrine of legitimacy allows foreign powers to arbitrarily decide whether a government is a government on the basis of its own values. The fact that some authors have argued that the Nazis were not the government of Germany during Second World War or that the Taliban were not the government of Afghanistan in the late 1990s is a good example of how the doctrine of legitimacy can be used to manipulate factual realities. One might think that not recognizing an effective but "illegitimate" government (in the absence of a treaty on collective recognition, what is or is not legitimate is simply left opened to interpretation) is actually favourable for the population of the State. Some authors have even advocated for the use of non-recognition of governments as a means to boycott regimes with a lousy human rights records (see Berlin 2009; Auron 2013). But the truth is that using effectiveness as the ultimate criterion for recognition is the best way to ensure that the international order is respected. The fact of denying recognition to a fully effective government can lead to counterproductive and undesirable results, especially in two interrelated domains of great importance, namely the use of force and the treatment of detainees during armed conflict. For instance, it can lead a foreign power to arbitrarily intervene in another State under the assumption that the effective government is not actually the government—i.e. the entity that can consent or oppose to the foreign intervention in the first place. The latter, in turn, could not only violate the prohibition against the use of force (*jus ad bellum*), with all its human consequences, but might also pave the way for legal fictions that could end up depriving human beings of some of their entitlements under IHL (*jus in bello*). We will come back to this in the last part of this article.

balance in its favour. In other words, the endorsement of a sufficient number of third States can help to *constitute* it as the government of the State if its internal effectiveness is equivocal.[98] Two well-known examples can help to clarify this situation.

In the late 1990s, the Taliban were in control of 90% of Afghanistan.[99] Despite their level of internal effectiveness, only three States recognized them as the legitimate government of Afghanistan: Saudi Arabia, Pakistan and the United Arab Emirates.[100] In this case, any act of recognition (or non-recognition) is merely declaratory. It has an impact on the possibility to establish diplomatic relations (or not) with the Taliban, but it does not change the fact that the Taliban were in fact the government of Afghanistan for the purposes of international law.[101] On the other hand, in the 2000s, Somalia had no internally effective government. For most of the decade, both the Transitional National Government (TNG) (2000–2004) and the Transitional Federal Government (TFG) (2004–2012) were circumscribed to certain neighbourhoods of Mogadishu and some other major cities. Al-Shabab, an organized armed group, controlled large parts of the territory. In addition, Somaliland—a northern region—claimed to be independent and was *de facto* administered by a different authority. And yet, the international community considered that first the TNG and then the TFG were the legitimate governments of Somalia. If one had only taken into account the level of internal effectiveness, it would seem that Somalia either was a failed State with no government—as perhaps it was—or was in fact governed by Al-Shabab. But when internal effectiveness is doubtful, either because one government is partially ineffective at the internal level, or because there are two or more entities fighting over the control of the State, then recognition can become constitutive. This is so because the act of recognition allows the recognized government to be more effective from an external point of view. Nevertheless, it must be reiterated that external recognition by itself would *a priori* be insufficient to argue that an entity with zero internal effectiveness is indeed the government—which is one of the reasons why it is debatable whether Somalia was a failed State (i.e. one with no government at all) during at least part of the 2000s, when its internal effectiveness was close to non-existent.[102]

There is no clear-cut formula to quantify the impact of recognition in each particular case. Suffice to say that recognition might contribute to consolidate—or maintain—a precarious government, provided that the recognizing State "is not

---

[98] Of course, this interpretation assumes that some internal effectiveness exists in the first place.

[99] Bellal, Giacca and Casey-Maslen 2011, p. 49.

[100] Ibid.

[101] This is demonstrated, *inter alia*, by the fact that the immense majority of scholars and practitioners classified the US-led invasion of Afghanistan in October 2001 as an international armed conflict. See, e.g., Bellal et al. 2011, pp. 51–52; see also the analysis made by Milanovic and Hadzi-Vidanovic on this same case: Milanovic and Hadzi-Vidanovic 2013, pp. 279–280.

[102] Khayre 2014, pp. 208–233.

acting in a merely opportunistic way".[103] In the case of two (or more) competing entities, recognition by a critical mass of States might tip the balance in favour of one of them. The opposite also holds true: when one of two (or more) competing entities is not completely effective internally and has not been recognized by a critical mass of States—i.e. it is not effective externally either—then there seems to be no legal reason to see that entity as a government. An example of this particular scenario is provided by the recent situation in Yemen. In February 2015, the Houthis took control over the Yemeni capital, Sana'a, dissolved the parliament and installed a transitional government.[104] However, despite administering—or partially administering—the capital, the Houthis were far from exercising effective control inside the country. Since they enjoyed zero international recognition, their contested internal effectiveness was paired with an absolute absence of external effectiveness. In view of such circumstances, the Houthis' transitional government could hardly be considered a government in the sense of public international law. The real question—which this author would not dare to answer—was whether President Hadi remained the representative of Yemen, a conclusion possibly underpinned by its external effectiveness, or whether Yemen was in fact a failed State due to President Hadi's very limited effectiveness inside the country.[105]

As a conclusion, governments should be recognized when they are effective.[106] In practice, however, States often base their decision to grant governmental recognition (or not) to a given entity upon political considerations. If the government is clearly effective at the internal level, non-recognition will not affect its status under international law. On the other hand, if there are doubts as to its internal effectiveness, recognition might provide the entity in question with ancillary external effectiveness, turning it into the government of the State. But sometimes, as in the case of Libya, the existence of competing entities can also give rise to two different types of government. Examining the modes of recognition can shed light on the legal obligations of each of these governments.

---

[103] Crawford 2006, p. 93. A third State would be opportunistic if it bases its decision to recognize a government solely on political considerations, without heeding the actual effectiveness of the entity in question.

[104] Al-Jazeera (2015) Yemen's Houthis Form Own Government in Sanaa. http://www.aljazeera.com/news/middleeast/2015/02/yemen-houthi-rebels-announce-presidential-council-150206122736448.html. Accessed 21 March 2016.

[105] The consequences of being a failed State will be briefly outlined further below.

[106] Lauterpacht argues that there is an international legal obligation to recognize effective governments, but most scholars do not see recognition of effective entities as a duty. State practice clearly supports the latter view. See, e.g., Institut De Droit International 1936, Article 10 (emphasis added): "The recognition of the new government of a State which has been already recognized is the *free act* by which one or several States acknowledge that a person or a group of persons are capable of binding the State which they claim to represent, and witness their intention to enter into relations with them".

1.4.2 *De Jure v. De Facto: Types of Recognition and Legal Consequences*

It is a general principle of international law that there can be but one government representing the same State. However, general principles also have exceptions. According to Article 11 of the *Resolution Concerning the Recognition of New States and New Governments* from the Institute of International Law, "[r]ecognition [of new governments] is either definite and complete (*de jure*) or provisional or limited to certain juridical relations (*de facto*)".[107]

It is important to note that the terms *de jure* and *de facto* have been used with different meanings in different types of situation. Talmon, arguably the scholar that has carried out the most thorough study on the issue of recognition over the past few decades, identifies no less than six different—and often contradictory—meanings to the term "*de facto* government".[108]

De jure recognition of a government usually means that the recognizing State considers the entity so recognized as the government of a sovereign State.[109] In other words, the recognizing State considers that the *de jure* government is the ultimate representative of the State. By itself, this type of recognition does *not* express a judgement upon the legitimacy of the recognized authority.[110] It only signifies that its claim to be endorsed as the government of the State in question is considered valid by the recognizing State. On the contrary, *de facto* recognition tends to imply that, in the opinion of the recognizing State, the recognized entity wields effective power in the territory under its control, but has not yet demonstrated that it will maintain its stability for a prolonged period of time and become the *de jure* government of that State.[111] As summarized by Shaw:

> *De facto* recognition involves a hesitant assessment of the situation, an attitude of wait and see, to be succeeded by *de jure* recognition when the doubts are sufficiently overcome to extend formal acceptance.[112]

---

[107] Institut De Droit International 1936, Article 11.

[108] Talmon 1998, p. 60.

[109] Ibid., p. 67.

[110] Menon 1991, p. 34.

[111] Ibid., p. 32; Shaw 2014, pp. 332–333. For Talmon, this is only one of the three main meanings of *de facto* recognition and not necessarily the most frequent. However, it is the one that better serves the purposes of this article. See Talmon 1998, p. 88: "*De facto* recognition may thus generally be employed in (at least) the following two meanings: it may indicate that, in the opinion of the recognizing State, the government so recognized is not a sovereign authority and/or it may express the recognizing State's general willingness to maintain relations with it. In addition, in the practice of individual States, it has been used in the meaning of a simple acknowledgement that a government exists and wields effective control over people and territory".

[112] Shaw 2014, pp. 332–333.

Despite the general rule that a State can only have one government, State practice and scholars agree that, in the event of a civil war, two or more entities can be recognized as governments of the same State. Nevertheless, this can only be done as long as only one of the rival governments is recognized *de jure*, and the other is recognized *de facto*. Alternatively, it is also possible to recognize both competing governments as *de facto* only.[113] Back in 2011, Libya was already a good example of this type of situation. A couple of months into the uprising against Gaddafi, once the National Transitional Council (NTC) started to exercise some effective governmental authority in the Western part of the country, and in particular around the city of Benghazi, some States granted *de facto* recognition to it.[114] A less recent—but much cited—example is that of the Spanish Civil War. During the last two years of that conflict, at a time in which each of the contenders controlled roughly half of the national territory, several European countries, including the UK, decided to recognize the Republican government as the *de jure* government and General Franco's administration as the *de facto* government.[115]

Obviously, these two types of recognition reflect the existence of two different types of government.[116] It is generally admitted that in reality there are very few meaningful differences between a *de jure* and a *de facto* government.[117] The legal validity of the *internal* acts carried out by a *de facto* government seems to be beyond dispute. In addition, both *de jure* and *de facto* governments are bound by international law and must respect the international legal obligations of the

[113] Ibid., p. 333; Talmon 1998, p. 105.

[114] Schuit 2012, pp. 395–396; Talmon 2011.

[115] Shaw 2014, p. 333.

[116] However, there is almost no literature focused on what it means to be a *de facto* government. The difference between a *de facto* and a *de jure* government is commonly analysed under the prism of recognition. In other words, scholars have continued to write about recognition as a *de facto* government, but not about *de facto* governments themselves. Arguably, this has been due to a switch on the object of debate. During the second half of the twentieth century, with the rise of human rights treaties, the literature has instead focused on how international law deals with non-State actors, marginalizing the figure of *de facto* governments. At the same time, contemporary international law scholars have continued to use the figure of *de facto* governments as one of the basic pillars of the law of recognition—despite the fact that the ultimate legal consequences of being a *de facto* government remain seriously understudied.

[117] Jennings and Watts 1992, pp. 156–157. For a more in-depth analysis of these differences, see Talmon 1998, pp. 105–106; Shaw 2014, p. 333; Peterson 1997, pp. 92–94; Lauterpacht 1947, pp. 341–346; Lauterpacht 1939, pp. 8–10.

State.[118] The main difference between these two types of governments lays in their capacity to carry out certain *external* acts. In the event of a conflict of interests between both entities regarding the external representation of the State, it is the *de jure* government which is entitled to speak on behalf of the State—and, consequently, to bind it *vis-à-vis* other States. For instance, only the *de jure* government is entitled to claim State property located in a foreign country—this is the reason why the Justice in charge of awarding control over Libya's $67-billion-worth wealth fund at the High Court in London needed to elucidate which of the two chairmen (if any) was actually speaking on behalf of the *de jure* government. Talmon provides another interesting example of this internal/external dichotomy. In October 1916, the UK recognized the pro-Entente Provisional Government of Salonika as the *de facto* government of Greece and the king, Constantine of Athens, as the *de jure* government. The former declared war on Germany in November 1916, whereas the latter followed the same course in June 1917. When the Reparation Commission established by the Treaty of Versailles had to determine the beginning of Greece's involvement in the war against the Central Powers, it considered that it was only after the *de jure* government of Greece had made its declaration. Although the validity of the internal acts of the *de facto* government of Salonika remained unchallenged, only the *de jure* government in Athens could issue a binding declaration of war.[119]

Interestingly, very little has been written on the arguments to consider that both *de facto* and *de jure* governments have international legal obligations, nor on the differences between *de facto* governments and non-State actors.[120] Although further research on this field is undoubtedly needed, it is submitted that the law on State responsibility and the law on treaties can help shed some light on the issue.

---

[118] Some of the scholarship of the first half of the twentieth century went as far as to suggest that both the *de facto* and the *de jure* governments must be treated as individual States in their respective areas of influence (see Baty 1921, pp. 483–487): "A government may have no reasonable prospect of recovering its authority throughout the old area of its sway. But it may have every prospect of maintaining itself indefinitely in some portion of it. It would be absurd to hold [...] that a state is necessarily one and indivisible, and that once the government is reduced to insignificance (and, in particular, turned out of the capital), it, and the region it occupies, become subject to the usurping government, as necessary parts of the whole, and thenceforth to be regarded as in mere rebellion. In the country which remains to it, and where, let it be assumed, it has every prospect of maintaining itself, it is surely as much entitled to be considered the government of a State as its rivals. The State, in short, in such a case is divided". More recently, scholars have also argued that the willingness of *de jure* and *de facto* governments to comply with treaty obligations has moved from a "condition of recognition" to an "established custom" (see Fenwick 1969, pp. 98–99).

[119] Talmon 1998, p. 106.

[120] Van Essen defines a *de facto* government (as opposed to national liberation movements, belligerent and insurgent groups or even *de facto* States) as "an entity which exercises 'at least some effective [...] authority over a territory within a State'. This degree of effective authority is coupled with a certain degree of political and organizational capacity. Moreover, this entity intends to represent the State of which it partially or completely controls the territory in the capacity of official government" (see Van Essen 2012, p. 32).

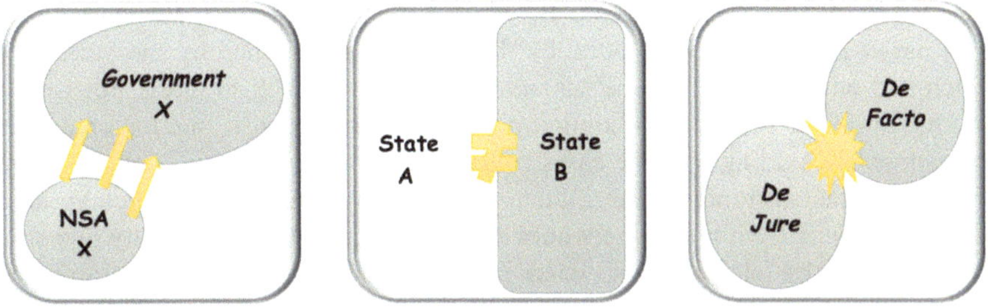

Fig. 1.1 Non-state actors, successor states and *de facto* governments

As stated in Article 10 of the *Articles on State Responsibility*, "the conduct of an insurrectional movement which becomes the new Government of a State shall be considered an act of that State under international law".[121] In other words, if a non-State actor succeeds in replacing the existing sovereign of the State and becomes the new government, that new government is responsible for the acts it carried out when it was just an insurrectional movement, i.e. before it actually represented the State (this situation corresponds to the first box in Fig. 1.1). Needless to say, this rule suggests that the new government can be held responsible for any violations of international law that it had committed during the uprising. The latter, in turn, means that the only way in which a successful insurrectional movement might elude its future responsibility is by respecting international law in the first place. According to the International Law Commission, Article 10 enshrines a "well-established principle of international law" which finds its basis on the continuity between the new government and the insurrectional movement.[122] On the opposite side of the spectrum, but with a similar logic, Article 34 of the 1978 *Vienna Convention on Succession of States in respect of Treaties* provides that when a part or parts of the territory of a State:

> separate to form one or more States, whether or not the predecessor State continues to exist […] any treaty in force at the date of the succession of States in respect of the entire territory of the predecessor State continues in force in respect of each successor State so formed.[123]

[121] UN General Assembly, above n 73, p. 50. See also Brownlie 1999, pp. 449–457.

[122] Ibid. For a brief analysis of the pre-eminence of the so-called principle of continuity in international law (see Pastor Ridruejo 1994, pp. 323–325). Nevertheless, some scholars have also contested this view and argued that the rule according to which violations of international law "by rebels that subsequently seize power are attributable to the State, rests neither on sound precedential nor systemic grounds" (see d'Aspremont 2009, pp. 427–442).

[123] It should be noted that only 22 countries have ratified the Vienna Convention on Succession of States in respect of Treaties, opened for signature 23 August 1978, 1946 UNTS 3 (entered into force 6 November 1996). However, its controversial nature is mostly due to a somewhat arbitrary distinction between former colonial States (which receive a so-called clean slate upon independence) and all other States, to which Article 34 would apply. See, e.g., Korman 1992–1993; Dumberry 2015.

This means that the new State B, which has acquired separate international legal personality, is initially bound by the treaties duly ratified by the State A to which it used to belong (cf. the second box in Fig. 1.1). Once more, this rule is also based on the principle of continuity. It is submitted that if international legal obligations—including in some cases those deriving from a treaty—can somehow precede the fact of representing a State and/or outlive its partial extinction, an *a maiore ad minus legal* reasoning would certainly support their continuity in a situation, such as the one in Libya, where a *de facto* government exercises a certain degree of sovereignty from the outset. As hinted by Van Essen, this could be related to the intent of the actor in question.[124] Unlike a non-State actor, whose aim is normally to replace the government and eventually represent the State, a *de facto* government already has a claim (albeit a partial one) to represent the State and would in principle—although this is of course debatable—consider itself bound by its international obligations.

Be it as it may, the bottom line is that both *de jure* and *de facto* governments are bound by the treaties duly ratified by the State they claim to represent, as well as by customary international law rules applicable to it.[125] However, in general terms, a *de jure* government is seen as the ultimate depositary of the sovereignty of the State. On the other hand, a *de facto* government is an entity that exercises a certain degree of effectiveness in representing the State, but that might never become a *de jure* government. In that sense, the fact of being recognized by a critical mass of States as the *de jure* government can be seen as a rebuttable presumption of being in fact the *de jure* government of that State, but only if a certain degree of internal effectiveness is also present. One of the reasons to argue in favour of this rebuttable presumption is that States are supposed to base their policies of government recognition upon the level of effectiveness of each entity—and not (just) upon political considerations. Furthermore, by supporting one among two or more competing entities, other States are vesting the chosen government with an extra degree of external effectiveness. The latter, in turn, might help the recognized government to successfully establish itself as the *de jure* representative of the State. However, as pointed out above, this is a question of degree in which one must simultaneously consider the levels of both internal and external effectiveness. A "merely opportunistic" recognition as a *de jure* government will not change the nature of a fully ineffective entity.

---

[124] Van Essen 2012, p. 32.

[125] Ibid., p. 39: "[T]he contemporary system of international law allows for the inclusion of regimes that are not in complete possession of (the classic form of) [international legal personality]. This proposition can be based on different arguments and explained by understanding [international legal personality] in different forms [...] These arguments and conceptions differ in their denial of the importance and norm-creating nature of [international legal personality], but a common thread can be distinguished from the variety of theorems. This commonality is the notion that full [international legal personality], as used before, is currently not considered necessary for an entity to function in international law". This reasoning seems more applicable to non-State actors than to *de facto* governments. The latter have been considered part of the international legal order for several centuries.

Finally, it should be noted that recognition as a *de jure* or a *de facto* government can be carried out in two different ways, namely in an expressed or an implied manner.[126] There is much confusion on which acts of a State can amount to a form of tacit recognition. But it is submitted that the European Union's attitude throughout most of 2015 towards the two competing governments in Libya is an example of tacit recognition of the GNC as a *de facto* government. As mentioned in Sect. 1.2, even though the European Union had initially recognized the government of Tobruk as the representative of the State of Libya, it repeatedly expressed its reluctance to launch a military intervention inside the country unless it obtained the consent of the two governments. In doing so, the European Union has arguably acknowledged that part of the sovereignty of the State of Libya falls upon the shoulders of the Tripoli-based GNC government.[127]

During 2015, it was unclear whether the Tobruk-based HoR was more effective than the GNC from an internal point of view. That said, as mentioned earlier, some analysts have in fact considered that the government of Tripoli controlled more territory, arms and militias than its rival in the west. But when it came to external effectiveness, the government of Tobruk had clearly the upper hand. The HoR had been recognized by dozens of States, including the members of the OPEC, and its representatives sat at the UN. The Tripoli-based GNC was supported only by Qatar, Turkey and Sudan.[128]

With all this in mind, it would seem that for the most part of 2015, the Tobruk-based HoR was being treated as the *de jure* government of Libya, whereas its rival, the Tripoli-based GNC, fitted the mould of a *de facto* government. This type of scenario is actually fairly common in the event of a civil war in which both sides rely on some type of governmental apparatus. The case of Yemen, mentioned earlier, might be seen from a similar perspective. Another recent example is that of Ivory Coast. In early 2011, the country was divided between forces loyal to long-time ruler Laurent Gbagbo and supporters of the recently elected Alassane Ouattara.[129] For several months, it was difficult to determine which of the two governments was more effective inside the country. However, Ouattara had been recognized by the large majority of States and was endorsed by the African Union, the Economic Community of West African States and the UN. Thanks to this, Ouattara was undoubtedly more effective than his rival and, therefore, could have arguably been considered the head of the *de jure* government of Ivory Coast even

---

[126] Menon 1991, pp. 20–31; Lauterpacht 1947, pp. 369–408; Peterson 1997, pp. 86–100.

[127] It is also quite significant that when the USA bombed the ISG inside Libya in February 2016, the Pentagon announced that the strike had been carried out "with the knowledge of Libyan authorities", but "declined to confirm who had been informed" (see BBC News (2016) Islamic State Camp in Libya Attacked by US Planes). http://www.bbc.com/news/world-africa-35613085. Accessed 21 March 2016.

[128] As a reminder, Jordan, Kuwait, Belarus and Serbia might have also backed the GNC, at least at its initial stages.

[129] Campbell J (2011) What to Do About Ivory Coast. http://www.nytimes.com/2011/01/12/opinion/12iht-edcampbell12.html?_r=0. Accessed 21 March 2016.

before his supporters took over the capital in late March 2011.[130] Laurent Gbagbo, in turn, had become the President of a *de facto* government—one with contested internal effectiveness and zero external effectiveness.[131]

It should be stressed one last time that the term *de jure* government is used here as a synonym for being more effective—considering both internal and external factors—and is not immediately related to being more or less legitimate than the competing entity.[132] With this in mind, it remains to be seen how this conclusion affects the scope of application of the laws of war.

1.5 Recognition in Libya and Its Impact on IHL

1.5.1 IHL Applicable to Non-International Armed Conflicts

As it is well known, IHL applies once there is either an international or a non-international armed conflict. According to the ICRC (emphasis in the original):

> Non-international armed conflicts are *protracted armed confrontations* occurring between governmental armed forces and the forces of one or more armed groups, or between such groups […]. The armed confrontation must reach *a minimum level of intensity* and the parties involved in the conflict must show *a minimum of organization*.[133]

These two criteria, i.e. the intensity of the violence and the organization of the parties, are meant to distinguish an armed conflict from "banditry, unorganized

---

[130] James J (2011) Inside Ivory Coast's Capture Capital. http://www.bbc.com/news/world-africa-12928358. Accessed 21 March 2016.

[131] Some authors have argued that there is a rebuttable presumption in favour of the pre-existing government. It is submitted that this presumption has no basis on current State practice. On the contrary, there have been abundant examples against it in the last few decades, e.g. Afghanistan in 2001–2002, Libya in 2011 or Ivory Coast in 2010–2011.

[132] Nevertheless, subjective notions of legitimacy can have an indirect impact on the definition of a *de jure* government proposed in this paper. If the *de jure* government is the most effective entity, and effectiveness is measured both internally and externally, it is then clear that the recognition of third States can have an impact on who is deemed the most effective government overall. Recognition policies should in principle be based on the notion of internal effectiveness. But, as explained earlier, States also take into account their own perceptions with regard to the legitimacy of certain actors, or even their own political interests, when they decide whether to recognize (or not) a particular government. If these subjective motives are incorporated by a critical mass of States into their decision to recognize one of two contesting governments, then the so-called legitimacy criterion can find its way into the notion of effectiveness defended herein.

[133] International Committee of the Red Cross 2008, p. 5. This definition is based on Pictet's Commentary to Common Article 3 to the Geneva Conventions and on case law stemming from international tribunals, in particular the International Criminal Tribunal for the Former Yugoslavia (ICTY). See ICTY, *Prosecutor v Dusko Tadić a/k/a "Dule"*, Opinion and Judgement, 7 May 1997, Case No. IT-94-1-T (*Tadić*), paras 561–568 and ICTY, *Prosecutor v Ljube Boškoski and Johan Tarčulovski*, Judgement, 10 July 2008, Case No. IT-04-82-T, paras 175–178.

and short-lived insurrections, or terrorist activities, which are not subject to international humanitarian law".[134]

Conducting an individualized analysis of each of the violent actors in today's Libya would be a lengthy and arduous task. It would require identifying each of the dozens of militias that participate in the conflict, analysing their structure and verifying the extent to which they participate in the different instances of violence. However, the factual information already provided in Sect. 1.2 seems to indicate that there is at the very least a non-international armed conflict between the Tobruk-based government and the ISG, and a second non-international armed conflict between the latter and the Tripoli-based government.[135]

With regard to the applicable IHL, all non-international armed conflicts are governed, as a minimum, by Article 3 common to the four 1949 Geneva Conventions (Common Article 3)[136] and by customary IHL applicable to this type of conflict. In addition, some non-international armed conflicts are also governed by Additional Protocol II. The threshold of application of this treaty is laid down in its first article, which provides that it will apply to conflicts:

> which take place in the territory of a High Contracting Party between its armed forces and dissident armed forces or other organized armed groups which, under responsible command, exercise such control over a part of its territory as to enable them to carry out sustained and concerted military operations and to implement this Protocol.[137]

This threshold of application is manifestly higher than the one required by Common Article 3 to the Geneva Conventions. Apart from requiring a certain degree of territorial control by (and a certain ability from) the organized armed group, it does not apply to conflicts taking place solely between such groups. Indeed, Article 1(1) establishes that Additional Protocol II will only apply to conflicts in which at least one of the parties is a government—or to be more precise, conflicts between an organized armed group and the armed forces of a High Contracting Party. (Libya became a High Contracting Party when it ratified the

---

134 *Tadić*, above n 133, para 562.

135 The relationship between Haftar's National Army and the HoR has been clearly established. However, one could doubt whether the Tripoli-based GNC actually controls the militias that underpin its government. This article takes the view that the link between the latter and the former is (at least in some instances) sufficiently strong to consider (some of) those militias as the armed forces of the GNC. This interpretation is supported by the fact that "the term 'armed forces' of the High Contracting Party should be understood in the broadest sense" (see Sandoz et al. 1987, para 4462). For a more detailed analysis of the indicative factors of the level of organization and the level of intensity that need to be assessed to determine the existence of a non-international armed conflict, see Müller et al. 2016, paras 422–437; see also Vité 2009, pp. 75–78.

136 The Geneva Conventions have been universally ratified. And even if this was not the case, Common Article 3 itself has been considered a "minimum yardstick" that reflects customary IHL. See ICJ, *Case Concerning Military and Paramilitary Activities in and against Nicaragua (Nicaragua v United States of America)*, Judgment, 27 June 1986, (1986) ICJ Rep 14 paras 218–219.

137 Additional Protocol II, above n 17, Article 1(1).

protocol in June 1978). This means that a conflict might fall under the umbrella of Common Article 3 without fulfilling the prerequisites of Additional Protocol II.[138] On the contrary, any internal conflict covered by Additional Protocol II would also be covered by Common Article 3.[139]

The problem in Libya, of course, is deciding who must be considered the government for the purposes of Article 1(1) of Additional Protocol II. An analysis of the *travaux préparatoires* of the 1977 Diplomatic Conference reveals that the participating delegates did not address the issue of *de facto* and *de jure* governments. This is unsurprising. Cassese has convincingly argued that States taking part in the conference "were clearly motivated by the desire to reduce rebels to the level of criminals devoid of any international status".[140] If this is true for matters such as the status of an organized armed group, it is obviously even more so when it comes to accepting the possibility to recognize a *de facto* government.

As shown in the previous section, international law binds not only *de jure* governments, but also *de facto* ones. This is so, *inter alia*, because both entities exercise a certain degree of effectiveness and have a claim to represent the State. The latter, in turn, also presupposes that the entity in question is able and willing to abide by the international legal obligations of the State, including the treaties ratified by previous governments. Therefore, it is only logical that both the *de facto* and the *de jure* governments of a High Contracting Party be called to respect Additional Protocol II, provided that they are involved in an armed conflict with an organized armed group that fulfils the rest of the requirements of Article 1(1). Apart from the arguments enunciated above regarding the legal obligations of *de facto* governments, such an understanding is also coherent with the general rules on treaty interpretation. Article 31 of the Vienna Convention on the Laws of Treaties provides that treaties shall be construed in good faith "in the light of its object and purpose". The stated aim of Additional Protocol II is to "ensure a better protection for the victims of [non-international armed conflicts]",[141] provided that one of the parties is a government. Considering that *de facto* governments are equally bound by Additional Protocol II is obviously more protective, and better aligned with the object and purpose of the treaty, than considering that it only applies to conflicts involving a *de jure* government.[142]

The current situation in Libya also leaves no doubt as to the fact that the ISG controls part of the national territory, it has the capacity to launch sustained and concerted military operations, and it can implement the protocol, as required by

---

138 Vité 2009, p. 79.

139 Ibid.

140 Cassese 2008, p. 153.

141 Additional Protocol II, above n 17, Preamble.

142 Furthermore, this approach is also more consistent with the fact that in the midst of an armed conflict, it is not always possible to establish unequivocally which of the two competing entities is more effective.

Article 1(1). Therefore, it is submitted that Additional Protocol II applies to both the non-international armed conflict between the Tobruk-based HoR government and the ISG, on the one hand, and to the non-international armed conflict between the latter and the Tripoli-based GNC government, on the other.[143] The last question that needs to be answered is whether Libya is also party to any international armed conflict.

1.5.2 Third States Involvement and Possible International Armed Conflict

Nowadays, it is common for a State to conduct military operations in the territory of a third State, often against organized armed groups. Such interventions have in fact proliferated since 11 September 2001.[144] In the case of Libya, the most prominent instances of foreign intervention have been those led by Egypt and the USA—all of them reportedly against the ISG, with the exception of one individual US air strike against Al-Qaeda-affiliated Mokhtar Belmokhtar in June 2015. On the one side, this requires an analysis of the legality of the use of force under international law (*jus ad bellum*), a topic that has been the focus of much scholarly attention.[145] On the other hand, from an IHL perspective (*jus in bello*), it raises the question of whether the foreign involvement triggers the existence of an international armed conflict between any of the intervening States (Egypt and the USA) and the territorial State (Libya).

An international armed conflict takes place "when one or more States have recourse to armed force against another State, regardless of the reasons for or the intensity of the confrontation".[146] However, it is generally accepted that an international armed conflict in the sense of Common Article 2(1) to the Geneva Conventions would also be triggered if the territorial State does not consent to a foreign intervention within its borders. This would be so regardless of whether the intervention is directed solely against an organized armed group—and regardless of whether a parallel non-international armed conflict between the organized

---

143 It is possible that Additional Protocol II, above n 17, also applies to other non-international armed conflicts within the country.

144 Moir 2015, p. 402.

145 See, e.g., Weller 2015; Okimoto 2011. For an analysis of the particular issue of government recognition and its impact on the legality of the use of force, see Doswald-Beck 1985, pp. 189–252; Roth 2001, pp. 253–320; Wippman 1995–1996, pp. 435–485.

146 Ferraro and Cameron 2016, para 218.

armed group and the territorial State, or even between the organized armed group and the intervening State, exists.[147]

Once more, the main difficulty lies in deciding which government can actually consent to such an intervention.[148] As stressed by Ferraro and Cameron, in order to preclude an international armed conflict "[consent] must be valid, i.e. given by an authority authorized to do so on behalf of the State, and given without any coercion from the intervening State".[149] But when there are two or more entities claiming to be the government, it is necessary to elucidate which of these entities can validly consent on behalf of the State.

Historically, States have tried to hide behind the issue of government recognition to try to avoid the application of IHL. That is one of the reasons why it makes full sense to use the doctrine of effectiveness (instead of other, more subjective criteria, such as legitimacy) to determine who is the government of a State. IHL scholars unanimously agree that the status of an entity claiming to be the government of a State must be assessed in terms of its effectiveness and not just in view of its level of recognition or other factors.[150] This is important, in addition, because the question of who is the government can have an impact not only on the initial classification of the conflict, but also on any subsequent reclassification.[151]

As discussed earlier, when two governments claim to represent the State, it is the *de jure* government that must be seen as the ultimate depositary of its sovereignty. Although both *de facto* and *de jure* governments are bound by international law, only a *de jure* government can speak on behalf of the State when it comes to binding it towards other States (and/or to exercising its sovereignty *vis-à-vis* such States). If it is assumed, as done earlier, that—in the light of a balanced assessment of both its internal and external effectiveness—the Tobruk-based HoR was the *de jure* government of Libya throughout 2015, one must equally accept that it is also this government that can validly consent to—or oppose—any foreign intervention.

---

147 Ibid., paras 257–263. See also Milanovic 2015, p. 50. Milanovic provides some very illustrative examples, for instance the incursions of Colombia into Ecuador in 2008. Although the incursions aimed at chasing members from the FARC, an organized armed group, the fact that Ecuador did not consent to such operations could have triggered an international armed conflict between Colombia and Ecuador. In this case, Colombia was in a parallel non-international armed conflict with the FARC.

148 The International Law Commission has argued that "valid consent by a State to the commission of a given act by another State precludes the wrongfulness of that act [...] provided the consent is valid and to the extent that the conduct remains within the limits of the consent given". See UN General Assembly, above n 73, p. 72.

149 Ferraro and Cameron 2016, para 263.

150 Ibid., paras 234–235; Milanovic and Hadzi-Vidanovic 2013, p. 279; Schindler 1979, pp. 128–130; Bellal et al. 2011.

151 Ferraro and Cameron 2016, para 232; Milanovic and Hadzi-Vidanovic 2013.

Sassòli has pointed out that a "*de jure* authority without *de facto* control" cannot validly consent to a foreign intervention.[152] This seems to signify that the consent of so-called *de jure* authorities that do not wield any internal effectiveness within the country is not valid. Although Sassòli appears to be using the term "*de jure* authority" in a sense that is closer to notions of legitimacy than effectiveness (and, thus, in a sense that might differ from the one put forth in this article), it is submitted that his conclusion is fully correct. A government that enjoys a high level of international recognition, or of constitutional legitimacy for that matter, but wields zero effectiveness within the country cannot be said to speak on behalf of the State. That is why, unless things change radically in the next few months, a hypothetical consent of the Tunis-based Government of National Accord—which has been backed by the UN, the USA and the European Union—can hardly be considered valid in order to preclude an international armed conflict. Indeed, as of the time of writing, the Government of National Accord enjoys no internal effectiveness inside the territory of Libya.

On the other hand, Sassòli also posits that "mere consent by authorities with *de facto* control against the will of the *de jure* authority is equally insufficient".[153] In the opinion of the author of this article, this is also correct, provided that "*de jure* authority" is here understood, once more, as referring to an entity that wields some type of internal effectiveness, and it is not just a synonym for "ineffective, but legitimate".[154] In the case of Libya in 2015, this could be translated as considering that the consent of the Tripoli-based GNC would not be deemed valid for the purposes of authorizing a foreign intervention, since during this period the GNC appeared to have been only a *de facto* government—and not one that could claim to exercise full sovereignty on behalf of the State.

The government of Tobruk explicitly acquiesced to Egypt's air strikes against the ISG in February 2015. Therefore, under the assumptions made in this article, this intervention would not have triggered an international armed conflict between Egypt and Libya. With regard to the US air strikes, the absence of protests from Tobruk could be seen as "a strong indicator of the existence of—at least—tacit consent".[155] If tacit consent was indeed present, then an international armed conflict in the sense of Common Article 2(1) would not have been triggered despite the US air strikes against Mokhtar Belmokhtar and the ISG. On the other hand, if

[152] Sassòli 2015, p. 1406. It should be kept in mind that Sassòli is referring here to consenting to a foreign occupation, but it is submitted that the argument can be extrapolated to the consent (or lack thereof) given to a third State to intervene against an organized armed group within the territory of the consenting State.

[153] Ibid.

[154] It needs to be reminded that the terms *de jure* and *de facto* governments have been used very differently both by scholars and in State practice. However, this is arguably the reading of Sassòli, since he later on writes that he "would not consider consent by an ineffective *de jure* government, perhaps in exile, as sufficient"—Sassòli 2015, p. 1403.

[155] Ferraro and Cameron 2016, para 263.

renewed factual evidence prompted a different understanding of the situation and it could be proved that the HoR actually opposed the US air strikes, then an international armed conflict between the two countries might have taken place.

Finally, a different scenario should be briefly mentioned, namely the possibility that during 2015 Libya was a failed State with no effective government. Some analysts have considered that neither the government of Tripoli nor its counterpart in Tobruk was actually in control of any substantive part of Libya. According to this view, the only entities that yielded any power within the country were its hundreds of militias. If this alternative reading was accurate, then it might be possible to consider that none of the two entities, i.e. neither the HoR nor the GNC, was a government in the sense of public international law and that hence, none of them could validly consent to a foreign intervention. Under such circumstances, it is usually accepted that any foreign incursion in the territory of the failed State would immediately trigger an international armed conflict.[156] In other words, if one believed that throughout 2015 Libya was a failed State with no government, then the air strikes carried out by Egypt and the USA would have given rise to an international armed conflict between these two States and the State of Libya.[157] This would not mean that the State was represented by an organized armed group, but rather that it lacked effective representation altogether. Under such circumstances, i.e. in the absence of a government, failed States can obviously not give their tacit consent to any intervention.

1.6 Conclusion: The Importance of Internal and External Effectiveness

Throughout most of 2015, two entities have been competing to represent the State of Libya: the Tobruk-based HoR and the Tripoli-based GNC. Arguably, the latter wielded more influence internally. However, the HoR had been recognized by a majority of States and was often referred to as the "legitimate" or "internationally recognized" government. This article has re-examined the notion of government and applied its findings to the situation inside Libya. Most notably, it has proposed to focus on a definition of government that takes into consideration not only the level of internal effectiveness of the entity in question, but also its external effectiveness.

---

[156] Sassòli 2015, p. 1403. See also International Committee of the Red Cross 2002, p. 23: "A consensus then developed among the experts that when foreign forces intervened in a 'failed State', consent must be presumed to be absent".

[157] With the factual information publicly available, the author of this article clearly favours the opposite view, i.e. that for most of 2015 Libya had two partially effective—and partially ineffective—governments, one of which was able to consent (or oppose) to such interventions.

The article has then addressed the issue of recognition under public international law. In particular, it has argued—as done in the *Tinoco* arbitration case—that recognition of governments by third States is merely declaratory if the recognized entity already enjoys sufficient internal effectiveness. However, in situations in which a government is only partially effective, or in which two different entities claim to be the government, recognition by third States can also be considered constitutive. The latter is based on the fact that by recognizing a particular entity as the legitimate representative of the State, that entity can better conduct State functions *vis-à-vis* the recognizing States. In other words, it is more effective from an external perspective.

With this framework in mind, the article has moved on to explore the different modes of recognition. It has shown that governments can be recognized *de jure* or *de facto*. *De jure* governments are the ultimate guardians of the State's sovereignty, but *de facto* governments also exercise some degree of effectiveness within the national territory. In view of the latter, it has been traditionally considered that both types of governments are bound by international law. However, only *de jure* governments can represent the State when it comes to certain external acts, including consenting to a foreign intervention. It has been submitted that, at the end of the day, the term *de jure* government should be understood as the entity that is more effective—and that this effectiveness must be measured with due regard to both internal and external factors. This interpretation seems to indicate that, at least throughout most of 2015, the Tobruk-based HoR was the *de jure* government of Libya. Indeed, the possibility that the government of Tobruk was slightly less effective at home (an unconfirmed hypothesis that would require an in-depth—and, under the circumstances, uncertain—factual assessment) was arguably compensated by its high level of effectiveness abroad.

When it comes to the laws of war, it is clear that Libya is undergoing several non-international armed conflicts governed by IHL. Although an exhaustive analysis of all the indicative criteria of organization and intensity has been omitted, this article has maintained that there is a non-international armed conflict between the Tobruk-based HoR and the ISG, and between the latter and the Tripoli-based GNC. In addition to Common Article 3 to the Geneva Conventions and customary IHL applicable to non-international armed conflict, it has been submitted that these two conflicts are also governed by Additional Protocol II to the Geneva Conventions. Since both *de jure* and *de facto* governments are bound by the international legal obligations of the State, it is only reasonable to assume that Additional Protocol II would apply to any internal armed conflict involving any of these two governments—provided that the other material elements, including control of the territory by the organized armed group, are met (as is the case with the ISG).

With regard to air strikes conducted by third States, it has been argued that only the *de jure* government, understood as the most effective entity in the light of both its internal and its external effectiveness, can validly consent to the involvement of foreign powers for the purposes of *jus in bello*. In other words, in the absence of consent from the *de jure* government, any foreign intervention would trigger an international armed conflict. It would seem that unless the government of Tobruk had consented (either explicitly or tacitly) to the air strikes launched by Egypt and the USA, the attacks of these two countries against the ISG might have triggered an international armed conflict—in addition to any parallel non-international armed conflict existing between the ISG and other parties inside Libya, or even between the ISG and any of these two third States.[158] In the case of Egypt, this possibility could be easily discarded, thanks to the explicit consent of the HoR.

Further research is clearly needed on the issue of *de facto* governments. Contemporary scholars have kept using this terminology when dealing with the issue of recognition. However, the international legal obligations of *de facto* governments themselves have received very little attention during the last few decades. Moreover, it would be necessary to further elaborate on the differences between *de facto* governments and non-State armed groups exercising governmental functions. It is submitted that the notion of intent, as well as the degree to which the entity in question considers itself the successor of the pre-existing government, and thus the heir of the State's international obligations, might be key in understanding this difference. In addition, it would also be interesting to further explore the notion of effectiveness and the way in which the interplay between internal and external effectiveness has been taken into consideration in State practice. Much scholarly attention has been paid to this issue from a *jus ad bellum* perspective, whereas the *jus in bello* landscape remains largely unexplored.

Finally, other notions used in this article, such as those of failed State, implied government recognition and tacit consent to a foreign intervention, could also benefit from additional research—both from the point of view of public international law in general and of IHL in particular.

It is often repeated that the number of foreign interventions in third countries has risen since the beginning of the twenty-first century. *A priori*, it would seem that government fragmentation and the proliferation of competing entities claiming to represent the same State has followed a similar ascendant trend. If Somalia was often quoted as the paradigm of a State without a government, in the last couple of years several countries are arguably vying for the same position. The situation in Libya in early 2016 clearly reflects this trend. Not only has the power struggle between the HoR and the GNC not ceased, but there is now a third government claiming to represent the State. Interestingly, despite its absolute lack of internal effectiveness, this third government has been backed by the UN, the USA and the European Union. Only the future will tell if recognition of governments will continue to rely on the notion of effectiveness. For the sake of IHL and other branches of international law, one would hope so.

Acknowledgments The author would like to warmly thank Prof. Sarah Knuckey for sponsoring his stay at the Human Rights Institute at Columbia Law School, where the bulk of this piece was researched and drafted. The author would also like to thank Keiichiro Okimoto and Tilman Rodenhäuser for sharing their insights and providing valuable comments to an early draft.

[158] See the beginning of Sect. 1.5.2 above.

References

Articles, Books and Other Documents

Auron D (2013) The Derecognition Approach: Government Illegality, Recognition, and Non-Violent Regime Change. The George Washington Int Law Rev 45:443–499
Baty T (1921) So-Called De Facto Recognition. The Yale Law J 31:469–488
Bellal A, Giacca G, Casey-Maslen S (2011) International Law and Armed Non-State Actors in Afghanistan. Int Rev Red Cross 93:47–79
Berlin A (2009) Recognition as Sanction: Using International Recognition of New States to Deter, Punish, and Contain Bad Actors. Univ Pennsylvania J Int Law 31:531–591
Brownlie I (1986) Recognition in theory and practice. In: Macdonald R, Johnston D (eds) The Structure and Process of International law: Modern Essays in Legal Philosophy. Doctrine and Theory, Martinus Nijhoff Publishers, Boston, pp 627–642
Brownlie I (1999) Principles of Public International Law. Oxford University Press, Oxford
Cassese A (2008) The Status of Rebels Under the 1977 Geneva Protocol on Non-International Armed Conflicts. In: Cassese A, Gaeta P, Zappala S (eds) The Human Dimension of International Law: Selected Papers of Antonio Cassese. Oxford University Press, Oxford, pp 148–171
Charlesworth H (1991) The New Australian Recognition Policy in Comparative Perspective. Melbourne Univ Law Rev 18:1–25
Chen T-C (1951) The International Law of Recognition, with special reference to practice in Great Britain and the United States. Praeger, New York
Crawford J (2006) The Creation of States in International Law. Clarendon Press, Oxford
d'Aspremont J (2009) Rebellion and State Responsibility: Wrongdoing by Democratically Elected Insurgents. Int Comp Law Q 58:427–442
Doswald-Beck L (1984) The Legality of the United States Intervention in Grenada. Neth Int Law Rev 31:355–377
Doswald-Beck L (1985) The Legal Validity of Military Intervention by Invitation of the Government. Br Yearb Int Law 56:189–252
Dugard J (1987) Recognition and the United Nations. Grotius Publications Limited, Cambridge
Dumberry P (2015) State Succession to Bilateral Treaties: A Few Observations on the Incoherent and Unjustifiable Solution Adopted for Secession and Dissolution of States under the 1978 Vienna Convention. Leiden J Int Law 28:13–30
European Commission (1999) Bulletin of the European Union 7/8:1–153
Evans M (2010) International Law. Oxford University Press, Oxford
Fauchille P (1923) Droit international public. Rousseau & Co., Paris
Fenwick C (1969) Recognition of De Facto Governments: Old Guidelines and New Obligations. Am J Int Law 63:98–100
Ferraro T, Cameron L (2016) Commentary to the Geneva Conventions: Common Article 2. International Committee of the Red Cross, Geneva
Galloway T (1978) Recognizing foreign governments: the practice of the United States. American Enterprise Institute, Washington
Gamboa F, Fernández M (2006) Tratado de Derecho Internacional Público y Derecho de Integración, LexisNexis
Henkin L (1990) International Law: Politics, Values and Functions. General course on Public International Law. Martinus Nijhoff Publishers, Dordrecht/Boston/London
Institut De Droit International (1936) Resolution Concerning the Recognition of New States and New Governments. Am J Int Law 30:185–187
International Committee of the Red Cross (2002) Occupation and Other Forms of Administration of Foreign Territory. Expert Meeting, Geneva
International Committee of the Red Cross (2008) How is the Term "Armed Conflict" Defined in International Humanitarian Law? Opinion paper, Geneva

International Crisis Group (2016) Libya: Getting Geneva Right. Middle East and North Africa Report No. 157

Jennings R, Watts A (1992) Oppenheim's International Law, Vol I. Longman, Essex

Kaczorowska A (2010) Public International Law. Routledge, London

Kelsen H (1941) Recognition in International Law. Am J Int Law 35:605–617

Khayre A (2014) Self-Defence, Intervention by Invitation, or Proxy War? The Legality of the 2006 Ethiopian Invasion of Somalia. Afr J Int Comp Law 22:208–233

Kimball W (1987) Churchill and Roosevelt. The Complete Correspondence, Vol 2. Princeton University Press, Princeton

Korman S (1992–1993) The 1978 Vienna Convention on Succession of States in Respect of Treaties: an Inadequate Response to the Issue of State Succession. Suffolk Transnational Law Rev 16:174–199

Lauterpacht H (1939) Recognition of Insurgents as a De Facto Government. Mod Law Rev 3:1–20

Lauterpacht H (1947) Recognition in International Law. Cambridge University Press, Cambridge

Lauterpacht H (1970) International Law: Collective Papers, Vol I. Cambridge University Press, Cambridge

Menon P (1990) Some Aspects of the Law of Recognition. Part III: Recognition of Governments. Revue de Droit International, de Sciences Diplomatiques, Politiques et Sociales 3:157–196

Menon P (1991) Some Aspects of the Law of Recognition. Part V: Modes of Recognition. Revue de Droit International, de Sciences Diplomatiques, Politiques et Sociales 1:19–49

Milanovic M, Hadzi-Vidanovic V (2013) A taxonomy of armed conflict. In: White N (ed) Research Handbook on International Conflict and Security Law: Jus ad Bellum, Jus in Bello and Jus Post Bellum. Edward Elgar, Cheltenham, pp 256–314

Milanovic M (2015) The Applicability of the Geneva Conventions to 'Transnational' and 'Mixed' Conflicts. In: Clapham A, Gaeta P, Sassòli M (eds) The Geneva Conventions: a commentary. Oxford University Press, Oxford, pp 27–50

Ministers of Foreign Affairs of France, Germany, United Kingdom, Italy, USA and EU (2016) Ministerial meeting in Paris: France, Germany, United Kingdom, Italy, USA, EU—Statement on Libya, EU Doc. 160313_01

Moir L (2015) The Concept of Non-International Armed Conflict. In: Clapham A, Gaeta P, Sassòli M (eds) The Geneva Conventions: A Commentary. Oxford University Press, Oxford, pp 391–414

Müller I, Henckaerts J, Cameron L, Demeyere B, Geiβ R, La Haye E, Droege C, Gisel L (2016) Commentary to the Geneva Conventions: Common Article 3. International Committee of the Red Cross, Geneva

Okimoto K (2011) The Distinction and Relationship Between Jus ad Bellum and Jus in Bello. Bloomsbury Publishing, Oxford

Pastor Ridruejo J (1994) Curso de Derecho Internacional Público y Organizaciones Internacionales. Tecnos, Madrid

Peterson M (1997) Recognition of Governments: Legal Doctrine and State Practice. St. Martin's Press, New York

Quoc Dinh N (2002) Droit international public. LGDJ, Paris

Roth B (2001) Governmental Illegitimacy in International Law. Oxford University Press, New York

Sandoz Y, Swinarski C, Zimmermann B (1987) Commentary on the Additional Protocols of 8 June 1977 to the Geneva Conventions of 12 August 1949. Martinus Nijhoff Publishers, International Committee of the Red Cross, Geneva

Sassòli M (2015) The Concept and Beginning of Occupation. In: Clapham A, Gaeta P, Sassòli M (eds) The Geneva Conventions: A Commentary. Oxford University Press, Oxford, pp 1389–1420

Schindler D (1979) The Different Types of Armed Conflicts According to the Geneva Conventions and Protocols. Recueil des Cours de l'Académie de Droit International de La Haye 163:128–130

Schuit A (2012) Recognition of Governments in International Law and the Recent Conflict in Libya. Int Community Law Rev 14:381–402

Shaw M (2014) International law. Cambridge University Press, Cambridge

Talmon S (1998) Recognition of Governments in International Law: With Particular Reference to Governments in Exile. Clarendon Press, Oxford

Talmon S (2011) Recognition of the Libyan National Transitional Council. Insights: American Society of International Law 15

Thibaudeau A-C (1828) Histoire générale de Napoléon Bonaparte, vol 2. Ponthieu et Comp, Paris

UN (2006) Reports of International Arbitral Awards: Aguilar-Amory and Royal Bank of Canada claims (Great Britain v. Costa Rica) 18 October 1923, vol I

UN General Assembly (2001) Draft Articles on Responsibility of States for Internationally Wrongful Acts with Commentaries, UN Doc. A/56/10

UN Security Council (1950) Letter Dated 8 March 1950 from the Secretary-General to the President of the Security Council Transmitting a Memorandum on the Legal Aspects of the Problem of Representation in the United Nations, UN Doc. S/1466

UN Security Council (2011) Resolution 1975 (2015), UN Doc. S/RES/1975

UN Security Council (2015) Resolution 2213 (2015), UN Doc. S/RES/2213

UN Security Council (2015) Resolution 2216 (2015), UN Doc. S/RES/2216

UN Security Council (2015) Resolution 2238 (2015), UN Doc. S/RES/2238

UN Security Council (2015) Resolution 2259 (2015), UN Doc. S/RES/2259

UN Security Council (2016) Report of the Secretary-General on the United Nations Support Mission in Libya, UN Doc. S/2016/182

Van Essen J (2012) De Facto Regimes in International Law. Utrecht J Int Eur Law 28:31–49

Verhoeven J (1975) La Reconnaissance Internationale dans la Pratique Contemporaine. Editions A, Pedone, Paris

Vité S (2009) Typology of Armed Conflicts in International Humanitarian Law, Legal Concepts and Actual Situations. Int Rev Red Cross 91:69–94

Warbrick C (1981) The New British Policy on Recognition of Governments. Int Comp Law Q 30:568–592

Weller M (2015) The Oxford Handbook of the Use of Force in International Law. Oxford University Press, Oxford

Wippman D (1995–1996) Change and Continuity in Legal Justifications for Military Intervention in Internal Conflict. Columbia Human Rights Law Rev 27:435–485

Case Law

ICJ, *Case Concerning Military and Paramilitary Activities in and against Nicaragua (Nicaragua v United States of America)*, Judgment, 27 June 1986, [1986] ICJ Rep 14

ICJ, *Legal Consequences of the Construction of a Wall in the Occupied Palestinian Territory*, Advisory Opinion, 9 July 2004, (2004) ICJ Rep 136

ICTY, *Prosecutor v Dusko Tadić a/k/a "Dule"*, Opinion and Judgement, 7 May 1997, Case No. IT-94-1-T

ICTY, *Prosecutor v Ljube Boškoski and Johan Tarčulovski*, Judgement, 10 July 2008, Case No. IT-04-82-T

Treaties

Montevideo Convention on the Rights and Duties of States, opened for signature 26 December 1933, 164 LNTS 19 (entered into force 26 December 1934)

Protocol Additional to the Geneva Conventions of 12 August 1949, and relating to the Protection of Victims of Non-International Armed Conflicts, opened for signature 8 June 1977, 1125 UNTS 609 (entered into force 7 December 1978)

Vienna Convention on Succession of States in respect of Treaties, opened for signature 23 August 1978, 1946 UNTS 3 (entered into force 6 November 1996)

Chapter 2
Puppet States: A Growing Trend of Covert Occupation

Bogdan Ivanel

Abstract This article deals with what it defines as *puppet states* or instances of *covert occupation*. In order to bypass the political burden and especially the legal obligations which international humanitarian law and general international law impose on the occupying power, a growing trend has come into place for states to create secessionist entities within another state. These secessionist entities, which have all outside aspects of a de facto state, are in fact effectively controlled by their sponsor state. Furthermore, the sponsor state not only establishes the puppet state through military force, but also controls its everyday life through the use of military, economic and political means, leading to a de facto annexation of the given territory. Five regions in the world are in this situation, while a sixth is under creation in Eastern Ukraine. Northern Cyprus, Nagorno-Karabakh, Transnistria, South Ossetia and Abkhazia can all be defined as puppet states. The unclear status of these regions makes them areas of impunity, regions which largely fall outside the implementation of international humanitarian law. The present paper intends to present this phenomenon and unveil the legal gaps that enable the use of puppet states for escaping the burden of international humanitarian law.

Keywords Puppet state · Covert occupation · International humanitarian law · Human rights law · Statehood · Occupation · Armed conflict · Transnistria · Independence

---

B. Ivanel (✉)
L'Institut D'études Politiques (IEP) de Paris (Sciences Po Paris) Law School, Utrecht, The Netherlands
e-mail: bogdanivanel@gmail.com; bogdan.ivanel@sciences-po.org

T.D. Gill et al. (eds.), *Yearbook of International Humanitarian Law 2015*,
Yearbook of International Humanitarian Law 18,
DOI 10.1007/978-94-6265-141-8_2

Contents

2.1 Introduction

An interesting phenomenon has gained traction around the world in the last couple of decades, namely the phenomenon of puppet states.[1] While they are by no means a new occurrence, the post-war development of international law in the direction of human rights accountability, the development of the body of international humanitarian law (IHL) and, most importantly, the exclusion of occupation as a legitimate title to territory have presented the puppet state as roughly the only solution for translating military and economic might into additional territory while circumventing most legal and political hurdles. In other words, in a world where annexation by occupation is both made illegal and de-legitimised at a political level and where occupation comes with a restraining set of rules and obligations, a puppet state offers the perfect venue for occupation with impunity. In this sense, a puppet state is a form of covert occupation, offering all of the advantages of occupation while eluding the direct political costs and the obligations imposed by IHL. In a further sense, this covert occupation translates into a prolonged state of *de facto* annexation.

By far the most enduring example of a puppet state is that of Northern Cyprus. However, the fall of Yugoslavia and of the Soviet Union brought a boom to this phenomenon. While the puppet states of the former Yugoslavia have all been liquidated in one form or another, the puppet states of the former Soviet Union, including Abkhazia, South Ossetia, Transnistria and Nagorno-Karabakh, have become near permanent realities of today's world. Most disturbingly, Russia is in

[1] While being mainly used in political science literature, the term "puppet state" (or "état fantoche" in French) has been adopted by a handful of legal scholars to refer to entities which, while preserving the external appearance of a regular state, are fully dependent on and controlled by a foreign state. Among the legal scholars who used this term more than in passing are Krystyna Marek, James Crawford and Joe Verhoeven. However, none of them dwelled on the topic at length: a more extensive study on puppet states is yet to be written. Despite the use by some legal scholars, the term has never made its way into mainstream legal scholarship or practice nor has been used by any relevant source of law so far.

the process of creating yet another puppet state in Eastern Ukraine. Veiling occupation as statehood has essentially become an open road to circumventing IHL and achieving territorial expansion at the cost of another state. This road is not only available to powerful countries such as Russia, but to all sorts of states, notwithstanding their power or influence, as it has been proven by the example of Armenia's puppet Nagorno-Karabakh.

Even more alarming than the phenomenon itself or its solidity are the grave effects that accompany it, which can hardly be overstated. Not only do the sponsors of these entities escape the burden of IHL, but puppet states essentially constitute black holes in international law as far as human rights protection is concerned as well as easy venues for trafficking and illegal arms sale for the benefit of their sponsor state, making them zones of almost total impunity.

As will be described, this impunity comes largely from a regulation gap in international law. With the exception of two isolated instances of case law which will be discussed below, there is, at this point, no source of law defining these entities or dealing with them directly. Unfortunately, this gap in law has not been satisfactorily filled by academic work either. While there is some scarce scientific debate in the field of political science on this subject, the legal research on the issue has been almost nonexistent. Only a handful of legal scholars, such as James Crawford[2] or Joe Verhoeven,[3] briefly discuss puppet states but unfortunately dedicate just a few paragraphs at most to them. However, the great majority of legal scholars that do discuss these entities force them, for the sake of consistency, into models that do not suit them, and thus cannot explain them. In most cases, the puppet states are forced under the large and vague umbrella of unrecognised states or de facto states, with important qualifications being sidelined in the process of fitting them within this category. Unfortunately, wrongly categorising these entities is misleading. Exactly what separates puppet states from de facto states makes them cases of covert occupation. By using the wrong terminology of de facto or unrecognised states, these authors perpetuate the confusion that allows the perpetrators to bypass international law regulations.

The standpoint from which the current research starts is that until these entities are not correctly defined in their own right, they will continue to satisfy their role as a veil for occupation, sheltering their sponsor from the outreach of IHL. The current paper attempts to explain the way in which puppet states function as tools for circumventing IHL. In doing so, it starts from three hypotheses: (1) puppet states constitute a separate category of territorial entities which should be understood in their own right, (2) puppet states are a form of covert occupation and (3) the regime of covert occupation shields the sponsor state from responsibility under IHL.

---

[2] Crawford 2006, pp. 63, 75, 78–83, 87 and 156–157.

[3] Referring to puppet states in French as "états fantoche". See Verhoeven 2000, pp. 57 and 70; and Verhoeven 1975, pp. 54 and 64.

2.2 Defining the Concept of Puppet States

An encompassing debate over statehood in general falls beyond the limited scope of the present paper. However, in order to be able to place puppet states within their context, some brief background should be given. Due to the lack of any codification of what a state is, the criteria laid down in the 1933 Montevideo Convention on the Rights and Duties of States has become the point of reference in defining statehood. The four Montevideo criteria are as follows: (1) a permanent population, (2) a defined territory, (3) government and (4) capacity to enter into relations with the other states. While the first two requirements and the last requirement are of a more straightforward nature, in discussing the third a certain nuance needs to be highlighted. It has been established in international law that the requirement is one for an effective and independent government and not just any form of government. Effectiveness refers predominantly to the existence of a coherent structure of authority, taking whatever form, and which is able to administer and regulate the territory that it controls.[4] In addition, most international law scholars agree on the point that an effective government is one that is independent of any other authority.[5] This criterion of non-dependence as a basis for an effective government can be found in opinions of international legal bodies and in the *opinio juris* and practice of states; as such, it can be considered to have become a principle of customary international law.[6]

The debate over whether recognition should be one of the criteria for statehood, coupled with the fact that without a certain degree of recognition, the ability of a state to effectively act within the world community is fundamentally impaired, gave birth to the separate category of de facto states. These are entities that satisfy the Montevideo criteria but are not yet widely accepted by the other states. What sets the puppet states apart from the de facto states is exactly their lack of independence as defined above. Their existence is fundamentally dependent upon the support of another state (termed *sponsor state* in this paper).

Some international legal scholars propose a further category of states: nascent states or states in *statu nascendi*, meaning states in the process of formation. These entities share with the puppet state their usual dependence on foreign assistance. Nonetheless, three factors separate them from the puppet states. First and foremost, there is, in the case of nascent states, a wide agreement within the international community on the opportunity of creating a new state. The claim to statehood of such an entity has gained wide enough acceptance at the international level, but the state still has to develop itself into a full-fledged state with an efficient and independent administration.

Secondly, despite the factual dependency on the assistance it receives, a nascent state acts largely independently from its sponsors and not as an appendix of

[4] Wallace-Bruce 1994, p. 66.

[5] Wallace 2005, p. 63.

[6] Ibid.

their interests, as is the case for puppet states. The best example in this sense is the one of Kosovo. The extensive role of foreign troops in maintaining both the internal and the external security of Kosovo still keep it in the ranks of nascent states. However, while maintaining diplomatic links with 94 states that recognise it, a number of NATO member states that maintain troops in Kosovo and thus sustain its existence, such as Romania or Spain, do not recognise Kosovo as a state. Moreover, they were very vocal in their opposition to Kosovo's statehood, submitting opinions in this sense to the International Court of Justice (ICJ) in the wake of its *Advisory Opinion on Kosovo*. Thus, support for a nascent state does not automatically translate to political synchronisation, not to speak of a top-down type of political command as it is the case for most puppet states.

Lastly, being in *statu nascendi* is, as the name itself denotes, a transitory phase and not one which is intended as permanent. A nascent state's birth is being sponsored by the international community as long as it is in the process of attaining the institutions and administrative controls needed for its functioning. The objective of this project was to bring the nascent state to self-sustainability. Once this process reaches its goal, the new state is left in an independent position. Many former colonies, protectorates or trust territories went through a period of being nascent states before being able to fulfil factual statehood criteria. One of the newer examples is East Timor, whose path to statehood was recognised in 1999 by UN Security Council Resolution 1272,[7] and it was subsequently aided by the other states and the organisation in attaining this goal. Now East Timor is a full-fledged state.

Therefore, it can be summarised that there are four criteria that define a puppet state, or rather sets one apart from either de facto states or nascent states. First, puppet states are not self-sustainable. The existence of all of them is insured by the sponsor state, either economically, militarily, politically or in all these respects. Puppet institutions dramatically rely economically or militarily, or in both regards, on the assistance of another state.

Secondly, this reliance is also translated at the political level. The sponsor controls, fully or in part, the politics of its puppet. Moreover, political decisions are mostly passed down to the puppet by its sponsor. In a better case scenario, the sponsor and the puppet act in concert in their political decision-making. In other words, the puppet acts as an appendix of its sponsor, as if it would be just a part of the sponsor's state or, at most, an autonomous region. This does not mean that the puppet does not retain some degree of autonomy or that it does not exert its own type of influence on the sponsor, but never to the degree to which it could be able to undermine the sponsor's control.

Thirdly, the community of states do not acknowledge its existence. Puppet states are (1) totally unrecognised, as in the case of Transnistria or Nagorno-Karabakh; (2) only recognised by their respective sponsor states, like Northern Cyprus; or (3) recognised by their sponsor state and other countries with strong political links with the sponsor state, as in the cases of South Ossetia and

[7] UN Security Council (1999) Resolution 1272 (1999), UN Doc. S/RES/1272.

Abkhazia. Thus, they never command the support of enough states to enable them to function in the international arena by joining international organisations or signing up to multilateral treaties. It goes without saying that such a state of affairs only consolidates the dependency of the puppet on its sponsor.

Fourth and lastly, the existence of a puppet state is devised to be quasi-permanent. Differently put, in contrast with de facto states or nascent states, the objective of a puppet state is not its independence, but rather its integration with the sponsor state. While that cannot be achieved, maintaining the status-quo is the main objective as it represents a form of de facto annexation. This having been said, it does not mean that changing political context cannot bring the end of a puppet state, as happened in the cases of Republika Srpska or Herceg-Bosna in today's Bosnia and Herzegovina. What matters is that the objective of its creation remains that of bringing its territory under the control of its sponsor, and not its eventual independence.

From the four criteria described above, it can be concluded that in effective terms, a puppet state is nothing else than a form of occupation, what the present paper terms a *covert occupation*. For the sake of better understanding the mechanics of a covert occupation, the example of Transnistria (Pridnestrovian Moldavian Republic or PMR) will be discussed below.

2.3 Transnistria: A Puppet State Case Study

For over two decades, Transnistria has been the puppet state of the Russian Federation on the territory of the Republic of Moldova. The decision to choose Transnistria rather than the latest puppet state, the Confederation of Novorossiya in Eastern Ukraine, as a case study for this paper is based on three considerations. Firstly, an already formed puppet state with a longer history can be better used to illustrate how such an entity is formed and maintained. Secondly, access to accurate information on Novorossiya is hard to obtain at this moment, taking into account the fact that the entity is currently in the process of formation. Thirdly, Transnistria and Novorossiya share not only the same sponsor, Russia, but also the tools used by it to support and exert influence upon these regions.

To start with, Transnistria's economic survival is almost entirely dependent on Russia. The most crucial means of economic support come through Russia's delivery of free gas to Transnistria.[8] These free gas deliveries currently amount to a sum exceeding one billion Euros.[9] The PMR authorities gather money from the population for this gas that they receive for free, thus collecting important budgetary revenues.[10] This type of economic support from the sponsor is doubled by

[8] Stăvilă 2010, interview with author.

[9] Popescu 2006, p. 12.

[10] Stăvilă 2010, interview with author.

large subsidies from Moscow that keep the Transnistrian industry alive.[11] Furthermore, Russia's control over Transnistrian industrial assets is not only done by capitalisation and subsidising but also by direct ownership. Russian capital close to the governing circles of the Kremlin owns all relevant industry in Transnistria,[12] including the Rabnita steel plant and most importantly the vast electric plant of Cuciurgeni, which functions on free Russian gas and is the main source of revenue in the PMR.[13] Moreover, by any standards, the Transnistrian market is almost fully incorporated in the Russian one at all levels,[14] most importantly in the banking and financial sectors.

Additionally, in the social sphere, Russia took over most of PMR's social responsibility role by paying benefits to the people in the region. Among others, it officially pays all retired people living in Transnistria an important bonus to their pension, notwithstanding the passport they hold, be it Moldavian, Transnistrian, Ukrainian, Russian, Romanian or still Soviet.[15] Moreover, Russia directly pays to Transnistrian mothers the sum of 5000 US Dollars upon giving birth to a child.[16] This policy of the Russian state only covers the territory of the Russian state and Transnistria. Such sums are not being paid to ethnic Russian mothers or even Russian citizen mothers living abroad, either in Moldova proper, in other states, or in any other breakaway republic in the former USSR, showing in a straightforward manner that Russia deals with the territory and population of Transnistria as de facto its own. By all standards, in the terms used by Nicu Popescu,[17] Transnistria outsourced its statehood to Russia.

Last but not least, the economic support lent by Russia to Transnistria is coupled with economic pressure on Moldova.[18] Russia has consistently raised gas prices to Moldova and has repeatedly imposed restrictions on meat, vegetables or wine imports from Moldova. It is relevant to note that these restrictions were always imposed whenever Moldova tried to take bolder steps in the Transnistrian issue or distance itself from the Muscovite standpoints. Subsequently, as Moldova's economic balance largely depends on its exports to Russia, these trading restrictions applied at the right moments often managed to bring Moldova into compliance with Russian positions and interests.

Yet the outsourcing of statehood does not limit itself to the economic sphere—it is also translated into the government, administration and defence spheres.

[11] Popescu 2006, p. 12.

[12] What is also pertinent to note at this point is the quite massive armament producing plants in Transnistria which are also controlled by Russia. Such plants like Electromash Tiraspol export arms to states in conflict and other secessionist entities—Deleau 2005, Document 2 of the annexes.

[13] Stăvilă 2010, interview with author.

[14] Ibid.

[15] Ibid.

[16] Ibid.

[17] Popescu 2006.

[18] Ibid., p. 12.

Russia has been crucial in the administration of the PMR. The security institutions and even key ministries in Transnistria are traditionally headed by Russian citizens and officials directly delegated by state institutions of the Russian state[19] with eloquent examples being the secret services, the Defense Ministry and the Transnistrian Central Bank.[20] Going one step further, few of the PMR officials are born in Transnistria or have any link with the region. The former long-standing PMR President himself, Igor Smirnoff, moved to Transnistria from the Soviet Far East in 1987, just two years before the conflict started.

In the military sphere, the support of the Russian 14th Army in creating and maintaining the PMR cannot be overstated. Not only did it ensure the creation of the PMR by defeating the Moldavian Army, but Russian peacekeepers have been de facto protecting the borders of the Transnistrian secessionist entity. A massive number of officers and even simple soldiers of the Russian 14th Army moved to the Transnistrian military forces. As it stands now, the Transnistrian military forces are mainly composed of Russian soldiers and officers formerly or still part of the Russian 14th Army stationed in the region.[21] To give only the most relevant example, in December 1991, the Russian 14th Army's highest commander left his post and became head of the newly formed military forces of the PMR. He was followed by his Chief of Staff who became PMR's Defense Minister.[22] It is hard to imagine that such an act would happen without the acknowledgement and control of the Russian forces and that the line of command with Moscow would have been broken. This process sealed the creation of the so-called Dniester Guards of the PMR, which is nothing more than an appendage to the Russian troops. Furthermore, as already shown, the commanders of the Russian forces in Transnistria not only gathered a lot of indirect political power, but held official positions in the PMR hierarchy.[23] Most importantly, the Russian troops were primordial in the creation of the PMR, and this was indirectly acknowledged by the fact that the 1992 ceasefire 'bilateral agreement' was signed by Russia and Moldova as combating parties, without including the PMR in any way.

Furthermore, there is ample evidence of the premeditated intervention of the Russian 14th Army in the conflict and of the arm and ammunition transfers from Russian to Transnistrian forces not only before and during the 1992 war,[24] but also after the ceasefire agreement had been signed.[25] On 20 March 1998, Russia even signed an official agreement with the PMR by which it transferred "weapons, ammunition and surplus military property" as well as "immovable [military]

---

[19] Ibid., p. 11.

[20] King 2001, p. 539.

[21] Vahl and Emerson 2004, p. 8.

[22] King 2001, p. 539.

[23] Ibid.

[24] King 2000, pp. 194–196.

[25] Akgün, p. 54.

property" to the Transnistrian forces and equally shared the benefits of selling the rest of the armament.[26]

The European Court of Human Rights (ECtHR) recognised this situation in its decision in the *Ilascu* case:

> the authorities of the Russian Federation contributed both militarily and politically to the creation of a separatist regime in the region of Transdniestria, which is part of the territory of the Republic of Moldova [...] and even after the ceasefire agreement of 21 July 1992 the Russian Federation continued to provide military, political and economic support to the separatist regime [...], thus enabling it to survive by strengthening itself and by acquiring a certain amount of autonomy vis-à-vis Moldova.[27]

Similar states of affairs are present in all the other puppet states. The modes of operation might take different forms, but the effect is the same: a state of covert occupation. The hypothesis of the present research, that a puppet state is nothing but an appendix of its sponsor and a case of covert occupation, is supported by the two instances of case law which directly dealt with this question. The first time international law was confronted in a plenary manner with the phenomenon of puppet states was during the early 1930s in the Manchurian crisis. The so-called Lytton Commission was requested to present a report to the League of Nations on the Empire of Japan's seizure of Manchuria. The Lytton Commission Report unequivocally concluded that Manchukuo, the quasi-stately entity established by Japan in Manchuria, was not "a genuine and spontaneous independence movement"[28] due to its lack of an independent government. The second example comes in the context of the disbanding of Yugoslavia. The International Criminal Tribunal for the Former Yugoslavia (ICTY) concluded in the *Prosecutor v Rajic* case that Croatia exercised such control over Herceg-Bosna that the latter was not in fact a state, but an extension of the former.[29]

2.4 Puppet States as Areas of Impunity

After proving that puppet states are a category in themselves and should not be confused with either de facto states or nascent states, and that in fact they are instances of covert occupation, the present research moves to show how such a state of covert occupation benefits the sponsor state. As hypothesised, compared to

---

[26] Agreement on Questions Relating to Military Property (Russian Federation and the Moldavian Republic of Trandniestria), signed on 20 March 1998 in Odessa, Ukraine, Articles 1 and 5.

[27] ECtHR, *Case of Ilaşcu and others v Moldova and Russia,* Grand Chamber Judgment, 8 July 2004, Appl. No. 48787/99 (*Ilaşcu*), para 382.

[28] The League of Nations 1932.

[29] ICTY, *Prosecutor v Ivica Rajić*, Review of the Indictment Pursuant to Rule 61 of the Rules of Procedure and Evidence, 13 September 1996, Case No. IT-95-12-R61, para 26.

a regular form of occupation, this form of covert occupation not only has a lower reputational cost on the sponsor state, but it enables it to act outside the limits imposed by IHL.

2.4.1 Obligations of the Sponsor State Under IHL

2.4.1.1 Responsibility Under Common Article 2(1) of the Geneva Conventions

To start with, the sponsor state holds total responsibility under IHL over the acts of its own organs during the armed conflict.[30] According to Common Article 2(1), the Geneva Conventions apply even if the state of war is not recognised by one of the belligerents.[31]

The situation becomes much more complicated in respect of the sponsor state's responsibility over the humanitarian law violations of its puppet. The ICJ decided in the 1986 *Nicaragua* case that in order for the USA to be responsible for humanitarian law and human rights violations of the Nicaraguan Contras, "effective control over the military or paramilitary operations in the course of which the violations occurred" needs to be proven.[32] The threshold of effective control imposed by the Court was an exceptionally high one. In the eyes of the ICJ, the "decisive" financing, organising, training and supplying of a military force do not transfer responsibility of its humanitarian law violations to the sponsor.[33] Not even when the sponsor plans the military operations of the given force and has an overall control over it, is it responsible under the law of war. The Court offers in fact its test for "effective control": violations of international humanitarian law are attributed to the sponsor state when it plans, directs and supports the military operation directly, with only the execution, or part of it, being outsourced to the military group it controls.[34] In other words, the test is not one of dependence (not even

---

[30] If it is clear when the application of Common Article 2(1) commences [see Article 6(1)], it is more challenging to identify the end moment of its application. The reading of Article 6 of the Geneva Convention (IV) relative to the Protection of Civilian Persons in Time of War, opened for signature on 12 August 1949, 75 UNTS 287 (entered into force 21 October 1950) (GC IV), Article 2 of Protocol Additional to the Geneva Conventions of 12 August 1949, and relating to the Protection of Victims of Non-International Armed Conflicts, opened for signature 8 June 1977, 1125 UNTS 609 (entered into force 7 December 1978), and the ruling at para 70 in ICTY, *Prosecutor v Duško Tadić*, Judgement, 15 July 1999, Case No. IT-94-1-A (*Tadić*) leads to the conclusion that a conflict does not come to conclusion simply when a peace or ceasefire agreement is signed, but when the intensity of fighting on the ground subsides below the intensity of an armed conflict.

[31] GC IV, above n 30.

[32] ICJ, *Case Concerning Military and Paramilitary Activities in and against Nicaragua (Nicaragua v United States of America)*, Judgment, 27 June 1986, [1986] ICJ Rep 14, para 115.

[33] Ibid.

[34] Ibid., para 86.

one of complete dependence), but one of a high degree of effective control, including the command over each military operation in which violations occurred.

The ICTY's 1999 *Tadić* case has been cited as proof that the threshold for the attribution of conduct on the basis of direction or control has been lowered from "effective control" to "overall control".[35] However, regardless of the ICTY's convincing arguments, the ICJ firmly dismissed the move towards a test of "overall control" in its *Bosnia Genocide* judgement, pointing out the fact that the ICTY was adjudicating on a completely different matter and in a completely different context.[36]

As it stands now, the test put forward by the ICJ effectively thickens the smokescreen that shelters sponsor states from responsibility under the law of war. The main reason for such a statement is that the ICJ's test paradoxically requires a higher level of proof in order for violations of humanitarian law by the puppet state to be attributable to the sponsor than that required for the attribution of acts of its own organs. Consequently, the use of puppet states becomes especially advantageous in this context. On the one hand, under Article 7 of the International Law Commission Draft Articles on State Responsibility, a state is responsible for the acts of its organs or of a person empowered to exercise elements of governmental authority even when they exceed their authority or contravene instructions that they were given, whenever they act in their official capacity.[37] The commentaries to this article make plain that even *ultra vires* or unauthorised acts are attributable to the state and entail the state's responsibility.[38] On the other hand, the state can take refuge behind the very same excuses if it chooses to create and use a puppet state instead of its own organs. If, for example, a soldier of the sponsor state breaches IHL provisions following no official instructions, he nonetheless triggers his state's responsibility for the act. If the same soldier is transferred to the military forces of the puppet state, which are under the overall control and direction of the sponsor, and he commits the same humanitarian law violations, still without following any official instructions, his act is not attributable to the sponsor state. Just a change of uniform, with no alteration of circumstances or level of control protects the sponsor state from responsibility under IHL. Regrettably, the high threshold imposed by the ICJ acts as yet another incentive for a state to act covertly through the use of a puppet state, rather than overtly through the use of its own organs in the context of an international armed conflict.

[35] *Tadić*, above n 30, paras 116–145.

[36] ICJ, *Case Concerning Application of the Convention on the Prevention and Punishment of the Crime of Genocide (Bosnia and Herzegovina v Serbia and Montenegro)*, Judgment, 26 February 2007, [2007] ICJ Rep 43, paras 399–400.

[37] International Law Commission 2001, Article 7.

[38] Ibid.: "The State cannot take refuge behind the notion that, according to the provisions of its internal law or to instructions which may have been given to its organs or agents, their actions or omissions ought not to have occurred or ought to have taken a different form. This is so even where the organ or entity in question has overtly committed unlawful acts under the cover of its official status or has manifestly exceeded its competence. It is so even if other organs of the State have disowned the conduct in question".

The ICJ's test is so restrictive that it makes it very hard, if not impossible, to ever demonstrate the required level of *effective control* before this Court. The fact that this argument could never be made successfully before the ICJ speaks for itself. In conclusion, the very high qualification threshold imposed by ICJ's *effective control* test virtually shields the sponsor state when making use of the armed forces of its puppet.

2.4.1.2 Responsibility Under Common Article 2(2) of the Geneva Conventions

Common Article 2(2) deals with the application of IHL during a situation of occupation. The law of belligerent occupation can apply in two different circumstances. Firstly, it can apply concomitantly with Article 2(1). According to the commentary to the Geneva Conventions:

> So far as individuals are concerned, the application of the Fourth Geneva Convention does not depend upon the existence of a state of occupation within the meaning of the Article 42 [of the 1907 Hague Conventions] referred to above. The relations between the civilian population of a territory and troops advancing into that territory, whether fighting or not, are governed by the present Convention. There is no intermediate period between what might be termed the invasion phase and the inauguration of a stable regime of occupation. Even a patrol which penetrates into enemy territory without any intention of staying there must respect the Conventions in its dealings with the civilians it meets.[39]

Thus, the law of occupation applies in respect of the relation with the civilians encountered as soon as soldiers of the sponsor state advance into the territory of the mother state.

Secondly, the law of occupation applies once "a stable regime of occupation" begins. This takes place after the initial invasion and once the puppet state is firmly established and in control of the given territory. This stage is typically simultaneous with the moment when the military situation on the ground subsides and the hostilities habitually end. Using a term favoured by political scientists, for all intents and purposes, the conflict "freezes" and little, if any, military clashes occur. With the end of hostilities, IHL ceases to apply under Common Article 2(1) of the Geneva Conventions.[40] Nonetheless, IHL can continue to apply under Common Article 2(2) of the Conventions which covers occupation.

According to Article 42 of the 1907 Hague Conventions: "Territory is considered occupied when it is actually placed under the authority of the hostile army. The occupation extends only to the territory where such authority has been established and can be exercised." Yet, puppet states are created by design and often with the intent to evade the test put forward by Article 42. There certainly are a few forthright cases in which the sponsor state deployed its army in big numbers in support of its puppet. Northern Cyprus is one such case. Consequently, in the

[39] Pictet, Article 2.

[40] See above n 30.

case of Northern Cyprus, we can speak of a clear instance of occupation under the definition above, and thus falling under IHL rules. There is thus no covert occupation in Northern Cyprus, the establishment of the puppet state of the Turkish Republic of Northern Cyprus being a political calculation meant to diminish the reputational cost on the part of Turkey, rather than a way of circumventing IHL. Consequently, the sponsor state, Turkey, is bound by the provisions of the 1949 Fourth Geneva Convention (GC IV), especially Section III (Articles 27–34 and 47–78) dealing specifically with belligerent occupation.

The law of belligerent occupation found in the aforementioned section of the GC IV regulates the relationship between the occupier, the occupied state and the population under occupation. Article 29 of the Convention clearly lays the responsibility for the occupied territory and its inhabitants on the shoulders of the occupying power: "The Party to the conflict in whose hands protected persons may be, is responsible for the treatment accorded to them by its agents, irrespective of any individual responsibility which may be incurred."[41]

Important to note is the fact that the Article stresses the dual responsibility under international law of the individual who commits the violation and of the state whose agent he is. These two responsibilities apply in parallel, being complementary to one another. The Convention continues by spelling out the rights enjoyed by the population of the occupied territory, such as the prohibition of any reprisals against civilians and their property (Article 33), the prohibition of deportation (Article 49), the prohibition against compelling the occupied population to serve in the armed forces of the occupier (Article 51) or to take part in military operations against their country (Article 52), respect for the person, honour, family rights, religious convictions and other customs or cultural and spiritual heritage monuments of the occupied population (Article 27), the obligation to offer humane conditions to the detained persons and to allow these detainees to be visited by delegates of the protecting power and of the International Committee of the Red Cross (Article 76), and the obligation to provide medical care, public health and hygiene to the occupied population (Article 56), as well as allowing the functioning of the National Red Cross or Red Crescent Society and other relief societies on the occupied territory (Article 63).

Furthermore, under Articles 54 and 64 GC IV, the occupying power should, as a general rule, keep in place the national laws and institutions of the occupied state. Very little leeway is offered to the occupier to alter the laws or make changes in the institutional makeup of the region they control. The two exceptions under which the occupier can modify the legislation of the occupied territory are spelled in Article 64 of GC IV: (1) "in cases where they [the laws] constitute a threat to its security or an obstacle to the application of the present Convention" and (2) under the need to enact "provisions which are essential to enable the occupying power to fulfil its obligations under the present Convention, to maintain the orderly government of the territory and to ensure the security of the occupying power, of the

[41] GC IV, above n 30.

members and property of the occupying forces or administration, and likewise of the establishments and lines of communication used by them".[42] Thus, these exceptions only allow the occupying state limited leeway in bringing about changes to the legal or institutional make-up of the region under occupation. Article 54 further lays down the condition that public officials may only be removed when they refuse to fulfil their tasks.[43] Nevertheless, judges cannot be removed from their posts for any reason.[44]

However, as shown above, the main purpose of establishing a puppet state is to achieve a state of *covert occupation*. In these cases, the occupation is instituted and maintained by the military troops of the puppet state and not of the sponsor state. Nevertheless, this army of the puppet state is often made up of former troops of the sponsor state and is under direct, yet covert, command and support of the sponsor state. In other words, as with the entire entity itself, its army is just a façade behind which stands the sponsor state's military.

In this context, it would follow that an occupation by the forces of a puppet state is merely an occupation by its sponsor, and thus imposed upon this sponsor are all the aforementioned obligations of GC IV and the Additional Protocols. However, despite the apparent logic of this argument, it needs to be stressed that at this point, there is no state practice or case law that could prove the acceptance of such a synonymy by the international community.[45] On the contrary, all United Nations Security Council Resolutions on the situation name the puppet state as the occupier, with very few allusions to the control of the sponsor. To give only one example, Resolution 822 (1993) concerning the Nagorno-Karabakh conflict speaks of the "local Armenian forces", with just vague hints to the involvement of Armenia.[46]

Thus, there currently seems to be a gap in the application of IHL. If the sponsor state has effective control over a territory through its command over the puppet regime, but its forces do not directly occupy the territory under question, the sponsor state escapes the burdens imposed by IHL. Moreover, not only does the sponsor state escape any obligations imposed by IHL, but these obligations are not transferred to

---

[42] Ibid.

[43] Ibid.

[44] Ibid.

[45] A possible exception might be found in the UK Military Manual, which reads at paragraph 11.3.1 that "[i]n some cases, occupying troops have operated indirectly through an existing or newly appointed indigenous government. This type of occupation is not discussed in detail in this chapter. In such cases, despite certain differences from the classic form of military occupation, the law relating to military occupation is likely to be applicable. Legal obligations, policy considerations, and external diplomatic pressures may all point to this conclusion."—UK Ministry of Defence 2004. It is, however, unclear if this passing and un-detailed mention applies to the case of puppet states. Anyhow, due to the use of the word likely, paragraph 11.3.1 can only be read as a guideline or recommendation, leaving the question of whether the creation and maintenance of puppet states should be equated with a state of occupation open. Moreover, such a stance has not been reflected in British state practice.

[46] UN Security Council (1993) Resolution 822 (1993), UN Doc. S/RES/822.

any other entity. The only way this set of obligations could be transferred to the puppet authorities is under the auspices of Common Article 3 of the Geneva Convention. This article deals with non-international armed conflicts. However, international law prescribes that an intervention by a state in support of armed opposition groups in another country internationalises the armed conflict if the intervening state is either controlling the military opposition group or is itself conducting military operations within the foreign territory.[47] This position is supported by the ICTY in its Appeals Chamber decision in the *Tadić Case*, which stated that:

> [i]n the light of the above discussion, the following conclusion may be safely reached. In the case at issue, given that the Bosnian Serb armed forces constituted a 'military organization', the control of the FRY authorities over these armed forces required by international law for considering the armed conflict to be international was overall control going beyond the mere financing and equipping of such forces and involving also participation in the planning and supervision of military operations. By contrast, international rules do not require that such control should extend to the issuance of specific orders or instructions relating to single military actions, whether or not such actions were contrary to international humanitarian law.[48]

Therefore, if the sponsor state controls a territory mainly through the puppet state's forces, rather than deploying its own in larger numbers, a vacuum is created in the application of IHL. On the one hand, the support of the sponsor state internationalises the conflict, making Common Article 3 of the Geneva Conventions inapplicable and consequently releasing the humanitarian law burden from the shoulders of the puppet state. On the other hand, the limited use of its forces on the territory controlled by the puppet puts the sponsor state under the threshold of belligerent occupation, absolving it of any obligations under IHL.

2.4.2 *Obligations of the Sponsor State Under Human Rights Law*

It should be nonetheless mentioned that the sponsor state does not escape the burden of international human rights law. Responsibility for wrongful acts is primarily based on effective control over the territory where such an act is committed.[49] It is, however, very important to note that the *effective control* test for the application of human rights law is different from, and should not be confused with, the ICJ's homonymous *effective control*/Nicaragua test for the application of IHL discussed above. As it will be shown below, the effective control test in human rights law, as defined by the ECtHR, has a much lower qualification threshold.

---

[47] Fleck 2008, p. 606.

[48] *Tadić*, above n 30, para 145.

[49] ICJ, *Legal Consequences for States of the Continued Presence of South Africa in Namibia (South West Africa) notwithstanding Security Council Resolution 276* 1970, Advisory Opinion, 21 June 1971, [1971] PCIJ Rep 16, para 118.

All through a long line of case law on the issue of human rights responsibility in puppet states, the ECtHR consistently upheld the principle according to which primary responsibility and liability for human rights violations in a puppet state rests with the sponsor state. The first case in which the ECtHR dealt with the issue of a puppet state is the *Loizidou v. Turkey Case*. In its judgement on the preliminary objections, the Court refuted Turkey's claim that the Turkish Republic of Northern Cyprus (TRNC) is not a puppet state but a democratic state established on the basis of its right of self-determination, and thus fully responsible for the breaches of law occurring on its territory.[50] The Court came to the conclusion that:

> [b]earing in mind the object and purpose of the Convention, the responsibility of a Contracting Party may also arise when as a consequence of military action - whether lawful or unlawful - it exercises effective control of an area outside its national territory. The obligation to secure, in such an area, the rights and freedoms set out in the Convention derives from the fact of such control whether it be exercised directly, through its armed forces, or through a subordinate local administration.

In this connection, the respondent government have acknowledged that the applicant's loss of control of her property stems from the occupation of the northern part of Cyprus by Turkish troops and the establishment there of the "TRNC". Furthermore, it has not been disputed that the applicant was prevented by Turkish troops from gaining access to her property.[51]

Therefore, apart from clearly establishing responsibility of the sponsor state for the human rights violations of the puppet state, the Court also stresses that the exercise of effective control does not need to be done through military means, as it is needed for the application of humanitarian law, but can also be achieved through the subordination of the puppet state's administration.

In *Ilaşcu and Others v Moldova and Russia* case, the ECtHR goes into a broader discussion on the ways in which the sponsor state can control its puppet. These means cover a wide range, from political, financial or economic support to the more straightforward military backing. According to the Court's judgement:

> [t]he 'MRT', set up in 1991-1992 with the support of the Russian Federation, vested with organs of power and its own administration, remains under the effective authority, or at the very least under the decisive influence, of the Russian Federation, and in any event that it survives by virtue of the military, economic, financial and political support given to it by the Russian Federation.
>
> That being so, the Court considers that there is a continuous and uninterrupted link of responsibility on the part of the Russian Federation for the applicants' fate, as the Russian Federation's policy of support for the regime and collaboration with it continued beyond 5 May 1998, and after that date the Russian Federation made no attempt to put an end to the applicants' situation brought about by its agents, and did not act to prevent the violations allegedly committed after 5 May 1998.[52]

---

[50] ECtHR, *Case of Loizidou v Turkey*, Preliminary Objections, 23 March 1995, Appl. No. 15318/89, para 54.

[51] Ibid., para 62.

[52] *Ilaşcu*, above n 27, paras 392–393.

It follows from the argument of the Court that even after the sponsor state vests the puppet with its own administration or military, it continues to be liable for its action if it has either (1) decisive influence over the decisions of the new administrative organs and/or (2) its aid, either military, financial, political, economic or of any other nature is indispensable to the puppet's survival.

In conclusion, under human rights law, the sponsor state has the full burden of responsibility for violations occurring on the territory of its puppet. In order to retain this responsibility, effective control of the sponsor does not need to be exercised through military means but can also be done through the subordination of the puppet state's administration. On the other hand, the sponsor state holds responsibility over the puppet state under the law of belligerent occupation only if it militarily occupies the territory in a direct manner using its own troops. If the occupation is done primarily through the troops of the puppet, the sponsor state escapes any obligations and responsibility under IHL, thus transforming the puppet states into a grey zone of total impunity for violations of the laws of war.

2.4.3 Obligations of the Puppet State

It is important to explain at this point that the puppet regime itself escapes any burden of responsibility under international law. As a general rule, states are traditionally seen as the primary guarantors and violators of human rights. Few exceptions exist from this rule. The first exception is made in the case of insurgencies. Despite the lack of agreement on a legal definition of insurgency, there is wide consensus in the academic and legal world that insurgents are actors in an internal conflict[53] and their obligations stem primarily out of Common Article 3 of the 1949 Geneva Conventions. However, as clarified above, the support offered to the puppet by the sponsor state internationalises the conflict, taking it out of the civil war framework and deeming Common Article 3 inapplicable to their case.

A second exception is that of national liberation movements (NLMs). These are in the words of Article 1(4) of the 1977 Additional Protocol I to the Geneva Conventions:

> peoples [...] fighting against colonial domination and alien occupation and against racist regimes in the exercise of their right of self-determination, as enshrined in the Charter of the United Nations and the Declaration on Principles of International Law concerning Friendly Relations and Co-operation among States in accordance with the Charter of the United Nations.[54]

Therefore, NLMs derive their status out of their right to self-determination. However, the right to self-determination only applies to a very limited number

[53] Schoiswohl 2004.

[54] Protocol Additional to the Geneva Conventions of 12 August 1949, and relating to the Protection of Victims of International Armed Conflicts, opened for signature 12 December 1977, 1125 UNTS 3 (entered into force 7 December 1979).

of qualified peoples. The right exists either in the colonial context or as remedial secession in cases where the rights of a people were violated by the state, and no internal self-determination remedy was offered. However, none of the puppet states discussed in this research fulfils this set of criteria. Nonetheless, a case where a genuine claim for self-determination is supported and advanced with the critical aid of a third party state is not unthinkable. On the other hand, in these cases, the genuine self-determination claim gains the wide support of the international community, placing the entity under the category of a nascent state. State practice does not record any instance in which a genuine self-determination claim was solely advanced through the aid of a third party state against the will of the international community at large. Consequently, it is safe to conclude on this matter that while none of the regimes of the current puppet states qualify as NLMs, there is also little chance that any future such regime will.

A third exception is represented by the de facto states. The reasons puppet states do not qualify as de facto states were discussed in the first part of the paper. However, international case law exhibits an interesting paradox in this respect. While there is no instance of equating puppet states with de facto states for the purpose of establishing liability of these entities per se for breaches of international law, the differentiation was blurred when it came to the responsibility of the authorities of the puppet state or of private individuals acting on the territory of these entities for violations of international law.

The major break came with the establishment of the ICTY. Dealing with the crimes committed by individuals on the territory of the former Yugoslavia, the Court was directly faced with the issue of puppet states and the subsequent question of the extent of their leaders' liability before the Court. The Court saw fit to counter this possible issue of jurisdiction by laying down the broadest possible definition for a state. Rule 2 of the ICTY Rules of Procedure and Evidence stipulates in this respect that a state is a:

(i) A State Member or non-Member of the United Nations;
(ii) An entity recognised by the constitution of Bosnia and Herzegovina, namely the Federation of Bosnia and Herzegovina and the Republic Srpska; or
(iii) A self-proclaimed entity de facto exercising governmental functions, whether recognised as a State or not.[55]

Thus, the only characteristic required of an entity to qualify under this definition is for it to exercise governmental functions within a territory. No threshold for this capacity is further required. The objective of this broad definition is purely pragmatic. It attempts to make sure that no gaps would exist that could be construed to limit the Court's jurisdiction over exactly such entities as puppet states. The Court indeed indicted a number of senior leaders of puppet states like Republic Srpska, ranging from simple individuals to the political head of the regime, Radovan Karadžić.

---

[55] UN 2009 International Tribunal for the Prosecution of Persons Responsible for Serious Violations of International Humanitarian Law Committed in the Territory of the Former Yugoslavia since 1991: Rules of Procedure and Evidence, UN Doc. It/32/Rev.44, Rule 2.

The United States Court of Appeals followed suit. In its *Kadic v Karadžić* case, it equated Republic Srpska with a state in order to ensure that no impunity would follow from the unclear status of the entity. The Court highlighted in this respect that "[t]he inquiry, after all, is whether a person purporting to wield official power has exceeded internationally recognised standards of civilised conduct, not whether statehood in all its formal aspects exists".[56]

The importance of this case law lies in the fact that while individual responsibility exists for genocide and crimes against humanity, the prohibition of torture on the other hand is still linked to the state. Article 1 of the 1984 Convention against Torture and Other Cruel, Inhumane or Degrading Treatment or Punishment limits the definition of torture to acts "inflicted by or at the instigation of or with the consent or acquiescence of a public official or other person acting in an official capacity".[57] The broader definition of the state in the understanding of the ICTY and the US Court of Appeals serves to make the officials of all stately entities, including puppet states, liable for the crime of torture.

As previously mentioned, there is also a well-established general prohibition of genocide and crimes against humanity. Private individuals bear criminal responsibility under international law for the perpetration of such crimes. The US Court of Appeals in the *Kadic v Karadžić* case underlined in this respect that:

> [w]e do not agree that the law of nations, as understood in the modern era, confines its reach to state action. Instead, we hold that certain forms of conduct violate the law of nations whether undertaken by those acting under the auspices of a state or only as private individuals.[58]

Article 4 of the 1951 Convention on the Prevention and Punishment of the Crime of Genocide further stipulates that: "Persons committing genocide or any of the other acts enumerated in Article 3 shall be punished, whether they are constitutionally responsible rulers, public officials or private individuals."[59]

In the same way, the statutes of all international criminal courts do not require any proof of official capacity for inferring criminal responsibility of private persons for crimes of genocide or crimes against humanity.[60] However, authorities of the puppet states do not face international criminal responsibility for any other crimes or human rights violations outside the scope of the prohibition of genocide, torture and crimes against humanity.

---

[56] *Kadic v Karadžić*, US Court of Appeals 2nd Circuit, 13 October 1995 (*Kadic*), para 158.

[57] Convention against Torture and Other Cruel, Inhumane or Degrading Treatment or Punishment, opened for signature 10 December 1984, 1465 UNTS 85 (entered into force 26 June 1987).

[58] *Kadic*, above n 56, para 152.

[59] Convention on the Prevention and Punishment of the Crime of Genocide, opened for signature 9 December 1948, 78 UNTS 277 (entered into force 12 January 1951).

[60] Rome Statute of the International Criminal Court, opened for signature 17 July 1998, 2187 UNTS 90 (entered into force 1 July 2002), Articles 6 and 7; UN Security Council 1993 Report of the Secretary-General pursuant to para 2 of Security Council Resolution 808 (1993), UN Doc S/25704, Annex: Statute of the International Tribunal, Article 5; UN Security Council 1994 Resolution 955 (1994), UN Doc. S/RES/955, Annex: Statute of the International Tribunal for Rwanda, Article 3.

Unfortunately, outside the three exceptions presented above, there are no legal obligations vested in puppet states. There is no treaty law or customary international law dealing with the obligations of puppet states. Little as it may be, the only exception is that of individual responsibility for crimes against humanity, genocide and torture. Apart from this exception, the organs of the puppet state together with the people who commit human rights violations in these territories fall between the lines of international law in a grey zone of impunity.

Various attempts have been made to fill this gap. Professor Theodor Meron was the first to open the debate with his 1984 article in the American Journal of International Law, *Towards a Humanitarian Declaration on Internal Strife.*[61] 1988 saw Meron publish the Draft Model Declaration on Internal Strife,[62] while Hans-Peter Gasser wrote the Code of Conduct in the Event of Internal Disturbances and Tensions[63] in an attempt to summarise all international standards on the subject. Finally, one year later, the Oslo Statement on Norms and Procedures in Times of Public Emergency or Internal Violence[64] emerged, followed by the 1990 Declaration of Minimum Humanitarian Standards at Turku/Abo (Turku Declaration).[65] The latter attempted to provide humanitarian standards meant, in the terms of Article 2, to "be respected by, and applied to all persons, groups and authorities, irrespective of their legal status and without any adverse discrimination".[66] Unfortunately, all of these attempts remained in the realm of academic endeavours, with no response so far in the sphere of applicable law.

Summing up, no responsibility of the puppet state for international law violations exists. The few attempts to fill this liability gap and enact rules on this matter unfortunately remained just at the level of academic wishful thinking, never seeing their reflection in hard law. On the other hand, international law clearly establishes private responsibility for individuals committing a series of grave human rights violations on the territory or in the name of a puppet state.

---

61 Meron 1984.

62 Meron 1988, pp. 59–76.

63 Gasser 1988, pp. 51–53.

64 UN General Assembly 1987 Letter dated 26 June 1987 from the representative of Norway to the commission on Human Rights addressed to the Under-Secretary-General for Human Rights (transmitting the Oslo Statement on Norms and Procedures in Times of Public Emergency or Internal Violence), UN Doc. E/CN.4/Dub.2/1987/31.

65 Expert Meeting (1990) Declaration of Minimum Humanitarian Standards, Adopted by an expert meeting convened by the Institute for Human Rights, Åbo Akademi University, in Turku/Åbo, Finland, 2 December 1990. http://www.ifrc.org/Docs/idrl/I149EN.pdf. Accessed 14 June 2016.

66 Ibid.

2.5 Conclusion

As shown above, the use of fake secessionist claims materialised as puppet states offers the perfect venue for a state to escape the constraints of international law, especially those of IHL, and perform de facto annexations. This consequently leads to prolonged instances of covert occupation. As long as the sponsor states are able to frame such entities in terms of statehood and equate them with de facto states, the situation is not likely to change. On the contrary, neither the world community nor international legal scholars have concerned themselves with this issue so far. In the meantime, while states, big and small, are able to use this gap within international law to pursue their imperialist agendas under a legal veil, principles like the illegality of annexation seem to be dead letters. Maybe the most worrying part of this state of affairs is that international law itself is defeated by the use of its own criteria. Instead of effectively outlawing annexation, the current rules of international law offer the tools to effectively, even if covertly, achieve it. While the law can be bypassed using its own criteria, law cannot be enforced, and an unenforceable law has little, if any, meaning in practice.

The present paper's main intention is to present this problem and to call attention to the growing trend of covert occupation. The first and most urgent step in dealing with this is piercing the veil by correctly defining the phenomenon at hand. These entities should not be seen in terms of statehood anymore, but in terms of occupation. They are not states, or de facto states—they are puppet states and by this they are instances of covert occupation. Once this is fully acknowledged, the gap that currently exists in IHL needs to be closed by establishing that this form of *covert occupation* is occupation nonetheless, and by treating it as such.

References

Books, Articles and Other Documents

Crawford J (2006) The Creation of States in International Law. Oxford University Press, Oxford
Deleau X (2005) Transnistrie: La Poudriere de l'Europe. Hugodoc, Paris
Fleck D (2008) The Handbook of International Humanitarian Law, 2nd edn. Oxford University Press, Oxford
Gasser H (1988) Code of Conduct in the event of internal disturbances and tensions. International Review of the Red Cross 262:38–58
International Law Commission (2001) Draft Articles on Responsibility of States for Internationally Wrongful Acts. Yearbook of the International Law Commission Vol II: Part 2
King C (2000) The Moldovans: Romania, Russia, and the Politics of Culture. Hoover Institution Press, Stanford
King C (2001) The Benefits of Ethnic War: Understanding Eurasia's unrecognized states. World Polit 53:524–552
Meron T (1984) Towards a humanitarian declaration on internal strife. Am J Int Law 78:859–868

Meron T (1988) Draft Model Declaration on Internal Strife. Int Rev Red Cross 262:59–76
Pictet J (1952) Commentary on the Geneva Conventions of 12 August 1949. International Committee of the Red Cross, Geneva
Popescu N (2006) 'Outsourcing' de facto Statehood: Russia and the Secessionist Entities in Georgia and Moldova. CEPS Policy Brief 109:1–8
Schoiswohl M (2004) Status and (Human Rights) Obligations of Non-Recognized De facto Regimes in International Law: The Case of 'Somaliland', Martinus Nijhoff Publishers
Stăvilă I (2010) Personal interview with the author on 13 January 2010
The League of Nations (1932) Appeal by the Chinese Government: Report of the Commission of Enquiry, Series of League of Nations Publications, Official No. C.663.M.320
UK Ministry of Defence (2004) The Joint Service Manual of the Law of Armed Conflict. Joint Service Publication 383
UN (2009) International Tribunal for the Prosecution of Persons Responsible for Serious Violations of International Humanitarian Law Committed in the Territory of the Former Yugoslavia since 1991: Rules of Procedure and Evidence, UN Doc. It/32/Rev.44
UN General Assembly (1987) Letter Dated 26 June 1987 from the Representative of Norway to the Commission on Human Rights Addressed to the Under-Secretary-General for Human Rights (transmitting the Oslo Statement on Norms and Procedures in Times of Public Emergency or Internal Violence), UN Doc. E/CN.4/Dub.2/1987/31
UN Security Council (1993) Report of the Secretary-General pursuant to Paragraph 2 of Security Council Resolution 808 (1993), UN Doc S/25704, Annex: Statute of the International Tribunal
UN Security Council (1993) Resolution 822 (1993), UN Doc. S/RES/822
UN Security Council (1994) Resolution 955 (1994), UN Doc. S/RES/955, Annex: Statute of the International Tribunal for Rwanda
UN Security Council (1999) Resolution 1272 (1999), UN Doc. S/RES/1272
Vahl M, Emerson M (2004) Moldova and the Transnistrian Conflict. J Ethnopolitics Minor Issues Eur 1 (Chap. 4)
Verhoeven J (1975) La reconnaissance internationale dans la pratique contemporaine. Bruillant
Verhoeven J (2000) Droit international public. De Boeck & Larcier
Wallace-Bruce N (1994) Claims to Statehood in International Law. Carlton Press, New York
Wallace R (2005) International Law. Sweet & Maxwell, London

Case Law

ECtHR, *Case of Ilaşcu and others v Moldova and Russia,* Grand Chamber Judgment, 8 July 2004, Appl. No. 48787/99
ECtHR, *Case of Loizidou v Turkey*, Preliminary Objections, 23 March 1995, Appl. No. 15318/89
ICJ, *Case Concerning Application of the Convention on the Prevention and Punishment of the Crime of Genocide (Bosnia and Herzegovina v Serbia and Montenegro),* Judgment, 26 February 2007, [2007] ICJ Rep 43
ICJ, *Case Concerning Military and Paramilitary Activities in and against Nicaragua (Nicaragua v United States of America)*, Judgment, 27 June 1986, [1986] ICJ Rep 14
ICJ, *Legal Consequences for States of the Continued Presence of South Africa in Namibia (South West Africa) notwithstanding Security Council Resolution 276 (1970)*, Advisory Opinion, 21 June 1971, [1971] PCIJ Rep 16
ICTY, *Prosecutor v Duško Tadić*, Judgement, 15 July 1999, Case No. IT-94-1-A
ICTY, *Prosecutor v Ivica Rajić*, Review of the Indictment Pursuant to Rule 61 of the Rules of Procedure and Evidence, 13 September 1996, Case No. IT-95-12-R61
Kadic v Karadžić, US Court of Appeals 2nd Circuit, 13 October 1995

Treaties

Agreement on Questions Relating to Military Property (Russian Federation and the Moldavian Republic of Trandniestria), signed on 20 March 1998 in Odessa, Ukraine

Convention against Torture and Other Cruel, Inhumane or Degrading Treatment or Punishment, opened for signature 10 December 1984, 1465 UNTS 85 (entered into force 26 June 1987)

Convention on the Prevention and Punishment of the Crime of Genocide, opened for signature 9 December 1948, 78 UNTS 277 (entered into force 12 January 1951)

Geneva Convention (IV) relative to the Protection of Civilian Persons in Time of War, opened for signature on 12 August 1949, 75 UNTS 287 (entered into force 21 October 1950)

Montevideo Convention on the Rights and Duties of States, opened for signature 26 December 1933, 164 LNTS 19 (entered into force 26 December 1934)

Protocol Additional to the Geneva Conventions of 12 August 1949, and relating to the Protection of Victims of International Armed Conflicts, opened for signature 12 December 1977, 1125 UNTS 3 (entered into force 7 December 1979)

Protocol Additional to the Geneva Conventions of 12 August 1949, and relating to the Protection of Victims of Non-International Armed Conflicts, opened for signature 8 June 1977, 1125 UNTS 609 (entered into force 7 December 1978)

Rome Statute of the International Criminal Court, opened for signature 17 July 1998, 2187 UNTS 90 (entered into force 1 July 2002)

Chapter 3
Humanitarian Law at Wits' End: Does the Violence Arising from the "War on Drugs" in Mexico Meet the International Criminal Court's Non-International Armed Conflict Threshold?

Carrie A. Comer and Daniel M. Mburu

Abstract The determination of whether there is an actual non-international armed conflict (NIAC) in the context of the violence in Mexico among the drug cartels themselves and with Mexican governmental authorities is controversial. This paper reopens the debate as to whether the violence meets the Rome Statute's NIAC threshold when assessed against the International Criminal Court (ICC) tripartite criteria of duration, organisation and intensity. It concludes that the violence generally regarded *prima facie* meets these criteria and that the ICC's war crimes provisions would provide an opportunity for accountability for acts of criminality expressly proscribed by Article 8 of the Statute in relation to war crimes, but not expressly criminalised by Article 7 on crimes against humanity.

Keywords Mexico · Armed conflict · NIAC · International humanitarian law · Applicability of IHL · Organised crime · War on drugs · Drug cartels

---

The views expressed in this article are those of the authors and do not necessarily reflect the views of either the FIDH or the STL.

Carrie A. Comer was in no way involved in drafting the 2014 report by FIDH referenced in this article.

C.A. Comer (✉)
International Federation for Human Rights, The Hague, The Netherlands
e-mail: cacomer@gmail.com

D.M. Mburu
Special Tribunal for Lebanon, The Hague, The Netherlands
e-mail: danmwihia@yahoo.com

T.D. Gill et al. (eds.), *Yearbook of International Humanitarian Law 2015*,
Yearbook of International Humanitarian Law 18,
DOI 10.1007/978-94-6265-141-8_3

Contents

3.1 Introduction

The aim of this paper is to reopen a debate as to whether the violence in Mexico involving a number of highly organised armed criminal drug cartels, either directly with the Mexican state or with rival cartels, has, in the course of the period between 2005 and present, risen to the Rome Statute Article 8 non-international armed conflict (NIAC) threshold. The authors posit that the violence has *prima facie* risen to the threshold of a single NIAC or multiple NIACs over a varying geographical and temporal scope. The militarised response by the government in the context of the so-called "war on drugs"[1] since 2006 suggests that the Mexican state may indeed be engaged in suppressing more than isolated disturbances or criminal activity. Nonetheless, there are significant objective difficulties in establishing the facts amidst a continually developing body of law, as well as political difficulties in determining the existence of a NIAC in Mexico.

On 12 September 2014, the International Federation for Human Rights (FIDH) together with two Mexican human rights NGOs submitted a communication to the Office of the Prosecutor (OTP) of the International Criminal Court (ICC) urging it to open a preliminary examination in Mexico. While the 2014 communication to the ICC Prosecutor presents an opportunity for accountability, it only urges the prosecutor to investigate crimes against humanity. It is silent on war crimes, thereby avoiding controversially qualifying the violence as a NIAC within the ICC framework. It is therefore crucial that the debate on the qualification of the violence be reopened as some provisions within the Rome Statute relating to war crimes may provide an opportunity for accountability for criminal acts committed on all sides.

[1] The term 'war' is employed here and elsewhere this paper in a loose metaphorical sense, rather than as a legal term, to abbreviate the totality of the violence involving drug cartels between themselves and with Mexican governmental authorities between 2005 and the present.

This first part introduces the paper. The second part provides a background on the violence committed in the context of the so-called Mexican "war on drugs". The third part will attempt to situate violence arising from the "war on drugs" within the rubric of IHL and discuss the tripartite criteria used by the ICC in qualifying a situation as a NIAC. The final part will conclude with the authors' reflections on the qualification of the violence as a NIAC.

3.2 Background to the Violence

Mexican drug cartels have produced marijuana and opiates and trafficked in Andean cocaine for decades.[2] However, under the 70-year rule of the Institutional Revolutionary Party (PRI), cartels flourished relatively peacefully, accumulating considerable economic and political power amidst widespread impunity and allegations of government corruption.[3] Only in 2005, shortly after the PRI lost power, did serious cartel violence erupt.[4] Violence escalated exponentially when Felipe Calderón took office in 2006.[5] President Calderón, expanding an approach developed by his predecessor, Vicente Fox, militarised the so-called "drug war" by deploying thousands of soldiers in areas plagued by heavy drug trafficking.[6] Calderón initiated offensive operations in multiple states, utilised sophisticated military air and sea equipment, in part provided by the USA, increased military presence in urban areas and made use of a highly controversial rhetoric, framing the conflict as "a fight against enemies of the nation".[7]

Though more than two-dozen cartel leaders were captured under Calderón's presidency, the conflict between the cartels and the Mexican government continued at a stalemate.[8] Recent efforts to dismantle cartel leadership have been fraught with missteps and slow advances, including the capture, escape and eventual recapture of the kingpin of the infamous *Sinaloa* Cartel, Joaquin *El Chapo* Guzman.[9]

---

[2] For a history on the Mexican drug trade, see Grillo 2012.

[3] Bolton G (2012) Calderón's Drug War: Was the juice worth the squeeze? http://www.coha.org/calderons-drug-war-was-the-juice-worth-the-squeeze/. Accessed 9 April 2016; Carpenter 2013, p. 163.

[4] Vulliamy E (2014) Mexico: How arrest of the last don heralds ruthless new drugs era. http://www.theguardian.com/society/2014/oct/05/mexico-war-on-drugs-hidden-story-joaquin-guzman-war-us. Accessed 9 April 2016.

[5] Grillo 2012, p. 10.

[6] Mirnoff N and Booth W (2013) Mexico's drug war is at a stalemate as Calderon's presidency ends. http://www.washingtonpost.com/world/the_americas/calderon-finishes-his-six-year-drug-war-at-stalemate/2012/11/26/82c90a94-31eb-11e2-92f0-496af208bf23_story.html. Accessed 9 April 2016.

[7] Grillo 2012, pp. 109–130.

[8] Ibid.

[9] Agren D (2016) Mexico recaptures drug cartel kingpin El Chapo after humiliating prison escape. http://www.theguardian.com/world/2016/jan/08/mexican-drug-lord-el-chapo-recaptured-president-says. Accessed 9 April 2016.

In recent years, unspeakable atrocities have been committed both by the state and by drug cartels. All in all, a death toll of approximately 70,000 was linked to Calderón's militarised strategy,[10] with homicide rates rising rapidly between 2007 and 2010.[11] Estimates of those who were forcibly displaced from their homes during that period range from 115,000[12] to 160,000.[13] Further, approximately 24,000 people were forcibly disappeared.[14] These numbers have not diminished in recent years; rather, a victim toll of 100,000 since 2007 is the often-cited current estimate.[15]

The most violent cartels began employing more gruesome tactics as militarisation increased. For example, Mexican prosecutors indicate that over 1300 people were beheaded between 2007 and 2011.[16] The rolling of decapitated heads onto the floor of discotheques,[17] the massacre of 72 Central American migrants, the hanging bodies from bridges, the bombing of a casino killing 52[18] and the "cleansing" of entire cities[19] are among the tactics employed in recent years. In addition to the violent brutality displayed through these crimes, cartels have recruited an estimated 30,000 children,[20] many of whom are transformed into *sicarios* (hitmen).[21] Cartels have also expanded into sex trafficking and the trafficking of Central American migrants, kidnapping, extortion and piracy to fund their operations.[22]

---

[10] FIDH et al. (2014) Comunicación de acuerdo con el artículo 15 del Estatuto de Roma de la Corte Penal Internacional sobre la presunta comisión de crímenes de lesa humanidad, en México entre 2006 y 2012. https://www.fidh.org/International-Federation-for-Human-Rights/americas/mexico/16028-human-rights-groups-call-on-the-icc-to-proceed-with-the-preliminary. Accessed 9 April 2016.

[11] Bolton, above n 3. FIDH estimates 70,000 deaths.

[12] Rosenberg M (2011) Mexico's Refugees: A Hidden Cost of the Drugs War. http://www.reuters.com/article/2011/02/18/us-mexico-drugs-idUSTRE71H0EQ20110218. Accessed 9 April 2016.

[13] FIDH et al., above n 10, p. 3.

[14] Ibid.

[15] Graham D (2014) Mass graves with charred victims found in southern Mexico. http://www.reuters.com/article/2014/10/05/us-mexico-violence-idUSKCN0HT0QB20141005. Accessed 9 April 2016.

[16] Mirnoff and Booth, above n 6.

[17] Marquez J (2006) Decapitan a 5 en Uruapan tiran cabezas en un bar. http://www.eluniversal.com.mx/estados/62434.html. Accessed 9 April 2016.

[18] Alexander H (2013) Crimes of the Zetas—Mexico's most notorious cartel. http://www.telegraph.co.uk/news/worldnews/centralamericaandthecaribbean/mexico/10182412/Crimes-of-the-Zetas-Mexicos-most-notorious-cartel.html. Accessed 9 April 2016.

[19] Vulliamy, above n 4.

[20] FIDH et al., above n 10, p. 4.

[21] Burnett J (2009) Mexican Drug Cartels Recruiting Young Men, Boys. http://www.npr.org/templates/story/story.php?storyId=102249839. Accessed 9 April 2016.

[22] Seelke C and Finklea K (2014) U.S.-Mexican Security Cooperation: The Mérida Initiative and Beyond. https://fas.org/sgp/crs/row/R41349.pdf. Accessed 9 April 2016.

Though the cartels perpetrate the most visible violence as part of a well-planned propaganda strategy that couples positive "narco-culture" with publicised terror-inducing crimes,[23] state security forces have increasingly been implicated in extrajudicial executions, disappearances, torture, rape and other forms of sexual violence, and arbitrary detentions.[24] Human rights complaints received by the Secretary of National Defence increased by nearly 700 % in a span of three years, from 182 in 2006 to 1230 in 2008.[25]

The UN Special Rapporteur on Torture indicated that torture by state officials was "*generalizado*" (widespread or generalised) in Mexico.[26] A pattern has been observed, beginning with arbitrary or illegal detention, six to twenty-four hours of torture in an unauthorised detention facility, and ending with transfer to the Public Prosecutor's office. Such cases increased under Calderón's leadership.[27] Further, a 2012 report by the Nobel Women's Initiative found that government officials and their security forces were often the worst perpetrators of sexualised violence and used it as a tool to "intimidate and subdue" women. The militarisation of certain zones under Calderón's administration contributed to a growing culture of violence and fear, especially for women.[28]

Enforced disappearances have also been attributed to the armed forces, or to security services in collusion with non-state groups. In one recent example of brutality and collusion between state and non-state actors, police in the state of Guerrero shot and killed six civilians before illegally detaining and subsequently "disappearing" 43 protesting university students. The police handed the students to the *Guerreros Unidos,* a cartel, who then killed them and likely incinerated their bodies.[29] During the search for the missing students, multiple mass graves con-

---

[23] Guevara 2013, p. 133: "Mexican drug cartels have actively sought to transform the Mexican populace with their intense forms of propaganda as they use violence, introduced the 'narco' concept, the narco-culture, narco-saints, intimidation tactics, and intent to control the media. Their use of propaganda is also intended to create immense fear among rivaling cartels and public/elected officials, defend their plazas, and provide a warning sign for those who dare cross their path.".

[24] Human Rights Watch (2011) Neither Rights Nor Security: Killings, Torture and Disappearances in Mexico's "War on Drugs". http://www.hrw.org/reports/2011/11/09/neither-rights-nor-security-0. Accessed 9 April 2016; Wright J (2012) Women Under Siege Project- Conflict Profiles: Mexico. http://www.womenundersiegeproject.org/conflicts/profile/mexico. Accessed 9 April 2016.

[25] FIDH et al., above n 10, p. 4.

[26] UN General Assembly (2014) Human Rights Council: Informe del Relator Especial sobre la tortura y otros tratos o penas crueles, inhumanos o degradantes, UN Doc. A/HRC/28/68/Add.3, para 23.

[27] FIDH et al., above n 10, p. 9.

[28] Nobel Women's Initiative and Just Associates (2012) From Survivors to Defenders: Women confronting violence in Mexico, Honduras and Guatemala. http://nobelwomensinitiative.org/wp-content/uploads/2012/06/Report_AmericasDelgation-2012.pdf. Accessed 9 April 2016, p. 9.

[29] Carlsen L (2014) Impunity and Mass Disappearance in Ayotzinapa. https://nacla.org/news/2014/10/29/impunity-and-mass-disappearance-ayotzinapa-0. Accessed 9 April 2016; Peralta E (2015) Mexico Officially Declares 43 Missing Students Dead. http://www.npr.org/blogs/thetwo-way/2015/01/28/382103750/mexico-officially-declares-43-missing-students-dead. Accessed 9 April 2016.

taining scores of unidentified human remains were discovered in the region.[30] Investigations by the attorney general indicate that the local mayor ordered the attack.[31] Journalists and rights activists have also accused the military of complicity and collaboration in the crimes, though these accusations are not currently being publicly investigated.[32] The Interdisciplinary Group of International Experts appointed by the Inter-American Commission on Human Rights (IACHR) found that a "massive attack" was perpetrated against the students, involving different groups of state agents, and contradicting the Mexican government's official version of events.[33]

However, even beyond these events, the incidence of enforced disappearances has become a "massive phenomenon" in Mexico, according to the IACHR[34] and was also strongly condemned by the UN Committee on Enforced Disappearances in February 2015.[35]

3.2.1 NGO Communication to the ICC Prosecutor

On 12 September 2014, the FIDH together with two Mexican human rights NGOs, the Mexican Commission for the Defense and Promotion of Human Rights and the Citizens' Commission of Human Rights of the Northeast, requested that the prosecutor of the ICC open a preliminary examination in Mexico. The prosecutor was asked to examine allegations of torture, severe deprivation of liberty and enforced disappearances allegedly committed by Mexican armed forces and police in Baja California, Mexico, between 2006 and 2012.[36] The NGO allegations relating to Baja California focus on 30 cases involving 95 victims which they claim provide a reasonable basis to believe that crimes amounting to crimes against humanity were committed in Baja California, namely the crimes of murder, rape, torture, illegal

---

[30] BBC (2014) Mexico mass grave found near Iguala after protests. http://www.bbc.co.uk/news/world-latin-america-29493797. Accessed 9 April 2016.

[31] Malkin E (2014) Mexican Official Links a Mayor to Missing College Students. http://www.nytimes.com/2014/10/23/world/americas/mexican-official-links-a-mayor-to-missing-college-students.html?_r=2&gwh=DA2F5BDA18F742E1028E27FB2F53D26F&gwt=pay&assetType=nyt_now. Accessed 9 April 2016.

[32] Hernandez A and Fisher S (2014) Iguala: la historia no oficial. http://www.proceso.com.mx/?p=390560. Accessed 9 April 2016.

[33] Grupo Interdisciplinario de Expertos Internacionales (2015) Informe completo Ayotzinapa. http://big.assets.huffingtonpost.com/Informe.pdf. Accessed 9 April 2016.

[34] Schoichet CE (2012) Vanishing victims: The 'open wounds' of Mexico's drug war. http://edition.cnn.com/2012/01/16/world/americas/mexico-disappeared. Accessed 9 April 2016.

[35] UN Committee on Enforced Disappearances (2015) Concluding Observations Version Avanzada no Editada, 8th Session, 2-13 February 2015. http://tbinternet.ohchr.org/_layouts/treatybodyexternal/SessionDetails1.aspx?SessionID=972&Lang=en. Accessed 9 April 2016.

[36] FIDH et al., above n 10.

imprisonment and enforced disappearance as criminalised by Article 7 of the Rome Statute.[37]

The most recent request to the ICC Prosecutor to open an investigation in Mexico did not allege the commission of war crimes. However, in a 2011 submission, Mexican human rights organisations had asked the ICC Prosecutor to look into the possible commission of war crimes by the government and the cartels.[38] In response, the Mexican government asserted that: "the Mexican government is not at war, and there is no generalised or systematic attack against civilians, nor any government policy in that direction".[39]

3.3 Qualifying the Violence Involving the Mexican Government and Drug Cartels as a NIAC Under the ICC Framework

According to common Article 2 to the Geneva Conventions (GCs), an international armed conflict (IAC) occurs whenever there is an armed conflict between two or more High Contracting Parties. While there appears to be a single definition of an IAC, there are at least two types of NIACs.[40] The first is the Common Article 3 to the Geneva Conventions (CA3) NIAC. This NIAC is defined, by omission, as an armed conflict not of an international character occurring in the territory of one of the High Contracting Parties. The second NIAC variety is defined in Article 1(1) of Additional Protocol II to the Geneva Conventions (APII). This provision goes beyond the ambiguous wording of CA3 to apply to a specific brand of NIACs, that is those which take place in the territory of a state between its armed forces and dissident armed forces (or other organised groups) which, under responsible command, exercise such control over a part of its territory as to enable them to carry out sustained and concerted military operations and to implement

[37] Rome Statute of the International Criminal Court, opened for signature 17 July 1998, 2187 UNTS 90 (entered into force 1 July 2002) (Rome Statute), Article 17.

[38] Associated Press (2011) Mexican Activists File War-Crimes Complaint Against President Calderon And Drug Lords. http://www.cnsnews.com/news/article/group-files-war-crimes-complaint-against-calderon. Accessed 9 April 2016; See also the Guardian (2011) Activists accuse Mexican president of war crimes in drug crackdown. http://www.theguardian.com/world/2011/nov/26/mexican-president-war-crimes-drug. Accessed 9 April 2016.

[39] Ibid.

[40] On this point, the authors take a different position from the International Committee of the Red Cross (ICRC) whose view is that although AP II does not apply to all situations of NIAC, there are not two different types of NIAC. The ICRC considers that there are two criteria for determining whether a situation of violence qualifies as a NIAC: organization of the armed group(s) involved and intensity of the violence. See ICRC (2008) How is the Term "Armed Conflict" Defined in International Humanitarian Law? https://www.icrc.org/eng/assets/files/other/opinion-paper-armed-conflict.pdf. Accessed 9 April 2016.

the protocol. As such, APII and CA3 hold NIACs to different standards, with APII having a higher threshold.

Though the Rome Statute may at first blush appear to have collapsed these two types of NIACs into one, a closer reading of Article 8(2)(c) and 8(2)(d) on the one hand and Article 8(2)(e) and 8(2)(f) on the other hand reveals that there is not one but two NIAC varieties within Article 8 of the Rome Statute. The first, in Article 8(2)(c) and 8(2)(d), replicates the Common Article 3 NIAC variety. In this regard, Article 8(2)(d) provides that:

> Paragraph 2 (c) applies to armed conflicts not of an international character and thus does not apply to situations of internal disturbances and tensions, such as riots, isolated and sporadic acts of violence or other acts of a similar nature.

The second NIAC variety is in Article 8(2)(e) and 8(2)(f), the latter of which provides that:

> Paragraph 2 (e) applies to armed conflicts not of an international character and thus does not apply to situations of internal disturbances and tensions, such as riots, isolated and sporadic acts of violence or other acts of a similar nature. It applies to armed conflicts that take place in the territory of a state *when there is protracted armed conflict* between governmental authorities and organized armed groups or between such groups.[41]

As the drafting history of Article 8(2)(e) and 8(2)(f) reveals, states were uncomfortable with treating the crimes presently enumerated at Article 8(2)(c) and Article 8(2)(e) within the framework of a singular NIAC definition.[42] They were also opposed to the introduction of the higher APII threshold for crimes not falling within CA3 as such a threshold would have been overly strict and even regressive in the light of the nature of armed conflicts that the world had witnessed over the past few years.[43] The compromise proposed by Sierra Leone introduced the present "protracted armed conflict" requirement in the second sentence of Article 8(2)(f), thereby doing away with the more demanding APII requirement for responsible command, control over territory, the conduct of sustained and concerted military operations and state involvement in hostilities.[44] The reference to "protracted armed conflict" in Sierra Leone's proposal, which eventually became Article 8(2)(f) of the Statute, appears to have been lifted from the *Tadić* jurisdictional appeal decision where a NIAC had been defined as "protracted armed *violence* between governmental authorities and organised armed groups or between such groups

---

[41] Emphasis added.

[42] UN Diplomatic Conference of Plenipotentiaries on the Establishment of an International Criminal Court (1998) Report of the Preparatory Committee on the Establishment of an International Criminal Court, UN Doc. A/CONF.183/2/Add.1, p. 22. See Kritsiotis 2010, pp. 288–289; Cullen 2008, pp. 428–429.

[43] UN Diplomatic Conference of Plenipotentiaries on the Establishment of an International Criminal Court (1998) Committee of the Whole: Summary Record of the 35th Meeting, UN Doc. A/CONF.183/C.1/SR.35 (UNConf), p. 2. See also Kritsiotis 2010, pp. 288–289; Cullen 2008, p. 429.

[44] UNConf, above n 43, para 8. See also Cullen 2008, p. 432.

within a state".[45] Article 8(2)(f) may hence be seen as introducing a third type of NIAC under international law with a threshold higher than that of CA3 but lower than the APII standard.[46]

Regardless of the various NIAC typologies that may exist under international law, this paper's focus is on the NIAC concept under the Rome Statute and how it may apply to the Mexican situation at hand. The ICC's first two trial judgments in *Lubanga* and *Katanga* have both dealt with the qualification of NIACs according to the Article 8(2)(f) threshold. In this regard, the court has held there are three criteria required for a situation to be classified as a NIAC: (i) the protracted nature of the armed conflict;[47] (ii) the involvement of organised armed groups;[48] and (iii) the intensity of conflict.[49] In comparison, the International Committee of the Red Cross (ICRC) takes into account only two criteria: (i) the organisation of the armed group and (ii) the intensity of the conflict. The ICRC considers "protractedness"/duration to be an indicator of the intensity of the violence rather than as a stand-alone criterion to determine the existence of a NIAC.[50] In contrast, the court treats "duration" and "intensity" as distinct criteria, the sole purpose of "intensity" being "to distinguish an armed conflict from banditry, unorganised and short-lived insurrections, or terrorist activities, which are not subject to international humanitarian law".[51]

The next section considers the ICC tripartite NIAC criteria of duration, organisation and intensity and how these criteria may apply to the Mexican situation.

---

[45] ICTY, *Prosecutor v Duško Tadić a/k/a "Dule"*, Decision on the Defence Motion for Interlocutory Appeal on Jurisdiction, 2 October 1995, Case No. IT-94-1-AR72 *(Tadić)*, para 70. Emphasis added.

[46] For an overview of the debate concerning the Article 8(2)(f) threshold, see Cullen 2008, pp. 435-445.

[47] ICC, *Prosecutor v Thomas Lubanga Dyilo,* Judgment Pursuant to Article 74 of the Statute, 14 March 2012, Case No. ICC-01/04-01/06-2842 *(Lubanga* 2012), para 536; ICC, *Prosecutor v Germain Katanga*, Jugement rendu en application de l'article 74 du Statut, 7 March 2014, Case No. ICC-01/04-01/07-3436 *(Katanga)*, para 1185.

[48] *Lubanga* 2012, above n 47, para 536; *Katanga*, above n 47, para 1185. It should also be noted that the *Katanga* Trial Chamber included the necessity of being able to implement IHL as a condition for being sufficiently organised. However, if able to meet other requisite standards, it is the authors' view that a group would also be capable of implementing IHL.

[49] *Lubanga* 2012, above n 47, para 538; *Katanga*, above n 47, para 1187.

[50] International Committee of the Red Cross (2012) Internal conflicts or other situations of violence—what is the difference for victims? https://www.icrc.org/eng/resources/documents/interview/2012/12-10-niac-non-international-armed-conflict.htm. Accessed 9 April 2016.

[51] *Lubanga* 2012, above n 47, para 538, quoting ICTY, *Prosecutor v Vlastimir Đorđević*, Public Judgment with Confidential Annex—Volume I of II, 23 February 2011, Case No. IT-05-87/1-T, para 1522. However, see ICC, *Prosecutor v Jean-Pierre Bemba Gombo*, Judgment pursuant to Article 74 of the Statute, 21 March 2016, Case No. ICC-01/05-01/08-3343 (*Bemba* 2016), para 139, where the Court states that "the concept of 'protracted conflict' has not been explicitly defined in the jurisprudence of this Court, but has generally been addressed within the framework of assessing the intensity of the conflict".

3.3.1 Duration

3.3.1.1 ICC Framework

Duration within the ICC framework is a problematic concept given the difference in wording between Article 8(2)(c) and 8(2)(f) in relation to the requirement by the latter provision for the existence of a "protracted armed conflict" in order for Article 8(2)(e) to be engaged. While the trial judgments of the court in *Lubanga* and *Katanga* have made it clear that the Article 8(2)(f) threshold is lower than the APII one,[52] these two judgments relate to accused persons who have been charged with crimes under Article 8(2)(e), but not 8(2)(c). However, in the *Bemba* confirmation decision—where Bemba was charged with, *inter alia*, murder under Article 8(2)(c)(i) of the Statute, torture under Article 8(2)(c)(i) of the Statute and outrages upon personal dignity under Article 8(2)(c)(ii) of the Statute—the Trial Chamber stated that:

> The Chamber is also mindful that the wording of Article 8(2)(f) of the Statute differs from that of Article 8(2)(d) of the Statute, which requires the existence of a 'protracted armed conflict' and thus may be seen to require a higher or additional threshold to be met—a necessity which is not set out in Article 8(2)(d) of the Statute. *The argument can be raised as to whether this requirement may nevertheless be applied also in the context of Article 8(2)(d) of the Statute.* However, irrespective of such a possible interpretative approach, the Chamber does not deem it necessary to address this argument, as the period in question covers approximately five months and is therefore to be regarded as 'protracted' in any event.[53]

Although the court is yet to definitively determine the NIAC threshold for Article 8(2)(c), the above pronouncement shows a tendency in favour of extending the "protracted" requirement in Article 8(2)(f) to the war crimes in Article 8(2)(c) instead of viewing it as a term whose aim is to distinguish a NIAC from internal tensions and disturbances as was the case in *Tadić,* ultimately rendering it a superfluous definitional element for a NIAC.[54] Such an interpretive approach would mean that the CA3 NIAC threshold as set out in Article 8(2)(c) is illusory and that in reality, the court, in pursuing such an interpretive approach, would have merged Article 8(2)(c) and 8(2)(f) to create a unitary concept of a NIAC that lies somewhere between the CA3 lower threshold and the APII upper threshold.[55]

Accepting the *Tadić* formulation that a NIAC exists when there is "protracted armed *violence* between governmental authorities and organised armed groups or

---

[52] *Lubanga* 2012, above n 47, para 536. See also *Katanga*, above n 47, para 1186.

[53] ICC, *Prosecutor v Jean-Pierre Bemba Gombo*, Decision Pursuant to Article 61(7)(a) and (b) of the Rome Statute on the Charges of the Prosecutor Against Jean-Pierre Bemba Gombo, 15 June 2009, Case No. ICC-01/05-01/08-424 (*Bemba* 2009), para 235. Emphasis added.

[54] Contrary to the suggestion by Fleck 2008, p. 611.

[55] For the view that the NIAC referred to in Article 8(2)(f) has the same threshold of applicability as Common Article 3 and that the Statute did not intend to infer a different trigger, see Pejic 2011, p. 193.

between such groups within a state",[56] then implicit in Article 8(2)(f) is a prerequisite for double protraction: the violence in question must, in the first instance, be protracted in order to cross the threshold from internal disturbance/tension to NIAC; and having done so, the NIAC would additionally need to be protracted in order to engage the application of Article 8(2)(e) of the Statute.[57] Despite the court's pronouncement in the above-cited *dicta* in *Bemba,* it does not appear to have interpreted Article 8(2)(f) as requiring "double protraction". In *Lubanga,* the Trial Chamber held "that Article 8(2)(f) of the Statute only requires the existence of a 'protracted' *conflict* between 'organised armed groups'".[58] In *Katanga,* the Trial Chamber held that "Trial Chamber I in Lubanga stated that article 8(2)(f) of the Statute requires only the existence of a 'protracted' *conflict* between 'organised armed groups'".[59] In the *Mbarushimana* confirmation decision, the Trial Chamber held that:

> [T]he designation 'conflicts of a non-international character' applies to armed conflicts that take place in the territory of a state, when there is a protracted armed conflict between government authorities and organised armed groups or between such groups. Consistent with the case law of the Chamber, for the purpose of Article 8(2)(f) of the Statute, an organised armed group must have 'the ability to plan and carry out military operations for a prolonged period of time'.[60]

Duration therefore appears to have been considered *vis-à-vis* the "conflict" rather than "armed conflict", thereby suggesting that the ICC's omission of the word "armed" in its analysis is in effect a consideration of the duration of the "violence" rather than the NIAC, thus reverting to the *Tadić* "violence" standard.

It would be interesting to compare the ICC's requirement that a "conflict" be protracted with the IACHR's conclusion that the hostilities against *La Tablada* military base, lasting a mere 30 hours, qualified as a NIAC.[61] Though this example represents the lowest end of the scale (and has been criticised),[62] violence need not last months or years in order to be considered a NIAC under Article 8(2)(c) if it meets the organisation and intensity requirements as discussed below. With regard to the term *"protracted"* in the ICC's jurisprudence, the court in the *Bemba* confirmation decision held that the requirements of intensity and a conflict's protracted nature are distinct and separate, but that a period covering approximately five months is regarded as "protracted" in any event.[63]

---

[56] *Tadić*, above n 45, para 70. Emphasis added.

[57] Cryer et al. 2008, pp. 237–238.

[58] *Lubanga* 2012, above n 47, para 536.

[59] *Katanga*, above n 47, para 1185.

[60] ICC, *Prosecutor v Callixte Mbarushimana,* Decision on the Confirmation of Charges, 16 December 2011, Case No. ICC-01/04-01/10-465-Red (*Mbarushimana*), para 103.

[61] IACommHR, *Case 11.137 Juan Carlos Abella (Argentina)*, Merits, 30 October 1997, Report No. 55/97, Doc No. 38, No. OEA/Ser/L/V/II.97.

[62] Dinstein 2014, p. 34.

[63] *Bemba* 2009, above n 53, para 235.

3.3.1.2 Application to the Mexican Situation

One question that the court has not squarely addressed is whether, in determining whether a conflict or violence has been protracted for the purposes of its qualification as a NIAC, such violence or armed conflict must have been continuously sustained and, if so, between the same parties and the same geographical area in order to be considered "protracted".[64] The Heidelberg Institute for International Conflict Research (HIIK)'s annual Conflict Barometer dates the beginning of the violence between the Mexican government and cartels to 2006 and inter-cartel violence to 2005.[65] If the violence is considered to begin in earnest with Calderón's military incursions in 2006, then it has been going on for at least ten years. The duration of the violence under discussion here far exceeds the five-month period cited in *Bemba*. If an analytical approach that regards the violence as a whole is adopted, a decade would certainly meet the Article 8(2)(f) threshold.

However, the case may be different if an analytical model that considers the duration of the violence between specific cartels that meet the "organisation" requirement is adopted. If the decade-long violence is clinically dissected so as to determine which organised armed groups are engaging in violence against each other or against Mexican governmental authorities at which time, place and at what intensity, it may emerge that some cartels that meet the "organisation" requirement were never involved in violence during a particular stretch of time. For instance, HIIK reports that in 2014, "clashes" between government forces and armed groups took place almost daily.[66] This does not mean that all drug cartels in Mexico meeting the "organisation" requirement were involved in the violence. If such an approach were to be used, individual acts of violence between cartels meeting the "organisation" requirement or such cartels and government authorities would need to be individually assessed with a view to determine their duration. Nevertheless, it is unclear how many instances of violence would be required in order to satisfy the Article 8(2)(f) duration requirement. If such an analytical framework were adopted, Article 8(2)(d) may be more forgiving as it contains no express requirement that violence be protracted as long as such violence meets the "intensity" requirement and involved cartels meet the "organisation" criterion. The outcome of such an approach is likely to be multiple NIACs over varying different times and geographical locations.

---

[64] See for instance the Trial Chamber's analysis of the facts in *Lubanga* 2012, above n 47, paras 523–567, particularly at para 563 where the Court appears to adopt a general analytical approach. See also *Bemba* 2016, above n 51, para 140, where the Court states that the intensity and "protracted armed conflict" criteria do not require the violence to be continuous and uninterrupted.

[65] Heidelberg Institute for International Conflict Research (2015) Conflict Barometer 2014. http://www.hiik.de/en/konfliktbarometer/. Accessed 9 April 2016.

[66] Ibid., p. 100.

3.3.2 Organisation

3.3.2.1 ICC Framework

To rise above the status of a disturbance, an armed group must be "more than a ragtag mob".[67] "Some degree of organisation" was required by the ICTY in the light of the understanding that an armed group need not be as structured as government forces.[68] In the *Lukić and Lukić* case, the ICTY Trial Chamber provided some additional guidance on how to interpret organisation levels within a NIAC:

> [T]he evidence shows that during the indictment period there was an armed conflict […] both sides undertook offensive and defensive actions, a feature which, the Trial Chamber considers, demonstrates that they were engaged in military planning and tactics in order to achieve military objectives, including to establish control over portions of the territory […].The Trial Chamber notes in this regard the establishment of front lines by both forces, to which armed men were deployed.[69]

The Trial Chamber in *Haradinaj* identified the following indicative factors to determine a sufficient level of organisation: "the existence of KLA headquarters and command structure; the existence of KLA disciplinary rules and mechanisms; territorial control exerted by the KLA; the ability of the KLA to gain access to weapons and other military equipment; to recruit members; to provide them with military training; to carry out military operations and use tactics and strategy; and to speak with one voice".[70]

The ICC Chambers have reiterated their view that organisation means that it is necessary for armed groups to possess "the ability to plan and carry out military operations for a prolonged period of time".[71] Chambers has further accepted the ICTY's *Haradinaj* jurisprudence of potential factors to assess organisation.[72] Not all of these factors need be met—the list is non-exhaustive.[73]

To date, little factual guidance has been given by the ICC for the interpretation of these factors in practice. In one of the court's few cases, the Pre-Trial Chamber held that:

> […] the FDLR was a well-organised combatant force with a political wing, whose top leaders were based mainly in Europe, and a military wing stationed in the eastern DRC.

---

67 Dinstein 2014, p. 30.

68 ICTY, *Prosecutor v Ljube Boškoski and Johan Tarčulovski,* Judgment, 10 July 2008, Case No. IT-04-82-T (*Boškoski and Tarčulovski*), para 197.

69 ICTY, *Prosecutor v Milan Lukić and Sredoje Lukić,* Judgment, 20 July 2009, Case No. IT-98-32/1-T, para 880.

70 ICTY, *Prosecutor v Ramush Haradinaj, Idriz Balaj and Lahi Brahimaj*, Judgment, 3 April 2008, Case No. IT-04-84-T, para 64.

71 *Mbarushimana*, above n 60; ICC, *Prosecutor v Thomas Lubanga Dyilo,* Décision sur la confirmation des charges, 29 January 2007, Case No. ICC-01/04-01/06-803, para 234; *Bemba* 2009, above n 53, para 233.

72 *Lubanga* 2012, above n 47, para 537; *Katanga*, above n 47, para 1136.

73 *Lubanga* 2012, above n 47, para 537.

> These two branches of the organisation were coordinated by a Steering Committee, which was comprised of equal numbers of civilian and military leaders. [...] The evidence further shows that the FDLR was characterised by a hierarchical structure and a high level of internal organisation. Its constitutive instruments included a statute, a 'reglement d'ordre interieur' and a disciplinary code which provided the organisation's internal disciplinary system.[74]

The OTP has also analysed the level of organisation requirements in its Preliminary Examination Activities. For instance, in the situation of Nigeria, the OTP examined the organisational structure of Boko Haram by considering: its hierarchical structure; its command rules and ability to impose discipline among its members; the weapons used by the group; its ability to plan and carry out coordinated attacks; and the number of Boko Haram forces under command.[75]

3.3.2.2 Application to the Mexican Situation

As previously mentioned, multiple cartels exist within the Mexican territory and they have exerted different levels of dominance, violence and allegiances over the past ten years. As the cartels are far from homogenous, an assessment of each structure within a particular time frame would be necessary to identify with precision the existence and scope of a NIAC.

Nonetheless, some Mexican cartels, particularly the *Sinaloa* Cartel and *Los Zetas*, arguably encompass all of the factors necessary to determine the existence of the requisite level of organisation.[76] While some academics and policy makers have argued that the cartels are, in fact, merely loosely organised groups who rely too heavily on "enforcement" from street gangs, lack a hierarchical structure capable of controlling military action or are organised more like businesses with external contractors than a traditional army,[77] others insist otherwise. Bergal, citing information from the US Drug Enforcement Administration, notes,

> [T]he cartel's operative structure, which is comprised of an executive council made up of visible leaders within the government and 'clandestine leaders,' who are 'drug traffickers

[74] *Mbarushimana*, above n 60, para 104.

[75] ICC Office of the Prosecutor (2013) Report on Preliminary Examination Activities. https://www.icc-cpi.int/en_menus/icc/press%20and%20media/press%20releases/Documents/OTP%20Preliminary%20Examinations/OTP%20-%20Report%20%20Preliminary%20Examination%20Activities%202013.PDF. Accessed 9 April 2016, para 215.

[76] For more detailed guidance on how to judge a level of organisation within an armed group, see the complete discussion in *Boškoski and Tarčulovski*, above n 68, paras 199-204, which include, for example, the ability to authorise military action, assign tasks to individuals, issue political statements, the existence of a headquarters, internal regulations, the capacity to control territory, the effective dissemination of orders, the ability to recruit new members, the providing of military training, etc., which may be useful in determining NIAC status. See also Grillo 2012, p. 211.

[77] See, for example, Sánchez 2013, p. 485.

> from various municipalities.' Moreover, a 2007 US Congressional Research Service report found that the drug cartels have become 'increasingly sophisticated, three-tiered organization[s] with leaders and middlemen who coordinate contracts with petty criminals to carry out street work'.[78]

Others point to defined and functional command, though particularities are not homogenous between each cartel:

> The *Zetas* initially modelled this chain of command based on the Mexican army they came from. Ranks included first commanders and second commanders, just as in the military. But the war evolved their structure to become close to Latin America's guerrilla armies or right-wing paramilitaries, who use autonomous cells to coordinate thousands of men at arms. The Zetas trained *La Familia* members in this guerrilla warfare in 2005 and 2006.[79]

Cartel violence and the state's response should be viewed from the lens of the objectives of territorial and resource control and regional dominance. Further, cartels increasingly appear to be vying for political power itself as they expand into the more extensive business of control over local municipalities and conventional economic resources.[80] Scholar Vanda Felbab-Brown explained, for example, how:

> […] the *Zetas* in Mexico also seek to dominate the political life of a community, controlling the community's ability to organize and interact with the state, determining the extent and functions of local government, and sometimes even exercising quasi-control over the local territory.[81]

Some commentators have tried to skirt the implications of the level of cartel organisation by labelling them "criminal insurgencies", though the manner in which they plan and engage in strategic attacks remains similar to other cases of armed groups engaged in NIACs:

> Mexican cartels have employed psychological operations, fomented anti-government protests, attacked both police and military in infantry-style assaults, assassinated political officials [and] journalists, beheaded and maimed their victims, to amplify the strategic impact of their attacks, and co-opted and corrupted the military, police and political officials at all levels of government. The result is […] a set of interlocking 'criminal insurgencies' culminating in virtual civil war.[82]

Though territorial control is not a necessary requirement for the existence of a NIAC,[83] it is indicative of the level of capacity of an organisation. In Mexico, "parallel zones of sovereignty dominated by cartels" can be identified.[84] These

---

[78] Bergal 2011, p. 1071.

[79] Grillo 2012, p. 211.

[80] Grillo I (2016) Why Cartels are Killing Mexico's Mayors. http://www.nytimes.com/2016/01/17/opinion/sunday/why-cartels-are-killing-mexicos-mayors.html?_r=0. Accessed 9 April 2016.

[81] Felbab-Brown 2009, p. 5.

[82] Bunker and Sullivan 2010.

[83] *Bemba* 2009, above n 53, para 236.

[84] Bunker and Sullivan 2010, p. 3.

zones necessarily shift over time depending on advances within the conflict and alliances between cartels, but large swathes of territory are generally associated with specific cartels, with their control exerted to varying degrees.[85] Due to the nature of the cartels' resource and traffic-oriented objectives, the territory they expressly control is obtained to meet those needs. This may include, for example, less traditional territorial control, including border regions, coastlines and drug routes, which are peppered with extensive land, air and sea transportation circuits, including scores of underground tunnels.[86]

Additionally, the cartels have amassed an impressive arsenal, through both legal and illegal means, that potentially exceed those available to the Mexican government's forces.[87] Nearly 100,000 guns have been seized at drug-related crime scenes, and, for example, it has been estimated that cartels sometimes have ten times the amount of ammunition as security forces.[88] The cartels show sophisticated use of a wide variety of weaponry in coordinated operations as well. According to General Barry McCaffrey, former US director of the Office of National Drug Control Policy:

> Mexican law enforcement authorities face armed criminal attacks from platoon-sized units employing night vision goggles, electronic intercept collection, encrypted communications, fairly sophisticated information operations, sea-going submersibles, helicopters and modern transport aviation, automatic weapons, RPG's, anti-tank 66-mm rockets, mines and booby traps, heavy machine guns, 50 cal [sic] sniper rifles, massive use of military hand grenades and the most modern models of 40-mm grenade machine guns.[89]

Recruitment and maintenance of cartel forces is likewise strong. An estimated 150,000 soldiers have defected from the military since 2000, particularly in regions of high drug activity, likely joining the ranks of the more lucrative cartels after receiving combat training and weapons.[90] The *Zetas* are known to recruit from former military special forces members.[91]

From the foregoing, it is arguable that at least some drug cartels, such as the *Zetas* and *Sinaloa*, would have the required level of organisation to be considered an "organised armed group" within the meaning of Article 8(2)(c) and 8(2)(f) of the Rome Statute.

---

[85] See, for example, NPR (2009) Snapshot of 2007 cartel territory: Mexico Drug Cartel Territory. http://www.npr.org/news/graphics/2009/mar/mexico-cartels/. Accessed 9 April 2016.

[86] Kerr 2012, p. 203.

[87] Bergal 2011, p. 172.

[88] Grillo I (2011) Mexico's Drug Lords Ramp Up Their Arsenals with RPGs. http://world.time.com/2012/10/25/mexicos-drug-lords-ramp-up-their-arsenals-with-rpgs/. Accessed 9 April 2016; Bergal 2011, p. 172.

[89] Bloom 2012, pp. 345 and 370.

[90] Rodriguez R (2009) Army desertions hurting Mexico's war on drugs. http://edition.cnn.com/2009/WORLD/americas/03/11/mexico.desertions/. Accessed 9 April 2016.

[91] Ibid.

3.3.3 *Intensity*

3.3.3.1 ICC Framework

ICC jurisprudence has also provided guidance regarding how to judge the intensity of a conflict in order to classify it as a NIAC. In *Lubanga*, it was stated that proof of intensity should be "used solely as a way to distinguish an armed conflict from banditry, unorganised and short-lived insurrections or terrorist activities which are not subject to IHL".[92] Trial Chamber I has agreed with the approach of the ICTY Chambers and applied the following factors as relevant for the assessment of the intensity of the conflict:

> the seriousness of attacks and potential increase in armed clashes, their spread over territory and over a period of time, the increase in the number of government forces, the mobilisation and the distribution of weapons among both parties to the conflict, as well as whether the conflict has attracted the attention of the United Nations Security Council, and, if so, whether any resolutions on the matter have been passed.[93]

However, it should be noted that the use of military detachments in attempting to harness a situation of violence does not in and of itself imply that a NIAC is underway.[94] However, when armed forces surpass law enforcement standards regarding use of force as a last resort and begin to employ lethal weaponry against their adversaries in the first instance, this would give credence to claims of a de facto NIAC.[95]

The OTP has in addition to the above-mentioned criteria assessed other factual indicators such as the extent and sustained nature of incidents, the frequency and intensity of armed confrontations, and the number and composition of personnel involved on both sides.[96] For example, in its analysis of situation in Nigeria and the armed confrontations between Boko Haram and Nigerian security forces, the OTP has evaluated over 200 incidents occurring between July 2009 and May 2013. The OTP established a correlation between the deployment of the Nigerian Government Joint Task Force in June 2011 and an increase in frequency and intensity of the incidents between Boko Haram and security forces. It also took into consideration two declarations of a state of emergency in the north-eastern parts of Nigeria in December 2011 and May 2013 which were followed by a surge of

---

[92] *Lubanga* 2012, above n 47, para 538.

[93] ICTY, *Prosecutor v Fatmir Limaj, Haradin Bala and Isak Musliu,* Judgment, 30 November 2005, Case No. IT-03-66-T, para 90.

[94] ICTR, *Prosecutor v Alfred Musema*, Judgment and Sentence, 27 January 2000, Case No. ICTR-96-13-T, para 248.

[95] See, for example, Dahl and Sandbu 2006, pp. 369–388.

[96] ICC Office of the Prosecutor, above n 75, para 217; ICC Office of the Prosecutor (2012) Interim report on Colombia. https://www.icc-cpi.int/NR/rdonlyres/3D3055BD-16E2-4C83-BA85-35BCFD2A7922/285102/OTPCOLOMBIAPublicInterimReportNovember2012.pdf. Accessed 9 April 2016, para 126.

troops, increased security operations and renewed armed confrontations. It highlighted that the latter declaration defined Boko Haram's activities as an "insurgency".[97]

However, as case law has indicted, these factors should be assessed on a case-by-case basis and against the backdrop of the facts present in that specific situation. As such, the checklist for the factors to take into account in determining intensity is not set in stone.

3.3.3.2 Application to the Mexican Situation

The qualification of intensity should be assessed thoroughly within particular regions, among particular groups and during specific time frames. However, an overview of indications of the overall conflict is useful for a broad view of the Mexican situation.

In terms of the "seriousness of military involvement", drug cartels have faced an "increasing militarisation of the Mexican state's response".[98] In 2011, Human Rights Watch claimed over 50,000 soldiers were involved in anti-drug operations at that point.[99] Further, through joint security plans such as the Merida Initiative, the USA has appropriated $2.1 billion to the war on drugs in Mexico for both civilian and military operations and training since 2008.[100] The numbers of forces and financial support for the Mexican armed forces, particularly during Calderón's presidency,[101] suggest a response to an organised armed group.

As early as 2008, Calderón, in an attempt to minimise criticism of complaints of his increased domestic use of the military, claimed that it was "a temporary solution and that he plans to phase the armed forces out of that role".[102] This did not in fact occur under Calderón's leadership, nor under Enrique Pena Nieto's current administration. For example, 2500 federal troops were mobilised to the state of Tamaulipas in May 2014.[103]

---

[97] ICC Office of the Prosecutor, above n 75, para 217.

[98] Sullivan J and Elkus A (2010) Cartel v. Cartel: Mexico's Criminal Insurgency. http://smallwarsjournal.com/jrnl/art/cartel-v-cartel-mexicos-criminal-insurgency. Accessed 9 April 2016, p. 1.

[99] Human Rights Watch, above n 24, p. 4.

[100] US Department of state (2015) Merida Initiative. http://www.state.gov/j/inl/merida/. Accessed 9 April 2016.

[101] Current president, Enrique Peña Nieto, has claimed to redirect this strategy, focusing on institution-building and a new, more efficient 10,000-strong paramilitary force, 8000 of which will be members of the armed forces. Ince C (2013) President Peña Nieto and Mexico's On-Going War on Drugs. http://smallwarsjournal.com/jrnl/art/president-pe%C3%B1a-nieto-and-mexico%E2%80%99s-ongoing-war-on-drugs. Accessed 9 April 2016.

[102] Stratfor Global Intelligence (2008) Mexico Security Memo: Feb. 11, 2008 https://www.stratfor.com/analysis/mexico-security-memo-feb-11-2008. Accessed 9 April 2016.

[103] Heidelberg Institute for International Conflict Research, above n 65, p. 100.

Indeed, the scope and scale of the military's tasks exceeds those of assisting traditional law enforcement. The official tasks have included intelligence, detention and arrest, meth laboratory and crop eradication, raids, patrols and checkpoints.[104] In a situation of "mission creep" whereby the armed forces took on more and more law enforcement duties, the armed forces began to take on the "bulk of the manpower and coordination" of the cartel war.[105] These duties have been carried out amidst serious allegations of "unauthorised searches and seizures, rough treatment and torture of suspects (which in some cases have included police officers), and improper rules of engagement, which have led several times to civilian deaths when soldiers mistook them for hostile shooters".[106]

The number of members engaged by the drug cartels is similarly significant, even if many members would not be considered direct participants in hostilities assuming a continuous combat function. Seven major cartels currently operate in different territories, with the *Sinaloa* Cartel, the Gulf Cartel and the infamously violent *Zetas* being the strongest.[107] According to the US state Department, the *Sinaloa* Cartel and the *Zetas* alone consist of an estimated 100,000 foot soldiers.[108] To put these numbers in perspective, the USA currently has approximately 30,000 soldiers deployed in Afghanistan, and Taliban militants are estimated at 20,000.[109]

The frequency of clashes has remained steady or intensified over the ten-year period. For example, confrontations in 2013 led to over 17,000 killed and the emergence of numerous vigilante groups.[110] Cartel forces clashed with the government on a weekly basis though inter-cartel conflict caused the highest fatalities. In battles for control of certain northern cities in Tamaulipas, civilians were allegedly specifically targeted by both the *Zetas* and the Gulf Cartel.[111]

As mentioned above, in 2014 clashes between the government and cartels occurred nearly every day.[112] Clashes between cartels themselves were also

[104] Meiners S and Burton F (2009) The Role of the Mexican Military in the Cartel War https://www.stratfor.com/weekly/20090729_role_mexican_military_cartel_war. Accessed 9 April 2016.

[105] Ibid.

[106] Ibid.

[107] The most widely recognised cartels are the *Beltrán Leyva* Cartel, Gulf Cartel, *Juarez* Cartel, *La Familia Michoacán*, *Los Zetas*, *Sinaloa* Cartel and the *Tijuana/Arellano Felix* Cartel. Other important cartels, such as the Knights Templar and *Guerreros Unidos* have also gained prominence at times. See, for example: CNN (2016) Mexico Drug War Fast Facts. http://edition.cnn.com/2013/09/02/world/americas/mexico-drug-war-fast-facts/. Accessed 9 April 2016.

[108] Washington Times (2009) 100,000 foot soldiers in Mexican cartels. http://www.washingtontimes.com/news/2009/mar/03/100000-foot-soldiers-in-cartels/?page=all. Accessed 9 April 2016.

[109] BBC (2014) Q&A: Foreign forces in Afghanistan. http://www.bbc.com/news/world-south-asia-11371138. Accessed 9 April 2016.

[110] Heidelberg Institute for International Conflict Research, above n 65, pp. 15 and 85.

[111] Ibid., p. 85.

[112] Ibid., p. 100.

extremely violent.[113] Rather than decreasing, violence shifted regionally, with a subsequent military intervention as a response in Tamaulipas and an augmentation of federal troops in Michoacan.[114]

US Secretary of state affirmed to the Council of Foreign Affairs in 2010 that:

> We face an increasing threat from a well-organized network drug trafficking threat that is, in some cases, morphing into or making common cause with what we would consider an insurgency in Mexico and in Central America. [...] [The] drug cartels are now showing more and more indices of insurgency; all of a sudden, car bombs show up which weren't there before. [...] [I]t's looking more and more like Colombia looked 20 years ago, where the narco-traffickers control certain parts of the country.[115]

Though the Obama administration later rejected the comparison with Colombia, the recall appeared based more on diplomatic concerns than an assessment of the de facto situation in Mexico.[116]

The intensity of conflict can be measured not only by the numbers of casualties (as referred to in the second section of this paper), but also from the number of civilians displaced. As from December 2014, the Internal Displacement Monitoring Centre estimates that there were at least 281,400 internally displaced people (IDP) in Mexico, though Mexico does not officially recognise IDPs in its territory and will likely not allow international humanitarian intervention.[117]

In the light of the above, viewed as a whole the violence appears to satisfy the intensity requirement.

3.4 Conclusion

The multiplicity of organised groups, shifting alliances and varying degrees of intensity across territories and time periods render the violence challenging to qualify. Nevertheless, a *prima facie* and general assessment of the violence discussed in this paper suggests that each of the three criteria for the existence of a NIAC under the Rome Statute is satisfied: the violence has, on the whole, been protracted and intense and at least some the cartels involved in the violence, such as the *Sinaola* and *Los Zetas*, may be considered to be *organised* armed groups. Nevertheless, it is stressed that the present conclusion on the existence of a NIAC

[113] Ibid.

[114] Ibid., p. 89.

[115] James F (2010) Obama Rejects Hillary Clinton Mexico-Colombia Comparison. http://www.npr.org/sections/thetwo-way/2010/09/09/129760276/obama-rejects-hillary-clinton-mexico-colombia-comparison. Accessed 9 April 2016.

[116] Ibid.

[117] International Displacement Monitoring Centre (2015) New Humanitarian Frontiers: Addressing criminal violence in Mexico and Central America. http://www.internal-displacement.org/publications/2015/new-humanitarian-frontiers-addressing-criminal-violence-in-mexico-and-central-america. Accessed 9 April 2016.

is based on no more than a general assessment of publicly available material in relation to the wider context of the violence. An ICC Chamber presented with concrete evidence may be able to make a more specific assessment, including as to whether the three requirements coincide geographically and temporally, and relate to drug cartels with the requisite level of organisation. The NGO submission would be an ideal opportunity for the prosecutor to look more closely at the qualification of the violence in conducting her preliminary inquiries and investigations.

Nevertheless, to the extent that the application of IHL to the violence arising from the war on drugs would result in possible prosecutions for crimes that are expressly proscribed by the laws of war, but not canvassed by the provisions outlawing crimes against humanity, the qualification of the violence arising from the war on drugs as a NIAC would enhance accountability. For example, it is estimated that about 30,000 children have been recruited into the ranks of the cartels.[118] Under the Rome Statute, such recruitment—by and of itself—would not amount to a crime against humanity under Article 7 of the Rome Statute. However, recruitment of children under the age of 15 would amount to a war crime under Article 8(2)(e)(viii) in the context of a NIAC.[119] This would have a tangible impact as it would mean that those that have suffered harm as a result of the recruitment—such as parents whose children have been transformed into *sicarios*—can participate as victims in criminal proceedings at the ICC against individuals who are responsible for such recruitment[120] and they would also have the possibility of getting reparations.[121] Similarly, women suffering gender-based violence, including sexual slavery and forced prostitution, may have more recourse under the Rome Statute than domestic law.[122]

Acknowledgment The authors sincerely thank Prof. Dino Kritsiotis for his comments on an earlier draft of this paper. Any errors, however, remain entirely the authors'.

References

Articles, Books and Other Documents

Bergal C (2011) The Mexican Drug War: The Case for a Non-International Armed Conflict Classification. Fordham Int Law J 34:1042–1088

Bloom CA (2012) Square Pegs and Round Holes: Mexico, Drugs, and International Law. Houston J Int Law 24:345–414

---

[118] Burnett, above n 21.

[119] *Lubanga* 2012, above n 47.

[120] Rome Statute, above n 37, Article 68.

[121] Ibid., Article 75.

[122] Grillo I (2013) The Mexican Drug Cartels' Other Business: Sex Trafficking. http://world.time.com/2013/07/31/the-mexican-drug-cartels-other-business-sex-trafficking/. Accessed 9 April 2016.

Bunker R, Sullivan J (2010) Cartel Evolution Revisited: Third Phase Cartel Potentials and Alternative Futures in Mexico. Small Wars Insurgencies 21:30–54

Carpenter A (2013) Changing Lenses: Conflict Analysis and Mexico's 'Drug War'. Latin Am Politics Soc 55:139–160

Cryer R, Friman H, Robinson D, Wilmshurst E (2008) An Introduction to International Criminal Law and Procedure. Cambridge University Press, New York

Cullen A (2008) The Definition of Non-International Armed Conflict in the Rome Statute of the International Criminal Court: An Analysis of the Threshold of Application Contained in Article 8 (2)(f). J Conflict Secur Law 12:419–445

Dahl A, Sandbu M (2006) The Threshold of Armed Conflict. Revue de droit militaire et de droit de la guerre 45:369–388

Dinstein Y (2014) Non-International Armed Conflicts in International Law. Cambridge University Press, Cambridge

Felbab-Brown V (2009) The Violent Drug Market in Mexico and Lessons from Colombia. The Brookings Institution Policy Paper 12:1–29

Fleck D (2008) The Law of Non-International Armed Conflicts. In: Fleck D (ed) The Handbook of International Humanitarian Law, 3rd edn. Oxford University Press, New York, pp 581–610

Grillo I (2012) El Narco: The bloody rise of Mexican drug cartels. Bloomsbury Publishing, Great Britain

Guevara A (2013) Propaganda in Mexico's Drug War. J Strateg Secur 6:131–151

Kerr C (2012) Mexico's Drug War: Is it really a war? South Texas Law Rev 54:193

Kritsiotis D (2010) The Tremors of Tadić. Israel Law Rev 43:262–300

Pejic J (2011) The protective scope of Common Article 3: more than meets the eye. Int Rev Red Cross 93:189–225

Sánchez A (2013) Mexico's Drug War: Drawing a Line between Rhetoric and Reality. Yale Journal of International Law 38:467–509

UN Diplomatic Conference of Plenipotentiaries on the Establishment of an International Criminal Court (1998) Committee of the Whole: Summary Record of the 35th Meeting, UN Doc. A/CONF.183/C.1/SR.35

UN Diplomatic Conference of Plenipotentiaries on the Establishment of an International Criminal Court (1998) Report of the Preparatory Committee on the Establishment of an International Criminal Court, UN Doc. A/CONF.183/2/Add.1

UN General Assembly (2014) Human Rights Council: Informe del Relator Especial sobre la tortura y otros tratos o penas crueles, inhumanos o degradantes, UN Doc. A/HRC/28/68/ Add.3

Case Law

IACommHR, *Case 11.137 Juan Carlos Abella (Argentina)*, Merits, 30 October 1997, Report No. 55/97, Doc No. 38, No. OEA/Ser/L/V/II.97

ICC, *Prosecutor v Callixte Mbarushimana,* Decision on the Confirmation of Charges, 16 December 2011, Case No. ICC-01/04-01/10-465-Red

ICC, *Prosecutor v Germain Katanga*, Jugement rendu en application de l'article 74 du Statut, 7 March 2014, Case No. ICC-01/04-01/07-3436

ICC, *Prosecutor v Jean-Pierre Bemba Gombo*, Decision Pursuant to Article 61(7)(a) and (b) of the Rome Statute on the Charges of the Prosecutor Against Jean-Pierre Bemba Gombo, 15 June 2009, Case No. ICC-01/05-01/08-424

ICC, *Prosecutor v Jean-Pierre Bemba Gombo*, Judgment pursuant to Article 74 of the Statute, 21 March 2016, Case No. ICC-01/05-01/08-3343

ICC, *Prosecutor v Thomas Lubanga Dyilo,* Décision sur la confirmation des charges, 29 January 2007, Case No. ICC-01/04-01/06-803

ICC, *Prosecutor v Thomas Lubanga Dyilo,* Judgment Pursuant to Article 74 of the Statute, 14 March 2012, Case No. ICC-01/04-01/06-2842
ICTR, *Prosecutor v Alfred Musema,* Judgment and Sentence, 27 January 2000, Case No. ICTR-96-13-T
ICTY, *Prosecutor v Duško Tadić a/k/a "Dule"*, Decision on the Defence Motion for Interlocutory Appeal on Jurisdiction, 2 October 1995, Case No. IT-94-1-AR72
ICTY, *Prosecutor v Fatmir Limaj, Haradin Bala and Isak Musliu,* Judgment, 30 November 2005, Case No. IT-03-66-T
ICTY, *Prosecutor v Ljube Boškoski and Johan Tarčulovski,* Judgment, 10 July 2008, Case No. IT-04-82-T
ICTY, *Prosecutor v Milan Lukić and Sredoje Lukić,* Judgment, 20 July 2009, Case No. IT-98-32/1-T
ICTY, *Prosecutor v Ramush Haradinaj, Idriz Balaj and Lahi Brahimaj*, Judgment, 3 April 2008, Case No. IT-04-84-T
ICTY, *Prosecutor v Vlastimir Đorđević*, Public Judgment with Confidential Annex – Volume I of II, 23 February 2011, Case No. IT-05-87/1-T

Treaties

Rome Statute of the International Criminal Court, opened for signature 17 July 1998, 2187 UNTS 90 (entered into force 1 July 2002)

Other Consulted Sources

López JCA (2015) Reiteran petición de investigar a militares en Guerrero por caso Ayotzinapa. http://www.noticiasmvs.com/#!/noticias/reiteran-peticion-de-investigar-a-militares-en-guerrero-por-caso-ayotzinapa-843. Accessed 9 April 2016
UN Diplomatic Conference of Plenipotentiaries on the Establishment of an International Criminal Court (1998) Information conveyed by New Zealand—International Committee of the Red Cross: Concerns on Threshold for War Crimes Committed in Non-International Armed Conflicts as contained in the Bureau Proposal (A/CONF.183/C.1/L.59), UN Doc. A/CONF.183/INF/11

Chapter 4
The Armed Conflict(s) Against the Islamic State

Noam Zamir

Abstract International Humanitarian Law in general and the classification of armed conflicts in particular have been the subjects of a vast amount of scholarly writing, international jurisprudence, states' reports and international reports of IGOs and NGOs. Nevertheless, as exemplified by the armed conflicts with the Islamic State, important questions regarding various aspects of conflict classification remain. Since conflict classification has important practical ramifications, by analysing the armed conflicts with the Islamic State from the perspective of conflict classification, this article aims to frame these open questions and address them. As conflict classification is contingent on the status of the different actors in the battlefield, the article, *inter alia,* examines the following: whether the Islamic State can be regarded as a national liberation movement for the purposes of conflict classification; how international humanitarian law determines whether a group can be deemed as the Government of a given state; the effect of consent of the territorial state for intervention on the conflict classification; and, in cases where there is invitation of the territorial state for intervention, whether the foreign armed intervention should be considered separately or conjunctively with the ongoing non-international armed conflict of the territorial state.

Keywords Conflict classification · Islamic State · Syria · Iraq · Armed conflicts · International humanitarian law

N. Zamir (✉)
Assistant Professor, School of Law,
City University of Hong Kong,
Kowloon Tong, Hong Kong
e-mail: noam.zamir@cantab.net

T.D. Gill et al. (eds.), *Yearbook of International Humanitarian Law 2015*,
Yearbook of International Humanitarian Law 18,
DOI 10.1007/978-94-6265-141-8_4

Contents

4.1 Introduction

The conflict between the USA and its Western and Arab allies (Foreign Coalition)[1] against the Islamic State (IS)[2] involves complex legal issues and reveals that despite the increasing scholarly attention,[3] there are still important open questions regarding conflict classification in international humanitarian law (IHL). These open questions have a real impact on the legality of the actions committed by the various actors involved in the armed conflict, and therefore their importance goes well beyond the sphere of academic debate.

The effect of the open questions on conflict classification is augmented due to the difficulty of assessing the exact facts in most ongoing armed conflicts. While at times it is challenging to draw the line between the practical difficulties of applying the law to the facts and the theoretical questions regarding the content of the law, this chapter aims to map the theoretical questions and offer some thoughts on how they should be addressed by examining the armed conflicts between IS and the governmental forces of Iraq and Syria, and between IS and the Foreign

[1] Various states are involved in the Foreign Coalition. However, not all of them participate directly in the armed conflicts against IS. The main states that are involved, to some extent but not necessarily directly, in the Foreign Coalition are as follows: USA; UK; Jordan; Morocco; Australia; Belgium; Canada; Denmark; France; Germany; Italy; the Netherlands; New Zealand; Turkey; Bahrain; Qatar; Saudi Arabia; and United Arab Emirates. See discussion in section II.

[2] Also known as ISIS and ISIL—see discussion below in Sect. 2.

[3] See, for example, Milanović and Hadzi-Vidanović 2013; Lubell and Derejko 2013, p. 65; Wilmshurst 2012; Kreß 2010, p. 245; Vité 2009, p. 69.

Coalition.[4] Thus, the focus of this chapter is on the relevant theoretical questions that arise in the armed conflicts against IS, and less on covering all the precise small factual details, some of which are simply not publicly available, of the ongoing armed conflicts with IS. It should be stated that as the conflicts which involve IS are constantly developing and changing, the time frame for the examination of the conflict does not extend beyond August 2015.[5]

The chapter is structured as follows: Sect. 2 briefly summarises the factual background of the conflict(s) with IS; Sect. 3 discusses whether IS can be treated like a state for the purposes of IHL; Sect. 4 examines the armed conflicts between IS and Iraq, and IS and Syria; Sect. 5 analyses that armed conflict between IS and the Foreign Coalition; and Sect. 6 concludes the chapter.

4.2 The Conflict(s) with IS—Factual Background

IS emerged out of al-Qaeda in 2004 in Iraq and was known as al-Qaeda in Iraq (AQI).[6] In 2006, AQI created an umbrella organisation of various terror organisations and was known as the Islamic State in Iraq (ISI). In 2013, ISI extended its operations to Syria via the al-Nusra Front. By early 2013, the group was conducting dozens of armed attacks per month in Iraq. In April 2013, ISI decided to merge its forces in Iraq and Syria to create the Islamic State in Iraq and the Levant/Syria (ISIL/ISIS). Al-Qaeda objected to this move, severed its connections to ISIS and denounced the brutality of ISIS.[7] In June 2014, after consolidating its hold over

[4] Thus, it is beyond the scope of this chapter to examine other possible conflicts which take place in the territories of Iraq and Syria, including armed conflicts between other non-state groups and IS (e.g. the armed conflict between Hezbollah and IS). Also, the legality of armed interventions from the perspective of *jus ad bellum* does not fall within the scope of this chapter.

[5] Accordingly, the Russian military intervention against IS that started on Syrian soil in September 2015 is not examined in this chapter. In any case, the Russian intervention does not add any other significant open questions with regard to classification of conflicts.

[6] The organisational roots can be traced further back to 2002, and the activities of the late Abu Musab al Zarqawi in Iraq. For background information on IS, see Blanchard et al. 2014, pp. 10–11; UN General Assembly (2015) Human Rights Council: Report of the Independent International Commission of Inquiry on the Syrian Arab Republic. UN Doc A/HRC/28/69, paras 33–39; BBC News (2015) What is Islamic State? http://www.bbc.com/news/world-middle-east-29052144. Accessed 6 June 2016.

[7] See Malik S, Khalili M and Ackerman S (2015) How ISIS Crippled Al-Qaida. http://www.theguardian.com/world/2015/jun/10/how-isis-crippled-al-qaida. Accessed 6 June 2016; Sly L (2014) Al-Qaeda Disavows Any Ties with Radical Islamist ISIS group in Syria, Iraq. https://www.washingtonpost.com/world/middle_east/al-qaeda-disavows-any-ties-with-radical-islamist-isis-group-in-syria-iraq/2014/02/03/2c9afc3a-8cef-11e3-98ab-fe5228217bd1_story.html. Accessed 6 June 2016.

dozens of cities and towns in Iraq and Syria, ISIS declared the creation of a caliphate and changed its name to the Islamic State (IS).[8] The financial strength of IS is believed to be based on donations from wealthy individuals from the Gulf and Saudi Arabia, the oil fields in eastern Syria and Iraq and the capture of reserves of the Iraqi Central Bank held in Mosul that took place in June 2014.[9]

Various forces have been intervening in the ongoing conflict in Syria and Iraq.[10] It is difficult to establish the extent of the direct involvement of the state members in the Foreign Coalition because each state reports its specific activities differently, independently and on different timetables.[11] However, in the context of the specific armed activities of the Foreign Coalition against IS, the USA was the main state to start using direct force against IS. On 8 August 2014, the USA started bombing IS targets in Iraq.[12] By a letter dated 23 September 2014, the USA informed the UN Secretary General that it has started to carry out airstrikes on Syrian soil on the basis of Article 51 of the UN Charter due to the inability or unwillingness of the Syrian government to prevent the use of its territory for attacks carried by IS.[13] By the end of September 2014, the USA had conducted around 240 air strikes against IS in Iraq and Syria.[14] Other states joined, with different types of support, the Foreign Coalition. For example, Australia joined the air strikes in October 2014,[15] and the UK joined in September 2014 and conducted

8 Office of the High Commissioner for Human Rights and UN Assistance Mission for Iraq (2014) Report on the Protection of Civilians in the Non International Armed Conflict in Iraq: 5 June 2014–5 July 2014. http://www.ohchr.org/Documents/Countries/IQ/UNAMI_OHCHR_POC%20Report_FINAL_18July2014A.pdf. Accessed 6 June 2016, p. 1, note 3.

9 Ibid.

10 US Department of State (2016) The Global Coalition to Counter ISIL. http://www.state.gov/s/seci/. Accessed 6 June 2016; United States Central Command (2015) Counter-ISIL military coalition concludes operational planning conference. http://www.centcom.mil/news/news-article/counter-isil-military-coalition-concludes-operational-planning-conference. Accessed 6 June 2016.

11 Fantz A (2015) War on ISIS: Who's doing what? http://edition.cnn.com/2015/11/20/world/war-on-isis-whos-doing-what/. Accessed 6 June 2016.

12 Carter C, Cohen T and Starr B (2014) U.S. Jet Fighters, Drones Strike ISIS Fighters, Convoys in Iraq. http://edition.cnn.com/2014/08/08/world/iraq-options/index.html?hpt=hp_t1. Accessed 9 August 2014.

13 UN Security Council (2014) Letter dated 23 September 2014 from the Permanent Representative of the United States of America to the United Nations addressed to the Secretary-General, UN Doc. S/2014/695.

14 Sisk R (2014) Airstrike Agreement Keeps US Air Controllers Away From Combat. http://www.military.com/daily-news/2014/09/29/airstrike-agreement-keeps-us-air-controllers-away-from-combat.html. Accessed 6 June 2016.

15 Hudson P (2014) Cabinet Approves Australian Airstrikes in Iraq. http://www.theaustralian.com.au/in-depth/terror/cabinet-approves-australian-airstrikes-in-iraq/story-fnpdbcmu-1227078959113. Accessed 6 June 2016.

its first air strike on 30 September 2014.[16] Currently, while the members of the Foreign Coalition are involved to different extents in the conflict, none of these states has engaged its ground forces, with the exception of specific special operations, in the conflict.[17] Several of the states of the Foreign Coalition, such as the USA, UK and France, have explained that their use of force against IS in the territory of Iraq was based on Iraq's consent,[18] which was given explicitly.[19]

The classification of the armed conflicts to which IS is a party to is contingent on identifying the various actors involved and the hostilities among them. Thus, the first main question is whether IS can be treated like a state for the purposes of IHL. The second question is how to classify the conflicts between IS and the governments of Iraq and Syria. The third question is how to classify the conflict between IS and the Foreign Coalition.

4.3 Whether IS Can Be Treated like a State for the Purposes of IHL

IS can be considered a state for the purposes of IHL only if it is deemed to be Iraq, Syria or a new state—the so-called Islamic State. While IS has never claimed that it should be regarded as representing Iraq or Syria, the classification of conflicts is not dependent on the declaration of the different parties to the conflict. Thus, in any case, we first need to examine how IHL determines whether a certain group is deemed to be the government of a state in cases where there are different groups that struggle to control the said state and subsequently apply the law to the situation in Iraq and Syria. Then, we need to examine whether IS can be considered a new state.

---

[16] United Kingdom (2014) RAF Conducts First Air Strikes of Iraq Mission. https://www.gov.uk/government/news/raf-conducts-first-air-strikes-of-iraq-mission--2. Accessed 6 June 2016.

[17] "But the USA has ruled out using combat troops on the ground, as have Britain and other allies, even while agreeing to provide air power". See Sanger D and Barnard A (2014) US Defending Kurds in Syria, Expands Airstrikes Against Islamic State Militants. www.nytimes.com/2014/09/28/world/middleeast/us-strikes-isis-in-syria-to-defend-kurds.html?hp&action=click&pgtype=Homepage&version=LedeSum&module=first-column-region&region=top-news&WT.nav=top-news&_r=0t. Accessed 6 June 2016.

[18] See sources cited in Akande D and Vermeer Z (2015) The Airstrikes Against Islamic State in Iraq and the Alleged Prohibition on Military Assistance to Governments in Civil War. http://www.ejiltalk.org/the-airstrikes-against-islamic-state-in-iraq-and-the-alleged-prohibition-on-military-assistance-to-governments-in-civil-wars/. Accessed 6 June 2016.

[19] See UN Security Council (2014) Letter dated 20 September 2014 from the Permanent Representative of Iraq to the United Nations addressed to the President of the Security Council, UN Doc. S/2014/691, Annex: "It is for these reasons that we, in accordance with international law and the relevant bilateral and multilateral agreements, and with due regard for complete national sovereignty and the Constitution, have requested the United States of America to lead international efforts to strike ISIL sites and military strongholds, with our express consent".

4.3.1 *Can IS Be Deemed as the Government of Iraq or Syria?*

In international law, states act "through their agents and representatives"[20], and it is generally agreed that the government is the organ responsible for representing the state in international discourse.[21] It is also accepted that "there can be but one government in the same state at the same time".[22] Thus, in a civil war, while different groups may claim to represent the state or struggle to control it, only the group that is deemed to be the government of the state can represent that state.

In public international law, in general, the question of whether a new entity is considered a government becomes relevant only when there are competing groups claiming to be the legitimate government or when there is an unconstitutional change in the government.[23] Although there is no consensus on a specific test for determining when a group can be deemed to be the government of a state as the practice of recognition of governments has declined,[24] it is generally accepted that a state is represented by its *de facto* government and, therefore, a group that claims to be the government and exercises effective control, which is likely to continue,

[20] PCIJ, *Questions relating to Settlers of German Origin in Poland*, Advisory Opinion, 10 September 1923, [1923] PCIJ Rep Series B, No. 6, p. 22.

[21] Talmon 1998, p. 115 ("It is generally agreed that the organ representing the State in international intercourse is its government [...] The government, consequently possesses the *jus repraesentationis omnimodae*, i.e. the plenary and exclusive competence in international law to represent its State in the international sphere"); Cheng 1953, p. 184 ("States not only act through their government but through their government exclusively"). See Crawford 2012, p. 151 ("the legal entity in international law is the state; the government is in normal circumstances the representative of the state, entitled to act on its behalf"); Wilde R (2010) Recognition of States—the Consequences of Recognition or Non-Recognition in UK and International Law: Summary of the International Law Discussion Group meeting held at Chatham House on 4 February 2010. https://www.chathamhouse.org/sites/files/chathamhouse/public/Research/International%20 Law/040210il.pdf. Accessed 6 June 2016, p. 3 ("In international law, the connection between the two [i.e. the State and the government] is understood in terms of agency: the government is not itself a legal person, but, rather, the agent that acts on behalf of the legal person—the state—concerned. Its acts are the acts of the state").

[22] *Charles J Jansen v Mexico*, Mexico-US Claims Committee, 1868, reprinted in Moore 1898, p. 2928; American Law Institute 1965, p. 323 ("Customary, recognition of governments is made on a 'one of the other' basis"). See also Talmon 1998, pp. 105–107 and the sources cited therein.

[23] Shaw 2008, p. 454 ("Recognition will only really be relevant where the change in government is unconstitutional.").

[24] Although it is beyond the scope of this chapter to discuss the topic of recognition of governments, it suffices to say that while it is accepted that a government is not dependent on foreign recognition, states still use the tool of recognition explicitly or implicitly in order to engage in international discourse or to confer legitimacy. See in general, Talmon 1998, pp. 3–14.

over all or most of the state territory should be deemed as the government of a given state (hereinafter the *de facto* doctrine).[25]

Similarly, while this remains an open issue in the field of conflict classification, it has been argued that for the purpose of conflict classification, a state is deemed to be represented by the group that is considered its *de facto* government regardless of its legal standing or the extent of international recognition.[26] For example, despite the fact that the Taliban were never considered by the international community as the legitimate government of Afghanistan, they were still considered the *de facto* government and deemed to represent Afghanistan for the purpose of IHL. Hence, their armed conflict with the US-led coalition was considered international.[27]

Nevertheless, in the context of conflict classification, the *de facto* doctrine is not free from difficulties. First, in general, it is still an open question whether the *de facto* doctrine can be considered part of IHL. Second, it is not clear what a government is actually required to possess in order to be considered the *de facto* government. Does this government need to control 70 or 90 % of the territory? Or perhaps controlling 51 % of the territory or the capital is enough? Third, arguing that legal standing has no bearing may imply that every time rebels control most of the territory of a country, they could claim that they are the legitimate government for the purpose of conflict classification. This would, in turn, allow the rebels to claim that their soldiers are entitled to POW status when captured by a foreign state and, in other cases, it may open the door for a foreign state that intervenes against the established government to claim that it does not treat its armed conflict against the established government as international because the government is not the *de facto* government.

Thus, it is submitted that in the context of conflict classification, the *de facto* doctrine needs fine-tuning. Although the question of when a group is deemed to be

---

[25] *Great Britain v Costa Rica*, Arbitral Award, 18 October 1923, (1948) 1 UNRIAA 369, pp. 381–382 (*Tinoco Concessions* case); *Salimoff & Co and Others v Standard Oil Company of New York*, Court of Appeals of New York, (1933) 262 NYS 220, 227; Crawford 2012, p. 152 (referring to the *Tinoco Concessions* case and stating that "[i]n case of governments 'the standard set by international law' is so far the standard of secure *de facto* control of all or most of the state territory".); Shaw 2008, p. 455; Lauterpacht 1947, p. 98. See also Chen and Green 1951, p. 117.

[26] Dinstein 2014, pp. 95–107 (discussing the topic of recognition of governments and emphasising that "[g]eneral foreign recognition of a Government does not constitute a third condition for its existence, in addition to effectiveness and independence".); Milanović and Hadzi-Vidanović 2013, p. 279 ("[...] the position in modern IHL is that it is *de facto* government and not recognition that matters".); Arimatsu 2009, p. 175, note 97 ("State practice confirms that the legitimacy or *de jure* recognition of a government is irrelevant for the purpose of categorising a conflict as in the case of Afghanistan 2001".); Schindler 1979, pp. 128–130.

[27] Dinstein 2010, p. 29; Greenwood 2002, pp. 312–313; but see Wolfrum and Philipp 2002, p. 577 ("To sum it up: however, successful the Taliban were within their reign, the sole legitimate representative of the Islamic State of Afghanistan always was the former government under the leadership of its president Burhanuddin Rabbani. The *Taliban* were never considered to be the sole legitimate government of Afghanistan.").

the government of a given state should be based on its effective control over the state's territory, it is argued that legal standing of the given government still matters. For example, in the Mali civil war (2012–2015), despite the fact that the government lost control of a significant part of its territory,[28] it was generally accepted that it still represented Mali when it issued the invitation for French intervention in its favour. Therefore, the armed conflict between France and the rebels, who controlled vast areas in Mali, was regarded as non-international armed conflict (NIAC).[29] Another recent example is the Libyan civil war and the foreign intervention of the USA, UK and French forces in 2011 in favour of the rebels. Despite the fact that the UK and France recognised the rebels as the legitimate government, they still regarded Gaddafi's forces as representing the state for the purposes of conflict classification, even when those forces lost control over most of the territory.[30]

Focusing on the armed conflict with IS in Iraq and Syria, it is clear that the situation is complex. Though IS has never asserted that it should be regarded as the government of Iraq or Syria and IS' borders often change and their exact demarcation is unclear, it nevertheless controls large swaths of territory in north Iraq and Syria.[31] Moreover, IS seems to exercise its control over its territory in order to

---

[28] See Hadzi-Vidanović V (2013) France Intervenes in Mali Invoking both SC Resolution 2085 and the Invitation of the Malian Government—Redundancy or Legal Necessity? http://www.ejiltalk.org/france-intervenes-in-mali-invoking-both-sc-resolution-2085-and-the-invitation-of-the-malian-government-redundancy-or-legal-necessity/. Accessed 6 June 2016 (stating that "rebel groups control more than two thirds of the country's territory").

[29] E.g. United States Mission to the United Nations (2013) Remarks at a Press Gaggle Following UN Security Council Consultations on Mali. http://usun.state.gov/remarks/5641. Accessed 6 June 2016 (Susan Rice, the US Permanent Representative to the UN, just before the commencement of the French intervention, commenting that any state "can support and encourage the Malian government's sovereign request for assistance from friends and partners in the region and beyond [… and that] there was clear-cut consensus about the gravity of the situation and the right of the Malian authorities to seek what assistance they can receive"); Human Rights Watch (2013) Mali: All Sides Must Abide by Laws of War. https://www.hrw.org/news/2013/05/07/mali-all-sides-must-abide-laws-war. Accessed 6 June 2016 ("The current armed conflict between the Malian government and its allies and opposition armed groups is regulated by Common Article 3 to the Geneva Conventions of 1949, to which Mali is a party, and customary international humanitarian law").

[30] Although Libya (i.e. Gaddafi's governmental forces), and the UK and France did not officially classify their armed conflicts, there was no doubt that these states were engaged in an IAC against each other. See UN General Assembly (2011) Human Rights Council: Report of the International Commission of Inquiry to Investigate all Alleged Violations of International Human Rights Law in the Libyan Arab Jamahiriya, UN Doc. A/HRC/17/44, para 66; Arab Organization for Human Rights (2012), Report of the Independent Civil Society Fact-Finding Mission to Libya. http://reliefweb.int/sites/reliefweb.int/files/resources/Full%20Report_481.pdf. Accessed 6 June, para 63.

[31] Institute for the Study of War (2015) Iraq's Situation Report: April 21–22, 2015. http://www.understandingwar.org/backgrounder/iraq-situation-report-april-21-22-2015. Accessed 6 June 2016; The New York Times (2015) A Visual Guide to the Crisis in Iraq and Syria. http://www.nytimes.com/interactive/2014/06/12/world/middleeast/the-iraq-isis-conflict-in-maps-photos-and-video.html?_r=2. Accessed 6 June 2016.

collect taxes and enforce its laws.[32] Although this control might be loose and inconsistent in all its territory,[33] it seems that this control is nonetheless significant.[34] In addition, although other states ostensibly are not interested in having relations with IS,[35] it seems that IS, with its organisation skills, as demonstrated in its military campaign and propaganda, has the capacity to enter into relations with other states.[36] On the other hand, the established governments of Iraq and Syria, despite considerable loss of territory, still exercise control over some parts of their territories, including their capitals, assert authority, enjoy some international support and conduct armed resistance.[37] Thus, for the purposes of the discussion, it will be presumed that IS cannot be deemed as the government of Iraq or Syria. Nevertheless, admittedly, since IHL does not have an established test to determine which group represents the state for the purposes of conflict classification, the legal basis of this conclusion can be debated.

---

[32] Al Hayat Media Center (2014) This is the Promise of Allah. https://ia902505.us.archive.org/28/items/poa_25984/EN.pdf. Accessed 6 June 2016; March A and Revkin M (2015) Caliphate of Law—ISIS Ground Rules. https://www.foreignaffairs.com/articles/syria/2015-04-15/caliphate-law?cid=nlc-foreign_affairs_this_week-041715-caliphate_of_law_5-041715&sp_mid=48469002&sp_rid=cGF1bEB2b25tdWhsZW5kYWhsLmNvbQS2. Accessed 6 June 2016.

[33] The New York Times, above n 31; BBC News (2015) Battle for Iraq and Syria in Maps. http://www.bbc.com/news/world-middle-east-27838034. Accessed 6 June 2016.

[34] UN News Centre (2014) New UN report depicts 'relentless assault' on civilians inside ISIL-controlled Syria. http://www.un.org/apps/news/story.asp?NewsID=49338#.VUIqcyFVik. Accessed 6 June 2016; Packer G (2014) The Common Enemy. http://www.newyorker.com/magazine/2014/08/25/the-common-enemy. Accessed 6 June 2016.

[35] See e.g.: UK's Prime Minister Office (2014) Summary of the Government's Legal Position on Military Action in Iraq Against ISIL. https://www.gov.uk/government/publications/military-action-in-iraq-against-isil-government-legal-position/summary-of-the-government-legal-position-on-military-action-in-iraq-against-isil. Accessed 6 June 2016; Scheer A (2014) 41st Canadian Parliament, House of Commons Debates 2nd Session, vol. 147, no. 123. http://www.parl.gc.ca/HousePublications/Publication.aspx?Language=E&Mode=1&Parl=41&Ses=2&DocId=6717243. Accessed 6 June 2016; UN Security Council (2014) Resolution 2170 (2014), UN Doc. S/RES/2170.

[36] See Al Hayat Media Centre, above n 32; Becker O (2014) ISIS Has a Really Slick and Sophisticated Media Department. https://news.vice.com/article/isis-has-a-really-slick-and-sophisticated-media-department. Accessed 6 June 2016; UN Independent International Commission of Inquiry on the Syrian Arab Republic (2014) Rule of Terror: Living under ISIS in Syria. http://www.refworld.org/pdfid/5469b2e14.pdf. Accessed 9 June 2016, p. 3.

[37] Lister C (2014) Not Just Iraq: The Islamic State Is Also on the March in Syria. http://www.huffingtonpost.com/charles-lister/not-just-iraq-the-islamic_b_5658048.html. Accessed 6 June 2016; BBC News (2015) Syria: Mapping of the Conflict. http://www.bbc.com/news/world-middle-east-22798391. Accessed 6 June 2016; Noble Z (2014) The Government Still Controls Some Parts of This Country. Here's What It's Like to Live There. http://www.theblaze.com/stories/2014/11/02/the-government-still-controls-some-parts-of-this-country-heres-what-its-like-to-live-there/. Accessed 6 June 2016.

4.3.2 Can IS Be Deemed as an Independent State?

Some might dismiss the question whether IS can considered to be a state because not a single state has recognised IS as such. Others might argue that this question deserves a separate article due to the various factual and doctrinal questions that the case of IS presents. For the purposes of classifying the armed conflict with IS, we will try to address this question succinctly.[38]

There are basically two theories as to the nature of recognition of states. According to the constitutive theory, it is the act of recognition by other states that creates a new state and endows it with legal personality.[39] According to the declaratory theory, a new state will acquire capacity in international law not by virtue of the consent of others, but by virtue of a particular factual situation.[40] Other scholars have tried to suggest a middle position, according to which the act of recognition is an important indicator that the given state has conformed to the basic requirements of international law as to the creation of a state.[41]

While the debate between these two theories is still ongoing,[42] it seems that the constitutive theory has lost support in recent years, and state practice and academic writing have both demonstrated support of a more declaratory approach.[43]

As the application of both theories leads to the same result, there is no need to make any determination as to the correct theory of recognition of states. To start with the constitutive theory, it is clear that IS represents an extreme case of lack of recognition. No state has recognised IS as a state.[44] This wide lack of recognition resembles the status of Somaliland, which, despite its claim for statehood and its exercise of autonomous powers, does not enjoy any international recognition and therefore is not considered a state.[45] Thus, it is clear that this international consensus regarding the lack of recognition of IS as a state would preclude IS from achieving statehood according to the constitutive theory.

---

[38] See discussion in Shany Y, Cohen A and Mimran T (2014) ISIS: Is the Islamic State Really a State? http://en.idi.org.il/analysis/articles/isis-is-the-islamic-state-really-a-state/. Accessed 9 June 2016; similarly, on whether ISIS can govern, see Caris and Reynolds 2014, p. 4.

[39] Shaw 2014, p. 322; Lauterpacht 1947, p. 39; Jennings 1961, p. 9.

[40] Shaw 2014, p. 322; Crawford 1976, pp. 93 and 95.

[41] Crawford 1976, p. 106; Shaw 2014, p. 322.

[42] Lauterpacht 1947, p. 39; Dugard 2011, p. 47; International Law Association (2012) Sofia Conference (2012): Recognition/Non-recognition in International Law. file:///U:/!YIHL/16.06.03 %20-%20YIHL%20-%20Zamir/final_report_sofia_rev_aug_2014_42022.pdf. Accessed 9 June 2016, p. 4.

[43] International Law Association, above n 42; Peters 2010, p. 175.

[44] UN Security Council, above n 19; Presidentassad.net (2015) H.E. President Assad's Swedish Expression Newspaper Interview, April 17, 2015. http://www.presidentassad.net/index.php?option=com_content&view=article&id=1448:h-e-president-assad-s-swedish-expressen-newspaper-interview-april-17-2015&catid=314&Itemid=468. Accessed 6 June 2016.

[45] Eggers 2007, p. 211; Crawford 2006, p. 417; Kaplan 2008, p. 152; Adam 1994, p. 21.

With regard to the declaratory theory, the most common and often cited basis for statehood are the four conditions enshrined in Article 1 of the Montevideo Convention on the Rights and Duties of State:[46] (a) a permanent population; (b) a defined territory; (c) government; and (d) capacity to enter into relations with the other states. There are two other requirements, which are often regarded as cumulatively necessary—independence and respect for peremptory norms.[47]

It is clear that IS does not meet all these requirements. First, it seems that IS does not meet the requirement of permanent population.[48] Despite some signs of support from the local Iraqi and Syrian population, most of the individuals under IS' control did not choose to be part of this new state, and therefore we can assume that they do not identify themselves as part of this so-called state. It is possible that the fighters that are part of this state will be considered civilians of this state, but it is not clear to what extent its fighters actually feel bound to this entity and are going to stay. As the fulfilment of the first condition is disputable, it is reasonable to conclude that IS does not meet the conditions for statehood. However, even if one interprets these conditions more flexibly and reaches the conclusion that IS met these conditions, it would nevertheless be inconsistent with current state practice to argue that those suffice and that IS is therefore a state.[49]

As explained above, it is necessary to examine the two other requirements of statehood (i.e. independence of the new entity and its respect for peremptory norms).[50] The international community has so far been reluctant to acknowledge new entities lacking those requirements, despite their ability to fulfil all four conditions thus far presented.[51]

---

[46] Montevideo Convention on the Rights and Duties of States, opened for signature 26 December 1933, 164 LNTS 19 (entered into force 26 December 1934), Article 1. Crawford 2006, p. 45; Pellet 1992, Appendix: Opinions of the Arbitration Committee, Opinion No. 1, pp. 182–183; Tancredi 2006, p172; International Law Association, above n 42, p. 6; Eggers 2007, p. 214. However, it should be stated that some scholars have criticised these conditions as being insufficient for the determination of statehood. See, e.g. Grant 1998–1999, p. 434; Vidmar 2012, p. 704.

[47] Dugard 2011, p. 48; Vidmar 2012, p. 704; e.g. UN Security Council (1965) Resolution 217 (1965), UN Doc. S/RES/217 (Southern Rhodesia); UN Security Council (1984) Resolution 550 (1984), UN Doc. S/RES/550 (Cyprus).

[48] Duman 2014, p. 2; Abu-Nasr D (2015) Attacks on ISIS Show Local Resistance. http://www.dailystar.com.lb/News/Middle-East/2015/Mar-21/291645-attacks-on-isis-show-local-resistance.ashx. Accessed 6 June 2016.

[49] See e.g. Southern Rhodesia, above n 47; Cyprus, above n 47; UN General Assembly (1976) Resolution 31/6. Policies of *apartheid* of the Government of South Africa, UN Doc. A/RES/31/6 and UN Security Council (1976) Resolution 402 (1976), UN Doc. S/RES/402 (Bantustans States); UN Security Council (1992) Resolution 787 (1992), UN Doc. S/RES/787 (Republic of Srpska).

[50] Dugard 2011, above n 47; Vidmar 2012, above n 47.

[51] Southern Rhodesia, above n 47; Cyprus, above n 47; Bantustans State, above n 49; Republic of Srpska, above n 49.

Regarding the first requirement, it would seem that IS indeed enjoys independence. IS has thus far been able to maintain control over its territories, despite armed resistance and lack of support, both from the local population and from other states.[52] Similarly, it is operating functioning administrative systems, irrespective of the lack of outside help and including legislation, tax regulations and enforcement mechanisms.[53] Nevertheless, IS fails to meet the second requirement of respect for peremptory norms, such as the prohibition of torture. IS has gained control over its territories by using excessive force and while demonstrating clear disrespect for the inhabitants' human rights.[54] Therefore, IS' evident violations of peremptory norms preclude its establishment as a state under international law.[55]

To conclude, while it is possible that IS could qualify as a new state in the future, at this stage, IS does not meet all the requirements of a state and therefore it is to be considered as a non-state actor.

4.4 The Armed Conflicts Between IS and Iraq and IS and Syria

According to Common Article 2, the law of international armed conflicts (IAC) applies to any case of declared war or armed conflict between two or more states. The law of IAC also applies in cases of occupation, even if the said occupation is met with no armed resistance.[56] For states that are party to Additional Protocol I (AP I),

---

[52] UN Security Council (2014) Resolution 2161 (2014), UN Doc. S/RES/2161; UN Security Council (2015) Resolution 2199 (2015), UN Doc. S/RES/2199 (condemning any kind of trade with IS and reaffirming Iraq and Syria's territorial integrity).

[53] Al Hayat Media Center, above n 32, p. 5; March and Revkin, above n 32, p. 2; Zelin A (2014) The Islamic State of Iraq and Syria has a consumer protection office—a guide to how the militant group overrunning Iraq wins hearts and minds. http://www.theatlantic.com/international/archive/2014/06/the-isis-guide-to-building-an-islamic-state/372769/. Accessed 6 June 2016.

[54] UN Independent International Commission of Inquiry on the Syrian Arab Republic, above n 36, p. 3; UN Security Council, above n 35; Office of the High Commissioner for Human Rights (2014) UN Commission of Inquiry: Syrian Victims Reveal ISIS's Calculated Use of Brutality and Indoctrination. http://www.ohchr.org/EN/NewsEvents/Pages/DisplayNews.aspx?NewsID=15295&LangID=E#sthash.es5eEgN4.dpuf. Accessed 7 June 2016.

[55] It could be argued that states have a legal obligation not to recognise IS due to its violations of peremptory norms. However, a full discussion regarding the doctrine of non-recognition is beyond the scope of the present article. For further discussion, see: Dugard 1987, p. 135; ICJ, *Case Concerning East Timor (Portugal v Australia)*, Judgment, 30 June 1995, [1995] ICJ Rep 90, Dissenting Opinion of Judge Skubiszewski, para 125 .

[56] The customary definition of occupation is elaborated in Article 42 of the Regulations concerning the Laws and Customs of War on Land, Annex to the Hague Convention (IV) respecting the Laws and Customs of War on Land, opened for signature 18 October 1907, 205 CTS 277 (entered into force 26 January 1910) (Hague Regulations). For a discussion regarding the definition of occupation, see Benvenisti 2012, pp. 43–67.

according to Article 1(4), the law of IAC also applies to armed conflicts between states and armed groups fighting on behalf of people who are fighting "against colonial domination and alien occupation and against racist régimes in the exercise of their right of self-determination". The term "armed conflict" is not defined in the Geneva Conventions or in AP I. Nevertheless, it is commonly accepted that, as explained by the ICTY, an IAC would exist when there is "a resort to armed force between States".[57]

As IS is not a state and Iraq and Syria are parties to AP I, the question is whether IS could qualify as a group who fights on behalf of people who are fighting "against colonial domination and alien occupation and against racist régimes in the exercise of their right of self-determination". While IS does not claim that it is entitled to qualify as a movement that falls under of Article 1(4) of AP I, for the purposes of examining the theoretical aspects of the conflict, it is at least worth examining this question in brief.

As been noted by several scholars, Article 1(4) was mainly aimed at South Africa, Rhodesia (as it was then called), Portugal and Israel.[58] Thus, it appears that this provision was not intended to apply to regular civil wars or to NIACs between territorial states and non-state groups.[59] Since Iraq and Syria did not exercise "colonial domination" and "alien occupation" over their Sunni population, the focus of the question is whether IS could be considered as fighting on behalf of the Sunni people of Iraq and Syria against their "racist régimes". Alas, IHL does not contain a definition of a "racist regime".

Admittedly, the Sunni population in Iraq and Syria has complained against maltreatment and discrimination both in Iraq and Syria.[60] Nevertheless, although the term "racist" regime is not clearly defined in IHL, several points strongly support that the notion that the conflict between IS and Iraq and Syria cannot be qualified as an IAC under Article 1(4) of AP I. First, as explained above, while IS enjoys some signs of support from the local Iraqi and Syrian populations, most of the individuals under IS' control did not choose to be under IS' control. Thus, it is unreasonable to claim that IS fights on behalf of this population against the regimes of Syria and Iraq. Second, bearing in mind that the term "racist" régime was drafted in reference to South Africa, which implemented a regime based on

[57] ICTY, *Prosecutor v Duško Tadić a/k/a "Dule"*, Decision on the Defence Motion for Interlocutory Appeal on Jurisdiction, 2 October 1995, Case No. IT-94-1-AR72 (*Tadić* 1995), paras 70 and 184. See also ICC, *Prosecutor v Thomas Lubanga Dyilo*, Judgment pursuant to Article 74 of the Statute, 14 March 2012, Case No. ICC-01/04-01/06-2842 (*Lubanga* 2012), para 553; International Law Commission 2011, Article 2(b); UN General Assembly (2006) Human Rights Council: Report of the Commission of Inquiry on Lebanon pursuant to Human Rights Council resolution S-2/1, UN Doc. A/HRC/3/2, para 51.

[58] Aldrich 1991, p. 6; Draper 1979, p. 46.

[59] This is demonstrated also by the terms used in Article 1(4): "colonial domination", "alien occupation" and "racist regimes".

[60] Laub Z and Masters J (2015) The Islamic State. http://www.cfr.org/iraq/islamic-state/p14811. Accessed 6 June 106; Adnan and Reese 2014.

racist segregation, it is hard to stretch the meaning of this term to include all regimes that do not secure adequate equality between all the groups of their population. Finally, bearing in mind that Article 1(4) has never been formally applied in any armed conflict,[61] it could be well argued that the conflict between IS and Iraq and Syria does not fall within the ambit of Article 1(4) of API.

The next question is whether we can classify the armed conflicts between IS and Syria and Iraq as NIACs.

According to Common Article 3 of the Geneva Conventions, the law of NIAC is the law that applies in armed conflicts between states and non-state groups, and in armed conflicts among non-state groups.[62] Despite important dissenters,[63] it is commonly accepted that NIACs are not limited to purely internal armed conflicts (i.e. conflicts confined within the borders of a single state) as the law of NIAC is based on the identity of the fighting parties and not on the geographical location of the hostilities.[64]

It is well established that a conflict between states and non-state groups or a conflict among non-state groups must meet a twofold requirement of minimum organisation of the conflict parties and minimum intensity of the conflict itself in order to be classified as a NIAC.[65] Thus, in order to classify the armed conflicts between IS and Syria and Iraq as NIACs, it must be shown that the twofold requirement of organisation and intensity of the violence exist in both conflicts (i.e. between IS and Syria, and between IS and Iraq).[66] Otherwise, there are no NIACs, and the hostilities between IS and Iraq and Syria will be regulated under international human rights law (IHRL).

---

[61] Akande 2012, p. 49.

[62] See also the widely cited definition of NIAC in *Tadić* 1995, above n 57, para 70 (defining NIAC as "protracted armed violence between governmental authorities and organized armed groups or between such groups within a State").

[63] E.g. *Public Committee against Torture in Israel v Government of Israel*, Judgement, 13 December 2006, Case No. HCJ 769/02, para 18 ("This law [the law of IACs] applies in any case of an armed conflict of international character—in other words, one that crosses the borders of the state—whether or not the place in which the armed conflict occurs is subject to belligerent occupation") & para 21 ("[...] the fact that the terrorist organizations and their members do not act in the name of a state does not turn the struggle against them into a purely internal state conflict"); Dinstein 2012, p. 400.

[64] *Hamdan v Rumsfeld* 548 US 557, pp. 625–632; Sassòli 2006, pp. 8–9; Jinks 2006, pp. 188–189; Fleck 2008, p. 605.

[65] *Tadić* 1995, above n 57, para 70 ("A non-international armed conflict exists whenever there is [...] protracted armed violence between governmental authorities and organized armed groups or between such groups within a State"). This definition of NIAC has been applied in various ICTY case-law, see, e.g. ICTY, *Tadić* 1995, above n 57; ICTY, *Prosecutor v Fatmir Limaj, Haradin Bala and Isak Musliu*, Judgement, 30 November 2005, Case No. IT-03-66-T (*Limaj* et al.), paras 88-170; ICTY, *Prosecutor v Ramush Haradinaj, Idriz Balaj and Lahi Brahimaj*, Judgement, 3 April 2008, Case No. IT-04-84-T (*Haradinaj* et al.), paras 37–60.

[66] It should be noted that as Syria and Iraq are not parties to the Protocol Additional to the Geneva Conventions of 12 August 1949, and relating to the Protection of Victims of Non-International Armed Conflicts, opened for signature 8 June 1977, 1125 UNTS 609 (entered into force 7 December 1978), the question of its treaty applicability is irrelevant.

The Chambers of the International Criminal Tribunal for the former Yugoslavia (ICTY) have elaborated different indicators relevant to determining whether a non-state group is sufficiently organised. Although none of these indicators is central in itself, it is illustrative to state some of these indicators: the existence of a command structure and disciplinary mechanisms within the non-state group; governing by rules; the group's control over a certain territory; the group's unity in internal and external relations; and the group's ability to gain access to weapons, equipment, recruits and training.[67] In addition, international tribunals stated different factors for the requirement of intensity: the number of persons and type of forces in the fighting,[68] the type and quantity of weapons used,[69] the number of casualties,[70] the geographical spread and frequency of hostilities,[71] foreign involvement (either of the UN Security Council or of other states),[72] and the need for mobilisation of armed forces to counter the insurrection.[73] None of these factors is essential in itself for the requirement of intensity, and therefore the absence of one or several of these factors in a given conflict does not mean that the conflict should not be classified as a NIAC.[74]

These factors show that the conflict between IS and Iraq and Syria meets the twofold requirement of NIAC: first, IS is sufficiently organised as it has a central command which allows it to control vast territory,[75] and, as stated above, it seems that is has the ability to engage in internal and external relations;[76] second, the intensity of the conflict is very high as indicated by the vast amount of forces involved, weapons used, foreign involvement, and the geographical spread and frequency with which weapons are used.[77]

---

[67] *Limaj* et al., above n 65, para 90; *Haradinaj* et al., above n 65, para 60.

[68] *Haradinaj* et al., above n 65, para 48.

[69] ICTY, *Prosecutor v Ljube Boškoski and Johan Tarčulovski*, Judgement, 10 July 2008, Case No. IT-04-82-T, para 177.

[70] Ibid.

[71] *Limaj* et al., above n 65, para 168; ICTY, *Prosecutor v Slobodan Milošević*, Decision on Motion for Judgement of Acquittal, 16 June 2004, Case No. IT-02-54-T (*Milošević*), paras 28–29.

[72] *Haradinaj* et al., above n 65, para 49; ICC, *Prosecutor v Thomas Lubanga Dyilo*, Decision on the Confirmation of Charges, 29 January 2007, Case No. ICC-01/04-01/06-830-tEN, para 211.

[73] *Milošević*, above n 71, para 30.

[74] *Haradinaj* et al., above n 65, para 49; International Law Association (2010) The Hague Conference (2010) Use of Force: Final Report on the Meaning of Armed Conflict in International Law. http://www.ila-hq.org/download.cfm/docid/2176DC63-D268-4133-8989A664754F9F87. Accessed 9 June 2016.

[75] The New York Times, above n 31; Institute for the Study of War (2015) above n 31; see also: Laub and Masters, above n 60.

[76] See discussion between notes 34–36.

[77] Lister, above n 37; BBC News, above n 37; Ellis R (2015) War Against ISIS: Successes and Failures. http://edition.cnn.com/2015/05/18/asia/isis-success-and-failure/. Accessed 6 June 2016; Bender J (2014) As ISIS Routs The Iraqi Army, Here's A Look At What The Jihadists Have In Their Arsenal. http://www.businessinsider.com/isis-military-equipment-breakdown-2014-7?op=1. Accessed 6 June 2016.

Does the foreign intervention against IS by the US-led coalition change the qualification of the armed conflicts between IS and Iraq and IS and Syria from NIAC to IAC? The short answer is no. There is almost a consensus among IHL experts that foreign armed intervention does not, of itself, transform the NIAC between the territorial state and the non-state group into an IAC and therefore this type of intervention would result in two parallel NIACS (in case of foreign intervention in favour of the territorial state) or mixed armed conflicts—IAC and NIAC (in case of intervention against the territorial state).[78] This approach was taken by the ICJ in the Nicaragua case, where it ruled that the armed conflict in Nicaragua between the government and the *Contras* (the non-state group) was a NIAC while the armed conflict between the US and Nicaragua was an IAC.[79] This approach was also adopted in the classification of other conflicts by the International Criminal Court (ICC)[80] and the ICTY.[81] Nevertheless, it is important to state there are dissenting voices, which have argued that any direct foreign intervention will internationalise the NIAC between the territorial state and the non-state group into an IAC.[82] This suggestion is often called "the global approach".[83] However, there is very little judicial support for this argument[84], and most IHL scholars agree that direct military intervention does not *ipso facto* internationalise the NIAC between the territorial state and the non-state group.[85]

[78] Schindler 1979, pp. 150–151; Rosas 1976, p. 283; Gasser 1983, p. 147; Dinstein 2010, pp. 26–28; Milanović and Hadzi-Vidanović 2010, pp. 302–303; Greenwood 1996, pp. 270–272; Hoffmann 2010, pp. 20–22; Moir 2002, pp. 46–47.

[79] ICJ, *Case Concerning Military and Paramilitary Activities in and against Nicaragua (Nicaragua v United States of America)*, Judgment, 27 June 1986, [1986] ICJ Rep 14, para 219.

[80] *Lubanga* 2012, above n 57, para 540.

[81] *Tadić* 1995, above n 57, para 77; ICTY, *Prosecutor v Duško Tadić*, Judgement, 15 July 1999, Case No. IT-94-1-A (*Tadić* 1999), para 84; ICTY, *Prosecutor v Tihomir Blaskić*, Judgement, 3 March 2000, Case No. IT-95-14-T, Declaration of Judge Shahabuddeen ("[…] foreign intervention does not of necessity deprive an internal armed conflict of its internal character altogether […]").

[82] Byron 2001, p. 83 (suggesting that "a purposive interpretation of the Geneva Conventions leads to the conclusion that the substantial intervention of foreign troops in an armed conflict would convert the conflict into an international one"); Aldrich 2000, p. 63.

[83] For a general discussion regarding the "global approach/view", see Stewart 2003, pp. 333–335; see also Cryer 2002, pp. 43–45; Aldrich 2000, pp. 62–63; Byron 2001, pp. 82–83.

[84] This limited support is manifested in implicit statements in support of the "global approach" that are not limited only to cases of intervention in favour of the non-state group. E.g. see *Tadić* 1999, above n 81, para 84; *Democratic Republic of Congo Military Prosecutor v Bongi Massaba*, Criminal Trial Judgment and Accompanying Civil Action for Damages, 24 March 2006, Case No. RP No 018/2006; RMP No 242/PEN/06, para 85.

[85] See Fleck 2008, p. 605; Akande 2012, p. 62; Solis 2010, p. 154; Wills 2011, pp. 173 and 177; Moir 2002, p. 51.

4.5 The Armed Conflict Between IS and the Foreign Coalition

At present, various states are taking part, in one way or another, in the Foreign Coalition.[86] Due to the large number of states involved in the hostilities, it is beyond the scope of this chapter to examine the specific involvement of each state. Instead, this section will elaborate the relevant issues that must be addressed in classifying these hostilities.

At the outset, since it is the identity of the parties to the conflict that matters and not their geographical location, the main question should be whether the hostilities between IS, as a non-state group, and the Foreign Coalition could be regarded as a NIAC. While this certainly is the main question, there are other important open questions, which must also be answered in the process of classifying these hostilities. First, various states participate in the Foreign Coalition, which is led by the USA, against IS. Does that mean that we need to examine hostilities between each of these states and IS in order to determine that an armed conflict exists between them or can we treat all these states as participating in the same armed conflict and thus not evaluate the hostilities between each foreign state and IS? Following the same line, can we classify the foreign intervention in support of the Iraqi government as part of the ongoing NIAC between Iraq and IS? While the answer to the first question is relatively straight forward, the second question highlights another open issue in conflict classification. Second, as the government of Syria has not officially and explicitly pronounced its consent to the foreign intervention on its territory, how should we classify the armed activities of the Foreign Coalition that take place in the territory of Syria?

4.5.1 One NIAC or Multiply NIACs

States have fought together in different alliances throughout history. In terms of conflict classification, there is nothing unusual in a coalition of states fighting on the same side of an armed conflict. As explained above, one of the central issues regarding conflict classification is the identity of the parties to the conflict. A state becomes a party to an armed conflict by using its own forces or forces acting on its behalf.[87] In the context of the struggle against IS, not all the member states of the Foreign Coalition actually participate in the hostilities against IS. Moreover, even

[86] See states previously listed, above n 1; US Department of State (2016), above n 10.

[87] Pictet 1960, p. 23, note 8; Schmitt 2002, p. 374; Dinstein 2010, p. 1; *Lubanga* 2012, above n 57, para 541.

the states that do participate directly in the hostilities against IS are not doing it under the joint command of the Coalition. Thus, it is clear that it is artificial to treat all the member states as one organ. Therefore, we need to examine the specific involvement of each member state in the conflict.

Moving on to the second question, even if we examine the specific involvement of each member state, as these member states have been invited by the Iraqi government, can we consider their armed conflict as part of the ongoing NIAC between IS and the Iraqi government?

Several scholars have suggested that when the forces of a foreign state intervene, with the consent of the territorial state, in an ongoing NIAC against a non-state group, the NIAC between the foreign state and the non-state group could be considered part of the ongoing NIAC and not an independent NIAC.[88] It could be argued that this approach was supported by the ICC, when it classified the armed conflict in the Central African Republic (CAR) as a NIAC and, while not mentioning that the foreign intervention was a separate NIAC, simply stated that the foreign troops were there to support the governmental forces against the non-state group:

> […] the Chamber finds that the armed conflict on the CAR territory was not of an international character […] The presence of a limited number of foreign troops on the CAR territory, such as the MLC soldiers, Chadian mercenaries and the Libyan troops, was intended to support the CAR government authorities to counter the organized armed group led by Mr Bozizé, and was not directed against the State of the CAR and its authorities.[89]

The normative crux behind the approach of classifying consensual interventions against non-state groups as part of the ongoing NIAC between the territorial state and the non-state group is that it arguably allows the foreign state to use force under the rules of IHL even if the threshold of a NIAC (i.e. intensity and organisation) would not have been met if the foreign state and the non-state group were engaged in a separate NIAC. Or to put it differently, classifying foreign interventions as part of an ongoing NIAC means that instead of examining the threshold of

---

[88] Parkerson 1991, p. 42 ("If, however, the third state intervenor fights alongside the government forces, then the intervening state is effectively grafted onto the domestic state in a kind of 'agency' relationship so that the relationship of the intervening state with the rebels is the same as that existing between the two internal parties to the conflict. Consequently, for that relationship the conflict remains 'non-international,' and common Article 3 determines the extent of application of humanitarian law"); Lubell 2012, p. 438 (making this argument with regard to a possible classification of the hostilities between the US and non-state groups in Pakistan: "[it could] be argued that when the US is targeting Pakistani militants as part of a joint operation with the Pakistani government, such operations could come within the scope of the non-international armed conflict between Pakistan and these groups").

[89] ICC, *Prosecutor v Jean-Pierre Bemba Gombo*, Decision Pursuant to Article 61(7)(a) and (b) of the Rome Statute on the Charges of the Prosecutor Against Jean-Pierre Bemba Gombo, 15 June 2009, Case No. ICC-01/05-01/08-424, para 246.

intensity and organisation for every foreign intervention, the consent of the territorial state to the foreign state to take part in the civil war would be enough for the purposes of applying the rules of IHL between the foreign state and the non-state group. Thus, for example, from the moment that Iraq gave its approval for the foreign intervention, every attack of the foreign forces would be considered part of the ongoing NIAC without establishing the existence of intensity and organisation as would have been required by a stand-alone NIAC.[90]

The main problem with adopting the suggested approach is that it is accepted that states can operate within the boundaries of international law and that each state is responsible for the acts of its own armed forces.[91] The rights and obligations of IHL come into existence for a given state only when this specific state has met the conditions of applicability of IHL. In NIACs, this means that the state in question must be involved in intense hostilities against an organised non-state group. Thus, it could be well argued that the fact that another state (i.e. the territorial state) is involved in an ongoing NIAC and consequently enjoys the rights and obligations of IHL does not relieve the intervening foreign state from meeting the same conditions of applicability in order to enjoy the rights and obligations of IHL.

Moreover, adopting this suggested approach would mean changing the customary threshold of applicability of NIACs by adding that the law of NIAC would apply automatically to every consensual extraterritorial use of force by a foreign state in an ongoing NIAC in favour of governmental forces. Thus, the suggested approach requires additional examination in order to assess whether it enjoys sufficient state practice and *opinio juris*.

Therefore, although this topic is still debatable in IHL, it is submitted that the hostilities between each foreign state and IS must separately meet the threshold of intensity and organisation in order to be classified as NIACs. In cases where the hostilities between the foreign state and IS do not meet the required threshold for NIAC, the extraterritorial use of force of the foreign state will be regulated under

---

[90] See the similar argument that uses a different example in: Farley 2011, p. 73 (arguing that due to the intervention of the USA in Yemen's NIAC with AQAP in support of Yemen, "the United States is in a non-international armed conflict with AQAP even though the hostilities between the United States and AQAP, standing alone, are insufficient to constitute an armed conflict").

[91] Article 3 of the Hague Regulations, above n 56; Protocol Additional to the Geneva Conventions of 12 August 1949, and relating to the Protection of Victims of International Armed Conflicts, opened for signature 12 December 1977, 1125 UNTS 3 (entered into force 7 December 1979) (AP I), Article 91; ICJ, *Case Concerning Armed Activities on the Territory of the Congo (Democratic Republic of the Congo v Uganda)*, Judgment, 19 December 2005, [2005] ICJ Rep 168 (*Armed Activities*), para 214 ("According to a well-established rule of a customary nature [...] a party to an armed conflict shall be responsible for all acts by persons forming part of its armed forces"); Henckaerts and Doswald-Beck 2005, rule 149 (Responsibility for violations of International Humanitarian Law).

the framework of law enforcement and IHRL.[92] This submission is consistent with the basic benchmark of conflict classification; classification is contingent on the different parties to the conflict and the existence of hostilities between them. If a foreign state wants to use extraterritorial force against IS under the platform of IHL but without being a party to the conflict, it must integrate its forces under the control of one of the parties to the NIAC with IS.[93] However, it should be noted that this scenario rarely, if ever, occurs in practice.[94]

Since the mere existence of a NIAC between a territorial state and a non-state group is not enough to establish that every use of force by a foreign state against a non-state group would suffice to establish that the foreign state is involved in a NIAC, the foreign intervention, in order to be considered a NIAC, must meet the dual threshold of intensity and organisation.[95] However, the threshold of NIACs can constitute a problem when classifying interventions like the ongoing intervention in Iraq and Syria, where some foreign states' involvement is limited to surveillance missions, or small surgical and sporadic attacks on non-state groups. Thus, when assessing the threshold, two points should be borne in mind. First, the requirements of intensity and organisation should not be interpreted too rigidly. Intensity does not have to include high levels of violence at all times. Low intensity violence, when it is extended for a long period, can also be considered sufficient for establishing a NIAC.[96] Second, although the use of military force by a

[92] In extraterritorial use of force, it is generally accepted that IHRL applies when the foreign state has some control over a territory or a said individual that needs protection (see discussion in Happold 2013, pp. 453–463). Nevertheless, it is controversial whether IHRL in general and the right to life in particular are applicable in small operations, like targeted killings, which do not involve any control of the foreign state over the state or the individual (Droege 2007, pp. 334–335). While it is beyond the scope of this chapter to assess this question in depth, it is submitted that it is untenable to argue that IHRL and the right to life are not applicable in small operations like targeted killings. Thus, it is submitted that IHRL will be applicable even in limited military foreign interventions which do not involve territorial control or even ground forces. Any other position would mean that a foreign state is prohibited by IHRL from torturing an individual but could still kill the individual in a targeted killing because IHRL would be applicable only in the former scenario due to the control of the foreign state over the said individual. The position of wide applicability of IHRL to the extraterritorial use of force is supported by various scholars (e.g. Droege 2007, p. 335; Kreß 2010, p. 259, note 49; Kretzmer 2005, p. 185). But see Happold 2013, p. 458 ("Arguments have also been made that international human rights law applies more widely, to all extraterritorial uses of force [...] However, although it has some support in the jurisprudence of the International Court of Justice and the American Commission on Human Rights and in legal doctrine, the current case law of the European Court of Human Rights argues the contrary").

[93] Schindler 1979, p. 131 (stating that "[i]f troops of a third State take part in an armed conflict, and if these troops are not integrated in the forces of a party to the conflict, the third State itself becomes a party to the conflict within the meaning of the Geneva Conventions and the Protocol").

[94] Akande 2012, p. 55 ("The forces of a co-belligerent are not usually regarded as part of the armed forces of a Party").

[95] See discussion between notes 61–65.

[96] Sivakumaran 2012, p. 168; International Law Association, above n 74, p. 30.

foreign state in an existing civil war can be considered law enforcement that is subject to IHRL and not IHL, the fact that both the governments of Syria and Iraq have reached the point where they cannot operate under the framework of law enforcement and arrest militia members of IS is an indicator that any armed engagement (which is not limited to surveillance missions) of the foreign state, which have less control in these states, against IS, would meet the requirement of intensity.[97]

While it is beyond the scope of this chapter to classify the conflicts between IS and each state in the Foreign Coalition, at least with regard to states like the USA, UK and Jordan that use direct and intensive air force against IS, which is considered an organised non-state group for the purposes of conflict classification,[98] and it is reasonable to argue that they are involved in NIACs against the IS.

4.5.2 The Ramifications of Consent

While we are on safe grounds when classifying at least some of the hostilities that take place in Iraq between the foreign states and IS as NIACs, it is less clear how to classify the same hostilities that take place in Syria, where the government has not officially and explicitly pronounced its consent to the foreign intervention. IHL does not provide a clear answer to this issue.

Dapo Akande, notably, argues that in cases of lack of consent, not only the foreign state and the territorial state would be engaged in an IAC, but also the rebels who actually fight against the territorial state (i.e. the governmental forces) would be considered part of the IAC as unprivileged belligerents who do not belong to any side of the conflict.[99] Noam Lubell, on the other hand, rejects Akande's argu-

---

[97] It should be emphasised that this is just an indicator. It is possible that despite the fact that the territorial state is unable to deal with the non-state group under the platform of law enforcement, the foreign state would be able to use law enforcement mechanisms.

[98] See discussion between notes 52–55.

[99] Akande 2012, pp. 73–79. The ICJ implicitly supported this approach when it applied the law of IAC in Congo to the armed activities that took place, without the consent of Uganda, outside of the province of Ituri, which was held under Ugandan occupation. The ICJ application of the law of IAC was despite the fact that the Uganda used force in the territory of Congo primarily against non-state groups (see *Armed Activities*, above n 91, para 214). For further support of this approach, see also Fleck 2006, p. 607 ("The internationalization of an armed conflict has also been assumed when a state is engaged in military operations against a transnational group on the territory of a foreign state without the agreement of the latter, such as during the Israeli-Hizbollah war in Lebanon 2006"); Sassòli 2006, p. 5 ("the law of international armed conflicts applies when a state is directing hostilities against a transnational armed group on the territory of another state without the agreement of the latter state"); Stewart 2007, p. 1043.

ment and states that "[t]he underlying question for classification must be that of identifying the parties to the conflict, rather than consent".[100] The focus on the identity of the parties to the conflict rather than on consent is also advanced by many other IHL scholars.[101] According to Lubell, the territorial state and the foreign state could still be in an IAC if the use of force by the foreign state involves "large-scale attacks that damage national infrastructure and cause widespread harm".[102] However, according to Lubell, in this case, the IAC between the two states will be a separate armed conflict from the NIAC between the territorial state and the non-state group.[103]

Akande is right, to a certain extent, to argue that consent should matter. However, it should matter only for the purpose of classification of the armed conflict between the foreign state and the territorial state, and not for the conflict between the foreign state and the non-state group.

As explained above, IACs require the use of force by a state against another state.[104] Lack of consent with regard to the use of armed force by the foreign state means that there is a use of force by the foreign state against the territorial state.[105] While the requirement of intensity in IACs is still disputed, there is strong support for the argument that there is no threshold requirement of intensity in IACs.[106] In any case, it seems clear that the threshold of intensity in IACs will be much lower

---

[100] Lubell 2012, p. 433.

[101] Wills 2011, p. 177 ("The majority view, espoused by the ICRC and many leading experts in the field, is that a conflict between states must be one in which their governments are pitted against each other. Therefore conflicts in which the armed forces of one state are engaged in an armed conflict with non-governmental forces based in another state fall outside the scope of the laws of international armed conflict. Such conflicts will always be non-international, regardless of whether or not the government of the state in which the armed groups are based has consented to the use of force in its territory, regardless of whether or not the intervention is authorised by the Security Council and regardless of whether or not the intervention is lawful"); Blank and Farley 2011, p. 183 ("[it] is not clear that the territorial state's consent has any impact on the characterization of the armed conflict. Underlying the whole body of the law of armed conflict is a preference for fact-driven, objective analysis irrespective of technicalities").

[102] Lubell 2012, p. 433.

[103] Ibid (however, Lubell states that this may "change if the non-state actor became aligned with a State").

[104] See discussion between notes 55–56.

[105] See also Milanović and Hadzi-Vidanović 2013, pp. 301–302 (arguing that lack of consent can lead to an IAC between the territorial state and the foreign state).

[106] Pictet 1958, p. 20; Sandoz et al. 1987, para 62; see also Schindler 1979, p. 131; Akande 2012, p. 4; Schmitt 2012, pp. 459–460; Dinstein 2010, pp. 28–29; Kolb and Hyde 2008, p. 76. But see sources that support the argument that there is a requirement of intensity: Greenwood 2008, p. 48; Solis 2010, p. 151; International Law Association, above n 74, p. 28.

than the threshold of intensity in NIACs.[107] Thus, arguably, even the use of a limited amount of force (and not only a large-scale attack) by the foreign state in the territory of the territorial state without the latter's consent would be enough to trigger an IAC between these states. However, as Lubell rightly argues, in this case, we may have parallel armed conflicts taking place in the territorial state because an IAC is an armed conflict between states.[108] Indeed, the approach of differentiating hostilities taking place on the same territory between IAC and NIAC based on the different actors is the dominant approach in cases of foreign intervention in an ongoing NIAC against a territorial state.[109]

Therefore, whether the armed activities of the Foreign Coalition can be regarded as not only an NIAC against IS but also as an IAC against Syria is contingent on whether we can deduce the consent of the government of Syria despite the fact that it did not officially and explicitly consent to the intervention.

As IHL does not provide any concrete answers as to how we should examine a state's consent to the use of force in its territory, we can rely on other areas of international law as a benchmark. Article 20 of the International Law Commission's (ILC) Articles on State Responsibility that focuses on consent as a circumstance that precludes international wrongfulness can provide us with such a benchmark. According to Article 20, "[v]alid consent by a State to the commission of a given act by another State precludes the wrongfulness of that act in relation to the former State to the extent that the act remains within the limits of that consent".[110] The ILC Commentaries clarify that "[c]onsent must be freely given and clearly established. It must be actually expressed by the State rather than merely presumed on the basis that the State would have consented if it had been asked".[111] While consent cannot be presumed, it is also established that consent can be given explicitly or implicitly.[112] For example, as highlighted by the ILC Commentaries,[113] in the Savarkar case, the arbitral tribunal considered that Britain did not violate French sovereignty because France has implicitly consented to Britain's actions.[114]

107 E.g. Milanović and Hadzi-Vidanović 2013, p. 274.

108 With regard to states parties to AP I, the law of IAC covers also armed conflicts between states and national liberation movements: AP I, above n 91, Article 1(4).

109 See discussion between notes 77–81.

110 See UN General Assembly (2001) Draft Articles on Responsibility of States for Internationally Wrongful Acts with Commentaries, UN Doc. A/56/10.

111 Ibid, p. 73, para 6.

112 Rosen 1991, p. 112, para 13 ("As in the case of other expressions of the will of the State, it may be tacit or implicit, provided, however, that it is always *clearly established*").

113 UN General Assembly, above n 110, p. 73, para 8.

114 *The Savarkar Case (France v Great Britain)*, Arbitral Award, 24 February 1911, (1961) 11 UNRIAA 252, pp. 252–255.

Focusing back on Syria, the Syrian government has not made an explicit or official statement in which it expressed its consent to the intervention of the Foreign Coalition. On the other hand, it did proclaim that "any strike which is not co-ordinated with the government will be considered as aggression".[115] Similarly, the Syrian government stated explicitly that "[a]ny action of any kind without the consent of the Syrian government would be an attack on Syria".[116] However, there are other indicators which suggest that Syria has implicitly consented to the intervention of the Foreign Coalition. First, the official Syrian news agency, Sana, has published that the Syrian authorities have been informed at the very outset of the foreign intervention,[117] without prompting any kind of protest, and the Syrian government had also taken a more conciliatory tone regarding the intervention of the Foreign Coalition.[118] In the same vein, Syria has argued that although there is no direct coordination with the Foreign Coalition, Iraq and other states do convey general information about the attacks.[119] While the USA has denied coordinating with the Syrian government,[120] it is possible that there is some indirect coordination between some states in the Foreign Coalition in Syria. Second, it is clear that the Syrian government has a clear interest in weakening IS.[121] Third, despite some military capabilities, which suggest that Syria could defend its airspace.[122] Syria has not tried to interfere with the foreign armed campaign against IS. While that might be understandable in the light of the need of the Syrian government to focus its sparse resources on IS and other rebel groups, one could at least expect Syria to condemn the ongoing airstrike of the Foreign Coalition and demand their

[115] The Guardian (2014) Syria offers to help fight Isis but warns against unilateral air strikes. www.theguardian.com/world/2014/aug/26/syria-offers-to-help-fight-isis-but-warns-against-unilateral-air-strikes. Accessed 6 June 2016.

[116] The Guardian (2014) Isis air strikes: Obama's plan condemned by Syria, Russia and Iran. http://www.theguardian.com/world/2014/sep/11/assad-moscow-tehran-condemn-obama-isis-airstrike-plan. Accessed 6 June 2016.

[117] Sana (2014) Ki-Moon: Syria didn't ask to carry out airstrikes on its lands, but it was informed of the operation. http://sana.sy/en/?p=13942. Accessed 6 June 2016.

[118] The Syria Times (2014) Minister al-Moallem: dual policy a recipe for more violence and terrorism. http://syriatimes.sy/index.php/arab-and-foreign-press/14651-minister-al-moallem-dual-policy-a-recipe-for-more-violence-and-terrorism. Accessed 6 June 2016.

[119] BBC News (2015) Assad says Syria is informed on anti-IS air campaign. http://www.bbc.com/news/world-middle-east-31312414. Accessed 6 June 2016.

[120] Ibid.

[121] A Syrian government spokesperson has reportedly stated, "We are facing one enemy. We should cooperate": Arimatsu L and Schmitt M (2014) The Legal Basis for the War Against ISIS Remains Contentious. http://www.theguardian.com/commentisfree/2014/oct/06/legal-basis-war-isis-syria-islamic-state. Accessed 6 June 2016.

[122] Atwood C and White J (2014) Syrian Air-Defense Capabilities and the Threat to Potential U.S. Air Operations. http://www.washingtoninstitute.org/policy-analysis/view/syrian-air-defense-capabilities-and-the-threat-to-potential-u.s.-air-operat. Accessed 6 June 2016.

cessation. Thus, while the facts remain unclear regarding the Syrian stance on the intervention of the Foreign Coalition, bearing in mind that consent should be interpreted in the light of the special feature of IHL,[123] which dictates that classification of conflicts is meant to be based on a factual analysis and only on formal declaration of states,[124] it is possible to argue that Syria has implicitly consented to the intervention and that there is no IAC between the foreign states and Syria.

4.6 Conclusion

Conflict classification is not an academic exercise without practical ramifications. On the contrary, the classification of armed conflicts affects the applicable law with regard to aspects such as the conduct of hostilities, the classification of the participants in the armed conflict and the treatment of those participants in case of capture by an opposing party. Thus, as epitomised by the conflict classification of IS and the different actors, the fact that IHL contains various open questions concerning conflict classification is concerning.

As conflict classification is contingent on the status of the different actors in the battlefield, our chapter revealed that IHL does not have an agreed test to establish which non-state group could be deemed to represent the state in cases where several groups struggle to control the state. Nevertheless, based on the fact that the governments of Iraq and Syria still exercise some amount of governmental control, it was submitted that IS cannot be deemed to represent the governments of Syria or Iraq.

Next, this chpater briefly assessed whether IS could be considered a state and submitted that it does not meet all the conditions of statehood. Finally, in the context of classifying the status of IS, this article examined whether IS could be classified as a national liberation movement fighting against a racist regime in accordance with Article 1(4) of AP I. This examination exposed again another open question of IHL—how to define racist regime. Despite not having an answer to this question, based on the fact that IS does not represent "people" and the historical context of Article 1(4) of AP I, it was submitted that IS could not be considered a national liberation movement for the purposes of conflict classification.

After substantiating that IS should be considered a non-state group, the chapter focused on whether the hostilities between IS and the other actors meet the threshold of NIAC or to put it in other words—whether the requirements of organisation and intensity were met.

---

[123] UN General Assembly, above n 110, p. 73, para 8 ("In considering the application of article 20 to such cases it may be necessary to have regard to the relevant primary rule.").

[124] Pictet 1958, p. 20; Greenwood 2008, p. 72.

With regard to the armed conflicts between IS and Iraq and IS and Syria—it was argued that it is beyond dispute that these conflicts involve a high intensity of violence and that IS is sufficiently organised. Thus, it was submitted that these conflicts should be considered NIACs.

The classification of the hostilities between IS and the other foreign states exposed two important open questions. First, whether each armed intervention should be considered separately or conjunctively with the ongoing NIAC between the territorial state and the non-state group (in cases where there is invitation of the territorial state for intervention). This question also pertains to whether all the intervening forces should be considered one force for the purposes of conflict classification or different forces. While admitting that there is no clear answer to the question, it was submitted that conflict classification should be based on an independent examination of the hostilities between each party to the conflict. Second, what is the effect of the lack consent of the territorial state for intervention on conflict classification? It was argued that the lack of consent will result in a parallel IAC between the foreign state and the territorial state, even if only a limited amount of force was used by the foreign state against the territorial state, as an IAC does not have the same threshold of intensity as a NIAC. In any case, in the context of Syria, it has been submitted that although it is uncertain, it seems that Syria, despite lack of official pronouncement of consent, has been implicitly consenting to the intervention. Thus, it could be argued there is no IAC between the foreign states and Syria.

The open questions in IHL with regard to conflict classification, as reflected in classifying the different armed conflict with IS, should be further analysed as they could have a significant impact on the applicable law in a given armed conflict. The hope is also expressed that states, especially those who are involved in armed conflicts, will take a more proactive approach towards the classification of conflicts and will reveal their opinion regarding the controversial issues in conflict classification.

Acknowledgements I would like to thank Tamar Drori for her excellent research assistance. In addition, I would like to express my thanks to Dr Paul von Mühlendahl and Dr Peretz Segal for their useful comments. Any errors or omissions are of course entirely mine.

References

Articles, Books and Other Documents

Adam H (1994) Formation and Recognition of New States: Somaliland in Contrast to Eritrea. Rev Afr Political Econ 21(59):21–38

Adnan S, Reese A (2014) Beyond the Islamic State: Iraq's Sunni Insurgency, Middle East Security Report 24, the Institute for the Study of War, United States of America

Aldrich G (1991) Prospects for United States Ratification of Additional Protocol I to the 1949 Geneva Conventions. Am J Int Law 85(1):1–20

Aldrich G (2000) The Laws of War on Land. Am J Int Law 94(1):42–63
Akande D (2012) Classification of Armed Conflicts: Relevant Legal Concepts. In: Wilmshurst Elizabeth (ed) International Law and the Classification of Conflicts. Oxford University Press, Oxford, pp 32–79
American Law Institute (1965) Restatement of the Law (Second): The Foreign Relations Law of the United States. St. Paul, Minnesota
Arimatsu L (2009) Territory, Boundaries and the Law of Armed Conflict. Yearb Int Humanitarian Law 12:157–192
Benvenisti E (2012) The International Law of Occupation. Oxford University Press, Oxford
Blanchard C, Humud C, Nikitin M (2014) Armed Conflict in Syria: Overview and U.S. Response, Congressional Research Service
Blank L, Farley B (2011) Characterizing US Operations in Pakistan: Is the United States Engaged in an Armed Conflict? Fordham Int Law J 34(2):151–189
Byron C (2001) Armed Conflicts: International or Non-International? J Confl Secur Law 6(1):63–90
Caris C, Reynolds S (2014) Middle East Security Report 22—ISIS Governance in Syria, Institute for the Study of War, the Institute for the Study of War, United States of America
Chen T, Green L (eds) (1951) The International Law of Recognition: With Special Reference to Practice in Great Britain and the United States. Praeger, New York
Cheng B (1953) General Principles of Law as Applied by International Courts and Tribunals. Cambridge University Press, Cambridge, UK
Crawford J (1976) The Criteria for Statehood in International Law. Br Yearb Int Law 48(1):93–182
Crawford J (2006) The Creation of States in International Law, 2nd edn. Oxford University Press, Oxford
Crawford J (2012) Brownlie's Principles of Public International Law. Oxford University Press, Oxford
Cryer R (2002) The Fine Art of Friendship: Jus in bello in Afghanistan. J Confl Secur Law 7(1):37–83
Dinstein Y (2010) The Conduct of Hostilities under the Law of International Armed Conflict. Cambridge University Press, Cambridge
Dinstein Y (2012) Concluding Remarks on Non-International Armed Conflicts. In: Watkin K, Norris A (eds) Non-International Armed Conflict in the Twenty-first Century: International Law Studies, Vol 88. Naval War College, Rhode Island, pp 399–421
Dinstein Y (2014) Non-International Armed Conflicts in International Law. Cambridge University Press, Cambridge
Draper G (1979) The Implementation and Enforcement of the Geneva Conventions of 1949 and the two Additional Protocols of 1978. Recueil des Cours 164:1–54
Droege C (2007) The Interplay between International Humanitarian Law and International Human Rights Law in Situations of Armed Conflict. Israel Law Rev 40(2):310–355
Dugard J (1987) Recognition and the United Nations. Grotius Publications, Cambridge
Dugard J (2011) The Secession of States and their Recognition in the Wake of Kosovo. Recueil des Cours de l'Académie de Droit International 357
Duman B (2014) The Effects of the ISIS Operations on the Turkmens. Orsam Rev Reg Aff 7:1–10
Eggers A (2007) When is a State a State? The Case for Recognition of Somaliland. Boston College Int Comp Law Rev 30(1):211–222
Farley B (2011) Targeting Anwar al-Aulaqi: A Case Study in U.S. Drone Strikes and Targeted Killing. Am Univ National Secur Law Brief 2(1):57–87
Fleck D (2008) The Law of Non-International Armed Conflicts. In: Fleck D, Gill T (eds) The Handbook of International Humanitarian Law. Oxford University Press, Oxford, pp 605–634
Gasser H (1983) Internationalized Non-International Armed Conflicts: Case Studies of Afghanistan, Kampuchea, and Lebanon. Am Univ Law Rev 33:145–161

Grant T (1998–1999) Defining Statehood: The Montevideo Convention and its Discontents. Columbia J Transnational Law 37:403–457

Greenwood C (1996) International Humanitarian Law and the Tadic Case. Eur J Int Law 7:265–283

Greenwood C (2002) International Law and the "War against Terrorism". Int Aff 78(2):301–317

Greenwood C (2008) Scope of Application of Humanitarian Law. In: Fleck D (ed) The Handbook of International Humanitarian Law. Oxford University Press, Oxford, pp 201–263

Happold M (2013) International Humanitarian Law and Human Rights law. In: Henderson C, White N (eds) Research Handbook on International Conflict and Security Law: Jus ad Bellum, Jus in Bello, and Jus post Bellum, Edward Elgar, pp 444–466

Henckaerts J, Doswald-Beck L (2005) Customary International Humanitarian Law—Volume I: Rules. Cambridge University Press, New York

Hoffmann T (2010) Squaring the Circle?—International Humanitarian Law and Transnational Armed Conflicts. In: Matheson M, Momtaz D (eds) Rules and Institutions of International Humanitarian Law Put to the Test of Recent Armed Conflicts, Hague Academy of International Law, The Netherlands, pp 217–274

International Law Commission (2011) Draft Articles on the Effects of Armed Conflicts on Treaties, with commentaries. Yearb Int Law Comm 2:Part 2

Jennings R (1961) The Acquisition of Territory in International Law. Manchester University Press, Manchester

Jinks D (2006) The Applicability of the Geneva Conventions to the "Global War on Terrorism". Virginia J Int Law 46:1–33

Kaplan S (2008) The Remarkable Story of Somaliland. J Democracy 19(3):143–157

Kolb R, Hyde R (2008) An Introduction to the International Law of Armed Conflicts. Hart Publishing, Oregon

Kreß C (2010) Some Reflections on the International Legal Framework Governing Transnational Armed Conflicts. J Confl Secur Law 15(2):245–274

Kretzmer D (2005) Targeted Killing of Suspected Terrorists: Extra-Judicial Executions or Legitimate Means of Defence? Eur J Int Law 16(2):171–212

Lauterpacht H (1947) Recognition in International Law. Cambridge University Press, Cambridge

Lubell N (2012) The War (?) against Al-Qaeda. In: Wilmshurst E (ed) International Law and the Classification of Conflicts. Oxford University Press, Oxford, pp 421–454

Lubell N, Derejko N (2013) A Global Battlefield? Drones and the Geographical Scope of Armed Conflict. J Int Crim Justice 11(1):65–88

Milanović M, Hadzi-Vidanović V (2013) A Taxonomy of Armed Conflict. In: White N, Henderson C (eds) Research Handbook on International Conflict and Security Law: Jus ad Bellum, Jus in Bello, and Jus post Bellum. Edward Elgar Publishing, UK, pp 256–314

Moir L (2002) The Law of Internal Armed Conflict. Cambridge University Press, Cambridge

Moore J (1898) History and Digest of the International Arbitrations to Which the U.S. Has Been a Party, US Government Printing Office, Washington

Parkerson J (1991) United States Compliance with Humanitarian Law Respecting Civilians During Operation Just Cause. Military Law Rev 133:31–140

Pellet A (1992) The Opinions of the Badinter Arbitration Committee: A Second Breath for the Self-Determination of Peoples. Eur J Int Law 3:178–185

Peters A (2010) Statehood after 1989: 'Effectivités' between Legality and Virtuality. In: Crawford J, Nouwen S (eds) Select Proceedings of the European Society of International Law, vol 3. Hart Publishing, Oregon, pp 171–184

Pictet J (ed) (1958) Geneva Convention Relative to the Protection of Civilian Persons in Time of War: commentary. ICRC, Geneva

Pictet J (ed) (1960) Geneva Convention Relative to the Treatment of Prisoners of War: Commentary. ICRC, Geneva

Rosas A (1976) The Legal Status of Prisoners of War: A Study in International Humanitarian Law. Suomalainen Tiedeakatemia, Helsinki
Rosen S (ed) (1991) The International Law Commission's Draft Articles on State Responsibility: Part 1, Articles 1–35. Martinus Nijhoff, Dordrecht
Sandoz Y, Swinarski C, Zimmerman B (eds) (1987) Commentary on the Additional Protocols of 8 June 1977 to the Geneva Conventions of 12 August 1949. International Committee of the Red Cross, Geneva
Sassòli M (2006) Transnational Armed Groups and International Humanitarian Law, Harvard University Program on Humanitarian Policy and Conflict Research. Occasional Paper Series No. 6
Schindler D (1979) The Different Types of Armed Conflicts According to the Geneva Conventions and Protocols. Recueil des Cours de l'Academie de Droit International de la Haye 163:117–164
Schmitt M (2002) Wired Warfare: Computer Network Attack and Jus in Bello. Int Rev Red Cross 84:365–399
Schmitt M (2012) Classification in Future Conflict. In: Wilmshurst E (ed) International Law and the Classification of conflicts. Oxford University Press, Oxford, pp 455–477
Shaw M (2008) International Law, 6th edn. Cambridge University Press, Cambridge
Shaw M (2014) International Law, 7th edn. Cambridge University Press, Cambridge
Sivakumaran S (2012) The Law of Non-International Armed Conflict. Oxford University Press, Oxford
Solis G (2010) The Law of Armed Conflict: International Humanitarian Law in War. Cambridge University Press, Cambridge
Stewart J (2003) Towards a Single Definition of Armed Conflict in International Humanitarian Law: A Critique of Internationalized Armed Conflict. Int Rev Red Cross 85:313–350
Stewart J (2007) The UN Commission of Inquiry on Lebanon: A Legal Appraisal. J Int Crim Justice 5:1039–1059
Talmon S (1998) Recognition of Governments in International Law: With Particular Reference to Governments in Exile. Clarendon Press, Oxford
Tancredi A (2012) A Mormative 'Due Process' in the Creation of States through Secession. In: Kohen M (ed) Secession: International Law Perspectives. Cambridge University Press, Cambridge, pp 171–207
UN General Assembly (1976) Resolution 31/6. Policies of apartheid of the Government of South Africa, UN Doc. A/RES/31/6
UN General Assembly (2001) Draft Articles on Responsibility of States for Internationally Wrongful Acts with Commentaries, UN Doc. A/56/10
UN General Assembly (2006) Human Rights Council: Report of the Commission of Inquiry on Lebanon pursuant to Human Rights Council Resolution S-2/1, UN Doc. A/HRC/3/2
UN General Assembly (2011) Human Rights Council: Report of the International Commission of Inquiry to Investigate all Alleged Violations of International Human Rights Law in the Libyan Arab Jamahiriya, UN Doc. A/HRC/17/44
UN General Assembly (2015) Human Rights Council: Report of the Independent International Commission of Inquiry on the Syrian Arab Republic. UN Doc A/HRC/28/69
UN Security Council (1965) Resolution 217 (1965), UN Doc. S/RES/217
UN Security Council (1976) Resolution 402 (1976), UN Doc. S/RES/402
UN Security Council (1984) Resolution 550 (1984), UN Doc. S/RES/550
UN Security Council (1992) Resolution 787 (1992), UN Doc. S/RES/787
UN Security Council (2014) Letter Dated 20 September 2014 from the Permanent Representative of Iraq to the United Nations Addressed to the President of the Security Council, UN Doc. S/2014/691
UN Security Council (2014) Letter Dated 23 September 2014 from the Permanent Representative of the United States of America to the United Nations Addressed to the Secretary-General, UN Doc. S/2014/695

UN Security Council (2014) Resolution 2161 (2014), UN Doc. S/RES/2161
UN Security Council (2014) Resolution 2170 (2014), UN Doc. S/RES/2170
UN Security Council (2015) Resolution 2199 (2015), UN Doc. S/RES/2199
Vidmar J (2012) Territorial Integrity and the Law of Statehood. George Wash Int Law Rev 44:697–770
Vité S (2009) Typology of Armed Conflicts in International Humanitarian Law: Legal Concepts and Actual Situations. Int Rev Red Cross 91(873):69–94
Wilmshurst E (ed) (2012) International Law and the Classification of Conflicts. Oxford University Press, Oxford
Wills S (2011) The Legal Characterization of the Armed Conflicts in Afghanistan and Iraq: Implications for Protection. Neth Int Law Rev 58(2):173–208
Wolfrum R, Philipp C (2002) The Status of the Taliban: Their Obligations and Rights Under International Law. Max Planck Yearb United Nations Law 6:559–601

Case Law

Charles J Jansen v Mexico, Mexico-US Claims Committee, 1868, reprinted in Moore J (1898) History and Digest of the International Arbitrations to Which the U.S. Has Been a Party, Vol III, US Government Printing Office, Washington, p 2902
Democratic Republic of the Congo Military Prosecutor v Bongi Massaba, Criminal Trial Judgment and Accompanying Civil Action for Damages, 24 March 2006, RP No 018/2006; RMP No 242/PEN/06
Great Britain v Costa Rica, Arbitral Award, 18 October 1923, (1948) 1 UNRIAA 369
Hamdan v Rumsfeld 548 US 557
ICJ, *Case Concerning Armed Activities on the Territory of the Congo (Democratic Republic of the Congo v Uganda)*, Judgment, 19 December 2005, [2005] ICJ Rep 168
ICJ, *Case Concerning East Timor (Portugal v Australia)*, Judgment, 30 June 1995, [1995] ICJ Rep 90
ICJ, *Case Concerning Military and Paramilitary Activities in and against Nicaragua (Nicaragua v United States of America)*, Judgment, 27 June 1986, [1986] ICJ Rep 14
ICTY, *Prosecutor v Duško Tadić a/k/a "Dule"*, Decision on the Defence Motion for Interlocutory Appeal on Jurisdiction, 2 October 1995, Case No. IT-94–1-AR72
ICTY, *Prosecutor v Duško Tadić*, Judgement, 15 July 1999, Case No. IT-94–1-A
ICTY, *Prosecutor v Fatmir Limaj, Haradin Bala and Isak Musliu*, Judgement, 30 November 2005, Case No. IT-03–66-T
ICC, *Prosecutor v Jean-Pierre Bemba Gombo*, Decision Pursuant to Article 61(7)(a) and (b) of the Rome Statute on the Charges of the Prosecutor Against Jean-Pierre Bemba Gombo, 15 June 2009, Case No. ICC-01/05–01/08-424
ICTY, *Prosecutor v Ljube Boškoski and Johan Tarčulovski*, Judgement, 10 July 2008, Case No. IT-04-82-T
ICTY, *Prosecutor v Ramush Haradinaj, Idriz Balaj and Lahi Brahimaj*, Judgement, 3 April 2008, Case No. IT-04-84-T
ICTY, *Prosecutor v Slobodan Milošević*, Decision on Motion for Judgement of Acquittal, 16 June 2004, Case No. IT-02-54-T
ICC, *Prosecutor v Thomas Lubanga Dyilo*, Decision on the Confirmation of Charges, 29 January 2007, Case No. ICC-01/04-01/06-830-tEN
ICC, *Prosecutor v Thomas Lubanga Dyilo*, Judgment pursuant to Article 74 of the Statute, 14 March 2012, Case No. ICC-01/04-01/06-2842
ICTY, *Prosecutor v Tihomir Blaskić*, Judgement, 3 March 2000, Case No. IT-95-14-T
Public Committee against Torture in Israel v Government of Israel, Judgement, 13 December 2006, HCJ 769/02

PCIJ, *Questions relating to Settlers of German Origin in Poland*, Advisory Opinion, 10 September 1923, [1923] PCIJ Rep Series B, No. 6
Salimoff & Co and Others v Standard Oil Company of New York, Court of Appeals of New York, (1933) 262 NYS 220
The Savarkar Case (France v Great Britain), Arbitral Award, 24 February 1911, (1961) 11 UNRIAA 252

Treaties

Montevideo Convention on the Rights and Duties of States, opened for signature 26 December 1933, 164 LNTS 19 (entered into force 26 December 1934)
Protocol Additional to the Geneva Conventions of 12 August 1949, and relating to the Protection of Victims of International Armed Conflicts, opened for signature 12 December 1977, 1125 UNTS 3 (entered into force 7 December 1979)
Protocol Additional to the Geneva Conventions of 12 August 1949, and relating to the Protection of Victims of Non-International Armed Conflicts, opened for signature 8 June 1977, 1125 UNTS 609 (entered into force 7 December 1978)
Regulations concerning the Laws and Customs of War on Land, Annex to Hague Convention (IV) respecting the Laws and Customs of War on Land, opened for signature 18 October 1907, 205 CTS 277 (entered into force 26 January 1910)

Chapter 5
Beyond the Pale? Engaging the Islamic State on International Humanitarian Law

Annyssa Bellal

Abstract This article discusses the possibility and desirability of engaging with a non-state armed group, such as the Islamic State (IS), on the topic of international humanitarian law (IHL). It first describes the structure and ideology of IS, and then, it proceeds to analyse the law applicable to armed groups as well as the challenges encountered when engaging these actors. In particular, it considers when such groups reject IHL as a common normative framework regulating armed conflicts. The last section of this article examines direct and indirect ways humanitarian actors have engaged armed groups, such as IS.

Keywords Non-state armed groups · Islamic State · International humanitarian law · Terrorism · Humanitarian engagement

Contents

A. Bellal (✉)
Geneva Academy of International Humanitarian Law and Human Rights, Geneva, Switzerland; Sciences Po, Paris, France
e-mail: annyssa.bellal@graduateinstitute.ch

T.D. Gill et al. (eds.), *Yearbook of International Humanitarian Law 2015*,
Yearbook of International Humanitarian Law 18,
DOI 10.1007/978-94-6265-141-8_5

5.1 Introduction

The expansion of the organization known as Islamic State (IS), operating mainly in Syria and Iraq, but also more recently in Libya,[1] raises several legal and political issues. The legality of the armed intervention of the international coalition led by the USA,[2] targeted killings,[3] or the status of foreign fighters under international law[4] is among the many *jus ad bellum* and *jus in bello* questions addressed by scholars and practitioners. The protection of cultural property in armed conflicts, a topic somewhat neglected by international lawyers, has also become an important issue.[5] This article, however, adopts a different angle of analysis and questions the possibility of engagement on humanitarian issues with a non-state armed group (NSAG), such as IS.

---

[1] Schmitt E (2016) U.S. Scrambles to Contain Growing ISIS Threat in Libya. http://www.nytimes.com/2016/02/22/world/africa/us-scrambles-to-contain-growing-isis-threat-in-libya.html?_r=0. Accessed 9 May 2016; El Amrani I (2016) How much of Libya does the Islamic State Control? http://foreignpolicy.com/2016/02/18/how-much-of-libya-does-the-islamic-state-control/. Accessed 9 May 2016; IS also claimed attacks in Yemen and Afghanistan, see Al-Jazeera (2015) ISIL claims suicide bombing in Yemen's Aden. http://www.aljazeera.com/news/2015/10/isil-claim-bombing-coalition-base-yemen-aden-151006144810019.html. Accessed 9 May 2016; Raghavan S (2015) Islamic State claims bombing in Afghanistan that kills dozens. https://www.washingtonpost.com/world/dozens-killed-in-suicide-bomber-attack-outside-an-afghanistan-bank/2015/04/18/3849f572-e59f-11e4-b510-962fcfabc310_story.html. Accessed 9 May 2016.

[2] See for example Coco and Maillard 2015, pp. 388–419; Weller M (2014) Islamic State crisis: What force does international law allow? http://www.bbc.com/news/world-middle-east-29283286. Accessed 9 May 2016; Arimatsu L and Schmitt M (2014) The legal basis for the war against Isis remains contentious. http://www.theguardian.com/commentisfree/2014/oct/06/legal-basis-war-isis-syria-islamic-state. Accessed 9 May 2016.

[3] Wintour P and Watt N (2015) UK forces kill British Isis fighters in targeted drone strike on Syrian city. http://www.theguardian.com/uk-news/2015/sep/07/uk-forces-airstrike-killed-isis-briton-reyaad-khan-syria. Accessed 9 May 2016.

[4] See Paulussen and Entenmann 2015, pp. 86–118; Kraehenmann 2014.

[5] See Hausler 2014, pp. 361–387.

Engagement with NSAGs with a view to a better understanding and implementation of international humanitarian law (IHL) has long been recognized as a necessity by humanitarian organizations, as well as scholars.[6] As noted by Marco Sassòli

> at least half the belligerents in the most widespread and most victimizing of armed conflicts around the world, i.e. non-international armed conflicts, are non-State armed groups […] It is urgent to improve the compliance with International Humanitarian Law […] by such armed groups (and by the parties for which they fight).[7]

Engagement with a wide range of armed groups will raise similar questions of security and access for humanitarian organizations. In many cases, NSAGs will find incentives in such engagement by, for instance, political recognition or access to basic resources for their group or constituency. For those organizations focusing on the dissemination of IHL rather than on providing humanitarian aid per se,[8] engagement will be difficult if the armed group totally rejects the international legal system as a valid normative framework regulating its actions. More generally, one could question the pertinence or even desirability of engaging with NSAGs that, like IS, not only reject the existing international legal framework, but also violate IHL and human rights law (HRL) as a method of warfare. In short: Is engagement with some NSAGs beyond the pale?

This article endeavours to demonstrate that humanitarian engagement with an armed group such as IS, even if it implies acute challenges, should not be disregarded. This article proceeds in three sections. The first describes the main

[6] Although intergovernmental organizations like the UN might have less flexibility to engage NSAGs, the UN Secretary-General (UNSG) has recognized, among the five core challenges to the protection of civilians, enhancing compliance by these actors. The UNSG noted in this regard that "armed groups are bound by international humanitarian law and must refrain from committing acts that would impair the enjoyment of human rights. For some groups, attacks and the commission of other violations against civilians are deliberate strategies, intended to maximize casualties and destabilize societies. Others may be less inclined to attack civilians deliberately, but their actions still have an adverse impact on the safety and security of civilians. We need urgently to develop a comprehensive approach towards improving compliance by all these groups with the law, encompassing actions that range from engagement to enforcement", UN Security Council (2009) Report of the Secretary-General on the protection of civilians in armed conflict: UN Doc. S/2009/277, para 39. More recently, in its report for the world humanitarian summit, the UNSG noted that "at a time when most conflicts are non-international, it is critical for impartial humanitarian actors to engage in dialogue with States as well as non-State armed groups to enhance their acceptance, understanding and implementation of obligations under international humanitarian and human rights law": UN General Assembly (2016) One humanity: shared responsibility—Report of the Secretary-General for the World Humanitarian Summit, UN Doc. A/70/709, para 51.

[7] Sassòli 2010, p. 6.

[8] Geneva Call, for instance, encourages NSAG to respect international humanitarian norms by signing unilateral declarations called "Deeds of Commitment", which prohibit the use of anti-personnel mines, the recruitment of children under 18 years of age, as well as the commission of sexual violence. The organization does not deliver aid or provide services, though it helps to facilitate collaboration between the armed groups with which it engages and humanitarian organizations, such as those specialized in demining; see: www.genevacall.org.

characteristics of IS, notably its origins and military strength, as well as its ideology. The second section reflects on the practice of engaging armed groups on IHL, with a particular focus on NSAGs claiming to act on the basis of Islamic law. This section concentrates on the definition of an NSAG and applicable international law. It suggests that IS has to be considered as a *de facto* (non-State) authority to which international human rights law is likewise applicable. It also addresses the question of the universality of IHL and its relation to Islamic law, as well as the problem of engaging armed groups that commit terrorist acts. The last section of this article suggests possible avenues for engagement with a group such as IS.

5.2 The Islamic State

5.2.1 Origins and Structure

The wider public came to know about the existence of IS in 2014, when the group experienced military success, capturing several major cities in Iraq and Syria, including Raqqa, Fallujah, and Mosul.[9] The first trace of IS, however, can be found in 1999, in Afghanistan, in a training camp for "jihadists" where a Jordanian man, Abu Musab al Zarqawi, was in charge.[10] Although the current IS leader is Abu Bakr al Baghdadi,[11] Zarqawi, who was killed in a drone strike in 2006, is indeed seen as the founding father of an organization, which has evolved over more than 15 years.[12] At first linked to al-Qaeda,[13] it has acted independently since February 2014.[14] After seizing Mosul in June 2014,[15] the group announced

[9] BBC (2015) What is Islamic State? http://www.bbc.com/news/world-middle-east-29052144. Accessed 9 May 2016.

[10] Hosken 2015, p. 9.

[11] BBC (2014) Profile: Abu Bakr al-Baghdadi. http://www.bbc.com/news/world-middle-east-28749734. Accessed 9 May 2016.

[12] Lister C (2014) Profiling the Islamic State. http://www.brookings.edu/research/reports2/2014/12/profiling-islamic-state-lister. Accessed 9 May 2016.

[13] In the context of the Iraqi conflict, Zarqawi pledged allegiance to al-Qaeda and Osama Bin Laden in September 2004: Ibid., p. 8; See also Hashim A (2014) Islamic State: From al-Qaeda Affiliate to Caliphate. http://www.mepc.org/journal/middle-east-policy-archives/islamic-state-al-qaeda-affiliate-caliphate. Accessed 9 May 2016.

[14] Lister, above n 12, p. 13; see also Al-Fajr Media (2014) On the Relationship of al-Qaeda and the Islamic State in Iraq and al-Sham. https://azelin.files.wordpress.com/2014/02/al-qc481_idah-22on-the-relationship-of-qc481idat-al-jihc481d-and-the-islamic-state-of-iraq-and-al-shc481m22-en.pdf. Accessed 9 May 2016.

[15] Chulov M (2014) Isis insurgents seize control of Iraqi city of Mosul. http://www.theguardian.com/world/2014/jun/10/iraq-sunni-insurgents-islamic-militants-seize-control-mosul. Accessed 9 May 2016.

the end of the "Sykes-Picot agreement"[16] and the establishment of the "caliphate", with Abu Bakr al Baghdadi designated as the ruler (Caliph). It also changed its name from the Islamic State in Iraq and Syria (ISIS) to the Islamic State.[17]

IS has been described "a well-run organization that combines bureaucratic efficiency and military expertise with a sophisticated use of information technology".[18] Many of its members were drawn from the former Baathist regime in Iraq, notably the armed forces, who were stripped of power through the process of "debaathification" put in place by the USA and who decided to join Zarqawi's organization.[19] IS's structure was revealed in the press when its strategic head, Haji Bakr, a former colonel in the intelligence service of Saddam Hussein's air defence force, was killed in January 2014.[20] According to the documents reporters found in Haji Bakr's home, administration of IS would cover areas such as finance, schools, day care, the media, and transportation. The documents also evidence a

> constantly recurring core theme, which is meticulously addressed in organizational charts and lists of responsibilities and reporting requirements: surveillance, espionage, murder and kidnapping. For each provincial council, Bakr had planned for an emir, or commander, to be in charge of murders, abductions, snipers, communication and encryption.[21]

IS also established a Sharia Council, a Sharia police, and Sharia courts.[22]

5.2.2 Military Strength

Currently, the group's precise size is unclear.[23] In September 2014, the CIA estimated the number of IS fighters to be between 20,000 and 31,500 across Iraq and

---

[16] The Sykes-Picot agreement is a demarcation of the border between Iraq and Syria, see Mezzofiore G (2014). Iraq Isis Crisis: Is This the End of Sykes-Picot? http://www.ibtimes.co.uk/iraq-isis-crisis-this-end-sykes-picot-1454751. Accessed 9 May 2016.

[17] The name Islamic State in Iraq and the Levant (ISIL) was also used by the group until June 2014, see the Stanford University database (2016) Mapping militant organisations: The Islamic State. https://web.stanford.edu/group/mappingmilitants/cgi-bin/groups/view/1. Accessed 9 May 2016.

[18] Ruthven M (2015) Inside the Islamic State. http://www.nybooks.com/articles/archives/2015/jul/09/inside-islamic-state/. Accessed 9 May 2016.

[19] Hosken 2015, p. 20.

[20] Reuter C (2015) The Terror Strategist, Secret Files Reveal the Structure of Islamic State. http://www.spiegel.de/international/world/islamic-state-files-show-structure-of-islamist-terror-group-a-1029274.html. Accessed 9 May 2016.

[21] Ibid.

[22] See also Revkin M (2014) The legal foundations of the Islamic State. http://www.joshualandis.com/blog/legal-foundations-islamic-state-mara-revkin/. Accessed 9 May 2016.

[23] In March 2016, documents were leaked allegedly revealing the identity of 22,000 IS fighters in Syria, see MacAskill E (2016) Isis document leak reportedly reveals identities of 22,000 recruits. http://www.theguardian.com/world/2016/mar/09/isis-document-leak-reportedly-reveals-identities-syria-22000-fighters. Accessed 9 May 2016.

Syria,[24] but a more recent report of the Agency announced a decrease in the number of fighters to the tune of several thousand.[25] In June 2014, the Sufan Group Research Centre estimated that 12,000 fighters from at least 81 countries had joined the conflict in Syria and that 2500 were from Western countries, including most members of the European Union, the USA, Canada, Australia, and New Zealand.[26] This number would likely have doubled by the end of 2015.[27]

Pledges of allegiance to IS have been made from a number of armed groups operating in countries such as in Libya, Nigeria, Pakistan, and Yemen, although not every pledge was publicly recognized by Baghdadi.[28] Some groups, such as Abu Sayyaf (Philippines), made a declaration of allegiance in order to attach their name to IS, but without having any operational ties to the group. IS claimed that some of the groups that pledged allegiance would not be accepted until they maintained a direct line of communication to Baghdadi and until he appointed or formally recognized the group's leadership.[29]

IS also possess sophisticated and powerful weapons systems, including tanks, armoured personnel carriers, field artillery, multiple rocket launchers, anti-tank guided missiles, anti-aircraft guns, and man-portable air-defence systems (MANPADs).[30] The group made major territorial gains in south-western Syria in 2015, but lost several key towns in Iraq, as well as parts of Syria's northern border with Turkey.[31] In particular, it lost the cities of Ramadi, Tikrit, Kobane, and Sinjar,

---

[24] Sciutto J, Crawford J and Carter C (2014) ISIS can 'muster' between 20,000 and 31,500 fighters, CIA says. http://edition.cnn.com/2014/09/11/world/meast/isis-syria-iraq/. Accessed 10 May 2016.

[25] See the White House: Office of the Press Secretary (2016) Press Briefing by Press Secretary Josh Earnest, 2/4/2016. https://www.whitehouse.gov/the-press-office/2016/02/04/press-briefing-press-secretary-josh-earnest-242016. Accessed 10 May 2016.

[26] The Soufan Group (2014) Foreign Fighters in Syria. http://soufangroup.com/foreign-fighters-in-syria/. Accessed 10 May 2016.

[27] Guardian (2015) Number of foreign fighters in Iraq and Syria doubles in a year, report finds. http://www.theguardian.com/world/2015/dec/08/isis-foreign-fighters-iraq-syria-doubles-report. Accessed 10 May 2016.

[28] Among the groups pledging allegiance that were recognized as such by IS, one can name Boko Haram (Nigeria) on 13 July 2014, Ansar al-Sharia (Libya) on 31 October 2014, Ansar Beit al-Maqdis/Sinai Province (Egypt) on 10 November 2014, and JundAllah (Soldiers of God) in Pakistan on 17 November 2014. See Ould Mohamedou 2015, p. 59.

[29] Stanford University database, above n 17. See also Other Solutions Consulting Ltd (2015) Mapping Jihadist groups alongside Current Humanitarian Action. http://othersolutions.eu/1565/. Accessed 9 May 2016.

[30] Lister, above n 12, pp. 16–17.

[31] See BBC (2016) Battle for Iraq and Syria in maps. http://www.bbc.com/news/world-middle-east-27838034. Accessed 10 May 2016.

but as of February 2016, the group still held a firm control over the regions and cities of Raqqa and (though to a lesser extent) Mosul.[32]

IS's takeover of one-third of Iraqi territory and one-quarter of Syrian territory made it the richest armed group in the world, primarily due to the oilfields in those areas which have produced revenues of hundreds of millions of dollars for the group. In Syria, IS seized eight oilfields in Raqqa and Deir el-Zour provinces. In Iraq, it has taken control of four fields in Saladin Province. At the end of 2014, the United Nations estimated that ISIS was making $1.6 million a day selling crude and refined oil on the black market.[33] In December 2014, Forbes listed IS among the richest "terrorist organizations", with an annual "turnover" of $2 billion, citing as funding sources the oil trade, kidnapping and ransom, collection of protection and taxes, bank robberies, and looting.[34] In 2015, however, US airstrikes have more systematically targeted IS-controlled oilfields, disrupting the group's main source of revenue.[35]

5.2.3 Ideology and Media Strategy

From the beginning of its existence, the establishment of an Islamic caliphate, regarded as the "most important sovereign institution of the history of Islam",[36] has been at the core of IS's political vision. As explained by Andrew March and Mara Revkin, the group

> sees itself as creating a distinctive and authentic legal order for the here and now, one that is based not only on a literal (if selective) reading of early Islamic materials but also on a long-standing theory of statecraft and legal authority […] On-going research shows that ISIS is using Islamic law not simply to terrorize foreign hostages and non-Muslim groups, such as Christians or Yazidis, but also to establish a social contract with the Muslim population it aspires to govern. Despite suggestion that ISIS has 'peaked' or is already in 'decline', its concern for establishing a law-based political order indicates that the group has aspirations for long-term governance –aspirations that should be taken seriously'.[37]

---

[32] Peçabha S and Watkins D (2015) 'ISIS' Territory Shrank in Syria and Iraq This Year. http://www.nytimes.com/interactive/2015/12/18/world/middleeast/Where-ISIS-Gained-and-Lost-Territory-Islamic-State.html?_r=0. Accessed 10 May 2016. See also Hawram F, Mohammed S and Shaheen K (2015) Life under Isis in Raqqa and Mosul: We're living in a giant prison. http://www.theguardian.com/world/2015/dec/09/life-under-isis-raqqa-mosul-giant-prison-syria-iraq. Accessed 10 May 2016.

[33] Feldman N (2015) How ISIS Became the World's Richest Terror Group. http://www.haaretz.com/middle-east-news/isis/1.686287. Accessed 10 May 2016.

[34] Forbes (2014) The World's 10 Richest Terrorist Organizations. http://www.forbes.com/sites/forbesinternational/2014/12/12/the-worlds-10-richest-terrorist-organizations/#1cd0988d2ffa. Accessed 10 May 2016.

[35] Gordon M and Schmitt E (2015) U.S. Steps Up Its Attacks on ISIS-Controlled Oil Fields in Syria. http://www.nytimes.com/2015/11/13/us/politics/us-steps-up-its-attacks-on-isis-controlled-oil-fields-in-syria.html?_r=0. Accessed 10 May 2016.

[36] Hosken 2015, p. 3.

[37] March A and Revkin M (2015) Caliphate of Law. https://www.foreignaffairs.com/articles/syria/2015-04-15/caliphate-law. Accessed 10 May 2016.

In 2005, the group articulated its ideology, which has been summarized as follows:

- Promote and defend monotheism (*tawhid*) and eliminate polytheism;
- Anyone not believing in the essential unity of God is an infidel and subject to excommunication and death (*takfir*);
- Secularism, nationalism, tribalism, communism, and baathism are considered blatant violations of Islam;
- Jihad is the duty of all Muslims if the Infidels attack;
- All Muslims, except the Shia, constitute one nation, subsumed in the establishment of the caliphate.[38]

The operationalization of IS's radical ideology is supported by a powerful media strategy and propaganda tools. The group uses movies, video games, and news channels to spread its message in several languages, but mainly in Arabic, German, English, and French, as well as social media, such as YouTube, Twitter, Instagram, and Tumblr.[39] It also has a propaganda magazine, "Dabiq", published only in English.[40] The level of sophistication of its use of the media marks IS out from its predecessor, notably al-Qaeda, though other armed groups such as the PKK (in Turkey) or the FARC (Fuerzas armadas revolucionarias de Colombia) also have TV channels, press agencies, and websites.[41] What differentiates IS's media strategy, however, is its ability to reach a worldwide audience, composed mainly of the young, thanks to use of a Westernized visual grammar that could compete with Hollywood movies and video game imagery in its sophistication. IS media strategy seems to have as its main objective the attraction and recruitment of fighters from outside the Middle East to join the group, an objective largely attained by the group so far, since foreign fighters compose many, if not the majority, of its military contingent.[42] IS media strategy is also congruent with the long relationship between media and terrorism, i.e. to provoke "irrational fear among large numbers of people in order to influence policymakers and thus advance their goals".[43]

---

[38] Hashim, above n 13.

[39] Rose S (2014) The Isis propaganda war: a hi-tech media jihad. http://www.theguardian.com/world/2014/oct/07/isis-media-machine-propaganda-war. Accessed 10 May 2016.

[40] The Clarion Project publishes the several editions of the magazine on its website, see http://www.clarionproject.org/news/islamic-state-isis-isil-propaganda-magazine-dabiq#.

[41] For the PKK, the website is http://www.pkkonline.com/en/. The FARC's website can be accessed at http://farc-ep.co/.

[42] Rose, above n 39. The reasons that draw thousands of men and women from all over the world to join IS go from a sheer feeling of being invested in some divine mission and a sense of holy war to save Islamic societies and restore the caliphate to feelings of oppression and dispossession for cultural specificities, see Chulov (2015) Why ISIS fights. http://www.theguardian.com/world/2015/sep/17/why-isis-fight-syria-iraq. Accessed 10 May 2016.

[43] Burke J (2016) How the changing media is changing terrorism. http://www.theguardian.com/world/2016/feb/25/how-changing-media-changing-terrorism. Accessed 10 May 2016.

5.3 Engaging with Non-state Armed Groups on International Humanitarian Law

Considerable literature concerns humanitarian engagement with non-state armed groups, and this article will not discuss in depth the contemporary practice of international humanitarian organizations in that area.[44] Instead, this section offers an overview of the main issues regarding engagement with NSAG, with a particular focus on radical armed groups that claim to be acting on the basis of Islamic law. But preliminary to this second section, a brief discussion of the different terminology used by scholars and journalists when referring to NSAG, such as IS, is warranted.

5.3.1 "Islamist", "Jihadist", or "Salafist" Armed Groups

The notion of "Islamism" refers to a spectrum of political ideologies that have roots dating to the end of the nineteenth century, developed by intellectuals wishing to solve the problems faced by Muslims because of imperialism and to build a utopian Islamic society using Islam as a guide to political and social life.[45] Over the years, however, "the more extremist Islamist trends were distilled in the context of authoritarianism and war [...] Currently, the majority of Islamist trends [...] tend to repudiate, rather than embrace modernity".[46] The term has been a source "of major controversy especially because of the divergence in Islamic interpretations"[47], and its wide application has encompassed different types of groups that advocate the implementation of Sharia law and pan-Islamic unity.

"Jihadism" should not be confused with "Islamism", but rather should be considered as a "violent subcategory of Islamism".[48] *Jihad* means "struggle" in Arabic and does not necessarily mean violence, but can refer to an individual internal struggle against more basic instincts.[49] Since the 1980s, however, the term has been widely used to designate the actions of armed groups such as al-Qaeda.

---

[44] See, for instance, Bongard and Somer 2011, pp. 673–706; Hofmann and Schneckener 2011, pp. 1–19 and more generally the special volume 93 of the *International Review of the Red Cross*, published in 2011, on "Engaging armed groups"; See also Bellal and Casey-Maslen 2011a.

[45] Saltman E and Winter C (2014) Islamic State: The Changing Face of Modern Jihadism. http://www.quilliamfoundation.org/wp/wp-content/uploads/publications/free/islamic-state-the-changing-face-of-modern-jihadism.pdf. Accessed 10 May 2016.

[46] Ibid.

[47] Other Solutions Consulting Ltd (2015) Key vocabulary of Terrorism. http://othersolutions.eu/key-vocabulary-of-terrorism/. Accessed 10 May 2016.

[48] Ibid.

[49] Ibid.

"Salafists" take their name from the term *salaf* ("predecessors" and "ancestors") referring to the practice of the seventh-century Muslims. As explained by Andrew Hosken,

> modern Salafis believe the first Muslims and the immediate successors of Muhammad exemplify most perfectly what it means to be a virtuous Muslim and later generations must emulate them. Islam must be purged of any impurities and shorn of any ambiguity or sentimentality about other religions.[50]

From this very short overview, one can say that none of these categorisations seems to be satisfactory when talking about NSAGs that claim to be acting on the basis of Islamic law, as they might fall into several different categories at the same time. Furthermore, "many Islamists believe in democracy and it is possible to be an Islamist extremist and not engage in violence. There are Salafis and Wahhabis who oppose IS and those who support them".[51] That said, in this article, the term "jihadist" NSAG might be used more frequently as a means to designate a group that totally rejects the existing international legal and political system and for which *Jihad* is not only defensive, but also offensive. As such, jihadist armed groups' ambitions are not confined to a single territory, but rather aim at spreading and establishing an often "Salafist" conception of Islam across borders. IS can be considered such a jihadist armed group, as can al-Qaeda and its affiliates.

5.3.2 Defining NSAGs

NSAGs are not defined in international law. Case law merely gives indications of the degree of organization; such groups should meet for the purpose of the application of IHL. The ICTY, for instance, listed some elements such as follows:

> the existence of a command structure and disciplinary rules and mechanisms within the group; the existence of a headquarters; the fact that the group controls a certain territory; the ability of the group to gain access to weapons, other military equipment, recruits and military training; its ability to plan, coordinate and carry out military operations, including troop movements and logistics; its ability to define a unified military strategy and use military tactics; and its ability to speak with one voice and negotiate and conclude agreements such as ceasefire or peace accords.[52]

Although useful this list can be to determine the threshold of application of IHL to violent situations involving NSAG, it has the disadvantage of focusing the attention on armed groups which are organized along lines similar to state armed forces, with a military structure (though it is one to which IS may certainly belong given its military aims). There is, however, a variety of NSAGs operating today.

---

[50] Hosken 2015, p. 13.

[51] Ibid, p. xiii.

[52] ICTY, *Prosecutor v Ramush Haradinaj, Idriz Balaj and Lahi Brahimaj*, Judgment, 3 April 2008, Case No. IT-04-84-T (*Haradinaj*), para 360.

Private security companies, crime groups (mafia), urban gangs, "vigilante", or "self-defence groups" do not necessarily all meet the threshold of organization required for the applicability of IHL, but they are active armed actors in many parts of the world. In that regard, another succinct but useful definition of armed non-state actors is the one proposed by Pablo Policzer, for whom armed groups can be described as any "challengers to the state's monopoly of legitimate coercive force".[53] This definition, alluding to Weber's description of the State as the only entity claiming the monopoly of lawful armed coercion,[54] would thus encompass a wider category of NSAG.

Despite the risk of its name leading to confusion,[55] it is clear that IS is a non-State armed group and cannot be considered a State under international law, as, for example, it does not fulfil the criteria enounced in Article 1 of the 1933 Montevideo Convention on the Rights and Duties of States. The treaty requires that "the State as a person of international law should possess the following qualifications: (a) a permanent population; (b) a defined territory; (c) government; and (d) capacity to enter into relations with the other states". Two additional criteria have also been suggested by practice and scholarship: the criteria of independence and legitimacy.[56] With regard to criteria (a), (c), and (d), there can be room for discussion as to what extent the people living under IS control will remain in the territory permanently or not, whether IS governing structures are effective, and whether IS does or does not want to enter into relations with other states despite its ability to do so. Arguably, since IS controls territory that crosses over the frontiers of two internationally recognized States (Iraq and Syria), criteria (b) seems not to be fulfilled. Finally, the issue of legitimacy can be regarded as a form of realization of the right to self-determination, including situations in which a people is subject to colonial rule, cases which there is a racist regime, or cases in which a people is suffering from serious human rights violations.[57] In the case of IS,

---

[53] Policzer P (2005) Neither terrorist nor freedom fighters. https://www.academia.edu/639782/Neither_terrorists_nor_freedom_fighters. Accessed 10 May 2016.

[54] In his famous lecture *Politics as a Vocation* (1918), the German sociologist Max Weber defined the state as a "human community that (successfully) claims the monopoly of the legitimate use of physical force within a given territory". The text is available at http://www.ucc.ie/archive/hdsp/Weber_Politics_as_Vocation.htm.

[55] Arango T (2015) ISIS transforming into functioning State that uses terror as tool. http://www.nytimes.com/2015/07/22/world/middleeast/isis-transforming-into-functioning-state-that-uses-terror-as-tool.html?_r=0. Accessed 10 May 2016. As noted by the Clarion project, "the Islamic State is not only a terrorist group. It is a political and military organization that holds a radical interpretation of Islam as a political philosophy and seeks to impose that worldview by force on Muslims and non-Muslims alike", The Clarion Project (2015) Special Report: The Islamic State. https://www.clarionproject.org/sites/default/files/islamic-state-isis-isil-factsheet-1.pdf. Accessed 10 May 2016.

[56] See for instance Crawford 1976, pp. 93–182.

[57] Shany Y Cohen A and Mimran T (2014) ISIS: Is the Islamic State Really a State? http://en.idi.org.il/analysis/articles/isis-is-the-islamic-state-really-a-state/. Accessed 10 May 2016.

> it cannot be argued that the establishment of the State was based on one of the scenarios that would justify the secession of a group from a region that is under the sovereignty of Iraq and Syria. In fact, it seems that it is actually the new regime that is systematically violating the human rights of the people in the territory, including the right to life, the right to liberty, freedom of religion, and freedom of expression.[58]

As a consequence, IS is only a State in name and not under international law. This conclusion, however, should be relativized as the group's complex structure and the fact that it administers a population and a territory need also to be taken into account as elements assessing the existence of a *de facto authority*, potentially changing the applicable legal regime as will be examined below.

De facto "regimes" or *de facto* "authorities" have been defined as "entities, which exercise effective authority over some territory, no matter whether they are engaged in warfare with the sovereign or are subsisting in times of peace".[59] The notion of "effective authority" is in itself subject to interpretation. Would it suffice, for instance, that the armed group exercise executive power without issuing any laws? In the 1939 *Arantzazu Mendi* case before the UK House of Lords, *de facto* administrative control was understood as the exercise of "all the functions of a sovereign government, in maintaining law and order, instituting and maintaining courts of justice, adopting or imposing laws regulating the relations of the inhabitants of the territory to one another and to the government".[60] In addition, the responsibility of *de facto* regimes was recognized by practice only when such a regime governed a specific territory for a *prolonged* period of time.[61]

While many fled, millions of people live under the control of IS. Congruent with the establishment of the caliphate, in 2014 IS built a holistic system of governance that includes educational, judicial, security, humanitarian, and infrastructure projects not only in Raqqa, but also in other towns of Syria.[62] IS divides governance in two categories, namely administration and Muslims services:

> Islamic outreach, Shari'a institutes, elementary education, law enforcement (both local and religious), courts, recruitment, and tribal relations fall under the administrative category. The provision of services, including humanitarian aid, bakeries, water and electricity falls under what ISIS calls the 'Department of Muslim Services'. The level of sophistication of the governance programs that appear in a given area are determined most directly by ISIS's level of control over that area. Where ISIS maintains greater dominance, it tends

---

[58] Ibid.

[59] Schoiswohl 2001, p. 50; Van Essen 2012, pp. 31–49.

[60] The *Arantzazu Mendi* case, House of Lords, Judgment of 23 February 1939, L.R., [1939] A.C. 256, reproduced in 1942 ILR 60, p. 65.

[61] See Frowein J (2016) De Facto Regime. http://opil.ouplaw.com/view/10.1093/law:epil/9780199231690/law-9780199231690-e1395?rskey=uRlfJm&result=1&prd=EPIL. Accessed 10 May 2016; Schoiswohl notes that "it is mainly the latter group of regimes exercising a high degree of effectiveness which raises issues of international legal personality, for they display a State-like structure demanding a more thorough treatment under international law than a group of somewhat organized rebels waging war against the 'parent' government": Schoiswohl 2001, p. 50.

[62] Caris C and Reynolds R (2014) ISIS Governance in Syria. http://www.understandingwar.org/sites/default/files/ISIS_Governance.pdf. Accessed 10 May 2016.

to deploy more sophisticated governance, making a substantial investment in developing lasting institutions.[63]

From these factual elements, even if IS territorial control might not be lasting, given the instability of the region, one can assume that the NSAG can be qualified as a *de facto* authority.

5.3.3 Applicable International Law to NSAGs

NSAGs are bound by Common Article 3 of the Geneva Conventions of 1949, Protocol Additional II of 1977 (APII), as well as by customary international humanitarian law when the requisite conditions are met.[64]

Historically, to what extent Common Article 3 directly addresses NSAG has been debated. As the article states that "each Party to the conflict shall be bound to apply, as a minimum" its provisions, it has sometimes been claimed that the term "each Party" does not apply to NSAGs, even though they may meet the criteria for being a party to the conflict, but only to government armed forces.[65] State practice, international case law, and scholarship have, however, confirmed that Common Article 3 applies to such NSAGs directly.[66] In addition, Common Article 3 offers a

[63] Ibid., p. 14.

[64] The two conditions of applicability of IHL, to non-international armed conflicts, i.e. protracted violence and level of organizations of the armed groups, have been spelled out by the ICTY, in the *Tadić* case. On a thorough review of the applicable IHL to NSAG, see Sivakumaran 2012; Geneva Convention (I) for the Amelioration of the Condition of the Wounded and Sick in Armed Forces in the Field, opened for signature 12 August 1949, 75 UNTS 31 (entered into force 21 October 1950) (GCI), Article 3; Geneva Convention (II) for the Amelioration of the Condition of Wounded, Sick and Shipwrecked Members of Armed Forces at Sea, opened for signature 12 August 1949, 75 UNTS 85 (entered into force 21 October 1950) (GC II), Article 3; Geneva Convention (III) relative to the Treatment of Prisoners of War, opened for signature 12 August 1949, 75 UNTS 135 (entered into force 21 October 1950) (GC III), Article 3; Geneva Convention (IV) relative to the Protection of Civilian Persons in Time of War, opened for signature on 12 August 1949, 75 UNTS 287 (entered into force 21 October 1950) (GC IV), Article 3; Protocol Additional to the Geneva Conventions of 12 August 1949, and relating to the Protection of Victims of Non-International Armed Conflicts, opened for signature 8 June 1977, 1125 UNTS 609 (entered into force 7 December 1978) (AP II).

[65] One of the arguments put forward has been that "Party" (with a capital "p") meant "High Contracting Party", i.e. states, and that it was used in a contracted form merely to avoid repetition. See, e.g. Zasova 2010, p. 58.

[66] In *Nicaragua v. United States of America*, for example, the International Court of Justice (ICJ) confirmed that Common Article 3 was applicable to the contras, the NSAG fighting the government: "The conflict between the contras' forces and those of the Government of Nicaragua is an armed conflict which is 'not of an international character'. The acts of the contras towards the Nicaraguan Government are therefore governed by the law applicable to conflicts of that character". See ICJ, *Case Concerning Military and Paramilitary Activities in and against Nicaragua (Nicaragua v United States of America)*, Judgment, 27 June 1986, [1986] ICJ Rep 14, para 219. See also Sassòli 2010, p. 12.

solid base for humanitarian engagement with NSAGs as it provides that any "impartial humanitarian body, such as the International Committee of the Red Cross, may offer its services to the Parties to the conflict" without implying any recognition on their legal status.[67]

With regard to AP II, in addition to the existence of an armed conflict between the insurgency and the government taking place in the territory of a High Contracting Party,[68] there are three cumulative material conditions under Article 1, para 1 for the treaty to be applicable to NSAGs: the organized armed group(s) must be under responsible command; it must exercise such control over a part of the national territory as to enable it to carry out sustained and concerted military operations; and territorial control must be such as to enable the group to be able to implement the protocol. Where these cumulative criteria for application of the protocol are objectively met, it becomes "immediately and automatically applicable", irrespective of the views of the parties to that conflict.[69]

Finally, customary international humanitarian law is applicable to all actors in a non-international armed conflict, including NSAGs that meet the necessary criteria.[70]

As of March 2016, the conflict in Syria can be qualified as a series of non-international armed conflicts opposing the Syrian armed forces and a number of organized armed groups, including IS, as well as between armed groups operating in several parts of the country. Thus, hostilities between these parties wherever they may occur in Syria are subject to the rules of IHL, in particular Common Article 3 and Customary IHL, as Syria is not a party to Additional Protocol II.[71] In addition, IHL is applicable to the different States that are conducting air strikes in Syria,

---

[67] GC I, GC II, GC III and GC IV, above n 64, common Article 3, para 2.

[68] In contrast to AP II, above n 64, Common Article 3 also regulates armed conflict that takes place only between NSAGs, for example in a failed state.

[69] See Sandoz et al. 1987, p. 1353; and ICTR, *Prosecutor v Jean-Paul Akayesu*, Judgement, 2 September 1998, Case No. ICTR-96-4-T, para 624.

[70] See, e.g. *Haradinaj*, above n 52, para 60; SCSL, *Prosecutor v Morris Kallon* and *Brima Buzzy Kamara*, Decision on Challenge to Jurisdiction: Lomé Accord Amnesty, 13 March 2004, Case Nos. SCSL-2004-15-AR72(E) and SCSL-2004-16- AR72(E), paras 45–47, which asserted that: "[T]here is now no doubt that this article [Common Article 3] is binding on states and insurgents alike, and that insurgents are subject to international humanitarian law [… a] convincing theory is that [insurgents] are bound as a matter of customary international law to observe the obligations declared by Common Article 3 which is aimed at the protection of humanity". See also Moir 2002, pp. 56–58; Bellal et al. 2011, pp. 47–79.

[71] See Bellal 2015, p. 265. The ICRC qualified the situation in Syria as a non-international armed conflict in 2012. As the level of intensity as well as of the organization of the main armed groups involved remains unchanged as of 2016, this qualification still holds today. See International Committee of the Red Cross (2012) Syria: ICRC and Syrian Arab Red Crescent maintain aid effort amid increased fighting. https://www.icrc.org/eng/resources/documents/update/2012/syria-update-2012-07-17.htm. Accessed 10 May 2016.

namely the USA, France, Russia, Australia, and Canada.[72] Iran is also bound by IHL since it has sent ground troops in support of the Syrian armed forces.[73] The role of Turkey's involvement in the conflict is less straightforward. While there have been instances of shelling of the Kurdish armed groups (YPG/YPJ) across the border, it is unclear at this stage whether the required threshold of violence has been reached in order for IHL to apply to Turkey with regard to the conflict in Syria.[74]

As for international human rights law, its applicability to NSAGs is still debated in public international law.[75] It is not possible within the framework of this article to address this controversy at length. For our purpose, it suffices to note that it is increasingly accepted that human rights law is applicable to non-State armed groups that exercise *de facto* control over a territory and population and exercise governmental functions.[76] In addition, NSAGs could be also bound by core human rights norms, whether or not they control territory.[77] As seen above, IS can be considered a *de facto* authority and is thus bound, theoretically at least, by international human rights law.

---

[72] Fantz A (2015) War on ISIS, who's doing what? http://edition.cnn.com/2015/11/20/world/war-on-isis-whos-doing-what/. Accessed 10 May 2016.

[73] Bastani H (2015) Iran quietly deepens involvement in Syria's war. http://www.bbc.com/news/world-middle-east-34572756. Accessed 10 May 2016.

[74] Gutman R (2016) Syria Cease-Fire brings Turkey closer to war. http://foreignpolicy.com/2016/02/16/syria-ceasefire-brings-turkey-closer-to-war/. Accessed 10 May 2016.

[75] It has been argued that human rights treaties are characterized as setting norms to regulate the relationship between a State and individuals under its jurisdiction and that such treaties would be "neither intended, nor adequate, to govern armed conflict between the State and armed opposition groups", see Zegveld 2002, p. 54. For a different opinion, see Clapham 2006, pp. 491–523.

[76] For instance, the Office of the High Commissioner for Human Rights has consistently taken the position that "non-State actors that exercise government-like functions and control over a territory are obliged to respect human rights norms when their conduct affects the human rights of the individuals under their control": UN General Assembly (2008) Human Rights Council: Human Rights Situation in Palestine and Other Occupied Arab Territories, UN Doc. A/HRC/8/17, para 9; and UN General Assembly 2009a, b Human Rights Council: Human Rights Situation in Palestine and Other Occupied Arab Territories, UN Doc. A/HRC/12/37, para 7. See also Rodley 1993. The International Commission on Libya, noted that "since the NTC has been exercising de facto *control* over territory akin to that of a Governmental authority, it will examine also allegations of human rights committed by its forces": UN General Assembly (2011) Human Rights Council: Report of the International Commission of Inquiry to investigate all alleged violations of international human rights law in the Libyan Arab Jamahiriya, UN Doc. A/HRC/17/44, para 72.

[77] The Independent Commission of Inquiry on Syria underlined in its February 2012 report that "at a minimum, human rights obligations constituting peremptory international law (*ius cogens*) bind States, individuals, and non-State collective entities, including armed groups. Acts violating *ius cogens*—for instance, torture or enforced disappearances—can never be justified": UN General Assembly (2012) Human Rights Council: Report of the independent international commission of inquiry on the Syrian Arab Republic, UN Doc. A/HRC/19/69, para 106.

5.3.4 Lack of Ownership of International Norms

Even if NSAGs are theoretically and legally bound by IHL and arguably also by (at least some) human rights norms in given circumstances, many difficulties in seeking to ensure compliance with international law by these actors remain. The reasons for the lack of compliance are diverse: strategic arguments (the nature of warfare in internal armed conflicts that may lead to the use of tactics that violate international law, such as launching attacks from within the civilian population); lack of knowledge of applicable norms; and lack of "ownership" over these norms. Indeed, since NSAGs are not entitled to ratify the relevant international treaties (as, by definition, they are not a State or other entity with the necessary international legal personality) and are generally precluded from participating as full members of a treaty drafting body, they could—and sometimes do—argue that they should not be bound to respect rules that they have neither put forward nor formally adhered to.[78]

Thus, while most NSAGs recognize IHL as a pertinent regulatory framework, some groups consider that either it is not their unique reference or that they will prioritise other types of rules, based on religion, ideology, or tradition, for instance. Choosing another moral and normative framework may also be a means for NSAGs to express their own voice in conducing the war or a way to criticize the state against which they are fighting and thereby legitimize their own struggle in the eyes of their or a wider constituency.[79] This, for instance, seems to be one of the tactics used by IS to undermine Saudi Arabia as the holder of the "true path to Islam". As explained by Malise Ruthven,

> in mounting its challenge to the Saudi monarch's quasi-caliphal claim to lead the Muslim world as 'Guardian of the Two Holy Shrines' (Mecca and Medina), ISIS highlights the royal family's love of luxury and acceptance of corruption which, it claims, renders its members ideologically and morally unfit for the task.[80]

More generally, despite some key differences, NSAGs such as IS, al-Qaeda, or the Taliban all claim Islam to be the basis of the normative and moral order they seek to establish and share a "rigidly Manichean worldview that sanctions political violence, pitting Muslims ('Good') against non-Muslims ('Evil') and necessitate the re-establishment of the caliphate as a solution to injustice and Muslim disempowerment".[81] As a result, many humanitarian organizations have attempted to bridge the gap between IHL and Islamic law as a means of dialogue and engagement.

---

[78] Bellal and Casey-Maslen 2011b, pp. 175–197.

[79] In some situations of armed conflicts, acts which are a flagrant violation of IHL, such as kidnapping and enslavement, can be justified by traditional laws of war, see Bangerter 2011, p. 370, giving the example of tribal practice in South Sudan or the *Pashtunwali* in Afghanistan and Pakistan.

[80] Ruthven, above n 18.

[81] Saltman and Winter, above n 45.

5.3.5 *Engaging "Jihadist" NSAGs on IHL*

Debates on the universality of international law took place mainly with regard to human rights law.[82] In the IHL world, other cultural voices were not really heard until the 1970s, during the negotiation of the two additional protocols to the 1949 Geneva Conventions, notably on the negotiation of article 1 of Additional Protocol I, which extended the protections of IHL to those fighting colonial domination, foreign occupation, or racist regimes.[83] The expansion of IS, and before them the Taliban and al-Qaeda, sparked this debate anew. It is, however, important to note that the critique of the "occidental" or Western origins of IHL is not only expressed by armed groups which claim to be acting on Islamic law. Maoist armed groups, for instance, may have a different interpretation of international humanitarian norms based on their specific ideology.[84]

5.3.5.1 Relativizing the Universality of IHL

While IHL was first conceived and based on the religious notions of "Christian charity",[85] Gustave Moynier understood that a universal and humanist approach was needed to succeed in the implementation of IHL despite the particularities of any one religion.[86] Islamic players did not have a role in the elaboration of early international humanitarian law. They

> were confined to this passive role of 'other', against which the international humanitarian law movement contrasted and defined itself, for some time. No Islamic State was present in the conference held in Geneva in 1863, which gave birth to the Red Cross Committee. Turkey did, however, ratify the 1864 Geneva Convention in 1865. Persia followed in 1874.[87]

The participation of the Ottoman Empire and Persia to the subsequent IHL negotiations secured the establishment of the emblems of the Red Crescent, and the Red Lion and Sun. However, during the inter-war IHL conferences, as well as the post-World War II period, the participation of Islamic delegations was not

[82] Sassòli M, Bouvier A and Quintin A (2012) How does law protect in war? International humanitarian law and cultural relativism. https://www.icrc.org/casebook/doc/book-chapter/fundamentals-ihl-book-chapter.htm#a_iii. Accessed 10 May 2016.

[83] Cockayne 2002, p. 614.

[84] As Olivier Bangerter recalls, "despite the emphasis in Maoist doctrine on respect for the 'people', a group adhering to that ideology may excuse one section of the civilian population from the 'people' whom they set out to protect, claiming that those excluded do not belong to the 'people' but to the 'enemies of the people' or 'class enemies'": Bangerter 2011, p. 383.

[85] As James Cockayne observes, if Henry Dunant was driven by basic internationalism when he presided over the creation of the Red Cross, his internationalism was also coloured by a Christian ethic: see Cockayne 2002, p. 600.

[86] Ibid., p. 601.

[87] Ibid.

framed "in terms of Islam, but public international law, and few Islamic scholars addressed, during this time, the relationship between a classical Islamic doctrine and humanitarian law".[88] The influence of Islamic participants (both States and non-States, such as the PLO) grew during the elaboration of the 1977 protocols, and Articles 43 and 44 of Additional Protocol I can be seen as their direct product. But here again, nationalism rather than Islam seems to have been the influential factor. The 1979 Islamic revolution in Iran changed the approach. During the Iran–Iraq war, the discourse adopted by Iran was no longer framed in international law arguments, but in Islamic law terms. Iranian military planners, for instance, announced they would "do away with conventional warfare methods in favour of Islamic warfare".[89]

5.3.5.2 Bridging the Gap Between IHL and Islamic Law

Scholars and practitioners have attempted to understand Islamic law approaches to war and compare them with both *jus ad bellum*[90] and *jus in bello*[91] frameworks, but the exercise has proven difficult for many reasons. First, international law and Islamic law are not conceived from on the same premises: one is a normative order based directly on religious and moral theories, while the other is a state-centric, secular ensemble of written norms elaborated from a rational rather than divine perspective. As Andrew March and Naz Modirzadeh have affirmed,

> *Shari'a* is not a settled body of law or legal doctrine, but an aspiration, like Justice, or an ontological concept, like Plato's Forms. If what we mean to inquire into is the field of reasoning and argument within which Muslim religious authorities attempt to justify various rules and doctrines as the most likely wordy simulacrum of divine *shari'a* (itself known infallibly only in God's mind), we are speaking of 'fiqh', or Islamic jurisprudence. If what we mean to inquire into is the authoritative, settled code of conduct within warfare accepted by Muslims, the Islamic analogue to the Geneva conventions, then, well, we are simply out of luck.[92]

While there are common values and aspirations in both IHL and Islamic law, such as the protection of the women, children and the elderly or some rules on the treatment of prisoners,[93] another challenge relating to the comparison of the two normative orders has to deal with the difficult reconciliation with Islamic law of some core notions of IHL, such as the notion of "civilians" or the prohibition of slavery.[94]

---

88 Ibid., p. 611.

89 Ibid., p. 618.

90 For example Shah 2013, pp. 343–365.

91 Badar 2013, pp. 593–625.

92 March and Modirzadeh 2013, p. 368.

93 Aly H (2014) Islamic Law and the rules of war. http://www.irinnews.org/analysis/2014/04/24/islamic-law-and-rules-war. Accessed May 2016.

94 Aly H (2014) Can Islamic law be an answer for humanitarians? http://www.irinnews.org/report/99989/can-islamic-law-be-an-answer-for-humanitarians. Accessed 10 May 2016.

That said, it is important to keep in mind that the interpretation of the rules of war in Islamic law made by some "jihadi" armed groups is far from being universally shared among all Islamic law scholars.[95] Even one of the most influential Islamist scholars in the Middle East, Abu Muhammad al-Maqdisi, distanced himself from Zarqawi's extremism and use of violence. In particular, he would emphatically reject Zarqawi's assertion that Shia Muslims were apostates and even non-Muslims and would also criticize the use of violence against civilians and mosques.[96]

In addition, the interpretation of Islamic laws on war by certain armed groups is not always static and may evolve over time. For example, between August 2006 and May 2010, the Taliban elaborated three different versions of the codes of conduct of their fighters under Islamic law with the rules changing several times.[97] In the latest (2010) version, section 57, clause (ii), declares that "A brave son of Islam should not be used for lower and useless targets. The utmost effort should be made to avoid civilian casualties".[98] In a statement of 22 February 2013, the Taliban added:

> According to us civilians are those who are in no way involved in fighting. The white-bearded people, women, children and common people who live an ordinary life, it is illegitimate to bring them under attack or kill them. But the police of Kabul admin, those personnel of the security companies who escort the foreigners' supply convoys and are practically armed, similarly those key figures of the Kabul admin who support the invasion and make plans against their people, religion and homeland, those people who move forward the surrender process for Americans in the name of peace and those Arbakis who plunder the goods, chastity and honour of the people by taking dollar salaries, all these people are civilian according to you. No Afghan can accept that the above mentioned people are civilian. […] They are directly involved in the protraction of our country's invasion and legally we do not find any difficulty in their elimination, rather we consider it our obligation.[99]

Even if this statement is not in full accord with IHL, notably with regard to those who are part of the administration that are directly targetable under the law, it is a starting point for the discussion and seems to open the possibility for humanitarian dialogue and engagement. In fact, engagement with some Salafist armed groups has been possible, even for those organizations that are not providing for humanitarian aid and focus on the promotion and dissemination of IHL. Geneva Call has for instance engaged directly with "Islamist", although not

---

[95] For instance, Turkey's official religious ministry has issued a 40 page report explaining how, to their mind, "IS deviates from Islamic norms, wreaks carnage on innocent people and defames the name of Islam": Akyol M (2015) Turkey takes on the Islamic State in 40-page report. http://www.al-monitor.com/pulse/originals/2015/09/turkey-offers-its-own-religious-case-against-islamic-state.html. Accessed 10 May 2016.

[96] Hosken 2015, p. 22.

[97] Munir 2011, p. 86.

[98] Ibid.

[99] Islamic Emirate of Afghanistan (2013) An Open Letter to the UNAMA about the Biased Behaviour of this Organization, 22 February 2013. https://blogs.mediapart.fr/lynx/blog/010313/open-letter-unama-about-biased-behavior-organization. Accessed 10 May 2016.

necessarily "jihadist" NSAGs, such as the Palestinian Islamic Jihad based in Lebanon, the Salafist armed group Ahrar al-Sham and the Islam Army in Syria.[100]

IS claims to be following Islamic laws of armed conflict. The group has published guidelines and legal opinions authored by affiliated clerics, so the group can claim that its fighters are acting lawfully according to the group's own rules, even if manifestly they do not comply with international law. The guidelines notably specify

> the conditions under which enemy combatants may be targeted, tortured, mutilated, or killed as well as rules governing the ransom of non-Muslim hostages. ISIS also has laws for the provision of security guarantees, called "aman documents", for journalists and humanitarian workers seeking access to ISIS-controlled area. Rules for the treatment of prisoners and slaves do include certain limitations, such as a prohibition on separating a mother from her young children, but they also permit sexual slavery as a legally permissible alternative to adultery.[101]

Obviously, these rules can hardly be reconciled with IHL and HRL. The fact that IS claims to be following Islamic laws on war, however, indicates that the group can be opened to some form of dialogue, if not with the international community, but with Islamic law scholars about their interpretation. As will be discussed below, this could be indeed one of the ways to engage IS on certain humanitarian issues.

5.3.6 Engaging with Armed Groups that Use Terror as a Strategy, and the Impact of Counter-Terrorism Legislation

There have been numerous reports of IHL and human rights violations committed by IS, such as the massacre of civilians, beheadings, mutilations, rape, and torture.[102] On 15 August 2014, the UN Security Council unanimously adopted Resolution 2170 (2014), condemning the "gross, systematic, and widespread abuses" of human rights by IS and imposing sanctions, such as travel restrictions and asset freezing, on its members.[103] IS has been listed as a foreign terrorist organization by the UN,[104] the EU,[105] and several other states, including the USA.[106]

---

[100] Geneva Call (2015) Syria. http://www.genevacall.org/country-page/syria/. Accessed 7 June 2016.

[101] March and Revkin, above n 37; See also Callimachi R (2015) ISIS enshrines a theology of rape. http://www.nytimes.com/2015/08/14/world/middleeast/isis-enshrines-a-theology-of-rape.html?_r=0. Accessed 10 May 2016.

[102] See, for instance, the UN General Assembly (2015) Human Rights Council: Report of the Office of the United Nations High Commissioner for Human Rights on the human rights situation in Iraq in light of abuses committed by the so-called Islamic State in Iraq and the Levant and associated groups, UN Doc. A/HRC/28/18.

[103] UN Security Council (2014) Resolution 2170 (2014), UN Doc. S/RES/2170 (2014).

[104] See UN Security Council Sanctions Committee, at: https://www.un.org/sc/suborg/en/sanctions/1267. Accessed 10 May 2016.

[105] See the EU terrorist list at: http://www.consilium.europa.eu/en/policies/fight-against-terrorism/terrorist-list/. Accessed 10 May 2016.

[106] See the list at: http://www.state.gov/j/ct/rls/other/des/123085.htm. Accessed 10 May 2016.

Terrorizing the population as well as the enemy, including in Muslim States, has been used as a strategy by IS: "far from being an undisciplined orgy of sadism, ISIS terror is a systematically applied policy that follows the ideas put forward in jihadist literature, notably in an online tract, The Management of Savagery, by the al Qaeda ideologue Abu Bakr Naji".[107] This document argues that carrying out campaigns of constant violent attacks in Muslim states will eventually exhaust these states' ability and will to enforce their authority and that chaos will ensue, allowing jihadist to take over the situation.[108] Coupled with a powerful media strategy, the display of horror and brutality gives an image of apocalyptic countries and instilled such fear among the enemy that some government troops in Iraq and Syria have fled rather than put up a fight.[109]

The existence of armed actors (be they state or non-State) that use terror as a strategy, and commit gruesome and horrific acts, is not a new phenomenon. Armed groups as diverse as the LRA (Lord's Resistance Army from Uganda) or the RUF (Revolutionary United Front) in Sierra Leone have, to a certain extent, used strategies terrorizing the population for tactical reasons.[110] It has been shown that some form of humanitarian engagement was possible even with extremely violent NSAGs, such as *Los Zetas* or the *Sinaloa Cartel* in Mexico, which, like IS, have committed beheadings, mutilations, child recruitment, and massacres.[111]

The use of the term "terrorist" to designate such armed groups is, however, problematic, as States will tend to label *any* armed group that opposes it as a "terrorist" group.[112] As noted by the International Committee of the Red Cross (ICRC),

> a recent challenge for IHL has been the tendency of States to label as terrorist all acts of warfare against them committed by armed groups, especially in non-international armed conflicts. This has created confusion in differentiating between lawful acts of war, including such acts committed by domestic insurgents against military targets, and acts of terrorism.[113]

---

[107] Ruthven, above n 18.

[108] Hashim, above n 13.

[109] Ruthven, above n 18.

[110] See Bangerter 2011, pp. 373–377.

[111] See Al-Gharbi M (2014) Mexican drug cartels are worse than ISIL. http://america.aljazeera.com/opinions/2014/10/isil-vs-mexican-drugcartelsunitedstatesislamophobia.html. Accessed 10 May 2016. For a discussion of how criminal gangs could be bound by IHL, and thus would also be considered to be a "party to a conflict" (Common Article 3 to GC I, GC II, GC III and GC IV, above n 64) or a "dissident armed forces" or "an organized armed group" (AP II, above n 64, Article 1), see Hazen 2010, pp. 369–386. For humanitarian engagement with such groups, see Bangerter 2010, pp. 387–406.

[112] In an article, Britain's chief broker of the Northern Ireland peace deal, Jonathan Powell, authored an article on "How to talk to terrorists", although he acknowledged the impropriety of this term to designate non-state armed groups generally (the author underlined he used "the word terrorist […] for sake of simplicity, but it isn't particularly helpful to define a group—terror is a tactic employed by governments, groups and individuals"): Powell J (2014) How to talk to terrorists. http://www.theguardian.com/world/2014/oct/07/-sp-how-to-talk-to-terrorists-isis-al-qaida. Accessed 13 June 2016..

[113] International Committee of the Red Cross (2013) Contemporary challenges for IHL: Overview. https://www.icrc.org/eng/war-and-law/contemporary-challenges-for-ihl/overview-contemporary-challenges-for-ihl.htm. Accessed 10 May 2016.

In addition, designating an armed group as a terrorist group can have serious implications as it can even encourage violations of IHL. Indeed, since it is typically far easier to be included on a list of terrorist organizations than it is to be removed from one, practical incentives to improve respect for IHL may be limited once an armed group has been so designated. In the USA, engaging with an armed group listed as a terrorist organization, such as IS or al-Qaeda, can trigger criminal responsibility.[114]

Even more problematic in that regard is the emerging conflict of norms between national and international counter-terrorism laws and some IHL provisions on health care and humanitarian assistance. In an interesting and detailed research, Dustin Lewis, Naz Modirzadeh, and Gabriella Blum give examples of medical doctors being imprisoned and judged in the USA and Syria for providing medical care to wounded fighters belonging to NSAGs listed as terrorist organizations, while caring for the wounded and sick is an obligation protected by both treaty law and customary IHL.[115] In that sense, it is regrettable that "the web of laws (on counter-terrorism) seems paralysing for humanitarian actors: an impossible regulatory framework in which success or compliance in one arena is likely to raise risks and liabilities in another".[116]

---

[114] In the controversial US Supreme Court decision of 21 June 2010, *Holder v Humanitarian Law Project* (2010) 130 S. Ct. 2705, the Court held that the training in international law for PKK members planned to be given by a US NGO (the Humanitarian Law Project) could be used by the PKK "as a part of a broader strategy to promote terrorism, and to threaten, manipulate, and disrupt". According to the Court, the planned training would thus rightly fall under the *Anti-terrorism and Effective Death Penalty Act of 1996* which criminalizes any material support given to terrorist groups. The fact that in the circumstances of the case, such a training was prohibited by the law was not found to be a violation of the First Amendment (freedom of expression) enjoyed by the NGO. See also the Washington Post (2010) The Supreme Court Goes too far in the Name of Fighting Terrorism. http://www.washingtonpost.com/wp-dyn/content/article/2010/06/21/AR2010062104267.html. Accessed 13 June 2016; and the New York Times (2010) What Counts as Abetting Terrorists? http://roomfordebate.blogs.nytimes.com/2010/06/21/what-counts-as-abetting-terrorists/. Accessed 10 May 2016.

[115] Lewis D, Modirzadeh N and Blum G (2015) Medical Care in Armed Conflict: International Humanitarian Law and State Responses to Terrorism. https://dash.harvard.edu/bitstream/handle/1/22508590/HLS_PILAC_Medical_Care_in_Armed_Conflict_IHL_and_State_Responses_to_Terrorism_September_2015.pdf?sequence=1. Accessed 10 May 2016. The rules protecting the wounded and sick and health care are numerous in treaty law, see notably GC I, above n 64, Articles 12, 15, 18, 19, 21, 22, 27, 35 and 36; GC II, above n 64, Articles 12, 18, 21 and 40; GC III, above n 64, Articles 14 and 22; GC IV, above n 64, Article 3; Protocol Additional to the Geneva Conventions of 12 August 1949, and relating to the Protection of Victims of International Armed Conflicts, opened for signature 12 December 1977, 1125 UNTS 3 (entered into force 7 December 1979) (AP I), Articles 8, 10, 12, 13, 15, 17, 21 and 28; AP II, above n 64, Articles 2, 7, 11 and 18. See also Rules 109–111 of the ICRC Study on Customary International Humanitarian Law, see Henckaerts and Doswald-Beck 2005, pp. 396–403.

[116] Modirzadeh et al. 2011, pp. 623–647.

5.4 Means to Engage the Islamic State on International Humanitarian Law

As of March 2016, to the extent of our knowledge, no humanitarian organization has engaged *directly* with IS *core* leadership.[117] However, although the practice of engaging NSAGs is not always visible and not systematically documented, humanitarian organizations have engaged or at least discussed humanitarian issues with armed groups such as the Taliban and al-Qaeda, as well as with commanders of IS, which are at the "periphery" of the group.

5.4.1 Direct Engagement

The ICRC, for instance, was able to visit detainees held by al-Qaeda in Yemen in 2013. As explained by the delegate who was in charge of the coordinating detention visits by the ICRC:

> We are currently focusing on visits to people detained by the State authorities to ensure that the detainees are being treated humanely, that living conditions are acceptable, and that the detainees can be in touch with their families. We even managed during the last couple of years to visit detainees held by Al Qaeda.[118]

As a much older example of direct engagement, one can mention the declaration made by the Taliban, under the name of the Islamic Emirate of Afghanistan, in October 1998, on the "total ban on the production, trade, stockpiling, and use of landmines". This declaration can be seen as the product of engagement efforts made by international NGOs advocating for the ban of anti-personal landmines, in coordination with the Afghan campaign to ban landmines.[119]

While direct engagement with IS core leadership has not been possible so far, there was some engagement made with IS local commanders on humanitarian issues. Former Médecins Sans Frontières (MSF) president Jean-Hervé Bradol wrote about his experience as a coordinator of hospitals for the organization in the town of Qabasin in Syria upon IS seizing of the town.[120] Bardol explains that IS

---

[117] This statement is made on the basis of interviews made with some persons working with key humanitarian organizations, including the International Committee of the Red Cross, Médecins Sans Frontières, and Amnesty International.

[118] International Committee of the Red Cross (2013) Yemen: Alleviating the suffering of detainees, Interview. https://www.icrc.org/eng/resources/documents/interview/2013/07-31-yemen-detainees-macsweeney.htm. Accessed 10 May 2016.

[119] Conference Organisers (2001) Engaging non-state actors in a Landmine Ban—A Pioneering Conference: Full Conference Proceedings. http://www.genevacall.org/wp-content/uploads/dlm_uploads/2013/11/20000325_engaging_nsa_in_landmine_ban_pioneering_conference1.pdf. Accessed 13 June 2016, p. 163.

[120] Bradol J (2015) Comment les humanitaires travaillent face à al-Qaeda et l'Etat islamique. http://www.msf-crash.org/drive/fdbc-1502_commentleshumanitaires.pdf. Accessible on 10 May 2016.

commanders in charge of the administration of the town asked MSF teams to continue working in the hospitals. The commander officially committed not to interfere with the administration of the hospital, not caring about international staff, whatever their nationality. The commander did not claim a strict separation between woman and men during their medical activities, and women could work while only covering their heads without hiding their faces. The hospital could treat the wounded and sick of the armed parties without discrimination, including the Kurdish forces. The commander's principal motivations, wrote Bradol, would be to not close the only hospital in the city upon his taking over of administrative functions.[121] Bradol concluded that the possibility to maintain the hospital in Qabasin was evidence that humanitarian aid was possible under the domination of an armed group as worrying as IS.[122]

Engagement with local commanders seems thus to be the more realistic solution for the time being with a group such as IS. As noted by one commentator,

> the Islamic State has a dominant leader, but it is also spread over a large territory where local leaders/middle managers hold significant power. This is buttressed by the fact that the group is increasingly welcoming allegiances to it, which means accommodation of a measure of decentralised power.[123]

Direct engagement would however not be necessarily impossible in the long run. Reflecting on his 30 years of experience working with MSF, notably in Chechenia, Afghanistan, Somalia, and Mali, Jean-Hervé Bradol also gave some insights on the "cycle of evolution" of the relationship between the "transnational jihadist" armed groups and the population they control. According to him, there are four phases in the cycle:

- "Knights of the faith": the first phase corresponds to a period when the armed groups are held in great esteem by either the people they control, and even humanitarians, as they are perceived as saving the people against tyranny or injustice;
- "Honeymoon": during this phase, the armed group has managed to secure law and order or to secure better prices on basic commodities, hence winning the support of the population;
- "Disappointment": administration becomes difficult, the war is costly, and the armed groups might need to prey on the local population to enhance their economic resources;
- "The Disaster": Pressure on the local population becomes too high, social discontent grows. As a response, repression is used by the armed group, fuelling the vicious circle of the conflict.

Bradol's interesting reflections show that humanitarian engagement might be possible with armed groups at a certain moment of the cycle he designated,

---

[121] Ibid.

[122] Ibid.

[123] Ould Mohamedou 2015, p. 60.

particularly during the "two first phases". This is corroborated by research on the practice of other humanitarian organizations. The Geneva Academy for International Humanitarian law and Human Rights' *Rules of Engagement* recommends, for instance, that:

> Those seeking to promote compliance with international norms should monitor the conflict for 'windows of opportunity' that may offer a greater chance for success of engagement on specific humanitarian concerns [...] The situation in any given conflict should be monitored for particular 'windows of opportunity' for engagement with ANSAs or a particular ANSA on international norms. A discussion of norms may more easily occur during a lull in fighting or a ceasefire, for example, than when conflict is intense. Leadership or military strategy may also change, helping to facilitate discussion of compliance with norms.[124]

5.4.2 Indirect Engagement

Apart from direct engagement, there are other "indirect" ways to talk with armed groups on IHL. This article suggests that engaging influential Islamic scholars or the constituency of the armed groups might be viable solutions to ensure some form of access to the civilian population under the control of armed groups such as IS.

5.4.2.1 Engagement Through Influential Scholars

In a fascinating article, Guardian journalists Shiv Malik, Ali Youned, Spencer Ackerman, and Mustafa Khalili explained how the FBI and a human rights lawyer, Stanley Cohen, "collaborated" with Islamic law scholar Abu Muhammad al-Maqdisi to try to free an American hostage held by IS named Peter Kassig.[125] The deal proposed was the following: in exchange for Maqdisi negotiations with IS chief scholar Turki al-Binali to free the hostage, supporters of al-Qaeda and IS

> would agree to stop denouncing each other as apostate and infidels. Then, if Isis agreed to stop taking hostages altogether, Maqdisi and the cohort of older al Qaeda religious scholars [...] would tone down their hostile rhetoric, potentially opening the door to a complete reconciliation between the two terrorist groups. As part of these larger agreements, Maqdisi would insist on Kassig's freedom. It would effectively be bundled into the negotiations as a gesture of good faith.[126]

The plan eventually failed as Maqdisi was arrested by the Jordanian authorities on October 27 2014. While the FBI declined to comment on the arrest, one could speculate that the geopolitical implications of a reconciliation between IS and

124 Bellal and Casey-Maslen 2011a, p. 20.

125 Malik S, Younes A, Ackerman S and Khalili M (2014) The race to save Peter Kassig. http://www.theguardian.com/news/2014/dec/18/-sp-the-race-to-save-peter-kassig. Accessed 10 May 2016.

126 Ibid.

al-Qaeda in Syria was a price too high to pay for the liberation of the hostage. Peter Kassig was later executed in November.

Though this story ends tragically and speaks of a State-led initiative rather than a pure humanitarian one, it shows that engagement with radical Islamist armed groups for certain punctual issues is possible through influential Islamic scholars. Indeed, some of these scholars have expressed strong disagreement over the interpretation made by IS of Islamic law on armed conflict.[127] It remains to be seen how and if they can influence the group's behaviour, but it might have more impact than concerns expressed by the broader international community, which is seen by IS as being an occidental, and thereby not legitimate voice.

5.4.2.2 Engagement Through the Constituency of the Armed Group

Another way humanitarian organizations have addressed humanitarian issues in conflict situations where access to the groups is difficult for either ideological or security reasons is to engage the constituency of these groups.

Geneva Call, for instance, on the basis of discussions and assessments that started in 2011, aims at working in Afghanistan "with a local partner to help community leaders enhance the protection of their communities through dialogue with ANSA (armed non-state actor) commanders on humanitarian norms".[128] While direct access to the Taliban is possible and necessary, many aid agencies seem also to "prefer an approach based on 'community acceptance' as providing the greatest guarantee of security for aid workers and those aim to help".[129]

Working with individuals close to IS, or through local NGOs, has also been one of the solutions to deliver some aid to IS controlled area, which would demonstrate that "although IS's rhetoric is clearly anti-Western, it is less clear whether or to what degree it is opposed to humanitarian agencies or humanitarian work more generally".[130] Finally, for those organizations not delivering humanitarian aid per se, opportunities may exist for dialogue with the "Islamist groups repelled by the violent excesses of some jihadist, as illustrated with disillusioned, former allies of

---

[127] RT news (2014) 24 reasons ISIS are wrong: Muslim scholars blast Islamic State. https://www.rt.com/news/190468-muslim-scholars-islamic-state/. Accessed 10 May 2016.

[128] Geneva Call (2015) Annual Report 2014: Protecting Civilians in Armed Conflict. http://www.genevacall.org/wp-content/uploads/dlm_uploads/2015/05/2014-Geneva-Call-Annual-Report-Short-version.pdf. Accessed 13 June 2016.

[129] Jackson A and Gisutozzi A (2012) Talking to the other side: Humanitarian engagement with the Taliban in Afghanistan. https://www.odi.org/publications/6993-aid-conflict-humanitarian-engagement-policy-taliban-afghanistan. Accessed 10 May 2016. See also Jackson A and Ayte A (2013) Talking to the other side: Humanitarian negotiations with Al-Shabaab in Somalia. https://www.odi.org/publications/8053-humanitarian-negotiations-al-shabaab-somalia-armed-group. Accessed 10 May 2016.

[130] IRIN/HPG Crisis Brief (2014) Aid and the Islamic State. http://www.odi.org/publications/9133-iraq-isis-isil-aid-humanitarian. Accessed 10 May 2016.

al-Qaeda in Iraq that have helped to marginalize the extremists in Al Anbar province".[131]

5.5 Conclusion

In 2009, during his visit to Afghanistan, the Special Rapporteur on Extrajudicial, Summary or Arbitrary Executions, Philip Alston, regretted that he did not speak with any formal representatives of the Taliban. Recognizing the political and security obstacles to engaging directly with the Taliban, Alston emphasized that there was no reason to assume that "the Taliban could never be persuaded to modify its conduct in ways that would improve its respect for human rights".[132] The Special Rapporteur would undoubtedly take the same position today with IS as he did for the Taliban, which was regarded by then as one of the most dangerous NSAGs.

It is true that IS represents a formidable challenge for the international community, not only because it embodies perhaps the "changing face of modern Jihadism".[133] The amount of the financial resources it can collect as well as the strength of its media and propaganda strategy, being notably able to attract an important number of fighters to join the group, are among the main reasons hindering engagement by humanitarian organizations, primarily because there will be no incentives for the group to respect international norms or to receive humanitarian aid.

However, irrespective of its motivations and actions, IS, like any other similar groups, is not and should not be beyond the pale of humanitarian engagement. While sporadic engagement with IS has been done in the past, notably through influential scholars or local partners, it is perhaps too early to say whether such engagement will be possible on a more general and long-term basis. This will depend partly on the capacity of the group to establish itself as an entity capable to provide in the long run for the constituency it claims to protect and represent.

References

Badar M (2013) Ius in Bello under Islamic International Law. Int Crim Law Rev 13:593–625

Bangerter O (2010) Territorial gangs and their consequences for humanitarian players. Int Rev Red Cross 92:387–406

Bangerter O (2011) Reasons why armed groups choose to respect international humanitarian law or not. Int Rev Red Cross 93:353–384

[131] Wither 2009, p. 21.

[132] UN General Assembly (2009a, b) Human Rights Council: Promotion and Protection of All Human Rights, Civil, Political, Economic, Social and Cultural Rights, including the Right to Development—Report of the Special Rapporteur on extrajudicial, summary or arbitrary executions, Philip Alston, UN Doc. A/HRC/11/2/Add.4, para 42.

[133] As analysed by Saltman and Winter, above n 45.

Bellal A (2015) Armed Conflicts in Syria in 2014. In: Bellal A (ed) The War Report 2014. Oxford University Press, Oxford, pp 265–281
Bellal A, Casey-Maslen S (2011a) Rules of Engagement, Protecting Civilians through Dialogue with Armed Non-State Actors. Geneva Academy of International Humanitarian Law and Human Rights
Bellal A, Casey-Maslen S (2011b) Enhancing Compliance with International Law by Armed Non-State Actors. Goettingen J Int Law 3:175–197
Bellal A, Giacca G, Casey-Maslen S (2011) International law and armed non-state actors in Afghanistan. Int Rev Red Cross 93:47–79
Bongard P, Somer J (2011) Monitoring armed non-state actor compliance with humanitarian norms: a look at international mechanisms and the Geneva Call Deed of Commitment. Int Rev Red Cross 93:673–706
Clapham A (2006) Human rights obligations of non-state actors in conflict situations. Int Rev Red Cross 88:491–523
Cockayne J (2002) Islam and international humanitarian law: From a clash to a conversation between civilizations. Int Rev Red Cross 84:597–626
Coco A, Maillard J-P (2015) The conflict with Islamic State: A critical review of international legal issues. In: Bellal A (ed) The War Report 2014. Oxford University Press, Oxford, pp 388–419
Crawford J (1976) The criteria for statehood in international law. Br Yearb Int Law 48:93–182
Hausler K (2014) The protection of cultural property in armed conflict. In: Casey-Maslen S (ed) The War Report 2013. Oxford University Press, Oxford, pp 361–387
Hazen J (2010) Understanding gangs as armed groups. Int Rev Red Cross 92:369–386
Henckearts J-M, Doswald-Beck L (2005) Customary International Humanitarian Law, Vol I, Rules. Cambridge University Press, Cambridge
Hofmann C, Ulrich Schneckener U (2011) Engaging non-state armed actors in state- and peace-building: options and strategies. Int Rev Red Cross 93:1–19
Hosken A (2015) Empire of Fear, Inside the Islamic state. Oneworld publications, London
Kraehenmann S (2014) Academy Briefing No. 7: Foreign Fighters under international law. Geneva Academy of International Humanitarian Law and Human Rights, Geneva
March A, Modirzadeh N (2013) Ambivalent Universalism? Jus ad Bellum in Modern Islamic Legal Discourse. Eur J Int Law 24:367–389
Modirzadeh N, Lewis D, Bruderlein C (2011) Humanitarian engagement under counter-terrorism: a conflict of norms and the emerging policy landscape. Int Rev Red Cross 93:623–647
Moir L (2002) The Law of Internal Armed Conflict. Cambridge University Press, Cambridge
Munir M (2011) The Layha for the Mujahideen: an analysis of the code of conduct for the Taliban fighters under Islamic law. Int Rev Red Cross 93:81–102
Ould Mohamedou M (2015) The Islamic State: Origins, evolution and implications for the United Nations. In: Understanding a new generation of non-state armed groups. United Nations System Staff College, pp 53–59
Paulussen C, Entenmann E (2015) Addressing Europe's Foreign Fighter Issue: Legal Avenues at the International and National Level. Secur Hum Rights 25:86–118
Rodley N (1993) Can Armed Opposition Groups Violate Human Rights? In: Mahoney K, Mahoney P (eds) Human Rights in the Twenty-first Century. Martinus Nijhoff, Leiden, pp 297–318
Sandoz Y, Swinarski C, Zimmerman B (eds) (1987) Commentary on the Additional Protocols of 8 June 1977 to the Geneva Conventions of 12 August 1949. Martinus Nijhoff Publishers, The Netherlands
Sassòli M (2010) Taking Armed Groups Seriously: Ways to Improve their Compliance with International Humanitarian Law. Int Humanitarian Legal Stud 1:5–51
Schoiswohl M (2001) De facto regimes and human rights obligations—the twilight zone of public international law? Austrian Rev Int Eur Law 6:45–90

Shah N (2013) The Use of Force under Islamic Law. Eur J Int Law 24:343–365
Sivakumaran S (2012) The law of non-international armed conflict. Oxford University Press, Oxford
UN General Assembly (2008) Human Rights Council: Human Rights Situation in Palestine and Other Occupied Arab Territories. UN Doc. A/HRC/8/17
UN General Assembly (2009a) Human Rights Council: Human Rights Situation in Palestine and Other Occupied Arab Territories, UN Doc. A/HRC/12/37
UN General Assembly (2009b) Human Rights Council: Promotion and Protection of All Human Rights, Civil, Political, Economic, Social and Cultural Rights, including the Right to Development—Report of the Special Rapporteur on Extrajudicial, Summary or Arbitrary Executions. Philip Alston, UN Doc. A/HRC/11/2/Add.4
UN General Assembly (2011) Human Rights Council: Report of the International Commission of Inquiry to investigate all alleged violations of international human rights law in the Libyan Arab Jamahiriya. UN Doc. A/HRC/17/44
UN General Assembly (2012) Human Rights Council: Report of the Independent International Commission of Inquiry on the Syrian Arab Republic, UN Doc. A/HRC/19/69
UN General Assembly (2015) Human Rights Council: Report of the Office of the United Nations High Commissioner for Human Rights on the human rights situation in Iraq in light of abuses committed by the so-called Islamic State in Iraq and the Levant and associated groups. UN Doc. A/HRC/28/18
UN General Assembly (2016) One humanity: shared responsibility—Report of the Secretary-General for the World Humanitarian Summit. UN Doc. A/70/709
UN Security Council (2009) Report of the Secretary-General on the protection of civilians in armed conflict, UN Doc. S/2009/277
UN Security Council (2014) Resolution 2170 (2014). UN Doc. S/RES/2170 (2014)
Van Essen J (2012) De Facto regimes in international law. Utrecht J Int Eur Law 28:31–49
Wither J (2009) Selective Engagement with Islamist Terrorists: Exploring the Prospects. Stud Confl Terrorism 32:18–35
Zasova S (2010) L'applicabilité du droit international humanitaire aux groupes armés organisés. In: Sorel J, Popescu C (eds) La protection des personnes vulnérables en temps de conflits armés. Bruylant, Brussels, pp 47–85
Zegveld L (2002) The Accountability of Armed Opposition Groups in International Law. Cambridge University Press, Cambridge

Case Law

ICJ, *Case Concerning Military and Paramilitary Activities in and against Nicaragua (Nicaragua v United States of America)*, Judgment, 27 June 1986, [1986] ICJ Rep 14
Holder v Humanitarian Law Project (2010) 130 S. Ct. 2705
ICTR, *Prosecutor v Jean-Paul Akayesu*, Judgement, 2 September 1998, Case No. ICTR-96-4-T
SCSL, *Prosecutor v Morris Kallon* and *Brima Buzzy Kamara*, Decision on challenge to Jurisdiction: Lomé Accord Amnesty, 13 March 2004, Case Nos. SCSL-2004-15-AR72(E) and SCSL-2004-16- AR72(E)
ICTY, *Prosecutor v Ramush Haradinaj, Idriz Balaj and Lahi Brahimaj*, Judgment, 3 April 2008, Case No. IT-04-84-T
The *Arantzazu Mendi* case, House of Lords, Judgment of 23 February 1939, L.R., [1939] A.C. 256, reproduced in 1942 ILR 60

Treaties

Geneva Convention (I) for the Amelioration of the Condition of the Wounded and Sick in Armed Forces in the Field, opened for signature 12 August 1949, 75 UNTS 31 (entered into force 21 October 1950)

Geneva Convention (II) for the Amelioration of the Condition of Wounded, Sick and Shipwrecked Members of Armed Forces at Sea, opened for signature 12 August 1949, 75 UNTS 85 (entered into force 21 October 1950)

Geneva Convention (III) relative to the Treatment of Prisoners of War, opened for signature 12 August 1949, 75 UNTS 135 (entered into force 21 October 1950)

Geneva Convention (IV) relative to the Protection of Civilian Persons in Time of War, opened for signature on 12 August 1949, 75 UNTS 287 (entered into force 21 October 1950)

Montevideo Convention on the Rights and Duties of States, opened for signature 26 December 1933, 164 LNTS 19 (entered into force 26 December 1934)

Protocol Additional to the Geneva Conventions of 12 August 1949, and relating to the Protection of Victims of International Armed Conflicts, opened for signature 12 December 1977, 1125 UNTS 3 (entered into force 7 December 1979)

Protocol Additional to the Geneva Conventions of 12 August 1949, and relating to the Protection of Victims of Non-International Armed Conflicts, opened for signature 8 June 1977, 1125 UNTS 609 (entered into force 7 December 1978)

Chapter 6
Trapped: Three Dilemmas in the Law of Proportionality and Asymmetric Warfare

Elad David Gil

Abstract The efforts to regulate asymmetric warfare, a generic term used to describe military clashes between state and non-state armed actors, are an ongoing challenge. Asymmetric warfare aggravates the dangers threatening civilians in armed conflicts. It renders their homes and public areas part of the battlefield, and too often indigenous armed groups utilize their vulnerability as a strategic asset. By analyzing the principle of proportionality, a prominent Law of War precept aimed at limiting harm to civilians caught in the line of fire, this chapter explores a few of the substantial methodological errors that arise when IHL is applied to asymmetric war environments. This chapter diagnoses three interpretive "traps" that threaten to prevent the proper application of proportionality and provides recommendations geared at avoiding, or at least mitigating each "trap" and its effects. This chapter concludes that the complexities of asymmetric warfare require a conceptual shift to a structured model of proportionality in IHL.

Keywords Proportionality · Asymmetrical warfare · Asymmetric armed conflict · Targeting law · Military advantage · Collateral damage · Israel · Gaza · Additional protocol I

Contents

I am grateful to Madeline Morris, Michael Schmitt, Pnina Sharvit Baruch, and Steven Ratner as well as the participants of the Michigan Law School Young Scholars' Conference for their comments and helpful suggestions. My thanks also go to Professor Jeremy Mullem for helpful advice and assistance.

E.D. Gil (✉)
Duke Law School, 210 Science Dr., Durham, NC 27708, USA
e-mail: elad.gil@duke.edu

T.D. Gill et al. (eds.), *Yearbook of International Humanitarian Law 2015*,
Yearbook of International Humanitarian Law 18,
DOI 10.1007/978-94-6265-141-8_6

6.1 Introduction

Despite the frequent eruption of asymmetrical wars in the recent years and the international legal attention they draw, it seems that the efforts to effectively regulate this form of warfare are failing. The 2014 conflict in the Gaza Strip between Israel and Palestinian armed groups, the third in six years, is illustrative of this point. This paradigmatic asymmetric armed conflict involved a superpower state employing its military might against a vastly outgunned enemy that, in an effort to compensate for this resource disparity, practiced unlawful methods of warfare directed primarily against civilians on both sides.

This chapter seeks to inquire into some of the methodological errors of international legal actors, as well as other participants in the international legal discourse, have made when applying international humanitarian law (IHL) to an asymmetric war environment. I identify these errors by examining how the principle of proportionality is applied in such conflicts.[1] Asymmetric warfare features unique challenges to the application of proportionality, while simultaneously requiring its application to virtually every instance of attack. In an age when hostilities have moved from remote frontlines to urban areas, incidental civilian loss remains a constant possibility—and commanders must undertake a proportionality assessment prior to every attack. In view of both its prominent role and the difficulty of its application, focusing on proportionality will, I expect, uncover vital insights into asymmetrical warfare and how it might be better regulated.

This chapter diagnoses three interpretive "traps" that threaten proportionality's purpose and efficacy in asymmetric armed conflicts. The "asymmetric effects"

[1] The principle of *in bello* proportionality prohibits attacks "which may be expected to cause incidental loss of civilian life, injury to civilians, damage to civilian objects, or a combination thereof, which would be excessive in relation to the concrete and direct military advantage anticipated." Articles 51(5)(b), 35(2), and 57(2)(a)(ii–iii) of Protocol Additional to the Geneva Conventions of 12 August 1949, and relating to the Protection of Victims of International Armed Conflicts, opened for signature 12 December 1977, 1125 UNTS 3 (entered into force 7 December 1979) (Additional Protocol 1). The norms incorporating the principle of proportionality in the context of rules of targeting discussed in this chapter are generally accepted as customary law applicable in both international and non-international armed conflict. See Henckaerts and Doswald-Beck 2009, rules 14, 15, 17, 18, 19, and 21. See also Schmitt and Widmar 2014 (arguing that the law of targeting is generally accepted as customary law applicable both in international and non-international armed conflicts).

trap, which I discuss in Sect. 6.3, describes a practice in which fatality rates and the destruction of private property are inappropriately used to heuristically determine disproportionality. In Sect. 6.4, I analyze the "formalist approach" trap. A formalist view on proportionality fails to consider the ways in which asymmetric warfare affects the balancing formula, specifically by incentivizing warfare techniques that deliberately endanger civilians. Finally, Sect. 6.5 discusses the "absolutist" trap, in which parties rely on proportionality as a categorical moral standard that should either shield civilians completely from the effects of war (from one point of view) or legitimizes attacks regardless of the risks to civilians (from another). The analysis is preceded by a brief introduction in Sect. 6.2 that outlines the characteristics of asymmetric warfare and the centrality of proportionality to the protection of civilians in asymmetric conflicts.

Of the three, I consider the third trap to be the most serious. While the "asymmetric effects" trap can easily be avoided with a proper invocation of the norm and the "formalist approach" trap can be mitigated by paying more attention to party incentives, the "absolutist" trap presents a real puzzle: The overly rigid proportionality test can embody both utopian and overly apologetic interpretations, and is particularly inadequate to counter legal manipulations effected in the fog of war. Addressing this problem will require a shift into a structured model of proportionality assessment—a doctrine widely accepted in modern constitutional jurisprudence as well as in other fields of international law.

The increase in military engagements with non-traditional actors employing unlawful warfare methodologies necessitates this shift. The current *in bello* proportionality assessment in IHL is a narrow and open-handed balancing test known as proportionality *stricto sensu*, which is only one of three sub-tests that together form the proportionality analysis prescribed by the comprehensive proportionality doctrine. Performing a structured proportionality analysis by reconfiguring already generally applicable norms will better tailor the standard to the complexities of asymmetric warfare; it will also ultimately provide a more nuanced and competent approach to the task of protecting civilians in the line of fire.

6.2 The Operation of Proportionality in Asymmetric War Environment

6.2.1 Regulating Asymmetric Conflicts

The increasing number of asymmetric conflicts in the recent years has drawn the attention of legal scholarship to the complexities involved with squaring the unique features of asymmetric warfare into the traditional system of the laws of war.[2] In this section, my purpose is to briefly summarize the characteristics of asymmetrical warfare that have set it apart from conventional warfare. That exercise will provide

---

[2] See generally, Schmitt 2008, pp. 2–7; Geiß and Siegris 2011, pp. 17–19; Pfanner 2005, p. 152; Wenger and Mason 2008, pp. 837–840.

the background necessary to understand and evaluate the response of the belligerent parties (specifically the non-state actor) to the manner in which the law is applied.

The principal feature of asymmetric warfare, and its primary point of contention with known legal paradigms of armed conflicts, resides in the identity of the warring parties; asymmetrical wars are waged by actors that had (and still have) no voice in shaping the rules under which wars are fought.[3] These actors use new weapons and new tactics,[4] and they seek different goals, respond to different incentives, and most often reject the Western-minded scheme of the current legal framework.[5] These actors are not nation states' regular militaries but rather non-state armed groups who gained enough power—political, military, or both—to challenge states by waging cross-borders hostilities against them.[6] The asymmetry between the warring parties does not end in their sovereign status (or lack thereof). Asymmetry is often invoked to describe the imbalance of military power between the parties, the different means and methods they employ to pursue their goals, and their acceptance or rejection of the laws of war as a binding legal regime.[7] Furthermore, asymmetric conflicts are characterized by asymmetric effects. The state actor's military edge enables it to dictate the intensity of hostilities, to hit harder than its opponent, and to push the combat zone away from its own territory toward the territory under the control of the non-state actor or its sponsor, thus putting the burden of the war mostly on the civilian population reside in that territory.

Somewhat less discussed but yet highly influential on the conduct of hostilities are *strategic-political asymmetries*. Due to its military deficiency, the non-state actor does not strive, de facto, to subdue its opponent on the battlefield, but rather to gain other political achievements from prolonging the hostilities and inflicting growing costs on the state's military and civilian population.[8] Contrary to the

---

[3] See Mohamedou 2007, pp. 21–25.

[4] Williamson 2010, pp. 459–460.

[5] McCready 2006, p. 470.

[6] Benvenisti 2010, pp. 339–342; Program on Humanitarian Policy and Conflict Research Harvard University (2006) Transnationality, war and the law: A report on a Roundtable on the Transformation of Warfare, International Law, and the Role of Transnational Armed Groups. http://hhi.harvard.edu/publications/transnationality-war-and-law-roundtable-report. Accessed 13 June 2016, pp. 4–7.

[7] For a broad analysis of the different forms of asymmetry in warfare see Schmitt 2008.

[8] For example, in what that has become known as the "Spider Web Speech" delivered in 2000 at the Lebanese town Bint Jbeil, Hezbollah leader Hassan Nasrallah pleaded before his crowd: "Our brothers and beloved Palestinians, I tell you: "Israel," which owns nuclear weapons and the strongest war aircraft in the region, is feebler than a spider's web—I swear to God." The Spider Web doctrine asserts that while Israel, as other forces of the West, possesses military superiority, its affluent society is weak, scared, and unwilling to make necessary sacrifices and lacks national resilience. Persistent, prolonged, and ongoing violence are strategic objectives of warfare and necessary components of a successful military campaign against a militarily superior state. Nasrallah elucidated it expressly, hoping to transit his perceived success to others: "Hence, we offer this noble Lebanese model to our people in Palestine. To free your land, you don't need tanks, a strategic balance, rockets, and cannons; you need to follow the way of the past self-sacrifice martyrs who disrupted and horrified the coercive Zionist entity." Nasrallah H (2000) Speech delivered on the Resistance and Liberation Day. http://breakingthespidersweb.blogspot.com/2011/05/nasrallahs-spider-web-speech.html. Accessed 13 June 2016.

conventional goal of warfighting, namely to win the war by a swift elimination of the enemy's armed forces, non-state armed groups' typical objective was to gain political leverage by prolonging the conflict and capitalizing on civilian suffering.

This objective lends itself to the military goals non-state armed groups pursue and dictates the means and methods of warfare they often employ. Belligerents who practice this type of asymmetric warfare discern basic concepts of war unlike their foes. "Military advantage," for example, is obtained chiefly from deliberate attacks on civilians and by spreading terror, notions completely antithetical to traditional military dogmas and laws of war. Another illustration is the capture of enemy's soldiers. Conventional military wisdom credits very limited military advantage to capturing of prisoners of war, which boils down to the removal of the prisoner's contribution to the fighting effort of the enemy. For the non-state armed groups, however, capturing even a single soldier amounts to a strategic military gain,[9] a gain that is designed to be utilized for other purposes, such as demonstration of force for uplifting its own troops and prospected recruits, demoralization of the adversary, eroding public support necessary to sustain military operation,[10] the use of captures as bargaining pawns, and so forth. Asymmetric warfare, therefore, is intended to strike differently than conventional warfare. Accordingly, opposing it possibly merits some grappling with the ways to prevent the adversary from attaining his goals.

The prevalent operation of various forms of asymmetry has complicated the invocation of IHL in contemporary conflicts. Asymmetric warfare has aggravated the risks and dangers incurred by civilians in armed conflicts. It has made their homes and public areas parts of the battlefield, and used their vulnerability to gain strategic advantages. Against this backdrop, proportionality has become a central tool in the effort to mitigate the effects of hostilities on civilians in asymmetric conflicts.

6.2.2 Proportionality Assumes a Vital Role in Asymmetric Conflicts

Proportionality considerations arise only when warfare takes place in vicinity of civilians and civilian objectives. Insofar as a military objective is identified and the

---

[9] Schmitt and Merriam 2015, pp. 129–130.

[10] As Charles Dunlap observes, asymmetrical warfare resorts to methods that seek to reduce the public support necessary to sustain the military effort. Dunlap illustrates this point with two examples. One, a remark by former North Vietnamese commander, saying "the conscience of America was part of its war-making capability, and we were turning that power in our favor. America lost because of its democracy; through dissent and protest it lost the ability to mobilize a will to win." Second, Dunlap notes the 1993 incident known as the battle of Mogadishu, demonstrating that "by dragging the body of a U.S. soldier through the streets of Mogadishu, the Somalis were able to destroy the public support upon which the United States and other Western democracies depend upon to sustain military operations." Dunlap 1998, p. 7.

military commander, acting reasonably and in good faith, concludes that there are no civilians in peril, balancing is not required by law.[11] Unfortunately, such "clean cases" are practically nowhere to be found in contemporary conflicts. The application of proportionality has become intricate because asymmetrical warfare had made it both paramount and almost unmanageable.

The main feature to account in that regard is the fighting terrain. Routinely, forces engage in close combat within densely populated urban areas in which: places of worship turn into weapon facilities; civilians are used as human shields to protect arms and militants; and rockets are launched from the protected civilian properties. The prevalence of such instances dictates a war environment in which proportionality considerations are an inherent feature.[12]

Bringing hostilities into the proximity of urban areas is obviously not a coincidental feature of asymmetric warfare, but rather a fighting philosophy designed to mitigate the military advantages of the adversary and optimize the gains of irregular methods of warfare resorted to by non-state belligerents. These methods seek to "make up" for an unbridgeable military disparity by making civilians, on both sides where feasible, an integral part of the combat.[13] For example, practicing warfare from within densely populated urban areas often entails an aggravated risk to the civilian population belonging to the attacker. Frequent use of human shields and deliberate blending within the civilian population are other examples of the aggravated risk constantly posed to civilians populating the territory from which the non-state belligerent acts. Asymmetric warfare further implicates civilians of the belligerent state, who may be turned into a strategic target for attacks and abductions. In summation, a battlefield in which one party deliberately and regularly draws civilians into the line of fire makes the task of minimizing collateral damage extremely difficult to manage. Proportionality, then, faces the danger of becoming apologetic, utopian, or both.

Conducting attacks in an asymmetric war environment poses three "traps" that threaten proportionality's purpose and efficacy: The "asymmetric effects" trap

---

[11] Article 51(5) of Additional Protocol 1, above n 1, constitutes the recent codification of *in bello* proportionality. The provision defines attacks as indiscriminate and thus forbids "an attack which may be expected to cause incidental loss of civilian life, injury to civilians, damage to civilian objects, or a combination thereof, which would be *excessive in relation to the concrete and direct military advantage anticipated.*" The Protocol's repetition of that formulation in two additional provisions prescribing precautions in attack suggests that proportionality governs various phases of a decision to plan and launch an attack, from the initial target selection process, choice of means and methods of attack, the decision to employ the attack itself, and the conduct throughout an ongoing attack. Belligerents must refrain from attacks that fail to maintain a proportionate relation between "*the concrete and direct military advantage anticipated*" and the expected "*incidental loss of civilian life, injury to civilians,* [or] *damage to civilian objects.*"

[12] Geiß and Siegris 2011, p. 29 ("In view of the blurred lines of distinction in asymmetric armed conflicts, carefully assessing the proportionality of an attack is ever more important and often ever more difficult").

[13] Ibid., p. 19 ("The constant evasion of direct military confrontation, the deliberate shifting of hostilities from one location to another, the adoption of population-centric approaches—all strategies frequently bringing hostilities into the proximity of urban and civilian surroundings—all aggravate the distinction between those who fight and protected civilians").

describes a practice in which fatality rates and the destruction of private property are inappropriately used to heuristically determine disproportionality; the "formalist approach" trap refers to a view on proportionality that fails to consider the ways in which asymmetric warfare affects the balancing formula, specifically by incentivizing guerrilla techniques that deliberately endanger civilians; and the "absolutist" trap by which parties rely on proportionality as a categorical moral standard that should either shield civilians completely from the effects of war (from one point of view) or legitimizes attacks regardless of the risks to civilians (from another). The analysis draws on the 2014 Gaza conflict (also known as Operation Protective Edge) and its aftermath to illustrate each trap and its effects. The outbreak of violence between Israel- and Palestinian-organized armed groups in 2014 was a paradigmatic illustration of an asymmetric armed conflict of one type, i.e., when the non-state party has effective control over a territory. Most contemporary asymmetric conflicts take place in similar settings, and thus, the Gaza conflict makes an effective test case for analysis.[14]

Proportionality lies at the heart of the fray over the Gaza conflict. Israel maintained to have integrated "the rule of proportionality [as] an operational mandate for its forces" throughout their conduct of operation.[15] In a recent examination of Israeli targeting policies, Michael Schmitt and John Merriam confirmed that the Israeli targeting procedures exert "capabilities [that] undeniably enhance the accuracy of likely military advantage and collateral damage estimations during the targeting process."[16] Other military experts who appraised the Israel Defense Force's (IDF) targeting decisions in the course of hostilities found they "went beyond the required legal principles of proportionality."[17] Against those who sided with the Israeli contention of adherence to the applicable law, human rights monitoring bodies assent to claims that Israel committed serious violations of the rule of proportionality.[18] Furthermore, the UN Human Rights Council's Independent Commission of Inquiry

[14] For factual background of the hostilities, see Human Rights Council (2015) Report of the detailed findings of the independent commission of inquiry established pursuant to Human Rights council resolution S-21/1, UN Doc. A/HRC/29/CRP.4 http://www.ohchr.org/EN/HRBodies/HRC/CoIGazaConflict/Pages/ReportCoIGaza.aspx#report. Accessed 2 June 2016 (McGowan-Davis Report), paras 53–58; State of Israel (2015) The 2014 Gaza Conflict 7 July–26 August 2014: Factual and Legal Aspects. http://mfa.gov.il/ProtectiveEdge/Documents/2014GazaConflictFullReport.pdf. Accessed 2 June 2016 (Israel's Gaza Conflict Report), pp. 9–57.

[15] Israel's Gaza Conflict Report, above n 14, p. 181.

[16] Schmitt and Merriam 2015, p. 126.

[17] See, e.g., High Level International Military Group (2015) The Gaza Conflict in 2014. http://blog.unwatch.org/wp-content/uploads/HLIMG-report-cover-letter-to-Judge-Mary-McGowan-Davis-UNHRC-31-May-2015.pdf. Accessed 2 June 2016 (The report issued was by a panel of retired military and diplomatic officials from NATO countries who visited Israel for a fact finding mission in 2015. The report concluded that "Israel not only met a reasonable international standard of observance of the laws of armed conflict, but in many cases significantly exceeded that standard").

[18] See, e.g., Amnesty International (2014) Families under the Rubble: Israeli Attacks on inhabited homes. https://www.amnesty.org/en/documents/MDE15/032/2014/en/. Accessed 2 June 2016; B'Tselem (2015) Black Flag: the Legal and Moral Implications of the Policy of Attacking Residential Buildings in the Gaza Strip, Summer 2014. http://www.btselem.org/publications/summaries/201501_black_flag. Accessed 2 June 2016.

report (the McGowan-Davis Report) noted several occasions in which it found "strong indications that [the] attacks could be disproportionate, and therefore amount to a war crime," while concluding in none of the instances examined that the civilian damage was proportionate.[19] The debate over the war in Gaza includes, undoubtedly, some partisan and political agendas. But it also illuminates valid legal questions and the effects of the three traps discussed in this article.

6.3 The "Asymmetric Effects" Trap

Ascribing civilian death or injury to unlawful behavior is as intuitive as it is tempting. It is also very wrong when dealing with *in bello* proportionality. Political bodies and other observers fell into this trap when hostilities in Gaza escalated rapidly last summer. In a special session held during the hostilities and facing with reports on growing numbers of civilian casualties, the UN Human Rights Council found the Israeli attacks in Gaza to be "disproportionate."[20] Days later, the UN Deputy Secretary-General said that it is plain to see that Israel's use of force has been disproportionate and that the Palestinian casualties have been excessive.[21] Governments, NGOs, and others have made similar statements in the wake of the Gaza conflict.[22] Some of these remarks could be understood alternatively as addressing *ad bellum* proportionality concerns (that is the obligation to exert the right of self-defense by resorting to proportionate force). Note, however, that *ad*

---

[19] Human Rights Council (2015) Report of the detailed findings of the independent commission of inquiry established pursuant to Human Rights council resolution S-21/1, UN Doc. A/HRC/29/CRP.4. http://www.ohchr.org/EN/HRBodies/HRC/CoIGazaConflict/Pages/ReportCoIGaza.aspx#report. Accessed 2 June 2016, para 221.

[20] Human Rights Council (2014) UN Human Rights Council Res. S-21/1 Ensuring respect for international law in the Occupied Palestinian Territory, including East Jerusalem, 21 Special Sess., Jul. 23, 2014, UN Doc. A/HRC/RES/S-21/1 http://www.ohchr.org/EN/HRBodies/HRC/SpecialSessions/Session21/Pages/21stSpecialSession.aspx. Accessed 2 June 2016.

[21] Hiatt A (2014) UN says Israel's use of force against Hamas is disproportionate. http://www.jpost.com/Middle-East/UN-says-Israels-use-of-force-against-Hamas-is-disproportionate-369503. Accessed 2 June 2016.

[22] Philip Luther, director of the Middle East and North Africa Program at Amnesty International, was quoted saying that "the repeated, disproportionate attacks on homes indicate that Israel's current military tactics are deeply flawed and fundamentally at odds with the principles of international humanitarian law." See Amnesty International (2014) Israeli forces displayed "callous indifference" in deadly attacks on family homes in Gaza. http://www.amnesty.org/en/news/israeli-forces-displayed-callous-indifference-deadly-attacks-family-homes-gaza-2014-11-05. Accessed 2 June 2016. Brazil recalled its Ambassador in Israel in light of Israel's "disproportionate" use of force in Gaza. The Brazilian Government issued a statement saying "The Brazilian government considers unacceptable escalation of violence between Israel and Palestine. We strongly condemn the disproportionate use of force by Israel in the Gaza Strip, from which large numbers of civilian casualties, including women and children resulted." Ravid B (2014) Brazil recalls Israel envoy to protest "disproportionate force" in Gaza. http://www.haaretz.com/news/diplomacy-defense/1.606979. Accessed 2 June 2016.

bellum proportionality does not mandate a proportionate ratio between civilian victims by both parties, but rather concerns the relation between the level of force exercised by the defending power and its overall legitimate objective. As on the *in bello* level, *ad bellum* proportionality does not establish liability-based solely on civilian harm.

The Commission of Inquiry on the Gaza Conflict was apparently aware of this slippery slope and noted at the outset of its analysis:

> the death of civilians during an armed conflict, no matter how grave and regrettable, does not in itself constitute a war crime. [IHL] and the Rome Statute permit belligerents to carry out proportionate attacks against military objectives, even when it is known that some civilian deaths or injuries will occur.[23]

Indeed, a disparity in civilian fatality rates, or the *asymmetric effects of a conflict* as termed previously, can serve neither as the sole evidence nor the decisive proof of the disproportionate use of force when isolated from the context of an attack and its military objectives.[24] Indeed, the lack of success by the non-state actor's attacks to cause substantial civilian damage may render the counter-attack's military advantage to be rather limited—and, thus, indirectly may affect the proportionality test. But nevertheless, death figures cannot substitute for comprehensive legal analysis weighing the anticipated military advantage against the expected civilian injury.[25] Something can never be proportionate, or disproportionate, to nothing. The equation prescribed by law does not compare the numbers of civilian victims on both sides, but rather weighs expected civilian loss against the military advantage anticipated. Laurie Blank rightly asserted that "effects-based analysis—that is, using the numbers of casualties and extent of destruction to make legal claims—is simply incorrect."[26]

The commission's task in that regard was virtually impossible due to the Israeli refusal to cooperate with the investigation and to grant access to Gaza, yet

---

[23] McGowan-Davis Report, above n 14, para 21.

[24] See NATO (2000) Final Report to the Prosecutor by the Committee Established to Review the NATO Bombing Campaign against the Federal Republic of Yugoslavia. http://www.icty.org/x/file/Press/nato061300.pdf. Accessed 2 June 2016, para 51. See also, Schmitt 2005, p. 456 (arguing that the principle of proportionality is often misapplied, *inter alia*, when "the mere quantum of collateral damage and incidental injury causes critics to condemn a strike as disproportionate").

[25] Assertions of disproportionality that rely merely on civilian casualty figures gathered in retrospect are at odds with international jurisprudence. In *Prosecutor v Blaškić*, the ICTY Appeals Chamber vacated conviction of a commander in the "Croatian Defense Council" concerning attacks carried on in the Bosnian town of Vitez, resulting in a substantial number of civilian casualties. The Appeals Chamber held that "civilian casualty figures in connection with the 16 April 1993 attack cannot be relied on in determining the nature of that attack." ICTY, *Prosecutor v Tihomir Blaškić*, Judgement, 29 July 2004, Case No. IT-95-14-A, paras 429–441.

[26] Blank L (2014) Asymmetries and proportionalities. http://thehill.com/blogs/pundits-blog/international/213546-asymmetries-and-proportionalities. Accessed 2 June 2016.

difficulties in analysis cannot justify flawed application of the law. As the reader plunges deep into the report, partial findings and cautious terminology turn into allegations of unlawfulness.[27] For example, in discussing the July 19 incident in Shuja'iya, for which the committee had no insight into the IDF's objectives or available information in real time, the report states:

> the fact that the attack was allowed to continue under these conditions evidences the commander's failure to comply with his obligation to do everything feasible to suspend an attack if it becomes apparent that it does not conform to the principle of proportionality.

In its concluding observations, the commission calls Israel to "break with its recent lamentable track record in holding wrongdoers accountable."

Evidently, the McGowan-Davis Report failed to meet its own standard of inquiry, despite the self-warning it did make allegations of possible war crimes (including violations of the principle of proportionality) without having access to the military advantage pursued by the IDF and without knowledge of the information possessed in real time by the military commanders. Its efforts to make up for the missing pieces were insufficient. For instance, the report makes use of an Israeli statement that "the IDF abandoned air strikes when the presence of civilians was detected" to conclude that "the IDF had the capacity to determine the civilian nature" of the vast majority of people around designated targets.[28] Such a deduction process implies the competence of the military commanders to accurately estimate civilian damage in each of the examined incidents, but has no merits. Furthermore, in assessing fifteen incidents of airstrikes that resulted in civilian casualties, the report found indications of possible military objectives in 9 cases and based its proportionality assessment on these findings.[29] But when the Israeli commanders who initiated the attacks are silent, when the commission is completely ignorant of the nature and use of each target, and when it cannot verify which of the casualties was a lawful target of attack, any attempt to determine the military advantage is merely speculation. The conclusions laid down in the report imply that the committee did fall into the trap. The effects of the fighting shaped its legal analysis despite its lack of key information to make conscious determinations.

---

[27] Wittes B and Schwartz Y (2015) What to Make of the UN's Special Commission Report on Gaza? http://www.lawfareblog.com/what-make-uns-special-commission-report-gaza. Accessed 2 June 2016 ("There's a bit of CYA work on the commission's part, mostly linguistic, to protect against this sort of criticism. The commission never specifically finds any incident a war crime. But the veil is thin and the modesty cosmetic. Despite the frequent appearance of hedging phrases like 'there are strong indications that' or that conduct 'may amount to war crimes', the report is in the business of drawing conclusions").

[28] McGowan-Davis Report, above n 14, para 230.

[29] Ibid., paras 219–221.

6.4 The "Formalist Approach" Trap

Asymmetric warfare features a different set of incentives and goals that shape the parties' conduct.[30] The formalist approach views proportionality as a mechanistic formula, or a game of numbers between fixed gains and losses. Formalism fails then, because it applies a rigid conventional war formula on settings that require interpretive adjustments to the realities of war.

6.4.1 Military Advantage and Asymmetric Warfare

In conventional warfare, attacks are generally motivated by the goal of impairing the adversary's ability to fight.[31] Elimination of a command post, for example, diminishes the ability of the enemy's forces to coordinate their operations and thus renders them less effective. Calculation of the anticipated military advantage is mostly determined then by its contribution to the goal of impairing the enemy's military force. Asymmetric fighting requires states to engage in a more nuanced calculation of "military advantage," one that is tailored to the *modus operandi* of the enemy and the different gains it seeks to attain in combat.

The first example to consider is the protection of civilians and prevention of terror among them as an *in bello* concern. Throughout Operation Protective Edge, Israel conducted a substantial volume of strikes against armed rocket launchers, shortly before they were about to fire rockets aimed at Israeli communities. Rocket launchers clearly qualify as military objectives, and therefore, their destruction can be justified under a narrow definition of military advantage. However, a closer look reveals that attacks of that kind are motivated primarily by the purpose of removing a threat, sometimes imminent, to civilian life.[32] It was not their contribution to the elimination of Hamas's military potential that defines their value but rather the humanitarian benefit of defending the civilian population in Israel from indiscriminate shelling. This example captures a much broader observation concerning asymmetric warfare: When the adversary systematically directs its military force against civilians, the defending power's response is aimed directly and primarily to protect the impaired civilian population and to prevent (or reduce) their terrorization. Calculation of the military advantage sought should consider the real motivation rather than be confined merely to the potential of weakening the enemy. Such a calculation closely links the conduct of hostilities and the goal of protecting

30 Benvenisti 2010, p. 4.

31 Declaration Renouncing the Use, in Time of War, of Explosive Projectiles under 400 Grammes Weight, opened for signature 11 December 1868, 1 AJILs 95 (entry into force 11 December 1868) (Saint Petersburg Declaration) (stating that "the only legitimate object which States should endeavour to accomplish during war is to weaken the military forces of the enemy").

32 See Rubinstein and Roznai 2011, p. 125 (advocating for adjusted application of proportionality when the attack is attained to remove an imminent threat).

civilians, a notion that is generally not considered in conventional conflicts on a tactical level (the level in which *in bello* proportionality operates). The conventional *in bello* framework concerns the relationship between the targeted military objective and the goal of diminishing the military potential of the enemy. It ignores the protection of civilians, which is less frequently required in conventional conflicts, as a tactical factor.[33] But asymmetric warfare summons that consideration on the tactical level of the conflict, thus making it an *in bello* consideration encompassed by "military advantage."[34] While attacks motivated by the protection of civilians have a rather moderate impact on the military strength of the adversary, they have a potential of paralyzing a strategic goal of the non-state actor's war doctrine, which seeks to maximize civilian casualties and to spread terror among them for the attainment of strategic achievements. These advantages should be calculated in the assessment of the direct anticipated military advantage of an attack.

Another illustration of the contextual nature of "military advantage" concerns the advantage gained from thwarting the capture of soldiers and civilians by the enemy. Abduction is evidently a practice that holds substantial military gain for non-state belligerents.[35] Reportedly, Hamas operates a specialized force called "Nuhba" which is dedicated to the sole purpose of kidnapping Israelis.[36] The IDF exerts special procedures, known as the "Hannibal Directive," to foil kidnapping attempts.[37] While the precise content of the directive is classified, it essentially "relaxes the rules of engagement" for forces engaged in frustrating kidnapping attempts,[38] possibly allowing them to employ means that may impose a greater risk on the hostage. Such risk is rationalized by the greater military advantage they have in asymmetric warfare than in conventional warfare. As Schmitt explains:

> foiling a capture is fairly considered by the IDF to be militarily advantageous and is appropriately factored into the proportionality analysis, not just in terms of securing the safety of the soldier concerned, but also with respect to denying the enemy an important military aim.[39]

The point here is not to argue that this specific directive is lawful, but rather to underscore how the military advantage sought in an asymmetric war is contextual and differs from an equivalent attack made in a conventional war.[40]

---

[33] Consideration of that kind is traditionally featured on the *jus ad bellum* level.

[34] See Rubinstein and Roznai 2011, pp. 123–126 (arguing that "[a] practice which would impair the right to individual self-defense might eventually impair the inherent rights of states to self-defense [on the *jus ad bellum* level]").

[35] See e.g., Schmitt and Merriam 2015, p. 46; Israel's Gaza Conflict Report, above n 14, p. 45.

[36] Israel's Gaza Conflict Report, above n 14, p. 45.

[37] Ibid., pp. 186–187.

[38] Schmitt and Merriam 2015, pp. 45–46.

[39] Schmitt M (2015) The Relationship between Context and Proportionality: A Reply to Cohen and Shany. https://www.justsecurity.org/22948/response-cohen-shany/. Accessed 2 June 2016.

[40] For a critical analysis of such contextual proportionality analysis see Cohen A and Shany Y (2015) Contextualizing Proportionality Analysis? A Response to Schmitt and Merriam on Israel's Targeting Practices. https://www.justsecurity.org/22786/contextualizing-proportionality-analysis-response-schmitt-merriam/. Accessed 13 June 2016.

A formalist approach to proportionality construes military advantage narrowly based solely on the attack's impact on the military potential of the enemy. It fails to give appropriate weight to the dominant motivation of attacks that aim to protect civilians from deliberate attacks or to prevent other strategic goals of asymmetric belligerency. Inevitably, formalism fails to properly measure the real "concrete and direct" military advantage that stems from potentially many attacks that occur in asymmetric conflicts. Attacks targeting rocket launchers or a single suicide bomber have a rather limited military advantage in terms of their impairment of the adversary's military potential. Their value lies in their humanitarian capacity and their potential to deprive the enemy from terrorizing civilians.[41] When the military and political goals of the adversary are to make civilians part of the combat, the calculation of "military advantage" should therefore correspond with the potential of attacks to foil these goals.[42]

The potential measurement of military advantage in the "currency" of civilian lives saved does bring to the analysis some new ethical misgivings. Consider a hypothetical strike against an armed rocket launcher that can prevent the expected killing of two civilians but anticipates collateral damage of three civilian casualties. When the anticipated military advantage of striking a target is termed in the protection of civilian life on the attacker's side, then perhaps the most difficult exercise in the business of *in bello* proportionality—factoring military gain against civilian injury—is arguably unraveled. In such instances, proportionality assessment will require calculation of civilian lives protected/endangered against each other and raise the question of what proportion would be morally and legally tenable. Attacks of this order virtually shift the burden of risks of war from one's own civilians to the civilian population occupying the enemy's territory. IHL generally forbids shifting of risk from combatants to civilians,[43] but encompasses far fewer guidelines on the liberty of states to prefer their own civilians over civilians on the other side, especially in settings when their enemy shows concern to none of them. Whatever targeting policies will emerge in future conflicts, factoring protection of civilian life as a "military advantage" element possesses novel ethical questions for states to answer.

---

[41] We should bear in mind that the instant civilian life-saving expectancy of such attacks might be modest, due to inaccuracy of the rockets fired at civilians, operation of defensive measures (e.g., Iron Dome), and other uncertainties. However, one ought to give weight to the overall destructive effect that deliberate and continuing targeting of civilians has in calculating the military advantage achieved from acting against them.

[42] See Rubinstein and Roznai 2011, p. 126.

[43] See *Adalah—The Legal Center for Arab Minority Rights in Israel* et al. *v GOC Central Command* et al., HCJ 3799/02, (2005) IDF 60(3) PD 67 (Isr.) (English version available at http://elyon1.court.gov.il/Files_ENG/02/990/037/A32/02037990.a32.htm) (finding the IDF's "Early Warning" procedure, by which Israeli soldiers wishing to arrest a Palestinian suspected of terrorist activity may be aided by a local Palestinian resident, "at odds" with international law). See further, Margalit and Walzer 2009 ("This is what each side should say to its soldiers: By wearing a uniform, you take on yourself a risk that is borne only by those who have been trained to injure others (and to protect themselves). You should not shift this risk onto those who haven't been trained, who lack the capacity to injure; whether they are brothers or others").

6.4.2 "Excessive" Collateral Damage

The perception of what is considered "excessive" (damage to civilians) may require adjustment when certain asymmetries operate. In an asymmetric warfare environment, when one party regularly resorts to methods of warfare that intentionally place civilians at risk, civilian suffering on both sides will be greater than otherwise. This is mainly because a "rational" law violating non-state actor potentially gains benefits from using civilians as human shields, placing military apparatus in places that enjoy special protection and other law-violating practices. In a formalistic proportionality assessment, which is essentially a mechanistic balancing formula, one's decision to place an increasing number of civilians in harm's way generates better protection of its military interests. So in effect, a formalist application of proportionality—while seeking to impose strict limitations on conduct that endangers civilians—incentivizes the systematic manipulation of the norm and erodes its potential for minimizing civilian suffering.

Hamas's conduct of hostilities in the recent conflict illustrates how well aware non-state actors are of the benefits that can be generated by endangering their own civilians. During the fighting in Gaza, Israeli forces obtained what was apparently Hamas Manuals on Urban Warfare.[44] The manuals delineate the benefits of maintaining a civilian presence on the battlefield (which it refers to as "pockets of resistance") and of the destruction of civilian property of Palestinians. One manual states that the destruction of civilian homes "increases the hatred of the citizens toward the attackers [the IDF] and increases their gathering [support] around the city defenders (resistance forces [i.e., Hamas])."[45] Another manual instructs militants to lay ambushes in residential areas rather than in open areas.[46] In the same vein, in response to Israel's policy of delivering warnings to civilians before bombing targets located near residential areas, Hamas's Ministry of Interior urged civilians to not comply with the warnings and remain in their homes.[47] Hamas's spokesperson reaffirmed this policy, saying "the fact that people are willing to sacrifice themselves against Israeli warplanes in order to protect their homes, I believe this strategy is proving itself, and we Hamas, call on our people to adopt this practice."[48]

These examples demonstrate an intentional abuse of the legal norm. A war practice that systematically sacrifices one's own civilian population to gain military advantage is at odds with the laws of war and basic morality, in which the protection of innocent civilians is a fundamental value. And yet, it is engaged in routinely by non-state armed groups. I point out these practices not to suggest

[44] Israel Defense Forces (2015) Special Report: Operation Protective Edge. http://www.idfblog.com/operationgaza2014/#Casualties. Accessed 2 December 2015. See also Israel's Gaza Conflict Report, above n 14, paras 125–126.

[45] Israel Defense Forces, above n 44.

[46] Israel's Gaza Conflict Report, above n 14, para 125.

[47] See Israel Defense Forces, above n 44.

[48] Ibid.

that state militaries should receive a *carte blanche* in operating against irregular forces in densely populated areas, but rather to argue that (1) a formalist approach that uses conventional war's balancing for determining when collateral damage is "excessive" in asymmetric warfare is erroneous and rewards practices that intentionally endanger civilians, and (2) the law must incorporate the conduct of hostilities of the counter-belligerent (here, the non-state actor) into the process that determines what collateral civilian damage is "excessive." Scrutiny of the conduct of operations of the state actor cannot turn a blind eye to the nature of warfare of its foe, which has direct bearing on the level of civilian damage inflicted. States should not be absolved of their responsibility to protect civilians even when they fight a law-violating enemy. But by the same token, they cannot bear the full responsibility for the greater risk this war environment entails for civilians.

For completeness, it is of interest to note that the formalist application of the norm may equally and erroneously support overly permissive targeting policies. Formalism is blind to context. It applies rules on predefined categories that may, or may not, fit with the realities of contemporary wars. The recently published US Defense Department's Law of War Manual's (US Law of War Manual) position on human shields provides an example.[49] The manual holds that injury to human shields shall be understood not to affect a proportionality assessment, while offering no distinction between different categories of civilians who shield military objectives.[50] The manual is of the view that people who voluntarily choose to shield targets should be treated equally as people who are forced to become human shields or who are unknowingly used by belligerents who conduct military activities in their vicinity. In my view, this is an ill-advised approach to take in an asymmetric warfare context, where the use of involuntary human shields is a common feature of the non-state party's conduct of operations. The law must be applied with concern to the context of hostilities and to treat differently voluntary human shields and civilians who are themselves victims to unlawful prosecution of war. The latter can never be dismissed in assessing proportionality.[51]

---

[49] US Department of Defense (2015) Law of War Manual. http://www.defense.gov/Portals/1/Documents/pubs/Law-of-War-Manual-June-2015.pdf. Accessed 2 June 2016.

[50] Ibid., Rule 5.12.3 ("Harm to the following categories of persons and objects would be understood not to prohibit attacks under the proportionality rule. (3) human shields. 5.12.3.3 If the proportionality rule were interpreted to permit the use of human shields to prohibit attacks, such an interpretation would perversely encourage the use of human shields and allow violations by the defending force to increase the legal obligations on the attacking force").

[51] The legal discourse is divided between two opposing views regarding the treatment of voluntary human shields. One view, reflected in the opinions of the Israeli Supreme Court and some commentators, is that by voluntary shielding a military objective, civilians are taking direct part in the hostilities. See e.g., *Public Committee against Torture in Israel and the Palestinian Society for the Protection of Human Rights and the Environment v the Government of Israel* et al., HCJ 769/02, (2006) 57(6) PD 285 (Isr.) (English version available at http://elyon1.court.gov.il/Files_ENG/02/690/007/A34/02007690.A34.HTM) (*Committee against Torture*), para 36 (Barak J.); and Schmitt and Merriam 2015, pp. 116–117. An opposing view is advocated by the ICRC, by which only voluntary shielding that physically (rather than legally) diminishes the capacity of the attacker to identify and destroy the shielded military objective may constitute direct participation in hostilities. See Melzer 2009, pp. 56–57.

6.4.3 *The Formalist Trap and Effective Protection of Civilians*

The approach advocated here is that the scope of "military advantage" and the benchmark for "excessiveness" are shaped by the nature of the warfare. Such a contextual view on *in bello* proportionality is better suited to positively affect the conduct of the law violating the non-state actor because it diminishes some of the gains sought in their resort to unlawful practices.[52] A formalistic approach tends to place all the burdens (in terms of minimizing civilian risk) on the state party and fails to acknowledge that the "regulation of asymmetric warfare requires a different structure of incentives to have any effect on the parties."[53] Put differently, placing all the responsibilities for the level of civilian damage incurred on the state party's side when, in effect, it is the conduct of the non-state party that causes most of the risk posed to civilians is counterproductive.

First, it signals to the non-state actor that practices which endanger civilians yield greater protection of its military interests. Indeed, as long as the law defines "excessive [civilian damage]" regardless of the tactics engaged by the non-state actor, frequent use of human shields as well as other conduct that put civilians as risk will be a rational choice for law-violating belligerents. Effectively, such non-state armed groups will be inclined to risk as many civilians are available to them.

Second, the formalist approach could eventually bring states to forsake their commitment to humanitarian concerns. The recent Gaza conflict presented a battlefield completely diffused into urban areas. In such a theater of war, virtually all attacks might be banned under a formalist view, especially when the non-state armed group exercises effective control of the territory and has the power to place civilians around every target. It would be erroneous to apply a rule that bans any effective war effort against an enemy that shields its weapons and combatants with civilians. States will be incentivized, inevitably, to disown a legal regime that bars effective countermeasures in this kind of situations.[54]

A conceivable critique of a view that concerns primarily to affect the conduct of the non-state party would be that it may diminish the accountability of the state party. Such an approach may turn out to legitimize attacks that cause greater collateral damage and erode the protection of civilians who reside in the territory from which the non-state actor operates. While the concerns surrounding the relaxation of the commitment by states to protect civilians in armed conflicts against law-violating armed groups are real, it is more likely under a formalistic proportionality regime that draws the line where no effective warfare is lawful. Proportionality seeks to promote a carefully crafted balance between military

[52] See Schmitt and Merriam 2015, pp. 129–130. Cf Cohen and Shany, above n 40.

[53] Benvenisti 2010, p. 4.

[54] Dinstein 2010, p xii; Rubinstein and Roznai 2011, p. 121.

necessity and humanitarian concerns.[55] It aims simultaneously to shield civilians from the tragic implications of war and to enable the conduct of war despite the potential of civilian harm.[56] In order to work, proportionality must advance both goals. It is a contextual view—in which a nuanced assessment of the variables is invoked—that strikes a right balance between military necessity and humanity. Nonetheless, even a successful application that avoids the formalist trap will not be able to crack other inherent limitations that proportionality, as other IHL norms, has in asymmetric conflicts. This final point is illustrated by the "absolutist" trap.

6.5 The "Absolutist" Trap

Perceiving proportionality as an absolute normative standard, when in effect it is a "rather loose"[57] principle, gives rise to the "absolutist" trap. Both human rights proponents and those who seek to legitimize aggressive military efforts in urban battlefields may fall into this trap by relying excessively on proportionality as a categorical justification for their political stance.[58]

6.5.1 The Absolutist Trap and States

States involved in asymmetric conflicts are affected by the absolutist trap when they rely on proportionality to vindicate attacks virtually regardless of the severity of civilian damage.

Asymmetric warfare produces many situations in which a decision to pursue or suspend an attack is attended by factual uncertainties and evaluative ambiguities. A warfare environment in which military operations are conducted in highly populated urban areas, the enemy regularly uses voluntary and involuntary human shields, civilian objects suddenly and temporarily transform into military objects and enemy combatants deliberately mingle with civilians possesses many dynamic variables that frequently cannot be accurately assessed by the military commander prior to the decision to launch an attack. In such environments, even attacks that hold extensive risk for civilians may not be seen as clearly disproportionate under positive law, which defers to the judgment of the commander based on the information available to him in real time. So in effect, a proportionality assessment may permit an attack despite its potential to harm civilians simply because the

[55] Schmitt and Widmar 2014, p. 2.

[56] See generally, Schmitt 2010.

[57] Cassese 2005, p. 417.

[58] Shany 2009, pp. 2–5.

legal test is ill-equipped for the complexities of asymmetric warfare. Legitimizing attacks on the ground that they are consistent with proportionality, or at minimum not clearly disproportionate,[59] could be seen then to have less normative validity and may overshadow other legal, moral, and policy considerations. Put differently, focusing the decision-making process on a narrow proportionality test, when in fact proportionality offers only a limited (albeit important) contribution to the entire scope of considerations, obscures the real problems that should be addressed. A sensible warfare strategy can and should avoid this trap.

6.5.2 The Absolutist Trap and Human Rights Proponents

Human rights proponents tend to construe proportionality as an absolute or near absolute prohibition against causing incidental civilian injury in armed conflicts.[60] While such an assertion has yet to openly be stated in the legal discourse, the fact that frequently the line is drawn where almost all attacks are unlawful whenever civilians are harmed seems to support such a view.[61] An absolutist view on proportionality may find doctrinal anchoring in the ICRC Commentary on the Additional Protocols.[62] The Commentary describes the prohibition on disproportionate collateral damage not with the relative term "excessive," as in the text of Article 51, but with the absolute term "extensive," suggesting that the norm prohibits extensive collateral damage.[63] However, such an absolute prohibition on extensive incidental civilian damage is not mandated by Article 51 proportionality and not supported by customary law. Proportionality mandates weighing any level of civilian damage against the anticipated military advantage.

In most cases, the absolutist view on proportionality is not so bluntly stated, but is realized through the application of the formula's components. This comes either by emphasizing the extensive civilian damage while narrowly defining the military

---

[59] In practice, international criminal law shows a tendency to outlaw only cases in which attacks are "*clearly* excessive." Article 8(2)(b)(iv) of the Rome Statute of the International Criminal Court, opened for signature 17 July 1998, 2187 UNTS 90 (entered into force 1 July 2002). See also NATO, above n 24, paras 50 and 77 (applying a standard of "clearly disproportionate" for criminal liability).

[60] Gabriella Blum contends in that context that "[h]umanitarian NGOs rarely concede that civilian casualties were the unfortunate outcome of legitimate military strikes." Blum 2011, p. 191. See also, Schmitt 2005, p. 455 (arguing that some of those who assess the conduct of hostilities are moving toward a stance by which there should be a rebuttable presumption that any civilian damage is a testimony of unlawful conduct by the attacker).

[61] Schmitt 2005, p. 455.

[62] Sandoz et al. 1987, p. 626.

[63] The Commentary contends that "[t]he Protocol does not provide any justification for attacks which cause extensive civilian losses and damages. Incidental losses and damages should never be extensive." Ibid., p. 626. Compare with Dinstein 2010, p. 131.

advantage or by assessing the attack *post-factum* without showing any level of consideration of the military commander's real choices before or during the attack. The McGowan-Davis Report provides a handful of examples. In none of the cases investigated did the mission find that the civilian damage was proportionate. In analyzing air and ground operations, the commission focused almost exclusively on the level of civilian damage incurred. When the military advantage sought by an attack was not clear, the mission applied the rule prescribed under Article 52.3 of Additional Protocol 1 (1977), providing that in case of doubt whether an object which is normally dedicated to civilian purposes is used for military action, it shall be presumed not to be so used.[64] This was a misapplication of the rule since there were no findings warranting the attribution of doubt to the commanders on the field. Rather, it was the mission of inquiry who lacked knowledge of the targets, an irrelevant factor in the legal analysis. In fact, the mission's ignorance of the military goals pursued and the lack of operational insights into specific attacks seem to be a crucial feature in the investigation and its conclusions.

Consider for example the mission's analysis of the battle in Shuja'iya.[65] On the evening of July 19, an IDF infantry convoy initiated a ground maneuver into the densely populated neighborhood located at the outskirts of Gaza. Things began to go badly when an explosive device was detonated on the convoy, causing the death of seven soldiers.[66] Heavy fighting followed the incident as the neighborhood rapidly transformed into a maze of sniper posts, anti-tank missile launch sites, booby-trapped buildings, and attacking tunnels.[67] The report provides a detailed account of the vast civilian damage inflicted during the hostilities, but in assessing the military advantages sought by the IDF, the commission presents the reader with a narrowly defined objective of force protection and very few details.[68] The report suggests that "intense shelling, combined with the use of a large number of one-ton bombs" was directed at a residential area for the sheer purpose of protecting one's own soldiers. In that context, it becomes easy for the commission to determine that the attack had to be suspended as it did not conform to the principle of proportionality.[69] But this is an incomplete context. Reading the Israeli report provides a better understanding of the military goals of the attack and the complexities faced by the forces in real time. Apparently, Shuja'iya was a Hamas stronghold "from which hundreds of rockets were fired at Israel" before the invasion.[70] Furthermore, the urban area held several cross-border tunnel entrances,

64 See e.g., McGowan-Davis Report, above n 14, paras 219 and 365.

65 Ibid., paras 251–299.

66 Ibid., para 259.

67 Israel's Gaza Conflict Report, above n 14, paras 19 and 93.

68 McGowan-Davis Report, above n 14, para 296 ("The objective of the shelling and heavy bombardment appears mainly to have been force protection").

69 Ibid., para 294.

70 Israel's Gaza Conflict Report, above n 14, para 19.

dozens of tunnel shafts, offensive and defensive military posts, and civilian houses rigged with booby traps.[71] The primary goal of the attack was apparently to establish "positions in order to undertake the lengthy and complicated task of dismantling" the tunnels.[72]

Neither the settings of the fighting and its direct military goals nor the strategic importance of Shuja'iya was grappled by the commission. And so its underlying conclusion was virtually predetermined. This sort of methodology is a common feature in human rights monitoring bodies' reports and characterizes their absolutist approach to proportionality.[73]

An absolutist approach to proportionality is an erroneous attempt to eliminate civilian suffering from the prosecution of war through an inappropriate modification of the law. But proportionality is a legal construction that, while seeking to minimize civilian suffering in war, is limited by the fact that the legal regime enables states to pursue the ultimate goal of defeating the enemy despite the unavoidable civilian suffering that it entails. In "rights terminology," proportionality both protects the right to life of civilians and limits that right in face of an armed conflict. For both practical and normative purposes, proportionality defers to the military commander's discretion so long as it is exercised reasonably.[74] It is inevitable that many cases will fall into gray zones, where despite the civilian damage, employing an attack will not be clearly beyond the limits of the norm.[75] Coloring these gray zones in unlawful black not only lacks a normative basis, but ultimately may be counterproductive to the humanitarian purpose of the law, especially in asymmetric conflicts when war is routinely fought in urban areas. It is the mirror problem to the practice of legitimizing attacks whenever the fog of war makes it difficult to predetermine that they are clearly disproportionate.

---

[71] Ibid., paras 19 and 93.

[72] Ibid., para 19.

[73] See Schmitt 2010, pp. 822–825 (arguing that NGO's perspective on IHL is far from neutral, often departing from that of states and demonstrate inherent bias). For examples of the NGO's application of proportionality see, e.g., Human Rights Council (2009) Human Rights in Palestine and Other Occupied Arab Territories: Report of the United Nations Fact-Finding Mission on the Gaza Conflict. UN Doc. A/HRC/12/48. http://www2.ohchr.org/english/bodies/hrcouncil/docs/12session/A-HRC-12-48.pdf. Accessed 2 June 2016, pp. 141–158 and 191–194; and Human Rights Watch (2003) Off Target: The Conduct of the War and Civilian Casualties in Iraq. https://www.hrw.org/sites/default/files/reports/usa1203.pdf. Accessed 2 June 2016, p. 9–10, 18–41 and 113–116.

[74] The Committee that was established to review the NATO Bombing Campaign against the Federal Republic of Yugoslavia noted in its report to the prosecutor that it expected that a military commander's view on proportionality will differ from a human rights lawyer's view. See NATO, above n 24, para 50 ("It is unlikely that a human rights lawyer and an experienced combat commander would assign the same relative values to military advantage and to injury to noncombatants"). See further, Geiß and Siegris 2011, p. 32 (noting that "[t]he value judgment inherent in the proportionality analysis is difficult to scrutinize").

[75] ICTY, *Prosecutor v Zoran Kupreškić, Mirjan Kupreškić, Vlatko Kupreškić, Drago Josipović, Dragan Papić and Vladimir Šantić*, Judgement, 14 January 2000, Case No. IT-95-16-T, para 526.

6.5.3 Moving to a Model of Structured Proportionality Analysis in IHL

So far I have demonstrated that both states and human rights proponents may adopt absolutist views on proportionality. These views can coexist because of the nature of *in bello* proportionality as an unconstrained and open-handed balancing formula, especially when applied in urban warfare situations replete with factual ambiguities. Can the law of proportionality generate a more principled assessment process to be invoked by military commanders, military lawyers and other observers conducting ex-post review of targeting decisions? It is my view that the answer is yes. We just have to look at the doctrine of proportionality in other places.

To begin to answer this question, it should be emphasized that the contemporary proportionality discourse in IHL is incomplete. It focuses on a narrow balancing test which is only one of three sub-tests that form together a complete proportionality analysis under the modern doctrine of proportionality. Drawing solely on the current narrow test, especially in asymmetric conflicts, presents proportionality with the danger of becoming a mechanistic, formalistic, and, in the hard cases, simply a meaningless norm. Performing a complete structured proportionality analysis in IHL will offer better tailoring of the legal norm to the complexities that arise in asymmetric warfare and thus advocated here. It does not require substantive changes in IHL, which already embodies each of the three sub-tests of proportionality in other rules. The following paragraph briefly introduces the modern doctrine of proportionality and discusses its components. Next, I establish the claim that the current legal framework of IHL encompasses all three sub-tests of proportionality. I then argue that performing a comprehensive structured proportionality analysis rather than focusing solely on proportionality *stricto sensu* will generate better regulation of hostilities, especially in asymmetric warfare situations.

The doctrine of proportionality has become a central concept in the modern constitutional law of many legal systems, serving as a methodological tool purporting to assess the lawfulness of governmental acts that derogate from human rights.[76] It is also a significant concept in several bodies of international law.[77]

[76] See generally Barak 2012, pp. 178–210; Beatty 2004, pp. 159–175; Grimm 2007, p. 383; Sweet and Mathews 2008, p. 74.

[77] See, e.g., ICJ, *Legality of the Threat or Use of Nuclear Weapons*, Advisory Opinion, 8 July 1996, (1996) ICJ Reports 226 (*Nuclear Weapons*), p. 257; Human Rights Committee (2001) General Comment 29: States of Emergency (Article 4), UN Doc. CCPR/C/21/Rev.1/Add.11; Human Rights Committee (1999) General Comment 27: Freedom of Movement (Article 12), UN Doc CCPR/C/21/Rev.1/Add.9 (finding that restrictive measures on the liberty of movement, protected under Article 12 of the International Covenant on Civil and Political Rights must comply with the principle of proportionality. The Committee maintained that restrictive measures "must be appropriate to achieve their protective function; they must be the least intrusive instrument amongst those which might achieve the desired result; and they must be proportionate to the interest to be protected"); and *Committee against Torture*, above n 51, paras 41–42 (Barak J.).

Proportionality is a legal construction designed to balance between ends and means.[78] It demands that a legal entity exercises its power rationally and reasonably "toward achieving a permissible goal, without unduly encroaching on protected rights" of others.[79] It relies on the premise that the end does not justify all means—that a legitimate social goal may become illegitimate due to the social costs to be incurred for its achievement.[80]

A proportionality analysis comprises a preliminary threshold requirement of "proper purpose" and three subsequent subtests: (1) suitability (known also as "rational connection"[81]), (2) necessity, and (3) proportionality *stricto sensu*.[82] The *proper purpose* threshold provides that only a legitimate objective may justify the limitation of a fundamental human right. If the measure in question (in our case, the measure being the attack) is not intended to achieve a legitimate objective (i.e., military advantage), it is *per-se* disproportionate. *Suitability* mandates that the chosen measure must be rationally capable of advancing the desired objective. A measure that has no rational connection with advancing the desired objective cannot survive proportionality scrutiny. *Necessity* requires that among all hypothetical suitable measures, the chosen measure is the one that minimally derogates from the right. Put differently, when various alternative measures can achieve the desired objective, it is disproportionate to use any measure other than the one that inflicts the minimal social costs necessary. Finally, *proportionality stricto sensu* is a cost/benefit analysis.[83] It entails a proper relation between the benefit gained by the objective sought and the adverse effect of the chosen measure. When a proportionate balance between the social benefit gained and the social cost incurred is not maintained, the chosen measure is rendered disproportionate. The three tests are complementary. Each of them must be satisfied for the scrutinized measure to survive proportionality assessment.

A complete doctrine of proportionality is neither prescribed under any IHL treaty nor acknowledged as a customary norm. Nonetheless, the historical development of targeting rules concerning the protection of civilians has incorporated, de facto, the tests of proportionality in specific and isolated norms:

---

78 For an overview see Barak 2012; Crawford 2011, pp. 533–539; Huscroft et al. 2016; and Pirker 2013.

79 Crawford 2011, p. 534.

80 See Barak 2012, p. 209.

81 See, e.g., *R v Oakes* (1986) 1 S.C.R. 103 (Can.) (*Oakes*); and *Beit Sourik Village Council v The Government of Israel and the Commander of the IDF Forces in the West Bank*, HCJ 2056/04, (2004) 58(5) 807 (Isr.) (English version available at http://elyon1.court.gov.il/Files_ENG/04/560/020/A28/04020560.A28.pdf), paras 43–44 (Barak J).

82 Crawford 2011, p. 534.

83 See, e.g., the Canadian model of proportionality assessment: in *Oakes*, above n 81, p. 103. See also Barak 2012, pp. 340–344; Crawford 2011, p. 534. Proportionality *stricto sensu* can be described as a manifestation of the Doctrine of Double Effect. See Blum 2011, p. 189 ("Following the Catholic-rooted doctrine of double-effect, the law prescribes that as long as civilian harm is the unintended—even if foreseen—outcome of an attack, such harm is a lawful cost of war. To be lawful, however, this unintended damage must not be excessive in relation to the overall military advantage that is anticipated from the attack").

- IHL imposes on the belligerent parties the threshold requirement of *proper purpose*, which is manifested in the fundamental principle of military necessity, prohibiting attacks that do not offer a definite military advantage.[84] The attainment of a military advantage is the only "proper purpose" that may justify military engagement.[85] In its absence, the attack is *per-se* unlawful, with no regard to the level of the collateral damage inflicted.
- *Suitability (rational connection)* is embodied, e.g., in the customary prohibition on attacks that are not directed at a specific military objective.[86] Such attacks fail to impact the military strength of the enemy and thus lack a rational connection between the chosen measure (the attack) and its legitimate objective (to eliminate the threat by impairing the military power of the opponent[87]).
- *Necessity*[88] is embodied in two *jus in bello* rules concerned with civilian protection, both prescribed under the obligation to employ precautions in attack.[89] The first is the duty to "take all feasible precautions in the choice of means and methods of attack with a view to avoiding, and in any event to minimizing, incidental loss of civilian life, injury to civilians, and damage to civilian objects."[90]

---

84 For the rule of Military Necessity, see Additional Protocol I, above n 1, Article 52(2). See also Dinstein 2010, pp. 4–5 (describing the principle of military necessity as the driving force of the laws of war).

85 Saint Petersburg Declaration, above n 31 ("the only legitimate object which States should endeavor to accomplish during war is to weaken the military forces of the enemy").

86 Additional Protocol I, above n 1, Article 51(4).

87 See, e.g., Saint Petersburg Declaration, above n 31.

88 Note that the discussion here on the concept of necessity refers to the second sub-test of proportionality and not to the general principle of military necessity, which prohibits attacks that do not offer a definite military advantage. For an analysis tying between the principle of military necessity and the necessity test, see Melzer 2006, pp. 98–100.

89 The requirement to supplement components of the necessity test to the traditional IHL proportionality assessment was first introduced in the Israeli Targeted Killings Case. Seemingly however, the Court anchored the requirement in the domestic doctrine of proportionality prescribed under Israeli administrative law. *Committee against Torture*, above n 51, para 40 (Barak J.). For a discussion on the least harmful means requirement in IHL see Melzer 2006, pp. 95–96.

90 This rule is codified under Additional Protocol I, above n 1, Article 57(2)(a)(ii). It is of a customary nature and appliesto both international and non-international armed conflicts. See Henckaerts and Doswald-Beck 2009, pp. 56–58. Limitations on choice of means and methods of attack apply also to protect combatants. Additional Protocol I, above n 1, Article 35(2) prohibits the employment of "weapons, projectiles, and Materials and methods of warfare of a nature to cause superfluous injury or unnecessary suffering." The prohibition against causing unnecessary suffering to combatants is also prescribed under Hague Convention (IV) Respecting the Laws and Customs of War on Land and Its Annex: Regulations Concerning the Laws and Customs of War on Land, opened for signature 18 October 1907, 187 CTS 227 (entered into force 26 January 1910), Article 23(e). In *Nuclear Weapons*, above n 77, para 78, the ICJ noted "it is prohibited to cause unnecessary suffering to combatants: it is accordingly prohibited to use weapons causing them such harm or uselessly aggravating their suffering. In application of that second principle, States do not have unlimited freedom of choice of means in the weapons they use." The ICRC commentary on the Additional Protocols contends that the prohibition to cause unnecessary suffering applies to both combatants and civilians. See Sandoz et al. 1987, p. 409.

The second mandates that "when a choice is possible between several military objectives for obtaining a similar military advantage, the objective to be selected shall be that the attack on which may be expected to cause the least danger to civilian lives and to civilian objects."[91] These rules establish a norm of necessity or, to put it differently, a "feasible minimization" requirement, in the choice of means, methods, and targets in attack when civilians are at risk. The attacker is directed to pursue the desired military goal while causing the least civilian damage as possible. For example, when an attacker seeks to destroy a tunnel used by the enemy to mobilize troops and weapons, and the path of the tunnel goes partly under populated areas, the strike should hit the component of the tunnel which is located as far away as possible from civilian communities. This is subject to the assumption that the goal of paralyzing the functionality of tunnel can be achieved by attacking less populated areas.
It is worth noting that the US Law of War Manual seems to reject the feasible minimization requirement concerning target selection as binding customary law.[92] Without getting into the correctness of the manual's assertions, this posture on targeting rules raises difficulties when these rules are analyzed under a proportionality requirement: Should the same military advantage be attainable by striking the tunnel away from the populated area, how can we call the collateral damage caused by striking it inside the populated anything other than "excessive."[93]
- *Proportionality stricto sensu* is manifested in the prohibition on causing excessive collateral damage, as discussed throughout this chapter.

Integrating military conduct that applies these tests under one structured proportionality assessment is advisable. Each sub-test serves the same function of promoting a rational decision-making process that carefully balances between military necessities and humanitarian considerations. Applied together, they generate a finer and more principled decision-making process. The absolutist problem can be contained, mostly by shifting some of the focus from the prohibition against excessive collateral damage, i.e., the proportionality *stricto sensu* test, to the norms concerning target selection and the choice of means and methods of attack that are incorporated in the necessity sub-test, the requirement of feasible minimization.[94]

Consider the following example: An attacker seeks to target X, the indispensable leader of a non-state armed group. X is hiding in an apartment located on the ninth floor of a ten-story building. In applying proportionality *stricto sensu* assessment, the military commander decides to authorize the attack. Based on

---

[91] This rule is codified under Additional Protocol I, above n 1, Article 57(3). It is unsettled whether state practice establishes the latter rule as a norm of customary law of non-international armed conflict. The ICRC study on customary IHL argues that "State practice establishes this rule as a norm of customary international law applicable in international, and arguably also in non-international, armed conflicts." Henckaerts and Doswald-Beck 2009, pp. 65–67.

[92] US Department of Defense, above n 49, Rule 5.11.5.

[93] See Haque A (2015) The Defense Department Stands Alone on Target Selection. https://www.justsecurity.org/24264/dod-stands-alone-target-selection/. Accessed 2 June 2016.

[94] Additional Protocol I, above n 1, Articles 57(2)(a)(ii) and 57(3).

the information available to him, he finds that the expected collateral damage of 8–12 civilian casualties, some of whom may be voluntary human shields, merits the military advantage in the elimination of X. However, in applying the rules of necessity concerning the choice of means, methods, and targets in attack, the military commander is faced with two additional questions: one, when to carry out the attack; and two, with what type of ammunition. Assume that if the attack is to be carried out at 10:00 AM rather than at 7:00 AM, fewer civilians will occupy the building; assume that if the attacking jet fighter uses a 500 kg bomb rather than 1000 kg bomb, it will destroy only the top floors and not the entire building. A military commander applying both assessments is expected to achieve the same military advantage with less civilian harm. As illustrated, norms of necessity which mandate feasible minimization advance proportionality with different tools than the prohibition against excessive incidental civilian damage, but seek to achieve the same goal of mitigating civilian suffering. They are, of course, supplemental to the prohibition to cause excessive incidental civilian damage.

Adoption of the structured proportionality model would beneficially enhance the military commander's decision-making process. The rules of *necessity* concerning choice of means and methods and target selection possess some clear advantages on *proportionality stricto sensu* (i.e., the prohibition to cause excessive collateral damage) in an asymmetric battlefield. First, they are less subject to manipulation by non-state actors who abuse the laws of war. Belligerents who are willing to sacrifice the lives of their own civilians by using them as human shields have incentive to manipulate the balancing formula of proportionality *stricto sensu* by loading military objectives with civilians and effectively raising the expected collateral damage against a specific military advantage.[95] Norms of necessity, which require feasible minimization of the damage, neither incentivize this sort of conduct nor are affected by it. They simply confine the attacker to means and methods of attack that will cause the minimal collateral damage, and call upon him to exhaust feasible alternative targets. His behavior in this context cannot be manipulated by the conduct of the non-state party. Second, norms of necessity are easier to implement and scrutinize because they are more principled and less subject to value determinations than proportionality *stricto sensu*. A choice between a 500 kg and a 1000 kg bomb to neutralize a target depends on a professional judgment call and does not involve moral value choices. Norms of necessity should then foster more consistent conduct among troops and provide another significant tool for minimizing the effects of war on civilians.

Furthermore, a structured proportionality analysis provides a relatively stable framework for resolving dilemmas in the heat of battle. The first and second subtests do not include a balancing exercise and in some cases will render it unnecessary. And finally, structured proportionality enhances transparency and thus advances more persuasive ex-post review of decisions, which would no longer settle with an unconstrained second guessing exercise, but rather would be held to the same structured process.

---

[95] Hamas, for example, frequently employed such tactics in the recent conflict. See Israel's Gaza Conflict Report, above n 14, paras 159–164.

To conclude, proportionality in attack will be best achieved through a complete multipart analysis, as administered in various constitutional courts and international bodies. In this assessment, each part serves as a check on the limitations and weaknesses of the other. Applied together, they generate a better and more rational process in evaluating attacks that may cause civilian harm. Inconsistent applications of proportionality, much like the US Law of War Manual's rejection of the feasible minimization requirement concerning target selection, would also be avoided should commanders be required to perform structured proportionality assessment when operating in the vicinity of civilians. All in all, the ultimate goal of targeting law to shield civilians from the risks of war will be better served through the invocation of structured proportionality assessment.

Epilogue

Proportionality has become a central tool in the effort to mitigate the effects of hostilities on civilians in asymmetric conflicts. It is a concept aimed to restrain violence when civilians and civilian property are at risk by imposing norms that integrate humanitarian considerations into the decision-making process of the military commander. Proportionality seeks to form a delicate balance between military necessity and humanitarian concerns. In this chapter, I argued that three interpretive "traps" may cause proportionality to fail to achieve this delicate balance. Invocations of proportionality that fail to avoid these traps would both encourage practices that deliberately risk civilians and condemn proportionality to be an irrelevant notion. At the same time, proportionality that fails to avoid the traps may be inappropriately exerted as a form of self-justification for conduct that shows little regard for humanitarian concerns.

The chapter provides recommendations aimed at avoiding or at least mitigating each trap and its effects. Yet, it would be naïve of me to presume that following the prescription advanced here will fix every problem involved with the operation of proportionality in asymmetric conflicts. One cannot escape from the conclusion that when states engage in asymmetric warfare against law-violating non-state armed groups, they should appreciate that proportionality has a limited set of tools for producing a satisfactory answer in these new war settings. They should avoid overly relying on proportionality, sometimes even when their decisions are seemingly consistent with the law. A workable warfare strategy would acknowledge the limited normative value of proportionality assessment and will not allow it to overshadow additional essential policy considerations that go beyond the confines of the current legal framework.[96]

[96] One can find guidelines in that spirit in the 2014 American Field Manual on Insurgencies and Countering Insurgencies. The manual concedes that "[a]ll interactions between security forces and the [civilian] population directly impact legitimacy" and further stipulates that "[t]he general rule for the use of force for the counterinsurgents is 'do not create more enemies than you eliminate with your action'." Restraints of that kind are not prescribed by the principle of proportionality, but seem to be closely connected to the goals of democracies when they fight asymmetric conflicts. Headquarters, Department of the Army (2014) Field Manual 3-24: Insurgencies and Countering Insurgencies. http://www.fas.org/irp/doddir/army/fm3-24.pdf. Accessed 2 June 2016, Rule 6.2.

References

Articles, Books and Other Documents

Barak A (2012) Proportionality: Constitutional Rights and their Limitations. Cambridge University Press, New York

Beatty D (2004) The Ultimate Rule of Law. Oxford University Press, New York

Benvenisti E (2010) The Legal Battle to Define the Law on Transnational Asymmetric Warfare. Duke J Comp Int Law 20:339–359

Blum G (2011) On a Differential Law of War. Harv Int Law J 52:164–218

Cassese A (2005) International Law, 2nd edn. Oxford University Press, New York

Crawford E (2011) Proportionality. In: Wolfrum R (ed) Max Planck Encyclopedia of Public International Law. Oxford University Press, Oxford, pp 533–539

Dinstein Y (2010) The Conduct of Hostilities under the Law of International Armed Conflict, 2nd edn. Cambridge University Press, United Kingdom

Dunlap C (1998) Preliminary Observations: Asymmetrical Warfare and the Western Mindset. In: Matthews L (ed) Challenging America Symmetrically and Asymmetrically: Can America be Defeated? Strategic Studies Institute, Carlisle, pp 1–17

Geiß R, Siegris M (2011) Has the armed conflict in Afghanistan affected the rules on the conduct of hostilities? Int Rev Red Cross 93(881):11–46

Grimm D (2007) Proportionality in Canadian and German Constitutional Jurisprudence. Univ Tor Law J 57:383–397

Henckaerts JM, Doswald-Beck L (2009) Customary International Humanitarian Law—Vol. 1: Rules. International Committee of the Red Cross, New York

Human Rights Committee (1999) General Comment 27: Freedom of Movement (Article 12). UN Doc CCPR/C/21/Rev.1/Add.9

Human Rights Committee (2001) General Comment 29: States of Emergency (Article 4). UN Doc. CCPR/C/21/Rev.1/Add.11

Huscroft G, Miller B, Webber G (eds) (2016) Proportionality and the Rule of Law: Rights, Justification, Reasoning. Cambridge University Press, USA

Margalit A, Walzer M (2009) Israel: Civilians & Combatants. New York Rev Books 56

McCready D (2006) Now More than Ever: Terrorism, Asymmetric Warfare, and the Just War Tradition. Polit Theol 7(4):461–474

Melzer N (2006) Targeted Killing or Less Harmful Means?—Israel's High Court Judgment on Targeted Killing and the Restrictive Function of Military Necessity. Yearb Int Humanitarian Law 9:87–113

Melzer N (2009) Interpretive Guidance on the Notions of Direct Participation under International Humanitarian Law. International Committee of the Red Cross, Geneva

Mohamedou M (2007) Understanding Al Qaeda: The Transformation of War. Pluto Press

Pfanner T (2005) Asymmetrical warfare from the perspective of humanitarian law and humanitarian action. Int Rev Red Cross 87(857):149–174

Pirker B (2013) Proportionality analysis and models of judicial review: a theoretical and comparative study. Europa Law Publishing

Rubinstein A, Roznai Y (2011) Human Shields in Modern Armed Conflicts: The Need for a Proportionate Proportionality. Stanf Law Policy Review 22:93–128

Sandoz Y, Swinarski C, Zimmerman B (eds) (1987) Commentary on the Additional Protocols to the Geneva Conventions of 8 June 1977 to the Geneva Conventions of 12 August 1949. International Committee of the Red Cross, the Netherlands

Schmitt M (2005) Precision Attack and International Humanitarian Law. Int Rev Red Cross 87(859):455–466

Schmitt M (2008) Asymmetrical Warfare and International Humanitarian Law. Air Force Law Rev 62:1–42

Schmitt M (2010) Military Necessity and Humanity in International Humanitarian Law: Preserving the Delicate Balance. Va J Int Law 50(4):795–839
Schmitt M, Merriam J (2015) The Tyranny of Context: Israeli Targeting Practices in Legal Perspective. Univ Pa J Int Law 37:53–139
Schmitt M, Widmar E (2014) "On Target": Precision and Balance in the Contemporary Law of Targeting. J Natl Secur Law Policy 7:379–409
Shany Y (2009) International Law and the hostilities in Gaza: Coordinating expectations. Hebr Univ Law Rev 1:2 (in Heb.)
Sweet A, Mathews J (2008) Proportionality Balancing and Global Constitutionalism. Columbia J Transnatl Law 47:72–164
Wenger A, Mason S (2008) The civilianization of armed conflict: trends and implications. Int Rev Red Cross 90(872):835–852
Williamson J (2010) Challenges of Twenty-First Century Conflicts: A Look at Direct Participation in Hostilities. Duke J Comp Int Law 20:457–471

Case Law

Adalah – The Legal Center for Arab Minority Rights in Israel et al. v GOC Central Command et al., HCJ 3799/02, [2005] IDF 60(3) PD 67 (Isr.).
Beit Sourik Village Council v The Government of Israel and the Commander of the IDF Forces in the West Bank, HCJ 2056/04, [2004] 58(5) 807 (Isr.).
ICJ, *Legality of the Threat or Use of Nuclear Weapons*, Advisory Opinion, 8 July 1996, [1996] ICJ Reports 226.
ICTY, *Prosecutor v Zoran Kupreškić, Mirjan Kupreškić, Vlatko Kupreškić, Drago Josipović, Dragan Papić and Vladimir Šantić*, Judgement, 14 January 2000, Case No. IT-95-16-T.
Public Committee against Torture in Israel and the Palestinian Society for the Protection of Human Rights and the Environment v the Government of Israel et al., HCJ 769/02, [2006] 57(6) PD 285 (Isr.).
R v Oakes [1986] 1 S.C.R. 103 (Can.).
ICTY, *Prosecutor v Tihomir Blaškić*, Judgement, 29 July 2004, Case No. IT-95-14-A.

Treaties

Protocol Additional to the Geneva Conventions of 12 August 1949, and relating to the Protection of Victims of International Armed Conflicts, opened for signature 12 December 1977, 1125 UNTS 3 (entered into force 7 December 1979)
Hague Convention (IV) Respecting the Laws and Customs of War on Land and Its Annex: Regulations Concerning the Laws and Customs of War on Land, opened for signature 18 October 1907, 187 CTS 227 (entered into force 26 January 1910)
Rome Statute of the International Criminal Court, opened for signature 17 July 1998, 2187 UNTS 90 (entered into force 1 July 2002)
Declaration Renouncing the Use, in Time of War, of Explosive Projectiles under 400 Grammes Weight, opened for signature 11 December 1868, 1 AJILs 95 (entry into force 11 December 1868)

Chapter 7
Generating Respect for International Humanitarian Law: The Establishment of Courts by Organized Non-State Armed Groups in Light of the Principle of Equality of Belligerents

Ezequiel Heffes

Abstract In the last few decades, different organized non-State armed groups have created judicial bodies in non-international armed conflicts. Despite their undisputed relevance, their establishment has not been thoroughly analysed, even if they could be included within those measures taken by these non-State entities in order to enhance respect for international humanitarian law. This article aims to explore some legal consequences of such actions. Mainly, two issues are dealt with: (a) the reasons why organized non-State armed groups are bound to respect IHL; (b) the lack of a unified view on which legal framework regulates the establishment of those "courts". In order to achieve an explanation that grasps the complexity of these issues, the article adopts an inclusive approach, which embraces the application of the principle of equality of belligerents as a basis to affirm that the regulation of these judicial bodies by the "laws" of armed groups is the most appropriate solution in order to generate compliance for IHL.

Keywords Organized Non-State armed groups · Equality of belligerents · International humanitarian law · Non-international armed conflicts · Courts

---

The views expressed here are solely those of the author in his private capacity and do not in any way represent the views of any institution.

E. Heffes LL.M. (✉)
University of Buenos Aires (UBA), Buenos Aires, Argentina;
Geneva Academy of International Humanitarian Law and Human Rights, Geneva, Switzerland
e-mail: ezequiel.heffes@geneva-academy.ch

T.D. Gill et al. (eds.), *Yearbook of International Humanitarian Law 2015*,
Yearbook of International Humanitarian Law 18,
DOI 10.1007/978-94-6265-141-8_7

Contents

7.1 Introduction

In today's contemporary international humanitarian law (IHL) context, the majority of armed conflicts include at least one non-State entity: an organized non-State armed group (NSAG).[1] For a long time, however, these entities and their acts were considered to be regulated only by the internal laws of the relevant State(s) and therefore they escaped from any form of international regime.[2] Under this view, NSAGs constituted a collective of common criminals who had to be punished for taking up arms against the legitimate authority of the state. Back then, admitting that hostilities were subject to international regulation was considered as intervening with the internal affairs of states, and NSAGs were generally granted some level of legitimacy only in instances where they attained victory in their struggle.[3]

This attitude has since changed dramatically, and today's reality continuously challenges states and their sacrosanct sovereignty. The humanitarian consequences for the civilian populations around the world caused by the intensity of non-international armed conflicts (NIACs) and their pre-eminence in the last few decades have shown the need for the development of effective IHL regulations. Yet, the shadow of state sovereignty has continually limited the evolution of this legal regime and the way it interacts with NSAGs in NIACs, even though it is presently recognized that IHL creates equal obligations upon these entities and states.[4]

---

[1] Recent surveys have concluded that the great majority of ongoing armed conflicts around the world are non-international in character. According to different sources, the total number of armed conflicts in recent years fluctuates between thirty and thirty-eight, and only two or three of them are considered to be international. See Casey–Maslen 2014, pp. 28–29.

[2] For a historical analysis, see Moir 2002, pp. 4–11 and Sivakumaran 2012, pp. 9–29.

[3] d'Aspremont 2008.

[4] La Rosa and Wuerzner 2008, pp. 327–329.

In the context of NIACs, NSAGs are bound by customary IHL,[5] Common Article 3 (CA3)[6] of the Geneva Conventions of 1949 (GCs)[7] as well as the 1977 Additional Protocol II (AP II)[8] to the GCs, taking into account the latter's more restricted scope of application, among a few other Conventions.[9]

Among those international obligations recognized by IHL, it is possible to find certain specific provisions regarding the administration of justice by NSAGs. In this sense, IHL seems to recognize their legal capacity to run a parallel judicial system—outside of and independent from the State's regular authority—to cater to those individuals who fall within NSAGs' ambits of control, should they be civilians, members of the armed forces opposing that group and even its own members. Interestingly, while these non-State actors do not always reach a high degree of organization or control over territory, which would make them incapable to fully implement judicial guarantees, IHL still binds these entities to respect certain safeguards in NIACs.[10]

This paper aims precisely to analyse the establishment and purpose of judicial bodies by NSAGs. Despite their undisputed relevance, the creation of a parallel

[5] It has become progressively clear that many rules that originally regulated international armed conflicts have over time also become applicable as customary law in non-international armed conflicts. ICTY, *Prosecutor v Duško Tadić*, Judgement, 15 July 1999, Case No. IT-94-1-A, paras 96–127. See also Kälin and Künzli 2009, pp. 67–76 and 158; Henckaerts and Doswald-Beck 2005 and International Committee of the Red Cross (2008) Improving Respect for International Humanitarian Law in Non-International Armed Conflicts. https://www.icrc.org/eng/assets/files/other/icrc_002_0923.pdf. Accessed 2 June 2016, pp. 9–10.

[6] See among others Moir 2002, pp. 52–88 and Pejić 2011, p. 189.

[7] Geneva Convention (I) for the Amelioration of the Condition of the Wounded and Sick in Armed Forces in the Field, opened for signature 12 August 1949, 75 UNTS 31 (entered into force 21 October 1950) (GC I); Geneva Convention (II) for the Amelioration of the Condition of Wounded, Sick and Shipwrecked Members of Armed Forces at Sea, opened for signature 12 August 1949, 75 UNTS 85 (entered into force 21 October 1950) (GC II); Geneva Convention (III) relative to the Treatment of Prisoners of War, opened for signature 12 August 1949, 75 UNTS 135 (entered into force 21 October 1950) (GC III); Geneva Convention (IV) relative to the Protection of Civilian Persons in Time of War, opened for signature on 12 August 1949, 75 UNTS 287 (entered into force 21 October 1950) (GC IV).

[8] Protection of Victims of Non-International Armed Conflicts, opened for signature 8 June 1977, 1125 UNTS 609 (entered into force 7 December 1978).

[9] See among others, the Hague Convention for the Protection of Cultural Property in the Event of Armed Conflict, opened for signature 14 May 1954, 249 UNTS 240 (entered into force 7 August 1956), Article 19; Protocol on Prohibitions or Restrictions on the Use of Mines, Booby-Traps and Other Devices (Protocol II as amended on 3 May 1996) annexed to the Convention on Prohibitions or Restrictions on the Use of Certain Conventional Weapons which may be deemed to be Excessively Injurious or to have Indiscriminate Effects, opened for signature 10 October 1980, 2048 UNTS 93 (entered into force 3 December 1998), Article 1.2; Optional Protocol to the Convention on the Rights of the Child on the Involvement of Children in Armed Conflict, opened for signature 25 May 2000, 2173 UNTS 222 (entered into force 12 February 2002), Article 4.

[10] Willms 2015, p. 151.

system separated from that of the state does not seem as simple as it looks. This is mainly because "the creation of a criminal justice system is a fundamental function of government, and states are vehement in their rejection of any kind of status for rebel groups".[11] Yet, they could also be included in those measures that armed groups can take to improve their respect for IHL. In this sense, the following pages will explore one of the main challenges regarding NSAG's courts: the lack of a unified view on which legal framework regulates them. Different alternatives will be addressed, and it will be argued, based on the principle of equality of belligerents, that the regulation of these judicial bodies by the 'laws' of an armed group is the most appropriate solution in order to deal effectively with IHL compliance issues.

7.2 The International Obligations of NSAGs

Accepting that NSAGs can create judicial bodies separated from the States' own and based on their internal legislations raises the question of what are the legal reasons to consider them actually bound by IHL in the first place.[12] This is mainly because the latter legal regime would be the basis to refer to their "laws". Therefore, to fully grasp the complexity of that question, it is necessary to understand why armed groups must observe those humanitarian rules.

7.2.1 Contemporary Explanations of NSAGs' Obligation to Comply with IHL

A classic approach to the traditional sources of international law is based on the consent given by states to be bound by an international norm. Depending on the type of source, this can occur in different ways: the regime of international treaties determines proceedings in order for states to express their consent to be bound by them; customary rules require, at least, that there has been no persistent objection to its formation; and general principles of law only emerge from rules already implemented by States' domestic legislation.[13] When it comes to armed groups, there is a general agreement regarding their obligation to comply with IHL, and there is no significant distinction between their international duties and those of

[11] Doswald-Beck 2015, p. 491.

[12] See Heffes et al. 2015, pp. 52–60 for an insightful analysis in this regard; and generally Clapham 2006, pp. 271–316; and Sivakumaran 2012, pp. 236–246.

[13] Klabbers 2013, pp. 21–40; and Clapham 2012, pp. 54–64, amongst many others.

states.[14] While CA3 affirms that "each party to the conflict shall be bound to apply, as a minimum" its provisions, AP II applies to those NIACs between state forces "and dissident armed forces or other organized armed groups".[15]

The reasons why NSAGs are bound by IHL, however, lie beyond merely accepting the existence of their obligations. Different views have been proposed in this sense. While some of them take into account their consent, others are based on their relationship with states. Implementing one or the other is not merely an intellectual exercise, and the alternative to be taken will certainly have a direct impact on the effectiveness of IHL as perceived by NSAGs.

Two traditional theories suggest that these entities are bound by IHL without considering their consent. The argument of effective sovereignty, on the one hand, focuses on armed groups' territorial link to a state party to the GCs. It was pointed out in the Commentary to GC I that they are bound by the international obligations of previous administrations in a similar way that successive governments are due to their claims to represent the country or part of it.[16] The domestic legislative jurisdiction argument, on the other hand, is the most commonly suggested, and it is based on the State's capacity to legislate for all its nationals.[17] As explained in the Commentary to GC II, "in most national legislations; by the fact of ratification, an international Convention becomes part of law and is therefore binding upon all the individuals of that country".[18]

These positions, nevertheless, raise some scenarios that are difficult to solve. With respect to the effective sovereignty over the territory argument, it derives NSAGs' rights and obligations exclusively from those already agreed upon by the state party to the conflict. Moreover, it is only applicable to the extent that the armed group itself purports to represent the state. Regarding the domestic legislative jurisdiction argument, it only focuses on the link between national legislation and those members of NSAGs, challenging the status of rebels not under domestic law but under international law *vis-à-vis* the government, third states and the international community.[19] Both arguments, in short, entail at least two practical problems for IHL implementation: (i) NSAGs that might be committed to observe humanitarian rules are unlikely to have any commitment to domestic national legislation;[20] and (ii) these theories do not explain some particular situations, such as when armed groups have effective control over a territory but do not claim to represent the state.[21]

---

[14] La Rosa and Wuerzner 2008, pp. 327–329.

[15] See generally Moir 2002, pp. 89–132; Sassòli et al. 2011, pp. 331–340; Stewart 2003, pp. 319–323; and Vité 2009, pp. 75–83.

[16] Pictet 1952, p. 51.

[17] Moir 2002, pp. 53–54; and Cassese 1981, p. 429.

[18] Pictet 1960a, p. 34.

[19] Cassese 1981, pp. 429–430.

[20] Moir 2002, p. 54; and Cassese 1981, pp. 429–430.

[21] For further critiques, see Henckaerts 2002, pp. 123–137; and d'Aspremont and de Hemptinne 2012, pp. 98–99.

There are also theories that actually recognize the direct relation between IHL and armed groups, highlighting the importance of their expressions of willingness. It has been suggested in this sense that NSAGs are bound to IHL by virtue of the customary status of its content,[22] which has been further explored by Somer who affirms that "in order for insurgents to be bound by a customary rule, their practice would be need to be taken into account".[23] The International Criminal Tribunal for the former Yugoslavia (ICTY) in the *Tadić* jurisdiction decision and the UN Commission of Enquiry's Report on Darfur have actually supported the view that armed groups already participate in the formation of customary IHL.[24] Sassòli has explained this view in the following way:

> A first step for creating a sense of ownership among armed groups is to involve them into the development and reaffirmation of the law. In my view, as far as customary IHL of non-international armed conflicts [...] this already is the case. Customary law is based on the behaviour of the subjects of a rule, in the form of acts and omissions or (whether qualified as practice *lato* sensu or evidence for *opinio iuris*) in the form of statements, mutual accusations and justifications for their own behavior.[25]

Although this remains still a minority view,[26] it is submitted that there is a good case to argue that NSAGs already participate in the formation of customary rules. This can be deduced not only by looking at their actions in the field but also by analysing their public statements, which can take the form of unilateral declarations, special agreements and codes of conduct. Their "internal" rules with respect to the establishment of judicial bodies, in fact, also follow this line of thought. Moreover, these sources serve the purpose of having NSAGs affirming their commitment to apply a set of international rules.[27] Only reviewing these expressions of willingness will make it possible to appreciate armed groups' practices and *opinio juris*.

Certainly, this view will have to face different challenges, such as selecting armed groups capable of doing it, monitoring and interpreting their *praxis* and *opinio juris*, and weighing it along with those of states and other armed groups, amongst many others. Moreover, it will have to struggle with the most difficult barrier: the erosion of the idea of states as the only international lawmaker entity.[28] Yet, one cannot ignore the value of NSAGs' public expressions of willingness in order to deal with IHL effectiveness issues.

---

[22] Somer 2007, p. 661; and Bellal et al. 2011, pp. 53–56.

[23] Somer 2007, pp. 661–662; and Heffes and Kotlik 2014 for an analysis on special agreements concluded in NIACs as sources of IHL.

[24] See ICTY, *Prosecutor v Duško Tadić a/k/a "Dule"*, Decision on the Defence Motion for Interlocutory Appeal on Jurisdiction, 2 October 1995, Case No. IT-94-1-AR72, paras 107–108; UN Security Council (2005) Letter dated 31 January 2005 from the Secretary-General addressed to the President of the Security Council, UN Doc. S/2005/60, Annex.

[25] Sassòli 2010, p. 13.

[26] Somer 2007, p. 662; and Heffes and Kotlik 2014, p. 1203.

[27] See generally Bangerter 2012.

[28] Several very interesting and even ground-breaking answers to some of these issues are proposed in Sassòli 2010, pp. 10–14.

7.2.2 Generating Respect for IHL and the Principle of Equality of Belligerents

The principle of equality of belligerents affirms that all the parties to an armed conflict have the same rights and obligations, regardless of their cause.[29] It is implied in CA3, which directly addresses "each party" to a NIAC, and by Article 1(1) of AP II. In the case of armed groups, their obligation to comply with those provisions remains despite any domestic legislation criminalizing their use of force against the state.[30]

Based on this principle, it is submitted that not only all parties to the conflict must be bound by IHL to the same extent but also for the same legal reasons, since the contrary would entail the subordination of NSAGs' rights and obligations to those previously accepted by states and would affect their equal status. Consequently, IHL's legitimacy as perceived by armed groups would be diminished by the fact that the rules would be exclusively imposed by the adverse party to the conflict, which is clear if the group was in an armed conflict against a state. That is precisely what occurs with the effective sovereignty argument and the domestic legislative jurisdiction perspective. They seem to fail when addressing NSAGs' actions or expressions, denying them any significance whatsoever, and therefore ignoring the participation of these entities. By challenging the equality of belligerents, they may actually affect IHL as an effective body of law.

On the contrary, the explanation that includes NSAGs in the creation of the law that regulates them represents an important improvement in terms of equality of the parties to NIACs.[31] Indeed, it is better placed to solve IHL effectiveness issues as they are caused by different circumstances (such as unwillingness to acknowledge that an armed conflict is taking place, the absence of incentives to comply, or even the lack of appropriate structures or resources to enable IHL compliance).[32] Bangerter has explained that IHL compliance will be enhanced only "if the reasons used by armed groups to justify respect or lack of it are understood and if the arguments in favour of respect take those reasons into account".[33] Recognizing that NSAGs play a relevant role in the formation of the law and particularly considering the value of their public expressions of willingness as useful tools is an important step in this direction.[34] In fact, NSAGs are keen on using unilateral declarations,

---

29 Somer 2007, pp. 661–662; and generally Greenwood 1983.

30 Sassòli 2007, p. 246.

31 Somer 2007, pp. 663–664; but see Bellal et al. 2011, p. 56; and Moir 2002, p. 99.

32 International Committee of the Red Cross (2003) Improving Compliance with International Humanitarian Law: ICRC Experts Seminars. https://www.icrc.org/end/assets/files/other/improving_compliance_with_international_report_eng_2003.pdf. Accessed 29 September 2015, pp. 20–21; and Bangerter 2011, p. 357.

33 Bangerter 2011, p. 383.

34 Heffes et al. 2015, p. 59.

special agreements and codes of conduct,[35] and their existence has been encouraged by states, international organizations, the International Committee of the Red Cross (ICRC) and non-governmental organizations.[36]

In sum, the proposed theory tries to narrow the breach between theoretical explanations and real strategies to address IHL compliance. To that end, a broad interpretation of the principle of equality of belligerents makes possible to take into account NSAGs' contributions, which in the end will serve for the purpose of ensuring the application of IHL equally and realistically.[37]

7.3 Non-State Armed Groups' Courts: An Inquiry into Their Legal Nature

While the administration of justice is a governmental function par excellence, IHL recognizes that during NIACs that NSAGs must respect judicial guarantees while passing sentences. The most basic provision in this respect is CA3, which affirms that "the passing of sentences and the carrying out of executions without previous judgments pronounced by a regularly constituted court, affording all the judicial guarantees which are recognized as indispensable by civilized people" is prohibited with respect to persons taking no active part in hostilities. It also contains a non-discrimination clause under which such individuals "shall in all circumstances be treated humanely, without any adverse distinction founded on race, colour, religion or faith, sex, birth or wealth, or any other similar criteria".

AP II develops and supplements CA3 without modifying its existing conditions of application. Its Article 6(2) includes several standards based on the more rigorous provisions of GC III and GC IV, and also from the International Covenant on Civil and Political Rights, particularly Article 15.[38] It is applicable "to the prosecution and punishment of criminal offences related to the armed conflict" and states that "[n]o sentence shall be passed and no penalty shall be executed on a person found guilty of an offence except pursuant to a conviction pronounced by a court offering the essential guarantees of independence and impartiality". As its commentary affirms, it applies equally "to civilians and combatants who have fallen in the power of the adverse party and who may be subject to penal prosecution".[39] In addition, Article 6(3) affirms that a convicted person "shall be advised on conviction of his judicial and other remedies and of the time limits within which they may be exercised".

---

[35] La Rosa and Wuerzner 2008, pp. 332–333.

[36] Sassòli 2010, p. 30.

[37] Ibid., pp. 13–26.

[38] Sandoz et al. 1987, p. 1397; International Covenant on Civil and Political Rights, opened for signature 16 December 1966, 999 UNTS 171 (entered into force 23 March 1976).

[39] Sandoz et al. 1987, p. 1397.

Therefore, both CA3 and AP II unequivocally grant NSAGs the possibility to entrust a body to pass judgment upon individuals under their control. Kleffner affirms in this line that these rules "imply that, in order to be compliant with IHL in adjudicating cases, parties to an armed conflict (including organized armed groups) must install judicial mechanisms that satisfy the mentioned requirements. To do so is not the concern of individual members but of the organized armed group as a whole".[40] Yet, the wording changes from one source to the other since a "regularly constituted court" is not included within the text of AP II. When dealing with states, this does not seem to be problematic since it is presumed that they have the capacity to run a proper judicial system. Non-State armed groups, nonetheless, present a different scenario since at the moment of drafting Article 6, "it was unlikely that a court could be "regularly constituted" under national law by an insurgent party".[41] But this scenario has changed since the Diplomatic Conference in which this provision was discussed, and nowadays there are different examples proving that NSAGs can actually establish courts to pass decisions.

7.3.1 The Legal Basis for NSAGs' Courts

7.3.1.1 NSAGs' Courts Through the Lens of State Law

The Customary IHL Study of the ICRC defines a "regularly constituted court" as one which "has been established and organized in accordance with the laws and procedures already in force in the country".[42] According to this view, IHL does not provide a legal basis for the establishment of courts by NSAGs, since this could only be achieved by virtue of the domestic legislation or constitution of a state—which would not allow NSAGs to set up a parallel judicial system completely separate from that of the state.

In the commentary to CA3 of 1952, Pictet does not actually analyse the legal basis of such courts, but instead concentrates on the prohibition of "summary justice"[43] from a State's judicial system perspective. In the recent commentary to CA3, this position seems to be justified by clarifying that the requirement of a regularly constituted court "focuses more on the capacity of the court to conduct a fair trial than on how it is established".[44] Moreover, instead of referring to

40 Kleffner 2011, p. 451.

41 Sandoz et al. 1987, p. 1398.

42 Henckaerts and Doswald-Beck 2005, p. 355.

43 Pictet 1952, p. 54.

44 International Committee of the Red Cross (2016) Commentary on Common Article 3 of the Geneva Convention for the Amelioration of the Condition of the Wounded and Sick in Armed Forces in the Field. www.icrc.org/applic/ihl/ihl.nsf/Treaty.xsp?documentId=4825657B0C7E 6BF0C12563CD002D6B0B&action=openDocument. Accessed 14 April 2016 (ICRC CA3 Commentary), para 678.

"civilized peoples" as CA3 does, Pictet points out that "[a]ll civilized *nations* surround the administration of justice with safeguards aimed at eliminating the possibility of judicial errors" (emphasis added).[45] He then recognizes that "it leaves intact the right of the state to prosecute, sentence and punish according to the law".[46] Notwithstanding the fact that CA3 addresses both parties to the conflict, Pictet does not seem to recognize a proper legal basis for the creation of judicial bodies by NSAGs, but only recognizes the prohibition incumbent upon NSAGs to not summarily execute someone who is taking no part in the hostilities, a practice that has been denounced by international bodies in different resolutions and reports.[47] As a result, as Zegveld has noted, the requirements of CA3 are actually "ambiguous".[48]

Other views have also argued in favour of the link with the national legal order of states. The United States Supreme Court in the *Hamdan* decision, for instance, has noted that a regularly constituted court is "not specifically defined in either CA3 or its accompanying commentary [of 1952–1960]".[49] In order to clarify its meaning, the majority looked at the commentary to Article 66 of GC IV which discusses "properly constituted courts" of an occupying power. Nonetheless, Justice Alito in his dissenting opinion follows the domestic law perspective as a basis for the establishment of courts in NIACs:

> In order to determine whether a court has been properly appointed, set up, or established, it is necessary to refer to a body of law that governs such matters. I interpret Common Article 3 as looking to the domestic law of the appointing country because I am not aware of any international standard regarding the way in which such a court must be appointed, set up, or established, and because different countries with different government structures handle this matter differently. Accordingly, "a merely constituted court" is a court that has been appointed, set up, or established in accordance with the domestic law of the appointing country.[50]

The practical consequences of only considering the link between courts established in NIACs with state legislation have not been thoroughly envisaged. There are, at least, two problems that this position cannot solve which are similar to those that serve to reject the theories that linked NSAGs' IHL obligations to State's domestic law.

Firstly, it is difficult to imagine the application of this legal regime in non-international armed conflicts fought only between NSAGs. If one adheres to the

---

45 Pictet 1952, p. 54.

46 Pictet 1958, p. 39.

47 See for instance UN Commission on Human Rights (1995) Situation of human rights in the Sudan. UN Doc. E/CN.4/RES/1995/77, para 15; and UN Commission on Human Rights (1989) Question of human rights and fundamental freedoms in Afghanistan, UN Doc. E/CN.4/RES/1989/67, para 11.

48 Zegveld 2002, p. 69.

49 *Hamdan v. Rumsfeld*, [2006] USSC, 548 U.S., p. 69.

50 Ibid., Dissenting Opinion of Judge Alito, p. 3.

view that domestic law governs such actions, thus making the establishment of any judicial body by an armed group illegal, then the judicial guarantees contained in CA3 and AP II seem to be stripped of any practical effect for those conflicts purely between non-State actors. Secondly, it is unclear how this position would operate in complex scenarios, such as in NIACs that take place in the territory of any given state between a NSAG and a third state. Would armed groups be in breach of the national law of the third state or should the one of the territorial state prevail? Determining domestic law as the only legal basis for the establishment of judicial bodies in NIACs would entail a number of complexities related to the aforementioned limitations, amongst others. Consequently, it is necessary to seek other alternatives.

7.3.1.2 A Promising Example: NSAGs' Courts and a Possible Argument of Customary International Law

As long as armed groups actually take part in the implementation of obligations of IHL, there may be chances to eventually identify signs of a nascent *praxis* and *opinio juris*. To that end, a broader interpretation based on the principle of equality of belligerents could authorize their existence based on NSAGs' own regulations.[51] Based on CA3 and AP II, both states and armed groups are required to comply with exactly the same rules irrespective of their causes. As explained above, where the parties to a NIAC are recognized as equal before law, there are more chances that a NSAG will show a willingness to conduct their actions in accordance IHL.[52]

Taking this into account, if the legal basis for the courts of states in NIACs can potentially be found in their domestic laws, NSAGs should be able to refer to their own "legislation" in order to justify their establishment of similar judicial bodies.[53] This was recently proposed by the ICRC in the commentary to CA3:

> Common Article 3 requires 'a regularly constituted court'. If this would refer exclusively to state courts constituted according to domestic law, non-State armed groups would not be able to comply with this requirement. The application of this rule in common Article 3 to 'each Party to the conflict' would then be without effect. Therefore, to give effect to this provision, it may be argued that courts are regularly constituted as long as they are constituted according to the 'laws' of the armed group.[54]

---

[51] See generally Greenwood 1983, pp. 221–234; and Heffes and Kotlik 2014, pp. 1201–1204.

[52] Sassòli et al. 2011, p. 347: "[i]f IHL did not respect the principle of the equality of belligerents before it in non-international armed conflicts, it would have an even smaller chance of being respected".

[53] Also in this line, Willms 2015, p. 152: "[i]f 'law' [in terms of CA3] is interpreted as state law only, this could be understood as prohibiting armed groups to operate courts. In the context of humanitarian law, the term 'law' could also include law by an armed group."

[54] ICRC CA3 Commentary, above n 44, para 692.

This seems to be a clear expression of the equality of belligerents. And it had been already articulated by Nigeria back at the 1974–1977 Diplomatic Conference. Its representative, Mr. Abdul-Malik, affirmed precisely this when he stated that "[r]ebels could certainly set up courts with a genuine legal basis [and] [i]t was only logical that if rebels could organize themselves sufficiently to observe the protocols, and thereby enjoy their protection, they could also organize a recognizable body of law".[55] The United Kingdom Manual of the Law of Armed Conflict follows the same idea, considering that the word "law" in Article 6(2)(c) of AP II "could also be wide enough to cover 'laws' passed by an insurgent authority".[56] Also, the commentary to AP II affirms "the possible co-existence of two sorts of national legislation, namely that of the state and that of the insurgents".[57] Sivakumaran advances on a similar point by affirming that "reference to law in this context should not be limited to state law. This would allow the courts of non-State armed groups to satisfy the necessary criterion".[58]

Therefore, bearing in mind that both CA3 and AP II create equal rights and obligations upon the Parties to the armed conflict and the views articulated above, it seems logical, coherent and consistent to argue that if states can rely on their own domestic systems as a legal basis for the establishment of courts in NIACs, NSAGs can do the same based on the principle of equality of belligerents. This alternative could actually solve some of the difficult situations raised above and also include those conflicts fought only between armed groups. In addition, this would increase the effectiveness of IHL, and it addresses a potential gap between theory and real-world problems and scenarios. Taking into account the practice of armed groups would give a real value to the rules, recognizing that the reasons why they are actually bound by them are the same as those of states. If only domestic legal frameworks governed the creation of such judicial bodies, then a differentiation between NSAGs and states would be created. Nonetheless, if both parties could refer to their internal laws, then equality between them would remain intact.

In addition, this position could also be based on the rules on interpretation of treaties codified in the Vienna Convention on the Law of Treaties (VCLT). Article 31(1) notes that a treaty shall be interpreted in good faith in accordance with the ordinary meaning to be given to the terms of the treaty in their context, and in the

---

[55] Federal Political Department (1978) Official Records of the Diplomatic Conference on the Reaffirmation and Development of International Humanitarian Law Applicable in Armed Conflicts (1974–1977): Volume 8. http://www.loc.gov/rr/frd/Military_Law/pdf/RC-records_Vol-17.pdf. Accessed 1 June 2016, p. 360, para 20.

[56] UK Ministry of Defence (2004) The Joint Service Manual of the Law of Armed Conflict. https://www.gov.uk/government/uploads/system/uploads/attachment_data/file/27874/JSP3832004Edition.pdf. Accessed 29 September 2015, p. 404, fn 94.

[57] Sandoz et al. 1987, p. 1339.

[58] Sivakumaran 2012, p. 306.

light of its object and purpose.[59] Together with the context, Article 31(3)(b) includes "any subsequent practice in the application of the treaty which establishes the agreement of the parties regarding its interpretation".[60] This is particularly relevant, since the Special Rapporteur of the International Law Commission has recently affirmed that subsequent practice also includes "practices by non-State entities which fall within the scope of what the treaty conceives as forms of its application".[61] With respect to IHL rules, it could be implied that not only the practice of states should be taken into account, but also that of NSAGs in order to interpret what "regularly constituted courts" mean.

This proposition is validated by real-world examples and practice of NSAGs.[62] It is therefore not merely an academic hypothetical. In 1991, for instance, the *Frente Farabundo Martí para la Liberación Nacional* (FMLN) in El Salvador issued a document entitled "Principles, Norms and Measures Ordered by FMLN in the Course of the War", where it established certain rules for its own penal system.[63] The fact that these provisions were reviewed by the UN Mission for El Salvador in order to assess to their conformity with IHL was taken by Zegveld as evidence that the Organization accepted the NSAG's competence to issue internal legislation. She points out in this regard that Article 6 of AP II refers not only to the laws of the state, but also to those adopted by the non-State entity.[64] Other internal laws of NSAGs also include similar provisions. The Constitution of the Republic of Somaliland—a breakaway region in Somalia—has an entire chapter on "The Judicial Branch" where it is affirmed that this non-State actor "shall have a judicial branch whose function is to adjudicate on proceedings between the Government and the public or between the various members of the public".[65] In Sudan, the Constitution of the Sudan People's Liberation Army provides the basis for the establishment of martial Courts,[66] and the Kurdistan Organization of the

---

[59] Vienna Convention on the Law of Treaties, opened for signature 23 May 1969, 1155 UNTS 331 (entered into force 27 January 1980), Article 31(1).

[60] Ibid., Article 31(3)(b).

[61] UN General Assembly 2014, p. 20, para 42.

[62] Bangerter 2012, p. 26 for a list of armed groups with disciplinary or penal codes.

[63] Principios, Normativos y Medidas Dispuestas por el FMLN en el Transcurso de la Guerra 1991, quoted in Zegveld 2002, p. 70.

[64] Zegveld 2002, p. 70.

[65] Republic of Somaliland (2000) The Constitution of the Republic of Somaliland. http://theirwords.org/media/transfer/doc/1_so_somaliland_2000_30-dd4d73a4d9dee6e847790e82b247d881.pdf. Accessed 29 September 2015, Article 97.

[66] The Sudan People's Liberation Army (SPLA) Act (2003). http://theirwords.org/media/transfer/doc/1_sd_splm_a_2003_03-5fd4e4fabf407e670f236c8d3ecaf381.pdf. Accessed 29 September 2015, Articles 60 and ff.

Communist Party had actually established back in 1985 regional and central levels of "Komala Revolutionary Courts" in order to administer justice in Kurdistan.[67]

These examples can serve as a promising road of action, proving a nascent *praxis* and *opinio juris* by armed groups to the extent that they comply with the requirements of giving a legal basis for the establishment of judicial bodies. Their internal laws, therefore, are tools used by certain NSAGs to actually incorporate IHL into a system of rules. While this scenario follows what the principle of equality of belligerents represents, an opposing view based on States' national legislation clearly diminishes the legitimacy of IHL as perceived by these entities. Placing the internal regulation of all the parties in an equal position can only work to enhance the respect for the rule of law, and even to encourage for their creation.

7.3.2 Challenges and Consequences

It shall be noted that the position advanced above raised some problematic scenarios. At least three can be identified. Firstly, it is not clear that it could be applied in practice to every NSAG. Certainly, their level of organization and, perhaps, control over territory are determinative factors. In fact, after receiving certain criticisms, the FMLN contended that its procedural law did not afford some fair trial guarantees because the obligations of AP II have to be "adapted to the conditions and capacity" of the warring parties.[68] This was also one of the approaches presented by Doswald-Beck recently when referring to CA3:

> The question [...] is whether, in situations where rebel groups do not possess sufficient territory and/or are not sufficiently organized to exercise governmental authorities, they should hold trials without being in automatically in violation of this provision. If the standard to be required is the expected of state authorities, the response would be that any attempt at holding a trial is bound to result in a violation. Therefore, one approach would be that Common Article 3 prevents such trials altogether.[69]

Moreover, some NSAGs do not have written rules, thus making it quite difficult to identify their "domestic" legislations. For instance, the Bemba's *Mouvement de Libération du Congo* had courts but did not have any publicly available penal code.[70] IHL, nevertheless, still binds these entities to respect certain safeguards in NIACs. This scenario seems to follow what Sassòli has called a "sliding scale of obligations". In his words, "[t]he better organized an armed group is and the more

[67] Komala Central Committee (1985) Penal Procedure and Revolutionary Courts of Komala. http://theirwords.org/media/transfer/doc/ut_ir_komala_1985_10-353859694966ca4cab2010fdf09 11b9e.pdf. Accessed 29 September 2015, Articles 1 and 4.

[68] Frente Farabundo Martí para la Liberación Nacional, Secretariat for the Promotion and Protection of Human Rights 1988, p. 20.

[69] Doswald-Beck 2015, p. 489.

[70] Willms 2015, p. 166.

stable control over the territory it has" the more IHL rules would become applicable.[71] This is the *rationale* behind the higher level of organization and control over territory required for AP II to be applicable.[72] One could expect from a highly organized NSAG exercising long-term control over a territory and having developed state-like institutions, including a judiciary, a higher degree of respect for international obligations with regard to fair trials guarantees. Yet, a minimum "recognized as indispensable by civilized people" should always be respected.

Secondly, there is nothing to prevent NSAGs from including within their internal laws certain provisions that could diminish the rights and obligations enshrined in IHL with respect to judicial guarantees. This could be the case of a provision explicitly preventing the independence of the tribunal, since most likely its members will also be part of the NSAGs, or a rule allowing for executions. For example, despite recognizing the existence of a judiciary system through sharia courts,[73] Article 11 of the Layha, or code of conduct, for Mujahideen affirms that:

> In case of the capture of contractors who transport and supply fuel, equipment or other materials for the infidels and their slave administration, as well as those who build military centres for them and those high – and low – ranking employees of security companies, interpreters of the infidels and drivers involved in enemy supply [business], if a judge proves the fact that the aforementioned persons are indeed involved in such activities, they should be punished by death.[74]

According to the obligations enshrined in CA3, the legality of such punishments could certainly be challenged. In any case, it is important to bear in mind that this humanitarian provision would still continue to apply regardless, as its rules constitute the minimum standards that protect individuals against any attempt to implement a lower threshold of protection.[75] If they were indeed implemented, members of NSAGs could potentially be committing war crimes.[76]

Thirdly, although the ICRC explores a different legal basis for NSAGs' judicial bodies, the new Commentary of CA3 notes that nothing in this provision "implies that a state must recognize or give legal effect to the results of a trial or other judicial proceeding conducted by a non-State Party to the conflict. This is consistent with the final paragraph of common Article 3 with respect to the legal status of such Parties".[77] This position is therefore linked to the final phrase of CA3, which affirms that its application "shall not affect the legal status of the

---

[71] Sassòli and Shani 2011, p. 430.

[72] Ibid., pp. 430–431.

[73] Munir 2011, Annex, p. 112, Article 38.

[74] Ibid., p. 107, Article 11.

[75] ICJ, *Case Concerning Military and Paramilitary Activities in and against Nicaragua (Nicaragua v United States of America),* Judgment, 27 June 1986, [1986] ICJ Rep 14, para 218.

[76] Rome Statute of the International Criminal Court, opened for signature 17 July 1998, 2187 UNTS 90 (entered into force 1 July 2002), Article 8(2)(c).

[77] ICRC CA3 Commentary, above n 44, para 695.

Parties to the conflict". Until now, this sentence had been understood as an explicit refusal by states to recognize that a non-State armed group has "any new international status, whatever it may be and whatever titled it may give itself or claim",[78] and had no relation with possible judicial procedures or decisions by armed groups' courts. In principle, by leaving to States' will the recognition of judicial processes carried out by these non-State actors, one could simply challenge the *effet utile* of the rule as such. What would be the purpose of requesting armed groups as parties to NIACs to follow a minimum of judicial guarantees if they could just be left without any legal effect, as if they were not respected at all?

Facing these difficulties in the link between internal legislation and the respect for humanitarian norms, some conclusions must be drawn in order to enhance the protection of individuals in NIACs. If a NSAG does not reach the level of organization required to create a judicial body (or whatever organ entrusted to that function) based on its internal "law",[79] then in order to respect the judicial guarantees enshrined in IHL, a combination of two complementary alternatives should be presented: a restrictive approach based on Pictet's theory, admitting that NSAGs could not exercise any type of judicial activity and the only prohibition would be not to summarily execute an individual, that is complemented by a Sassòlian sliding scale of obligations. The latter would allow the NSAG to be bound only by those provisions that it can practically (and realistically) fulfil.[80] While the former option is more restrictive, it assures a minimum of protection for every individual in NSAGs' hands. The complementarity of the sliding scale of obligations, however, faces a difficulty that should be noted—it could create an intermediate NIAC between CA3 and AP II without giving any clear criteria on how to determine its existence. It is therefore proposed to adopt the restricted alternative for every NSAG, and, only in so far as these entities have a proper legal

[78] Pictet 1960b, p. 44. According to Pictet in the Commentary to GC I, this provision was caused by States' fear that its application may interfere with their right to lawfully suppress NSAGs. Furthermore, it was not intended to "constitute any recognition by the de jure Government that the adverse Party has authority of any kind" or "to give [that party] any right to special protection or any immunity, whatever it may be and whatever title it may give itself or claim". Pictet 1952, p. 61.

[79] There is also the possibility that the group is unwilling to carry out judicial activities and to create bodies for those purposes. The Forces Nouvelles in Ivory Coast serve as an example of this scenario. International Committee of the Red Cross (2005) Annual Report. http://www.icrc.org/eng/resources/documents/annual-report/icrc-annual-report-2005.htm. Accessed 30 September 2015, p. 128: "In Forces Nouvelles-controlled areas, the ICRC was concerned about detention conditions, the absence of a functioning judicial system and the consequent lack of judicial guarantees. It raised these issues on several occasions with the detaining authorities and the Forces Nouvelles' leadership".

[80] It has been suggested that this is because NSAGs have fewer resources than states. Willms 2015, p. 175: "Indeed, armed groups have to devote a lot of their existing resources to their military because states usually try to defeat armed groups on their territory. Foreign states and the UN are, in most cases, not willing to provide aid in order to improve the judiciary of armed groups".

basis to be respectful of IHL, they would be entitled to establish a judicial body and exercise judicial functions.

The principle of equality of belligerents provides not only that the same rights and obligations bind all parties, but also that the source of those rights and obligations should be the same. This requires that all of them, including NSAGs, have a role in the process of creation and reaffirmation of the applicable rules. The contrary would lead to subordinating these non-State actors' obligations to those of the state, which appears to be an unacceptable scenario.

7.4 Concluding Remarks

This article has attempted to cover a specific challenge posed in NIACs—the legal basis for the existence of courts constituted by armed groups. In this regard, it has been suggested that based on the principle of equality of belligerents, these non-State actors should be able to rely on their "internal" legislation instead of referring to the State's domestic law. While this paper did not provide an answer for all the questions that are raised by the prospect of NSAGs having the legal capability to create judicial bodies in armed conflicts, the aim was to contribute to the ongoing study of their behaviours, especially to achieve enhanced IHL compliance by them.

First, different reasons to hold that armed groups are bound by IHL were presented. It was suggested that the customary status of this legal regime, which enables a broad interpretation of the principle of equality of belligerents, provides a plausible explanation of its binding nature for NSAGs in an effective manner. That theoretical framework led us to reject some existing theories concerning armed groups' obligations to comply with domestic legislations.

Following this rejection, the legal basis for the creation of judicial bodies in NIACs was explored in Section III. It proposed a complementary combination between the principle of equality of belligerents and the sliding scale of obligations approach. Taking these into account, both parties to a non-international armed conflict would be required to rely on their "internal" regulations in order to exercise judicial functions. This view rejected, at the same time, an alternative based purely on States' legal regimes, which would clearly diminish the legitimacy of IHL as perceived by NSAGs. Only by placing the parties in an equal position could the rule of law be better respected. Yet, it was also concluded that if the level of organization of the non-State entity was not enough to actually carry out full judicial functions, it would have to respect, as a minimum, the prohibition not to summarily execute individuals.

The above-mentioned proposals tried to open doors for new paradigms to be explored, particularly in the light of how NIACs operate in the real world. Some commentators, however, are likely to insist that accepting the premise that NSAGs could refer to internal norms with a similar hierarchy as those of states could legitimize their goals and aims. As Cismas has correctly suggested with respect to their subjectivity, "[l]egitimation may indeed take place, however, one needs to understand and emphasize that the resulting legitimation is that of the actor as rights-holder and duty bearer, not of its goals and conduct".[81] In practice, NSAGs will hardly need an academic paper to sanctify actions that they already carry out and to argue in favour of the existence of rules aiming to protect individuals held by these entities is a far better scenario than focusing merely on the actions of states. A perspective that neglects the equality of belligerents principle creates a differentiation that, in the end, leads down a road of negative consequences not for international law, but for those individuals in the hands of armed groups in NIACs.

Acknowledgments The author would also like to thank Manuel J. Ventura, Marcos D. Kotlik and Brian E. Frenkel for their comments and suggestions on earlier drafts.

References

Articles, Books and Other Documents

Bangerter O (2011) Reasons why armed groups choose to respect international humanitarian law or not. Int Rev Red Cross 93(882):353–384

Bangerter O (2012) Internal Control: Codes of Conduct within Insurgent Armed Groups. Small Arms Survey, Graduate Institute of International and Development Studies, Geneva

Bellal A, Giacca G, Casey-Maslen S (2011) International law and armed non-state actors in Afghanistan. Int Rev Red Cross 93(881):47–79

Casey-Maslen S (2014) The War Report: Armed Conflict in 2013. Oxford University Press, Oxford

Cassese A (1981) The Status of Rebels under the 1977 Geneva Protocols on Non-International Armed Conflicts. Int Comp Law Q 30(2):416–439

Cismas I (2014) Religious Actors and International Law. Oxford University Press, Oxford

Clapham A (2006) Human Rights Obligations of Non-State Actors. Oxford University Press, Oxford

Clapham A (2012) Brierly's Law of Nations. Oxford University Press, Oxford

d'Aspremont J (2008) La légitimité des rebelles en droit international. European society of international law Heidelberg Meeting

d'Aspremont J, De Hemptinne J (2012) Droit international humanitaire. Pedone, Paris

Doswald-Beck L (2015) Judicial Guarantees under Common Article 3. In: Clapham A, Gaeta P, Sassòli M (eds) The 1949 Geneva Conventions: A Commentary. Oxford University Press, Oxford, pp 469–494

Frente Farabundo Martí para la Liberación Nacional, Secretariat for the Promotion and Protection of Human Rights (1988) The Legitimacy of Our Methods of Struggle. Inkworth Press on behalf of FMLN, Berkeley

Greenwood C (1983) The relationship between ius ad bellum and ius in bello. Rev Int Stud 9(4):221–234

Heffes E, Kotlik M (2014) Special Agreements as Means to Enhance Compliance with IHL in Non-International Armed Conflicts: An Inquiry into the Governing Legal Regime. Int Rev Red Cross 96(895/896):1195–1224

Heffes E, Kotlik M, Frenkel B (2015) Addressing Armed Opposition Groups through Security Council Resolutions: A New Paradigm? In: Lachenmann F, Roder T, Wolfrum R (eds) Max Planck Yearbook of United Nations Law. Brill Nijhoff, Leiden/Boston, pp 32–67

[81] Cismas 2014, p. 75.

Henckaerts J-M (2002) Binding Armed Opposition Groups through Humanitarian Treaty Law and Customary Law. In: Proceedings of the Bruges Colloquium: Relevance of International Humanitarian Law to Non-State Actors, pp 123–137

Henckaerts J-M, Doswald-Beck L (2005) Customary International Humanitarian Law. Cambridge University Press, Cambridge

Kälin W, Künzli J (2009) The Law of International Human Rights Protection. Oxford University Press, Oxford

Klabbers J (2013) International Law. Cambridge University Press, Cambridge

Kleffner J (2011) The applicability of international humanitarian law to organized armed groups. Int R Red Cross 93(882):443–461

La Rosa A-M, Wuerzner C (2008) Armed groups, sanctions and the implementation of international humanitarian law. Int R Red Cross 90(870):327–341

Moir L (2002) The Law of Internal Armed Conflict. Cambridge University Press, Cambridge

Munir M (2011) The Layha for the Mujahideen: an analysis of the Code of Conduct for the Taliban fighters under Islamic Law. Int R Red Cross 93(881):81–102 and Annex

Pejić J (2011) The Protective Scope of Common Article 3: More than Meets the Eye. Int Rev Red Cross 93(881):189–225

Pictet J (ed) (1952) Commentary on the Geneva Convention (i) for the Amelioration of the Condition of the Wounded and Sick in Armed Forces in the Field. International Committee of the Red Cross, Geneva

Pictet J (ed) (1958) Commentary on the Geneva Convention (IV) Relative to the Protection of Civilian Persons in Time of War. International Committee of the Red Cross, Geneva

Pictet J (ed) (1960a) Commentary on the Geneva Convention (II) for the Amelioration of the Condition of Wounded, Sick and Shipwrecked Members of the Armed Forces at Sea. International Committee of the Red Cross, Geneva

Pictet J (ed) (1960b) Commentary on the Geneva Convention (III) Relative to the Treatment of Prisoners of War. International Committee of the Red Cross, Geneva

Sandoz Y, Swinarski C, Zimmerman B (1987) Commentary on the Additional Protocols of 8 June 1977 to the Geneva Conventions of 12 August 1949. Martinus Nijhoff Publishers, The Netherlands

Sassòli M (2007) Ius ad bellum and Ius in bello—The Separation between the Legality of the Use of Force and Humanitarian Rules to be Respected in Warfare: Crucial or Outdated? In: Schmitt M, Pejić J (eds) International Law and Armed Conflict: Exploring the Faultlines. Essays in Honour of Yoram Dinstein. Martinus Nijhoff Publishers, Leiden/Boston, pp 241–264

Sassòli M (2010) Taking Armed Groups Seriously: Ways to Improve their Compliance with International Humanitarian Law. J Int Humanitarian Legal Stud 1:5–51

Sassòli M, Shani Y (2011) Should the obligations of states and armed groups under international humanitarian law really be equal? Int Rev Red Cross 93(882):426–436

Sassòli M, Bouvier A, Quintin A (2011) How Does Law Protect in War?, 3rd edn. International Committee of the Red Cross, Geneva

Sivakumaran S (2012) The Law of Non-International Armed Conflicts. Oxford University Press, Oxford

Somer J (2007) Jungle justice: passing sentence on the equality of belligerents in non-international armed conflicts. Int Rev Red Cross 89(867):655–690

Stewart J (2003) Towards a single definition of armed conflict in international humanitarian law. A critique of internationalized armed conflict. Int Rev Red Cross 85(850):313–350

UN Commission on Human Rights (1989) Question of human rights and fundamental freedoms in Afghanistan, UN Doc. E/CN.4/RES/1989/67

UN Commission on Human Rights (1995) Situation of human rights in the Sudan, UN Doc. E/CN.4/RES/1995/77

UN General Assembly (2014) International Law Commission: Second Report on Subsequent Agreements and Subsequent Practice in Relation to the Interpretation of Treaties by Georg Nolte, Special Rapporteur, UN Doc. A/CN.4/671

UN Security Council (2005) Letter dated 31 January 2005 from the Secretary-General addressed to the President of the Security Council, UN Doc. S/2005/60
Vité S (2009) Typology of Armed Conflicts in International Humanitarian Law: Legal Concepts and Actual Situations. Int Rev Red Cross 91(873):69–94
Willms J (2015) Courts of armed groups—a tool for inducing higher compliance with international humanitarian law? In: Kriger H (ed) Inducing Compliance with International Humanitarian Law—Lessons from the African Great Lakes Region. Cambridge University Press, Cambridge, pp 149–180
Zegveld L (2002) The Accountability of Armed Opposition Groups in International Law. Cambridge University Press, Cambridge

Case Law

Hamdan v Rumsfeld [2006] USSC, 548 U.S
ICJ, *Case Concerning Military and Paramilitary Activities in and against Nicaragua (Nicaragua v United States of America),* Judgment, 27 June 1986, [1986] ICJ Rep 14
ICTY, *Prosecutor v Duško Tadić a/k/a "Dule"*, Decision on the Defence Motion for Interlocutory Appeal on Jurisdiction, 2 October 1995, Case No. IT-94-1-AR72
ICTY, *Prosecutor v Duško Tadić*, Judgement, 15 July 1999, Case No. IT-94-1-A

Treaties

Geneva Convention (I) for the Amelioration of the Condition of the Wounded and Sick in Armed Forces in the Field, opened for signature 12 August 1949, 75 UNTS 31 (entered into force 21 October 1950)
Geneva Convention (II) for the Amelioration of the Condition of Wounded, Sick and Shipwrecked Members of Armed Forces at Sea, opened for signature 12 August 1949, 75 UNTS 85 (entered into force 21 October 1950)
Geneva Convention (III) relative to the Treatment of Prisoners of War, opened for signature 12 August 1949, 75 UNTS 135 (entered into force 21 October 1950)
Geneva Convention (IV) relative to the Protection of Civilian Persons in Time of War, opened for signature on 12 August 1949, 75 UNTS 287 (entered into force 21 October 1950)
Hague Convention for the Protection of Cultural Property in the Event of Armed Conflict, opened for signature 14 May 1954, 249 UNTS 240 (entered into force 7 August 1956)
International Covenant on Civil and Political Rights, opened for signature 16 December 1966, 999 UNTS 171 (entered into force 23 March 1976)
Optional Protocol to the Convention on the Rights of the Child on the Involvement of Children in Armed Conflict, opened for signature 25 May 2000, 2173 UNTS 222 (entered into force 12 February 2002)
Protocol Additional to the Geneva Conventions of 12 August 1949, and relating to the Protection of Victims of Non-International Armed Conflicts, opened for signature 8 June 1977, 1125 UNTS 609 (entered into force 7 December 1978)
Protocol on Prohibitions or Restrictions on the Use of Mines, Booby-Traps and Other Devices (Protocol II as amended on 3 May 1996) annexed to the Convention on Prohibitions or Restrictions on the Use of Certain Conventional Weapons which may be deemed to be Excessively Injurious or to have Indiscriminate Effects, opened for signature 10 October 1980, 2048 UNTS 93 (entered into force 3 December 1998)
Rome Statute of the International Criminal Court, opened for signature 17 July 1998, 2187 UNTS 90 (entered into force 1 July 2002)

Vienna Convention on the Law of Treaties, opened for signature 23 May 1969, 1155 UNTS 331 (entered into force 27 January 1980)

Other Consulted Sources

Sivakumaran S (2011) Lessons for the law of armed conflict from commitments of armed groups: identification and legitimate targets and prisoners of war. Int Rev Red Cross 93(882):463–482

UN Security Council (1996) Letter Dated 11 December 1996 from the Permanent Representative of Sierra Leone to the United Nations Addressed to the Secretary General, with Annex: Peace Agreement between the Government of the Republic of Sierra Leone and the Revolutionary United Front of Sierra Leone, signed at Abidjan on 30 November 1996, UN Doc. S/1996/1034

Part II
Other Articles

Chapter 8
Defences for War Crimes and Crimes Against Humanity? Duress and the Rome Statute

Clare Frances Moran

Abstract Modern armed conflict has changed the way in which we understand the fighting of wars and the breakdown of diplomatic discourse. The Rome Statute, which was created to enforce the provisions of the law of war and international criminal law on a complementary basis, already appears dated because it deals with war crimes in a very traditional manner. At the same time, the Rome Statute has introduced a number of new ideas and new approaches. One such is the area of defences, which are now codified by the Rome Statute. This approach, of clarification through codification, is novel as the previous international criminal tribunals and domestic war crimes tribunals have dealt with the concept of defences on an *ad hoc* basis, or by excluding certain defences. The provisions in the Rome Statute codify six defences in total, one of which is duress. The defence of duress has not been accepted previously as a defence for serious crimes in international law and thus makes an interesting topic for discussion, particularly at this juncture where more and more cases are being heard by the International Criminal Court. This work examines the use of the defence of duress in international law and explores the problems of the current approach to defences in general, and duress in particular, in the Rome Statute.

Keywords Armed conflict · Defences · Duress · International criminal law · War crimes · Crimes against humanity

---

C.F. Moran (✉)
Edinburgh Napier University, Craiglockhart Campus, Colinton Road,
Edinburgh EH14 2DJ, Scotland, UK
e-mail: c.moran@napier.ac.uk

T.D. Gill et al. (eds.), *Yearbook of International Humanitarian Law 2015*,
Yearbook of International Humanitarian Law 18,
DOI 10.1007/978-94-6265-141-8_8

Contents

8.1 Introduction

The nature of armed conflict has changed dramatically. Wars are no longer fought as they once were: in defined battlefields, with artillery aimed at specific targets. Theatres of combat can now stretch to whole regions, and ordinary individuals may now be the targets of armed groups. Concurrently, there has been a change in the enforcement and regulation of armed conflict. The inception of the Rome Statute of the International Criminal Court (Rome Statute)[1] in 1998 created a permanent, international forum for the enforcement of violations of the law of armed conflict. In creating such an entity, a new system of "Rome law"[2] has emerged, bringing with it a new approach to a number of areas connected to the enforcement of the norms of international humanitarian law. Specifically, the Rome Statute now includes rights for victims,[3] enumerates significant rights for the accused[4] with the aim of ensuring a fair trial, and, notably, codifies defences which the accused may plead.[5] The latter issue, of defences, is the subject of this work, as the Rome Statute's codification of defences is the first formal acknowledgment in a treaty that defences could be available for war crimes and crimes against humanity.

The concept of defences for such crimes, and the discussion thereof at international criminal tribunals, is not new. During the cases heard by the war crimes tribunals of the Second World War, some of which are discussed below, a

[1] Rome Statute of the International Criminal Court, opened for signature 17 July 1998, 2187 UNTS 90 (entered into force 1 July 2002) (Rome Statute).

[2] A neat phrase distinguishing between international criminal law in general and the codified law in the Rome Statute used by Leila Sadat on a number of occasions. For a more specific discussion on codification and sources of law, see Sadat 2000.

[3] See, for example, Rome Statute, above n 1, Articles 68 and 75.

[4] Ibid., Article 67.

[5] Ibid., Articles 31–33.

number of defendants raised the possibility of defending their action by relying on the concepts of self-defence, necessity, and duress. The cases which were heard at this time represented, for the most part, traditional warfare: those indicted were soldiers and members of the armed forces. The difficulty in applying those defences was evident in the arguments put forward in their judgments. The past two decades have demonstrated that warfare has changed and that those outside the armed forces may now be more likely to commit war crimes and crimes against humanity. Indeed, the barbarous acts of entities such as Daesh demonstrate that warfare may no longer be limited to a geographical area or even one state entity. Armies no longer march to conquer or retreat as they once did: Daesh attacked Paris in November 2015[6] and swiftly left, using "soldiers" who were nationals of the very countries it sought to destroy. Where the crimes become more egregious and where the commission thereof diffuses through society in such a fashion, the issue of the impact of a defence, and the way in which criminal responsibility is affected, becomes more complex.

The most interesting inclusion in the Rome Statute, in the context of defences, is duress, for a number of reasons. It is not universally recognised as a defence to the most serious crime against the person at the domestic level, murder, and yet it appears in the Rome Statute which regulates the prosecution of "the most serious crimes of concern to humanity as a whole".[7] The provision of such a defence for certain situations where a person acts as a consequence of circumstances or a state of mind is not contested; it is the way in which the defence has been drafted that creates the issues discussed herein. The examination which follows explores the previous use of duress at war crimes tribunals and international criminal tribunals prior to the inception of the Rome Statute. The cases highlight the difficulty such tribunals had in applying duress, even to situations where individuals had suffered under great pressure, will be discussed, including an extensive examination of the decision in *Erdemović*[8] before the International Criminal Tribunal for the former Yugoslavia (ICTY). The inclusion of duress in the Rome Statute will then be discussed, using the work of the Preparatory Committee as well as the work of noted jurists to understand its inclusion. Finally, there is an application of "Rome law" to the case of Erdemović, to determine the efficacy and impact of the provisions under the Rome Statute: Would Erdemović's position be any different if the case came before the International Criminal Court (ICC)?

---

6 Fraser I and Henderson B (2015) Paris shooting: terrorists attack French capital—as it happened on Friday Nov 13. http://www.telegraph.co.uk/news/worldnews/europe/france/11995543/Paris-shooting-terrorists-attack-french-capital-as-it-happened-on-Friday-Nov-13.html. Accessed 1 March 2016.

7 Rome Statute, above n 1, Preamble. It is recognised that not all crimes within the scope of the ICC are crimes against the person, but the focus is on the availability of duress for such crimes, as the availability of duress for a property crime is not at issue in this work.

8 ICTY, *Prosecutor v Dražen Erdemović*, Judgment, 7 October 1997, Case No. IT-96-22-A (*Erdemović* 1997).

8.2 Duress Before International War Crimes Tribunals

Although its application may be elusive at the international level, the definition of duress is generally similar in both domestic law, where recognised, and in international law. The definition used in the Rome Statute relates to pressure, subdividing the defence into pressure which is generated by a threat of serious bodily harm from another and that which results from "circumstances beyond that person's control".[9] Taulbee notes that the formulation in the Rome Statute has "conflat[ed]"[10] the defences of duress and necessity, rather than supplying two different forms of duress. Indeed, duress and necessity may appear as separate defences in domestic law,[11] but they may also be conjoined as in the Rome Statute, albeit with theoretical differences in how both remove criminal liability.[12] Taulbee's argument, furthermore, relates to a greater extent about the concept of defences and how different types may remove liability at a theoretical level, without changing the final acquittal that both would generate.

However, there is a conspicuous lack of engagement with theory in the Rome Statute, precipitating the critique that its approach rejects the supposition that the defences are separate in character or application. The path chosen by the Rome Statute demonstrates the drafters' understanding of the defences as two different expressions of the same basic reasoning: those who are compelled to act, on whatever grounds, ought to be acquitted. Colvin's work appears to trace a similar model: he notes the importance of separating defences which relate to "contextual permission" and those which can be considered "defences of impairment".[13] He further discusses the difficulties inherent in the application of duress and necessity, noting the more consistent application of the principles underlying self-defence[14] and the general failure to clearly identify duress and necessity as justifications, excuses or, respectively, as an excuse and a justification. Colvin's conception would be to identify both as defences of contextual permission and then to develop a framework of principles around this notion. The framework he posits would correspond to the approach taken, not only by the Rome Statute, but also by many international criminal tribunals. Many of those from the era of the Second World War also had a limited engagement with theory, and none made a great deal of distinction between the theoretical roots of duress and necessity. The following discussion of the case law examines this point.

---

[9] Rome Statute, above n 1, Article 31(1)(d)(i).

[10] Taulbee 2009, p. 178.

[11] See, for example, in English law: Herring 2012, pp. 656–664 and 665–668; Padfield 2008, pp. 103 and 107; and *R v Howe*, Judgment of the Court of Appeal of England and Wales, [1987] AC 417, p. 453.

[12] See, for example, in German law: German Criminal Code 1994, ss 34–35; Bohlander 2008, p. 101.

[13] Colvin 1990, p. 407.

[14] Ibid., p. 401.

The *Ohlendorf*[15] case held that it was the "privilege" of the accused to raise a defence, with a corollary "duty" on the court to consider it.[16] In *Ohlendorf*, it was argued that the individuals were compelled to commit war crimes on account of the *Fuhrerprinzip,*[17] creating an obligation on all to obey Hitler's orders. Those accused argued that they had been subjected to pressure created by the Nazi hierarchy and made an argument for the application of the defence of duress, rather than superior orders, which was removed as a defence by the Nuremberg Charter. The tribunal held that although certain individuals may have felt pressure to conform during Hitler's reign in Germany, this pressure was insufficient to go beyond superior orders and could not stand alone as a case of duress. The tribunal distinguished between superior orders and duress[18] and held that in law, duress is a separate defence.[19] However, it also held that duress may be available in such a circumstance where the "will of the doer (does not) merge with the will of the superior".[20] Consideration of the unique circumstances in *Ohlendorf* did not demonstrate that the individuals had felt such pressure so as to be coerced into the acts libelled. Indeed, it was their willingness to act which undermined the plea of duress. Thus, the facts precluded the application of the defence in this instance, where it was unavailable simply because the facts demonstrated a degree of volition on the part of the accused.

The *Priebke*[21] case also discussed the concept of extenuating circumstances in a prosecution for the massacre of civilians. In this instance, both defendants had pleaded the existence of extenuating circumstances, which the tribunal acknowledged may constitute a defence. It held that the presence of superior orders and of military necessity may create extenuating circumstances for which the accused may be relieved of responsibility and that both are applicable during times of war.[22] The court noted, however, that a strict interpretation of the doctrines would apply in such a case and only where the participation of the individual in question was not critical to the execution of the task[23]: in other words, pressure from a superior which amounts to duress may only be pled as a defence where the individual is a lower-ranking officer. As in *Ohlendorf*, there was an element of volition demonstrated by the responsibility inherent in the planning and organisational role

---

15 *United States v Ohlendorf* et al., Judgment of the United States Military Tribunal Nuremberg, 8–9 April 1948.

16 Ibid., p. 468.

17 Ibid., p. 506.

18 Ibid., p. 471.

19 Ibid., p. 483.

20 Ibid., p. 480.

21 *Case of Hass and Priebke*, Sentencing Judgment of the Military Tribunal of Rome, 16 November 1998. http://www.asser.nl/upload/documents/DomCLIC/Docs/NLP/Italy/Hass_Priebke_CorteSupremaCasszione_16-11-1998.pdf. Accessed 12 May 2016.

22 Ibid., para 9.

23 Ibid., paras 9–10.

which Priebke had undertaken. Thus, the defence was unavailable in the circumstances.[24] The carefully circumscribed nature of the defence means that the defence of duress may relate to superior orders, but that the pressure which constitutes duress in law must be evidenced separately from the issue of orders from a superior. Both cases indicate that the pressure felt by orders from a superior must go further than simply feeling an obligation to act and, indeed, soldiers are not expected to act in an automatic, robotic fashion. For the defence to be available, an extensive degree of pressure needs to have been applied to the individual so as to overbear their will. If the will of the accused aligns with the act in the first place, the defence will be difficult to prove.

The *Flick* case also examined the availability of a defence of coercion in situations of war.[25] In this case, the defendants pleaded coercion, which was substantively the same as duress, as a defence to the war crimes, crimes against humanity, and crimes against property of which they were accused during the Second World War. In applying the law, the tribunal examined the Nuremberg tribunal's exclusion of the defence of superior orders when assessing the application of duress and concluded that it:

> might be reproached for wreaking vengeance rather than administering justice if it were to declare as unavailable to defendants the defense of necessity here urged in their behalf. This principle has had wide acceptance in American and English courts and is recognized elsewhere.[26]

There was limited further investigation in the bounds of the defence of duress, and indeed, it demonstrates the interchangeable usage of the defences of duress, necessity, and, now, coercion by the defendants and courts where the issue of removal of liability for acts committed under pressure arises. Once again, this tribunal accepted that the defence of duress may be raised, but that it had not to be applied in this instance as the necessary "compulsion and fear"[27] were not found to have been motives for their actions. Again, there was a failure to prove that the defendants were sufficiently pressurised so as to remove any freedom to act.

Thus, the unique situations in which war crimes are committed may make it difficult for a defence to be applied, even where it may be legally admissible. This is complicated further where the existence of duress is likely to relate, during armed conflict, to orders from a superior. As noted, the above tribunals have been able to distinguish between superior orders and to separately consider if the pressure applied to the individual pleading the defence ought to be considered duress. However, the individual is then bound to demonstrate a significant degree

---

[24] Ibid.

[25] The court was "a special tribunal constituted pursuant to a four-power agreement administering public international law", *U.S. v Flick* et al., Judgment of the United States Military Tribunal Nuremberg, 22 December 1947, para 1188.

[26] Ibid., para 1199.

[27] Ibid., para 1209.

of “compulsion or fear”. Furthermore, they must be acting against their own will: they must not support the aims of the war crimes. The cases thus far represent more straightforward examples in that the individuals were clearly not pressurised to act and, instead, were happy to comply with the orders given. The defence was thus not difficult to discount. However, in genuine cases of duress, this is quite a difficult point to prove for the defendant and raises the question of how their reluctance ought to be evidenced; if an individual is already working in a pressurised environment of battle or conflict, is he or she expected to withstand a greater degree of pressure? It would appear so, indeed that more would be expected of them than of the average person in a domestic criminal context. This discussion, which reinforces the conclusions of the tribunals immediately following the Second World War, demonstrates the incompatibility of the defence with the nature of armed conflict and of war crimes. Its lack of success for defendants often relates, as demonstrated, more to the context in which the events occurred, making it difficult for the individual to argue that he was sufficiently pressurised to benefit from the defence of duress. It is also worthwhile noting that these cases did not engage in an extensive exploration of the theory of such defences, nor in thorough comparative studies to support their acceptance of the availability of duress. The first case to carry out the latter task, at the international level, is one to which we now turn.

8.3 Duress and the International Criminal Tribunal for the Former Yugoslavia

The place of duress in international criminal law was discussed extensively in the case of *Erdemović*.[28] In an appeal from the original trial, the court undertook a wide comparative study of the nature of duress and concluded that there is no customary rule or general principle governing the application of the defence of duress. It was held that there is so much domestic dissonance over the defence that a clear rule could not be found. The lack of agreement centred on, firstly, whether the defence existed at the national level and then, where it existed, whether it could be applied to a charge of murder. No rule, thus, exists which is underpinned by *opinio juris*.[29] However, as highlighted above, this does conflict with previous practice at the international level which appeared to proceed on the issue without an extensive investigation of the existence of the defence at the national level. This exploration demonstrated the difficulty in the defence and thus made duress harder to plead at the ICTY than before previous tribunals. This resistance to the defence was mirrored at around the same time in domestic war crimes tribunals for

[28] *Erdemović* 1997, above n 8.

[29] Ibid., Joint Separate Opinion of Judge McDonald and Judge Vohrah, paras 48–51.

Rwanda.[30] Indeed, there appears to have been significant distaste for defences in general prior to the inception of the Rome Statute: The Amnesty International report[31] on principles of international criminal law, which was submitted to the Preparatory Committee during the Rome Statute negotiations, quoted Morris and Scharf's[32] work regarding the International Tribunal for the former Yugoslavia, where they noted that care ought to be taken when establishing defences for those accused of such serious crimes. It highlighted that "it is one thing to reduce the sentence to be imposed; it is quite another to negate the existence of any crime".[33] At this juncture, it is worth highlighting again that the issue of justifications and excuses is not dealt with extensively in international criminal law and, indeed, that no such classification has been discussed by tribunals or courts for the prosecution of war crimes or crimes against humanity. The distance between domestic criminal law theory and international criminal law has not been remedied, and so there remains, as of yet, no distinction between justifications and excuses in the realm of defences in the Rome Statute. No such distinction was made in the below case.

The trial, and subsequent appeal, of Dražen Erdemović[34] was heard in the months before the Rome Statute was created. His case was particularly important for the ICTY because, firstly, he was the first individual to be sentenced by the tribunal[35] and, secondly, because of the way in which it offered to shed light on the complex issue of defences for the tribunal. The case is often thought of as representing the first foray by an accused into the area of defences, but that is inaccurate: Erdemović did not lodge a defence with the tribunal. Rather, he made a statement with his guilty plea which amounted to a plea in mitigation. The court then discussed the potential of his plea as a full defence. Erdemović was an ordinary soldier, rather than an individual in any position of command responsibility, who had acted under orders and contributed to the Srebrenica massacre by the Bosnian Serb Army. Erdemović was initially charged with murder as a crime against humanity[36] and, in the alternative, violations of the laws and customs of war.[37] He pleaded guilty to the first charge, which was accepted, but was held not to have understood what this meant and the nature of his guilty plea,[38] with the caveat that he had no choice but to take part in the massacre, was

[30] *Affaire François Minani,* Judgment of the Tribunal of First Instance, Special Chamber, Gitarama, Rwanda, 25 September 1997. See Grover 2012, p. 212.

[31] Amnesty International 1997.

[32] Morris and Scharf 1995.

[33] Ibid., p. 111.

[34] *Erdemović* 1997, above n 8, and associated dissenting opinions.

[35] Ratner and Abrams 2001, p. 198.

[36] ICTY, *Prosecutor v Dražen Erdemović*, Sentencing Judgment, 29 November 1996, Case No. IT-96-22-T (*Erdemović* 1996), para 3.

[37] Ibid.

[38] *Erdemović* 1997, above n 8, Joint Separate Opinion of Judge McDonald and Judge Vohrah, para 15.

the subject of much discussion. Before remitting the case to a new Trial Chamber following this confusion, the Appeals Chamber discussed the defence of duress for war crimes and crimes against humanity extensively, despite neither Erdemović nor his defence counsel having requested that a defence be submitted.

The extent to which the accused may have the "right" has been endorsed by some authors: Knoops' idea is that the right to plead a defence is part of the right to a fair trial.[39] The rights of the defence before the court of the International Military Tribunal at Nuremberg also included a right to explain one's actions[40] as labelled by the court. At Nuremberg, this was the only reference made to any form of defence made by the accused during the proceedings, possibly to supplement any plea in mitigation that may be put forward. The Statute of the ICTY focused more on "fair trial" rights similar to those under the International Covenant on Civil and Political Rights,[41] although there is reference to defences in the Rules of Procedure and Evidence for the Tribunal.[42] The rules state that the prosecutor must be informed if the accused intends to submit a defence of alibi[43] or "any special defence"[44] with the examples of diminished or lack of mental responsibility offered. No mention of any other defences is made, although the list is not exhaustive by virtue of the way in which it has been drafted. There is no direct mention of duress, although there is evidence that the position at that time was greatly informed by the previous international criminal tribunals,[45] wherein the defence of superior orders was limited to a plea in mitigation.

It is argued that Erdemović made a plea in mitigation: he admitted that he had carried out the crimes, but stated that had he refused, he would have been killed.[46] The first Trial Chamber correctly noted that in cases in the previous international criminal tribunals had taken the concept of duress on a "case-by-case basis"[47] and that the idea of duress, "depending on the probative value and force" which may be attributed to the circumstances, could be considered a plea in mitigation or a defence.[48] Interestingly, the defence was not rejected on conceptual grounds, but

---

39 Knoops 2008, p. 2.

40 Agreement for the Prosecution and Punishment of the Major War Criminals of the European Axis, opened for signature 8 August 1945, 82 UNTC 280 (entered into force 8 August 1945), Charter of the International Military Tribunal (IMT Charter), Article 16(b).

41 International Covenant on Civil and Political Rights, opened for signature 16 December 1966, 999 UNTS 171 (entered into force 23 March 1976), Article 14.

42 International Criminal Tribunal for the former Yugoslavia (2015) Rules of Procedure and Evidence, UN Doc. It/32/Rev. 50, rule 67.

43 Ibid., rule 67(B)(i)(a).

44 Ibid., rule 67(B)(i)(b).

45 No reference was made to defences in the Statute of the ICTY; for further discussion on the legacy of Nuremberg, see Tomuschat 2006.

46 *Erdemović* 1996, above n 38, para 14.

47 Ibid., para 19.

48 Ibid., para 14.

rather on the basis of a lack of evidence.[49] This was overturned by the Appeals Chamber,[50] the judgment of which noted that the Trial Chamber had "occasioned a miscarriage of justice".[51] Despite this, it rejected the idea that duress could ever be a complete defence to a crime against humanity or a war crime where innocent lives were lost.[52] The Joint Separate Opinion of Judges Vorah and McDonald held that Erdemović did not understand what was meant by his guilty plea, because such a plea should usually be unequivocal.[53] His statement was taken as an intention to plead duress as a defence and the Chamber explored whether duress may constitute a full defence to a charge of crimes against humanity.[54] The Trial Chamber directed that Erdemović should be allowed to plead again in full knowledge of the consequences of his plea and he plead guilty to a charge of violating the laws and customs of war before a new Trial Chamber, which was accepted by the prosecutor.[55]

The Joint Separate Opinion undertook a survey of a number of legal jurisdictions and concluded that there was no single rule reflecting customary international law on the subject of duress.[56] This reflects well the contentious nature of duress, and the extensive survey of jurisdictions and international criminal tribunals[57] indicates that it is not possible to formulate a rule from such a disparate set of principles. It was on this reasoning that the judgment rested: where no rule on duress clearly existed, the tribunal could not accept the defence and was bound only to apply customary international law which was "beyond any doubt part of international humanitarian law" and contained within the conventions outlined in the Statute of the ICTY.[58]

On this basis, the tribunal held that the killing of innocents was not something that could be defended, espousing a binary perspective: Erdemović was either completely responsible and punished accordingly, or completely freed of responsibility through an acquittal. This offered nothing to the situation of a most reluctant, unwilling, and remorseful génocidaire. Indeed, Judge Li hinted at this point by highlighting the similarity between the repetition of the circumstances

[49] Ibid., para 20.

[50] *Erdemović* 1997, above n 8.

[51] Ibid., para 12.

[52] Ibid., para 19.

[53] Ibid., Joint Separate Opinion of Judge McDonald and Judge Vohrah, para 29.

[54] Ibid., para 15.

[55] ICTY, *Prosecutor v Dražen Erdemović*, Sentencing judgment, 5 March 1998, Case No. IT-96-22-T*bis*, (*Erdemović* 1998), para 8.

[56] *Erdemović* 1997, above n 8, Joint Separate Opinion of Judge McDonald and Judge Vohrah, para 49.

[57] Ibid., paras 59–65.

[58] UN Security Council 1993 Report of the Secretary-General pursuant to para 2 of Security Council Resolution 808 (1993), UN Doc S/25704, paras 34–35.

and the notion of a plea in mitigation, which would hint at the unequivocal nature of the guilty plea.[59] In more ways than this, the case demonstrates a missed opportunity: it provided an occasion on which to elucidate the grounds for a plea in mitigation and to contribute to international criminal legal theory in the area of defences by discussing the excusing and justificatory nature of certain defences.

The dissenting opinion of Antonio Cassese is the most notable aspect of the whole case, as Cassese disagreed fundamentally with the idea that an individual should be deprived of the defence of duress in the context of war crimes: his position can be summarised with reference to the oft-cited words that the law "should not set intractable standards of behaviour which require mankind to perform acts of martyrdom".[60] He held that the application of duress should be "realistic and flexible"[61] accepting that duress may be available

> when the killing would be in any case perpetrated by persons other than the one acting under duress (since then it is not a question of saving your own life by killing another person, but of simply saving your own life when the other person will inevitably die, which may not be "disproportionate" as a remedy).[62]

This raises the important issue of proportionality, which was highlighted as an ongoing problem with the defence of duress at the national level, as well as the international level, by van Sliedregt. Indeed, the issue hinges on "the concept of proportionality [... and] the weighing of human lives".[63] However, Cassese's point is that no weighing takes places: the accused had to comply or die and the victim would have died anyway. It should be said, however, that this should be regarded as a narrow, not to mention deeply theoretical, distinction: if all of the soldiers were to refuse and be killed, it would not be possible to massacre on the same scale. Indeed, the "arms and legs" of battalions are required to carry out large-scale attacks, and so there does exist an element of weighing one life against another, in that the accused person has chosen to act and kill in order to prevent his own death, which may or may not have been inevitable. By proceeding, and complying with the order, the inevitability of his or her death is never tested.

Thus, there appears to be little regard for any middle ground that could exist between the two situations, which may offer some succour to the victims without unduly punishing individuals who did not want to take part. This again demonstrates how difficult it can be to apply duress as a full defence to such serious crimes, particularly where there is no distinction between the types of defence. A broader approach, specifying not only full defences resulting in an acquittal, but also justificatory defences, excusatory defences, and pleas in mitigation, the latter of which formally acknowledges a reduction in punishment, may serve the

[59] *Erdemović* 1997, above n 8, Separate and Dissenting Opinion of Judge Li, paras 15 and 27.

[60] Ibid., Separate and Dissenting Opinion of Judge Cassese, para 47.

[61] Ibid.

[62] Ibid., para 12.

[63] van Sliedregt 2012, p. 258.

merciful purpose sought by Cassese without undermining the seriousness of the crimes in question. The idea of a need for such distinction is evident in the work of Cryer et al., in which the incongruity of codifying the defences in the Rome Statute, where the application of one of the defences had been rejected by the ICTY for a similarly serious crime, is highlighted.[64] Following this line of thought, the Rome Statute appears to have been influenced by the outcome of Cassese's opinion, without a deeper look at the underlying issues. It is to the drafting and operation of the Rome Statute that we now turn.

8.4 Duress, Proportionality, and the Rome Statute

The work of the Preparatory Committee for the Rome Statute and the discussions had by the members of the group in relation to grounds excluding criminal responsibility has not been discussed extensively,[65] reflecting the lack of focus on defences by the committee. Saland's chapter indicates that the work was the most contentious of all discussions on the general principles of law, given the distinctions between the domestic legal systems on the topic of defences.[66] It transpires that that the Canadian delegation initially proposed the defences as being part of the general principles of public international law. Saland then states that a proposal put forward by the Argentinian delegation and delegations from ten other legal systems represents the current formulation in the Rome Statute.[67] Indeed, the report on the work of the Preparatory Committee[68] appears to adopt the articles wholesale, and there is no substantive discussion on why these defences have been selected or why defences ought to be included in the first instance. Rather, the debate focuses on how the defences ought to be framed, and there is reference to duress as being limited to situations where the death of an individual was not likely. However, this proposal was not accepted and did not appear in the final draft.

As noted by Saland, it was desirable to have a proportionality test,[69] but the idea of what may be considered proportional in this context was not discussed. Given the significance of permitting a war crime, and the effect of labelling such

[64] Cryer et al. 2010, pp. 411–412.

[65] One of the few pieces of work was written by the Swedish delegation to the Preparatory Committee; see Saland 1999, pp. 189–216.

[66] Ibid., p. 206.

[67] Ibid.

[68] Preparatory Committee on the establishment of an International Criminal Court 1997 Decisions Taken by the Preparatory Committee at its Session held from 1 to 12 December 1997, UN Doc. A/AC.249/1997/L.9/Rev.1. http://www.iccnow.org/documents/DecisionsTaken18Dec97Eng.pdf. Accessed 9 June 2016.

[69] Saland 1999, p. 206.

action proportional, it is curious that there has not been further discussion of where the bounds of the doctrine of proportionality in this context may lie. The formulation of duress in Article 31(1)(d) of the Rome Statute is thus that which results:

> from a threat of imminent death or of continuing or imminent serious bodily harm against that person or another person, and the person acts necessarily and reasonably to avoid this threat, provided that the person does not intend to cause a greater harm than the one sought to be avoided. Such a threat may either be:

(i) Made by other persons; or
(ii) Constituted by other circumstances beyond that person's control.[70]

This formulation can be compared to the one noted by Cassese, in his dissenting opinion for *Erdemović*.[71] He noted that there were four main criteria for the defence to apply:

(i) the act charged was done under an immediate threat of severe and irreparable harm to life or limb;
(ii) there was no adequate means of averting such evil;
(iii) the crime committed was not disproportionate to the evil threatened (this would, e.g., occur in case of killing in order to avert an assault). In other words, in order not to be disproportionate, the crime committed under duress must be, on balance, the lesser of two evils;
(iv) the situation leading to duress must not have been voluntarily brought about by the person coerced.[72]

The defences are broadly similar, encompassing the requirements of a threat and a proportionate response. However, the "proportionality" test in the Rome Statute is more specific in that the action must be "necessary and reasonable", indicating that a higher standard must be met than simply the "lesser of two evils". In Cassese's eyes, the latter test would only have been met in "exceptional" circumstances, where the killing would have occurred with or without the participation of the accused.[73] This amounts to an acknowledgment that proportionality would not usually be available in the case of killing, a point made earlier in the opinion. Indeed, the killing committed by Erdemović was not simply the lesser evil, but rather his only option to avoid death. It is a highly specific test of proportionality in which participation in a massacre would be viewed as the lesser of two evils, with the caveat attached that participation in the violence by the individual was not key.

---

[70] Rome Statute, above n 1, Article 31(1)(d).

[71] *Erdemović* 1997, above n 9, Separate and Dissenting Opinion of Judge Cassese, para 16.

[72] Ibid.

[73] Ibid., para 12.

This is an unusual caveat attaching to proportionality, particularly where the action results in the death of another person. Drawing on German[74] and Israeli constitutional law,[75] as well as the common law approach to duress, the general rule is that one life cannot be balanced against another. Indeed, both sources, and the common law discomfort with the defence of duress to a charge of murder, indicate that the life of an aggressor ought not to be balanced against that of a victim. However, there is nothing said about exceptional circumstances in which there is no real balance between the life of the aggressor and the victim. Indeed, these forms of proportionality do not properly extend to a situation such as Erdemović, wherein there was strong evidence that his fate was sealed if he did not participate and that his refusal would have little effect on the death of thousands. Despite this, the domestic view of proportionality is more in line with that of the Rome Statute, which has created a higher standard of proportionality than those put forward by either Cassese or any previous tribunals.

The main components of the defence in the Rome Statute are the existence of a serious threat of physical violence and a necessary and reasonable response thereto, tempered by the lack of intention to cause a greater harm. The test of proportionality laid down indicates a higher standard that must be reached so that the defence may be applied. The difficulty here is not, thus, the balancing of one life against another, but the argument that the commission of a war crime was a "necessary and reasonable" act. Indeed, where the war crime in question was a crime against the person, this would be very difficult indeed. In the abstract, it would seem very difficult to argue that torture, murder, or slavery was a necessary or reasonable response to a situation. This is further complicated by the requirement that the act avoided a greater harm. Should the violence be done to more than one individual, it would then mean that this would need to be proved as a lesser harm than the violence which could be visited on the accused.

In the abstract, it is very difficult to see how these tests could be satisfied, particularly where they are more developed than before. It does not appear fair to supply the defence and then to limit it to only measured responses in the most difficult of circumstances. It is also unclear as to what may be considered a measured response under such circumstances. The difficulty in reaching the thresholds and arguing that any crime within the Rome Statute constituted a "reasonabl[e] and necessar[y]"[76] response does not appear to have been properly considered. Here, the problems generated by the lack of graduated removal of criminal responsibility are highlighted. Should the defence not apply, because the tests are not met, the individual is completely guilty. Should they apply, he or she would be completely exonerated. Little room is left for the grey areas created by hard cases. These issues are enormously difficult to consider in the abstract, and thus, it may be beneficial to examine how the tests could be applied to a real case. The next part will look at the application of Rome law to the case of *Erdemović*.

---

74 German Basic Law 2010, Article 1(1).

75 Israeli Basic Law: Human dignity and liberty 1992, Article 2.

76 Rome Statute, above n 1, Article 31(1)(d).

8.5 *Erdemović* Before the International Criminal Court

The discussion so far has highlighted how difficult it is to understand the contours of the defence of duress in the abstract. Thus, it is worth considering how the issues raised in *Erdemović* would be dealt with at the ICC, to determine how the Rome Statute's version of duress would operate. In the first instance, it should be noted that it is the policy of the prosecutor of the ICC[77] to ensure that "low-hanging fruit"[78] and lower-ranking soldiers become the focus of national prosecutions rather than those initiated by the ICC. Thus, it is likely that a case such as Erdemović would not have been prosecuted by the ICC, which may have focused its prosecutorial efforts on those who gave orders to carry out the massacre rather than those who fired the shots. However, if the scale of the disaster[79] had meant that Erdemović became a legitimate object of the court's attention, it is possible that such a case could be tried. The issues before the ICTY were twofold: firstly, whether a guilty plea must have been unequivocal in order to have been accepted; and secondly, whether duress was available in this instance. For the first issue, the Trial Chamber of the ICC is tasked with ensuring that the accused understands the charges,[80] the nature, and the consequences of a guilty plea[81] and ensuring that the plea is voluntary.[82] The latter requirement is evidenced through "sufficient consultation with defence counsel," but otherwise no further evidence needs to be produced. Therefore, Erdemović's plea of guilty and his accompanying statements could be accepted by the ICC without any further discussion.

However, given that defences are now codified within the statute, he may have wished to plead duress under the statute. Erdemović's circumstances would satisfy the criteria of a threat of imminent death and of that threat being made by a person. Using Cassese's conceptualisation of proportionality, the inevitability of the death of his victims would make his actions proportionate. However, the Rome Statute prefers the test of lesser harm generated by a reasonable and necessary response. The clear light of codification makes it difficult to argue that his actions at Srebrenica could ever be characterised as a necessary and reasonable response to a threat. The whole purpose of international criminal law is to ensure that individuals are held to account for their participation in serious violations of international criminal law, echoing the maxim that "crimes against international

---

[77] International Criminal Court Office of the Prosecutor (2003) Paper on some policy issues before the Office of the Prosecutor. http://www.icc-cpi.int/NR/rdonlyres/1FA7C4C6-DE5F-42B7-8B25-60AA962ED8B6/143594/030905_Policy_Paper.pdf). Accessed 12 May 2016, p. 3.

[78] William Schabas mentioned this idea at a lecture held in Dublin; Schabas 2011.

[79] See Bowers 2003.

[80] Rome Statute, above n 1, Article 64(8)(a).

[81] Ibid., Article 65(1)(a).

[82] Ibid., Article 65(1)(b).

law are committed by men, not by abstract entities"[83] and following the logic that each participant makes a contribution to the atrocity. Erdemović's situation, where he participated in the genocide in Srebrenica where over 7000 individuals died,[84] albeit against his will, may exclude the possibility of arguing duress, as formulated in the Rome Statute, in this instance. This supports the idea that to create a degree of distinction between the defences and to further engage with theory in this area may address the issue. The introduction of justifications, excuses, partial defences, and formal pleas in mitigation would allow for a degree of recognition that the individual in question was not fully responsible for the acts, or lacked the necessary will to freely carry out the acts.

The reduction in superior orders to a plea in mitigation by previous international criminal tribunals[85] is another indication of the lack of theoretical development in international criminal law, wherein one exception is made in order to exclude superior orders as a defence. Little effort was dedicated to the potential expansion of pleas in mitigation to other grounds, or to the broadening of the categories of defence which may exist. Indeed, the defences have high thresholds for use which may prevent their engagement—the provision of defences appears to have encouraged the creation of thresholds which make their application complex and difficult. The monochromatic approach in the Rome Statute, in that either the defence exonerates the accused or excuses them does not apply, leaves little room for a more nuanced approach, even through interpretation. On the idea of a distinction between complete exoneration and a reduction in penalty, Gross notes that "our response to crime must take its full circumstances into consideration and then decide how great a defection from a punitive response is possible without exciting the demons of impunity".[86] He further notes that the imposition of punishment on an individual must be justified and, in the case of serious violations of international criminal law, it would appear that a contribution to violence on a grand scale ought to be sufficient to justify this. Indeed, at the national level, sentencing and retributive policy in general would usually impose a punishment for crimes against the person, unless a defence could be sufficiently proved.

[83] *United States of America, French Republic, United Kingdom and the USSR v Hess, Goring* et al., Judgment of the International Military Tribunal in Nuremberg, 1 October 1946, para 447.

[84] See BBC News (2004) Serbs admit Srebrenica death toll. http://news.bbc.co.uk/1/hi/3743176.stm. Accessed 1 March 2016.

[85] IMT Charter, above n 42, Article 8; International Military Tribunal for the Far East, opened for signature 19 January 1946, 1589 Treaties and Other International Acts Series 20 (entered into force 19 January 1946), Article 6; ICTY (2009) Updated Statute of the International Criminal Tribunal for the Former Yugoslavia. http://www.icty.org/x/file/Legal%20Library/Statute/statute_sept09_en.pdf. Accessed 8 June 2016, Article 7(4); and International Criminal Tribunal for Rwanda (2010) Statute of the International Criminal Tribunal for Rwanda. http://unictr.unmict.org/sites/unictr.org/files/legal-library/100131_Statute_en_fr_0.pdf. Accessed 8 June 2016, Article 6(4).

[86] Gross 2012, p. 176.

However, the provisions discussed here do not appear to be drafted well enough in order to remove criminal liability in a "hard case" similar to that of *Erdemović*, where the test of proportionality may create a barrier to the application of duress.

8.6 Conclusion

The idea of duress in the Rome Statute has clearly been influenced by the jurisprudence of the ICTY, and there is evidence that the drafters of the Rome Statute would not wish to prosecute a future Erdemović, given the inclusion of duress in this Statute as a ground for excluding criminal responsibility. Although the inclusion of defences at this juncture is groundbreaking, the manner in which they have been drafted is not. More thought ought to have been given to the form and content of all of the defences, and particularly to duress.

The work of previous international criminal tribunals has demonstrated the incompatibility of duress with war crimes and crimes against humanity. Following the Second World War, it was possible to plead a defence of necessity, duress, or coercion. However, these pleadings were rarely accepted because of the failure to satisfy the grounds for duress, usually because the required pressure was not present. The situation in *Erdemović* finally surmounted this obstacle, because it could be proved that he was a genuinely unwilling participant. However, the defence was not accepted because of a lack of a customary rule regarding duress in international law, which allowed the tribunal to apply its own reasoning. The dissent of Cassese, arguing for the application of such a defence, thus, appears to have influenced the drafters of the Rome Statute.

The current position in the Rome Statute is that the defence is available to those who are able to meet the test of a "necessary and reasonable act" which does not cause a greater harm than the one sought to be avoided. Comparing this with the formulation in Cassese's dissent, to which a caveat of inevitable death was attached, it is clear that the standard of proportionality is too high for it to apply to a situation similar to that of Erdemović. His case is the clearest yet of "true" duress, in that he was genuinely compelled to act. The difficulty that the ICTY had in confirming his right to the defence is reflected in part by the provisions of the Rome Statute: the drafters have permitted the defence, but the tests make it difficult to see when the defence realistically may be accepted. Where the defence of duress, as drafted, was applied to the facts of Erdemović's case, it was still not available.

The issue of permitting duress at the international level clearly causes a degree of consternation, to the extent that it now appears impossible that it could ever be applied by the ICC. However, this supports the argument that the Rome Statute should engage further with criminal law theory and distinguish between the defences in a more graduated manner. This graduation would allow the distinction to be made between complete exoneration on the grounds of duress and partial removal of responsibility. Such a distinction would have perhaps allowed

Erdemović to plead differently before the ICTY. With the Rome Statute, there are fresh opportunities to revise and interpret these new codified provisions. Where battlefields modernise and conflict becomes more complex, greater precision in the attribution of liability is required, in the interests of fairness.

References

Articles, Books and Other Documents

Amnesty International (1997) Making the right choices, Part I: Defining the crimes and permissible defences and initiating a prosecution, AI Index IOR 40/01/97

Bohlander M (2009) Principles of German criminal law. Hart, Oxford

Bowers A (2003) A concession to humanity in the killing of innocents—validating the defences of duress and superior orders in international law. Windsor Rev Legal Soc Issues 15:31–72

Colvin E (1990) Exculpatory defences in criminal law. Oxford J Legal Stud 10:381–407

Cryer R, Friman H, Robinson D, Wilmshurst E (2010) An Introduction to International Criminal Law and Procedure. Cambridge University Press, Cambridge

Gross H (2012) Crime and punishment: a concise moral critique. Oxford University Press, Oxford

Grover S (2012) Child soldier victims of forcible genocidal transfer. Springer, Berlin

Herring JW (2012) Criminal law: text, cases and materials. Oxford University Press, Oxford

International Criminal Tribunal for the former Yugoslavia (2009) Rules of Procedure and Evidence, UN Doc. It/32/Rev. 44

Knoops GJ (2008) Defenses in contemporary international criminal law. Martinus Nijhoff, Leiden

Lee R (ed) (1999) The International Criminal Court: the making of the Rome Statute. Kluwer Law International, Alphen aan den Rijn

Morris V, Scharf M (1995) An Insider's Guide to the International Criminal Tribunal for the Former Yugoslavia: A Documentary History and Analysis. Transnational Publishers, London

Padfield N (2008) Criminal Law. Oxford University Press, Oxford

Preparatory Committee on the establishment of an International Criminal Court (1997) Decisions Taken by the Preparatory Committee at its Session held from 1 to 12 December 1997, UN Doc. A/AC.249/1997/L.9/Rev.1

Ratner S, Abrams J (2001) Accountability for human rights atrocities in international law. Oxford University Press, Oxford

Sadat L (2000) Custom, codification and some thoughts about the relation between the two. DePaul Law Review 49:909–923

Saland P (1999) International Criminal Law Principles. In: Lee R (ed) The International Criminal Court: The Making of the Rome Statute. Kluwer Law International, Alphen aan den Rijn, pp 189–216

Schabas W (2011) Unimaginable Atrocities, Speech. National University of Ireland, Dublin

Taulbee JL (2009) International crime and punishment: A guide to the issues. Praegar Security International, Santa Barbara

Tomuschat C (2006) The legacy of Nuremberg. J Int Crim Justice 4:830–844

UN Security Council (1993) Report of the Secretary-General pursuant to paragraph 2 of Security Council Resolution 808 (1993), UN Doc S/25704

van Sliedregt E (2012) Individual criminal responsibility in international criminal law. Oxford University Press, Oxford

Case Law

Affaire François Minani, Judgment of the Tribunal of First Instance, Special Chamber, Gitarama, Rwanda, 25 September 1997
ICTY, *Prosecutor v Dražen Erdemović*, Judgment, 7 October 1997, Case No. IT-96-22-A
ICTY, *Prosecutor v Dražen Erdemović*, Sentencing Judgment, 29 November 1996, Case No. IT-96-22-T
ICTY, *Prosecutor v Dražen Erdemović*, Sentencing Judgment, 5 March 1998, Case No. IT-96-22-T*bis*
R v Howe, Judgment of the Court of Appeal of England and Wales, [1987] AC 417
U.S. v Flick et al., Judgment of the United States Military Tribunal Nuremberg, 22 December 1947
United States of America, French Republic, United Kingdom and the USSR v Hess, Goring et al., Judgment of the International Military Tribunal in Nuremberg, 1 October 1946
United States v Ohlendorf et al., Judgment of the United States Military Tribunal Nuremberg, 8–9 April 1948

Treaties

Agreement for the Prosecution and Punishment of the Major War Criminals of the European Axis, opened for signature 8 August 1945, 82 UNTC 280 (entered into force 8 August 1945)
International Covenant on Civil and Political Rights, opened for signature 16 December 1966, 999 UNTS 171 (entered into force 23 March 1976)
International Military Tribunal for the Far East, opened for signature 19 January 1946, 1589 Treaties and Other International Acts Series 20 (entered into force 19 January 1946)
Rome Statute of the International Criminal Court, opened for signature 17 July 1998, 2187 UNTS 90 (entered into force 1 July 2002)

Chapter 9
Year in Review 2015

Bérénice Boutin, Kate Pitcher and Onur Güven

Abstract The year 2015 was marked by several noteworthy events with particular relevance to international humanitarian law, such as: the continuance of the conflict in Syria, the escalation of violence in Libya, and the eruption of a conflict in Yemen; the official closure of the International Criminal Tribunal for Rwanda (ICTR), and several key decisions by international, hybrid, and national courts related to the adjudication of war crimes, crimes against humanity, and genocide; the establishment by the United Nations (UN) and the Organisation for the Prohibition of Chemical Weapons (OPCW) of a Joint Investigative Mechanism in Syria, and the rising number of States that have ratified the Arms Trade Treaty. This chapter addresses a number of these issues amongst other events of note. The Year in Review is not intended to be a comprehensive summary of all events that occurred in 2015, but rather a sampling of events of note with particular relevance to the international humanitarian law.

Keywords International humanitarian law · International criminal law · Armed conflict · War crimes · Arms control · Terrorism

B. Boutin (✉) · K. Pitcher · O. Güven
T.M.C. Asser Instituut, The Hague, The Netherlands
e-mail: b.boutin@asser.nl

K. Pitcher
e-mail: k.pitcher@asser.nl

O. Güven
e-mail: o.guven@asser.nl

T.D. Gill et al. (eds.), *Yearbook of International Humanitarian Law 2015*,
Yearbook of International Humanitarian Law 18,
DOI 10.1007/978-94-6265-141-8_9

Contents

9.1 Ongoing Conflicts and Other Developments

9.1.1 Afghanistan

Following NATO's formal withdrawal from combat operations at the end of 2014,[1] the conflict in Afghanistan entered a new phase as of 2015, with the Afghan National Security Forces (ANSF) taking full responsibility for security. At the same time, there has been an upsurge in violence by the Taliban insurgency, which carried out numerous attacks against civilians and offensives against governmental forces.[2] According to the United Nations Assistance Mission in Afghanistan's (UNAMA) annual report on the Protection of Civilians in Armed Conflict in

[1] See Van Oijen and Dorsey 2016, p. 216.

[2] Human Rights Watch (2016) World Report 2016. www.hrw.org/world-report/2016. Accessed 13 April 2016, p. 55.

Afghanistan for 2015, civilian casualties for the year amounted to 3545 civilian deaths and 7457 injured, 62 % of which are attributed to the Taliban and other anti-government forces.[3] In September 2015, the Taliban took control of the city of Kunduz, which was recaptured by Afghan forces in October.[4] In the course of the counteroffensive, a US airstrike hit a hospital run by Médecins Sans Frontières (MSF), killing 12 staff members and 10 patients.[5]

9.1.2 Central African Republic

Since 2013, the Central African Republic (CAR) has been the theatre of sectarian violence with the Muslim Seleka rebels on the one hand and the Christian anti-Balaka groups on the other hand. Both sides have been carrying out widespread deadly attacks on civilians, often targeted on the basis of their (alleged) religion.[6] Despite efforts to reach a peace deal in May,[7] fighting continued and, in September, violent clashes erupted in the capital Bangui.[8] The continuing violence towards civilians resulted in scores of displaced persons; since 2013, more than 400,000 people have taken refuge in neighbouring countries, while the same number of people were internally displaced.[9] In this context, the mandate of the United Nations Multidimensional Integrated Stabilization Mission in the Central African Republic (MINUSCA) was renewed for one year.[10]

---

[3] UN Assistance Mission in Afghanistan (2015) Annual Report on the Protection of Civilians in Armed Conflict in Afghanistan. http://unama.unmissions.org/sites/default/files/poc_annual_report_2015_final_14_feb_2016.pdf. Accessed 13 April 2016, pp. 1–3.

[4] Nordland R (2015) Taliban End Takeover of Kunduz After 15 Days. http://www.nytimes.com/2015/10/14/world/asia/taliban-afghanistan-kunduz.html. Accessed 13 April 2016.

[5] Doctors Without Borders (2015) Afghanistan: MSF Demands Explanations After Deadly Airstrikes Hit Hospital in Kunduz http://www.doctorswithoutborders.org/article/afghanistan-msf-demands-explanations-after-deadly-airstrikes-hit-hospital-kunduz. Accessed 13 April 2016.

[6] Cadman T (2015) Religious war in Central African Republic. http://www.aljazeera.com/indepth/opinion/2015/06/religious-war-central-african-republic-150629104901894.html. Accessed 15 April 2016.

[7] Chonghaile CN (2015) Central African Republic militias poised to sign disarmament agreement http://www.theguardian.com/global-development/2015/may/08/central-african-republic-militias-disarmament-agreement-undp. Accessed 15 April 2016.

[8] The Guardian (2015) Central African Republic: violent sectarian clashes erupt in Bangui. http://www.theguardian.com/world/2015/sep/27/central-african-republic-violent-sectarian-clashes-erupt-in-bangui. Accessed 15 April 2016.

[9] UN High Commissioner for Refugees (2015) UN: Central African Republic at risk of becoming the world's largest forgotten humanitarian crisis. http://www.unhcr.org/553e49ec6.html. Accessed 15 April 2016.

[10] UN Security Council (2015) Resolution 2217 (2015), UN Doc. S/RES/2217.

Another notable event in CAR in 2015 was the revelations of sexual abuses by French soldiers deployed as part of Operation Sangaris,[11] as well as by United Nations (UN) peacekeepers from MINUSCA.[12] Apart from the abuses themselves, the alleged attempts by UN and French officials to cover up the abuses and the overall failure to address them were widely criticized.[13]

Turning to criminal prosecutions, Dominic Ongwen, who was subject to an arrest warrant of the International Criminal Court (ICC), surrendered in January to US forces in the south-east of the country and was then transferred to The Hague.[14] Finally, in April, a law creating a Special Criminal Court was adopted. The hybrid court will investigate and prosecute grave international crimes committed since 2003 and be composed of both national and international judges and prosecutors.[15]

9.1.3 Colombia

The ongoing conflict between the Colombian government and the Revolutionary Armed Forces of Colombia (FARC) guerrillas continued to result in attacks on civilians such as killings, kidnappings, and forced displacements.[16] At the same time, notable progress was achieved in the peace talks between the government and the guerrillas. In September, an agreement, described as historic, was reached, addressing transitional justice and reparations for crimes committed in the conflict.[17] Both sides agreed to establish a judicial body, the Special Peace

[11] Laville S and Willsher K (2015) France launches criminal inquiry into alleged sex abuse by peacekeepers. https://www.theguardian.com/world/2015/may/07/france-criminal-inquiry-alleged-sex-abuse-french-soldiers-un-central-african-republic. Accessed 16 June 2016.

[12] Al Jazeera (2016) 'Sickening' sex abuse alleged in CAR by UN peacekeepers. http://www.aljazeera.com/news/2016/03/sex-abuse-alleged-car-peacekeepers-160331183645566.html. Accessed 15 April 2016.

[13] Laville S (2015) UN human rights chief admits delay to inquiry into peacekeeper abuse claims. http://www.theguardian.com/world/2015/may/08/un-human-rights-peacekeeper-abuse-claims-inquiry-delay. Accessed 15 April 2016.

[14] The Guardian (2015) Senior Lord's Resistance Army commander surrenders to US troops. http://www.theguardian.com/world/2015/jan/06/lords-resistance-army-commander-surrenders-central-african-republic. Accessed 15 April 2016. See below, Sect. 9.2.1.4.

[15] Mattioli-Zeltner G (2015) Taking Justice to a New Level: The Special Criminal Court in the Central African Republic. http://www.jurist.org/hotline/2015/07/G%C3%A9raldine-Mattioli-Zeltner-CAR-Special-Court.php. Accessed 15 April 2016. See below, Sect. 9.2.3.3.

[16] Amnesty International (2016) Annual Report 2015/2016. https://www.amnesty.org/en/latest/research/2016/02/annual-report-201516/. Accessed 19 April 2016, p. 123.

[17] Brodzinsky S (2015) Farc peace talks: Colombia nears historic deal after agreement on justice and reparations. http://www.theguardian.com/world/2015/sep/24/farc-peace-talks-colombia-nears-historic-deal-after-agreement-on-justice-and-reparations. Accessed 19 April 2016.

Jurisdiction, to issue decisions on war crimes. Two types of procedures are envisaged: individuals acknowledging their responsibility would be sanctioned with an alternative punishment, while individuals who do not confess would face ordinary criminal sanctions.[18]

9.1.4 Egypt

Fighting between governmental forces and extremist insurgent groups escalated in 2015, particularly in the Sinai Peninsula.[19] An affiliate of the Islamic State (IS) terrorist group called Sinai Province carried out recurrent attacks targeting Egyptian military and police forces and resulting in civilian casualties. In retaliation, the Egyptian army intensified its offensive in the region.[20] Meanwhile, Egyptian security forces have been accused of numerous abuses against civilians, including extrajudicial executions, enforced disappearances, and torture.[21]

Other notable events of the year include the crashing of a Russian civilian plane above the Sinai, which was claimed by IS,[22] and the purportedly accidental killing of 12 civilians, including eight Mexican tourists, by Egyptian forces.[23]

9.1.5 Iraq

Since 2014, Iraq has been embroiled in a multilayered conflict involving IS, Iraqi governmental forces, Kurdish regional forces (Peshmerga), pro-government militias, various rebel groups, and Western forces supporting the Iraqi government through an aerial anti-IS campaign.[24]

At the beginning of 2015, IS controlled significant portions of the territory in the west of the country. Throughout the year, fighting has taken place, with each

---

[18] Carrillo-Santarelli N (2015) An Assessment of the Colombian-FARC 'Peace Jurisdiction' Agreement. http://www.ejiltalk.org/an-assessment-of-the-colombian-farc-peace-jurisdiction-agreement/. Accessed 19 April 2016.

[19] Human Rights Watch, above n 2, p. 225.

[20] Mohamed Y and Hassan A (2015) More than 100 dead as militants, Egyptian army clash in North Sinai. http://www.reuters.com/article/us-egypt-security-sinai-idUSKCN0PB3VJ20150701. Accessed 19 April 2016.

[21] Human Rights Watch, above n 2, pp. 227–228.

[22] BBC (2015) Sinai plane crash: Egypt dismisses IS claim. http://www.bbc.com/news/world-middle-east-34690936. Accessed 19 April 2016.

[23] BBC (2015) Mexican tourists killed by Egyptian security forces. http://www.bbc.com/news/world-middle-east-34241680. Accessed 19 April 2016.

[24] Human Rights Watch, above n 2, p. 319.

party successively capturing or recapturing areas. For instance, in January, Iraqi governmental forces recaptured the Province of Diyala, while Peshmerga forces pushed back IS from a large part of the territory surrounding Mosul.[25] In April, Iraqi forces launched an offensive to retake control of the Anbar Province, but IS carried out a counter-attack and captured the city of Ramadi.[26] One of the largest offensives was the Second Battle of Tikrit, which took place in March–April, and resulted in the recapture of Tikrit from IS. It involved more than 30,000 troops on the governmental side (Iraqi Army, Sunni militias, and Shiite militias) fighting an estimate of approximately 2000–3000 IS fighters.[27] Meanwhile, a coalition of States, including the US, the UK, Australia, and France, has carried out airstrikes targeting IS at the invitation and in support of the Iraqi government.[28] Estimates of civilians casualties in 2015 amounted to about 16,000 people, out of whom more than 7000 were killed by IS, and about 1200 were killed by airstrikes carried out by coalition forces or Iraqi forces.[29]

IS has been accused of gruesome abuses amounting to war crimes, including mass executions,[30] and killings "by extremely cruel and painful methods such as burning, drowning, electrocution, and stoning".[31] In particular, IS allegedly carried out systematic and widespread attacks on the Yezidi population, which, according to the Office of the United Nations High Commissioner for Human Rights

---

[25] Al Arabiya (2015) Iraqi forces 'liberate' Diyala from ISIS: officer. http://english.alarabiya.net/en/News/middle-east/2015/01/26/Iraq-forces-liberate-Diyala-province-from-ISIS-officer-.html. Accessed 25 April 2016; Morris L (2015) Kurds say they have ejected Islamic State militants from large area in northern Iraq. https://www.washingtonpost.com/world/middle_east/kurds-say-they-have-ejected-islamic-state-from-a-big-area-in-northern-iraq/2015/01/21/ac459372-a1c6-11e4-b146-577832eafcb4_story.html. Accessed 25 April 2016.

[26] Arango T (2015) ISIS Fighters Seize Government Headquarters in Ramadi, Iraq. http://www.nytimes.com/2015/05/16/world/middleeast/isis-fighters-seize-government-headquarters-in-ramadi-iraq.html. Accessed 25 April 2016.

[27] Micallef J (2015) Lessons From the Second Battle of Tikrit: March 2-April 4 2015. http://www.huffingtonpost.com/joseph-v-micallef/lessons-from-the-second-b_b_7049430.html. Accessed 25 April 2016.

[28] The Guardian (2015) US-led coalition launches air strikes in Iraq ahead of Mosul offensive. http://www.theguardian.com/world/2015/feb/20/coalition-air-strikes-isis-iraq-syria-mosul-kobani. Accessed 25 April 2016; Botelho G and Karadsheh J (2015) U.S.-led coalition launches 17 airstrikes on ISIS targets around Tikrit. http://edition.cnn.com/2015/03/26/middleeast/iraq-isis-tikrit/. Accessed 25 April 2016; Michaels J (2015) Intense U.S. airstrikes support Iraqi ground offensive in Ramadi. http://www.usatoday.com/story/news/world/2015/07/13/ramadi-offensive-militias-coalition-airstrikes/30096897/. Accessed 25 April 2016.

[29] IBC (2015) Iraq 2015: A Catastrophic Normal. https://www.iraqbodycount.org/analysis/numbers/2015/. Accessed 25 April 2016.

[30] Damon A, Alkhshali H and Ellis R (2015) Mass graves in Tikrit might contain 1,700 bodies. http://edition.cnn.com/2015/04/06/middleeast/iraq-mass-graves/. Accessed 25 April 2016; Saul H (2015) Isis mass execution: Soldier describes surviving brutal Tikrit massacre by playing dead. http://www.independent.co.uk/news/world/middle-east/isis-mass-execution-soldier-describes-surviving-brutal-tikrit-massacre-by-playing-dead-10159320.html. Accessed 25 April 2016.

[31] Human Rights Watch, above n 2, p. 321.

(OHCHR), "may amount to genocide".[32] IS also carried out recurrent terrorist attacks targeting civilians and Iraqi forces, amongst others, in the form of suicide bombings. For instance, on 17 July, more than 120 people were killed after a bomb hidden under an ice truck at a local marketplace was detonated.[33]

Finally, border incidents occurred with Turkey, which launched attacks against Kurdish militant camps in northern Iraq,[34] and deployed troops to fight IS without the consent of Iraq.[35]

9.1.6 Israel/Palestine

The conflict in Israel/Palestine continued throughout 2015, with an escalation of violence as of September 2015. During this wave of violence, dubbed by some as the "knife intifada", more than 200 stabbings of Israelis by Palestinians (leading to about 20 deaths) were reported, as well as shootings and car-ramming attacks. In the midst of the tension, about 200 Palestinians have reportedly been killed by Israeli forces.[36]

In June, a report by a UN Commission of Inquiry regarding the 2014 Israel–Gaza war[37] was released. It found that, on both sides, serious violations of international humanitarian law were committed. Amongst other things, Palestinian armed groups were accused of firing mortars and rockets into populated areas of Israel, while Israel reportedly used weapons indiscriminately in populated areas.[38]

---

[32] UN General Assembly (2015) Report of the Office of the United Nations High Commissioner for Human Rights on the human rights situation in Iraq in the light of abuses committed by the socalled Islamic State in Iraq and the Levant and associated groups, UN Doc. A/HRC/28/18. http://www.un.org/en/ga/search/view_doc.asp?symbol=A/HRC/28/18. Accessed 25 April 2016, p. 6.

[33] Conlon K, Hanna J and Tawfeeq M (2015) Sinister ISIS plot kills 120, wounds 140 in Iraq. http://edition.cnn.com/2015/07/18/middleeast/iraq-violence/. Accessed 25 April 2016.

[34] Yeginsu C (2015) Turkey Attacks Kurdish Militant Camps in Northern Iraq. http://www.nytimes.com/2015/07/26/world/middleeast/turkey-attacks-kurdish-militant-camps-in-northern-iraq.html. Accessed 25 April 2016.

[35] Karadeniz T and Gurses E (2015) Iraqi PM asks NATO to press Turkey to pull troops from north Iraq. http://www.reuters.com/article/us-mideast-crisis-russia-turkey-davutogl-idUSKBN0TR14F20151208. Accessed 25 April 2016.

[36] Beaumont P (2015) Israel-Palestine: outlook bleak as wave of violence passes six-month mark. http://www.theguardian.com/world/2016/mar/31/israel-palestine-violence-knife-attacks-west-bank-gaza. Accessed 6 May 2016.

[37] See Paulussen et al. 2015, pp. 224–225.

[38] UN General Assembly (2015) Report of the independent commission of inquiry established pursuant to Human Rights Council resolution S-21/1, UN Doc. A/HRC/29/52. http://www.un.org/en/ga/search/view_doc.asp?symbol=A/HRC/29/52. Accessed 6 May 2016.

Another notable event of the year 2015 was the accession of Palestine to the Rome Statute of the ICC.[39]

9.1.7 Libya

In the past years, Libya fell into a complex conflict involving two rival governments based, respectively, in Tobruk and in Tripoli, and a wide range of local actors including IS-affiliated groups, other armed groups, and tribal militias. Throughout the year, the two governments, "each supported by loose coalitions of armed groups and forces",[40] fought for control of part of the territory. Due to the lack of central authority, other actors, including IS-affiliated groups, increased their control of other areas.[41] In the course of the hostilities, IS militants have "maintained a reign of terror"[42] and committed numerous gruesome abuses amounting to war crimes. For instance, in February, they released a video showing the beheading of 21 Coptic Christians.[43] In response to this attack, Egypt carried out airstrikes against IS in the eastern part of Libya,[44] which, according to Amnesty International, might have been disproportionate and/or indiscriminate.[45] As a result of the hostilities in various parts of the country, civilians have suffered significant human and material casualties.[46] Towards the end of the year, it was reported that the US began to engage in airstrikes targeting IS militants in Libya.[47] In December, warring factions signed an agreement to form a national unity government, but the country remained highly unstable.[48]

---

[39] See below, Sect. 9.2.1.

[40] Amnesty International, above n 16, p. 321.

[41] Al-Warfalli A (2015) Islamic State fights rival group and eastern forces in Libya. http://www.reuters.com/article/us-libya-security-idUSKCN0QJ19420150814. Accessed 18 May 2016.

[42] Amnesty International, above n 16, p. 384.

[43] Al Jazeera (2015) ISIL video shows Christian Egyptians beheaded in Libya. http://www.aljazeera.com/news/middleeast/2015/02/isil-video-execution-egyptian-christian-hostages-libya-150215193050277.html. Accessed 18 May 2016.

[44] Malsin J and Stephen C (2015) Egyptian air strikes in Libya kill dozens of Isis militants. http://www.theguardian.com/world/2015/feb/16/egypt-air-strikes-target-isis-weapons-stockpiles-libya. Accessed 18 May 2016.

[45] Amnesty International (2015) Libya: Mounting evidence of war crimes in the wake of Egypt's airstrikes. https://www.amnesty.org/en/latest/news/2015/02/libya-mounting-evidence-war-crimes-after-egypt-airstrikes/. Accessed 18 May 2016.

[46] Human Rights Watch, above n 2, p. 378.

[47] Pengelly M and Stephen C (2015) Islamic State leader in Libya 'killed in US airstrike'. http://www.theguardian.com/world/2015/nov/14/us-airstrike-isis-leader-libya. Accessed 18 May 2016.

[48] El Yaakoubi A (2015) Libyan factions sign U.N. deal to form unity government. http://www.reuters.com/article/us-libya-security-idUSKBN0U00WP20151217. Accessed 18 May 2016.

9.1.8 Mali

Throughout the year, fighting continued between opposing armed groups, the UN Multidimensional Integrated Stabilization Mission in Mali (MINUSMA), and governmental forces.[49] Northern Mali has been the scene of violent clashes since 2012, involving separatist rebels of the National Movement for the Liberation of Azawad (MNLA), extremist groups such as Al-Qaeda in the Islamic Maghreb (AQIM) and Ansar Dine, and other rebel factions.[50] In 2015, violence spread into the rest of the country,[51] with clashes between opposing armed groups, Malian soldiers, and UN peacekeepers,[52] and terrorist attacks carried out by various groups in the capital Bamako and other cities.[53]

In June, a peace agreement was concluded by the government and various rebel groups, providing for the disarmament, demobilisation and reintegration of rebels, as well as political and institutional reforms, including the creation of elected regional assemblies.[54] Nonetheless, violence remained high, and, at the end of the year, hostilities were ongoing between the MNLA and AQIM.[55]

9.1.9 Myanmar

After a few years of relative calm, fighting between the army and various ethnic rebel groups reinvigorated in 2015. In the area of Kokang, located on the border with China, several clashes took place between the army and the Myanmar

[49] Amnesty International, above n 16, p. 395.

[50] Al Jazeera (2013) Making sense of Mali's armed groups. http://www.aljazeera.com/indepth/features/2013/01/201311395228l2326.html. Accessed 16 June 2016; Graham D (2015) Mali's Tangled Mix of Jihad and Civil War. http://www.theatlantic.com/international/archive/2015/11/mali-hotel-hostage-crisis/417021/. Accessed 3 May 2016.

[51] Human Rights Watch, above n 2, p. 395.

[52] UN Security Council (2015) Report of the Secretary-General on the situation in Mali, UN Doc. S/2015/426. http://www.un.org/en/ga/search/view_doc.asp?symbol=S/2015/426. Accessed 3 May 2016, pp. 4–6.

[53] RFI (2015) Mali: qui est derrière les attaques dans le centre du pays? http://www.rfi.fr/afrique/20150412-deux-soldats-maliens-tues-une-attaque-le-centre-pays/. Accessed 16 June 2016; Tapily M, Walker P and English C (2015) Mali attack: more than 20 dead after terrorist raid on Bamako hotel. http://www.theguardian.com/world/2015/nov/20/mali-attack-highlights-global-spread-extremist-violence. Accessed 3 May 2016.

[54] Al Jazeera (2015) Malian rivals sign peace deal. http://www.aljazeera.com/news/2015/06/malian-rivals-sign-peace-deal-150620173301883.html. Accessed 3 May 2016; Jezequel J (2015) Mali's peace deal represents a welcome development, but will it work this time? http://www.theguardian.com/global-development/2015/jul/01/mali-peace-deal-a-welcome-development-but-will-it-work-this-time. Accessed 3 May 2016.

[55] RFI (2015) Mali: dans le Nord, «terroristes» contre rebelles. http://www.rfi.fr/afrique/20151226-mali-rebelles-islamistes-nord-CMA-mnla. Accessed 3 May 2016.

National Democratic Alliance Army (MNDAA) insurgent group. Starting in February, the MNDAA and other rebel groups carried out attacks in an attempt to take control of the city of Laukkai.[56] The government declared a state of emergency in the region, and after a few months of fighting, a peace deal was reached in June.[57] As a result of the violence, tens of thousands of civilians were displaced.[58]

9.1.10 Nigeria

In 2015, the Islamist group Boko Haram continued to carry out countless horrific attacks on civilians and to engage in hostilities with Nigerian forces.[59] In January, the group carried out a particularly dreadful attack upon the north-eastern town of Baga.[60] In what Amnesty International called possibly the deadliest massacre in the history of Boko Haram, as many as 2000 people were allegedly killed.[61] The group overran a military base and stormed the town of Baga, destroying buildings, killing many, and forcing the rest to run for their lives.[62] Throughout the year, the group raided villages and carried out extremely violent attacks on civilians, including abductions,

---

[56] BBC (2015) Fighting continues in Myanmar's troubled Kokang region. http://www.bbc.com/news/world-asia-31527384. Accessed 16 June 2016; Al Jazeera (2015) Myanmar Kokang rebels 'kill dozens' of soldiers. http://www.aljazeera.com/news/2015/02/myanmar-kokang-rebels-kill-dozens-soldiers-150213072401121.html. Accessed 15 April 2016.

[57] Mclaughlin T and Yadana Zaw H (2012) Under pressure from China, Kokang rebels declare Myanmar ceasefire. http://www.reuters.com/article/us-myanmar-rebels-ceasefire-idUSKBN0OR0T120150611. Accessed 15 April 2016; Moe W (2015) Why Kokang Rebels Are Giving Fits to Burma's Military. http://foreignpolicy.com/2015/05/06/why-kokang-rebels-are-giving-fits-to-burmas-military-myanmar/. Accessed 15 April 2016.

[58] Al Jazeera (2015) Myanmar declares state of emergency in war-torn region. http://www.aljazeera.com/news/2015/02/myanmar-declares-state-emergency-war-torn-region-150217124515270.html. Accessed 15 April 2016.

[59] Human Rights Watch, above n 2, p. 422; Amnesty International, above n 16, p. 275.

[60] Mark M (2015) Boko Haram's 'deadliest massacre': 2,000 feared dead in Nigeria. http://www.theguardian.com/world/2015/jan/09/boko-haram-deadliest-massacre-baga-nigeria. Accessed 12 May 2016.

[61] Amnesty International (2015) Nigeria: Massacre Possibly Deadliest in Boko Haram's History. https://www.amnesty.org/en/press-releases/2015/01/nigeria-massacre-possibly-deadliest-boko-haram-s-history/. Accessed 12 May 2016. The exact number of dead remains unconfirmed.

[62] Fessy T (2015) Boko Haram attack: What happened in Baga? http://www.bbc.com/news/world-africa-30987043. Accessed 12 May 2016.

enslavement, torture, suicide bombings, mass killings, and decapitations.[63] In March, it declared allegiance to IS.[64] Nigerian forces were able to organise a number of rescue operations,[65] but, at the end of 2015, Boko Haram still held many hostages, including more than 200 schoolgirls kidnapped in April 2014.[66] The group also continued to use children as suicide bombers.[67]

Elections took place relatively peacefully in March and April,[68] but the newly elected President Buhari has not been able to reduce the violence.[69] Moreover, in their response to Boko Haram, governmental forces have also been accused of committing abuses amounting to humanitarian law violations, including torture and other ill-treatment.[70] In its 2015 Report on Preliminary Examination Activities released in November, the ICC's Office of the Prosecutor identified several possible cases of crimes against humanity and war crimes perpetrated by both Boko Haram and the Nigerian Army.[71]

---

63 See, e.g., BBC (2015) Boko Haram attack caps week of bloodshed in Nigeria. http://www.bbc.com/news/world-africa-33401810. Accessed 16 June 2016; Dutta K (2015) Boko Haram 'has abducted, raped and enslaved 2,000 women in reign of terror'. http://www.independent.co.uk/news/world/africa/boko-haram-has-abducted-raped-and-enslaved-2000-women-in-reign-of-terror-10174152.html. Accessed 16 June 2016; Sieff K (2015) War-torn Nigerian town shows devastating legacy of Boko Haram. https://www.washingtonpost.com/world/africa/war-torn-nigerian-town-shows-devastating-legacy-of-boko-haram/2015/04/11/d7628ce6-dcad-11e4-b6d7-b9bc8acf16f7_story.html. Accessed 16 June 2016; Abubakar A (2015) Boko Haram blamed for decapitations. http://edition.cnn.com/2015/03/28/world/boko-haram-nigeria-village-raid/. Accessed 12 May 2016.

64 Boffey D (2015) Boko Haram declares allegiance to Islamic State. http://www.theguardian.com/world/2015/mar/07/boko-haram-suicide-bombers-50-dead-maiduguri. Accessed 12 May 2016.

65 The Guardian (2015) Nigerian army 'rescues 200 girls and 93 women' in strike against Boko Haram. http://www.theguardian.com/world/2015/apr/28/nigeria-army-rescue-boko-haram-girls-sambisa-forest. Accessed 16 June 2016; Karimi F and Abubakar A (2015) Nigeria: 160 more women, children rescued from Boko Haram camp. http://edition.cnn.com/2015/04/30/africa/nigeria-boko-haram-hostages-rescued/. Accessed 12 May 2016.

66 Muscati S and Segun M (2015) One year after #BringBackOurGirls, Boko Haram still holds hundreds. http://www.msnbc.com/msnbc/one-year-after-bringbackourgirls-boko-haram-still-holds-hundreds. Accessed 16 June 2016; Alter C (2015) 200 Girls Rescued From Boko Haram Camps Are Not the Chibok Schoolgirls http://time.com/3839035/nigeria-boko-haram-girls-rescue/. Accessed 12 May 2016.

67 Human Rights Watch, above n 2, p. 423.

68 Al Jazeera (2015) Buhari secures historic election victory in Nigeria. http://www.aljazeera.com/news/2015/03/opposition-party-declares-victory-nigeria-election-150331135603507.html. Accessed 12 May 2016.

69 Human Rights Watch, above n 2, p. 424.

70 Amnesty International, above n 16, p. 275.

71 ICC (2015) Report on Preliminary Examination Activities 2015. https://www.icc-cpi.int/iccdocs/otp/OTP-PE-rep-2015-Eng.pdf. Accessed 12 May 2016, pp. 44–51.

9.1.11 Pakistan

In the region of Waziristan, in the north-west of the country, the army of Pakistan continued military operations launched in 2014 against extremist armed groups such as the Tehrik-i-Taliban Pakistan (TTP), Al-Qaeda, and IS.[72] Amnesty International noted that "[d]ue to the lack of transparency of the operations and independent media coverage, and previous concerns of disproportionate use of force in similar operations",[73] the operation raised serious concerns. Throughout the country, violence remained high, as extremist groups continued to carry out deadly attacks against civilians. Examples include a series of suicide bombings in a Christian neighbourhood of the city of Lahore,[74] an attack on a bus in the city of Karachi that killed more than 40 people,[75] and the bombing of a Shia mosque in southern Pakistan.[76] Meanwhile, the US reportedly continued to carry out drone strikes targeting suspected members of extremist groups,[77] one of which killed two foreign aid workers who had been held hostage by Al-Qaeda.[78]

9.1.12 Somalia

The ongoing conflict in Somalia showed no sign of appeasement in 2015. In the course of hostilities involving the Islamist group Al-Shabaab, Somalian governmental troops and allied forces, and the African Union Mission in Somalia (AMISOM), various abuses possibly amounting to war crimes have been reported.[79]

---

72 Amnesty International, above n 16, p. 282; BBC (2014) Pakistan army launches 'major offensive' in North Waziristan. http://www.bbc.com/news/world-asia-27858234. Accessed 18 May 2016.

73 Amnesty International, above n 16, p. 282.

74 Saifi S and Mullen J (2015) Suicide bombings in Christian area of Pakistani city kill at least 14. http://edition.cnn.com/2015/03/15/asia/pakistan-violence/. Accessed 18 May 2016.

75 Hashim A (2015) Pakistan's Ismaili community hit by deadly attack. http://www.aljazeera.com/news/2015/05/pakistan-karachi-bus-gunmen-150513053952497.html. Accessed 18 May 2016.

76 BBC (2015) Pakistan Shia mosque blast in Shikarpur kills dozens. http://www.bbc.com/news/world-asia-31056086. Accessed 18 May 2016.

77 BBC (2015) Pakistan Taliban: US drone 'kills militants' in tribal region. http://www.bbc.com/news/world-asia-30671107. Accessed 16 June 2016.

78 Whitlock C, Ryan M and Miller G (2015) Obama apologizes for attack that killed two hostages. https://www.washingtonpost.com/world/national-security/us-operation-kills-al-qaeda-hostages-including-american/2015/04/23/8e9fcaba-e9bd-11e4-aae1-d642717d8afa_story.html. Accessed 18 May 2016.

79 Human Rights Watch, above n 2, p. 507.

Throughout the year, Al-Shabaab continued to carry out attacks, including an attack on a hotel in the capital Mogadishu which killed at least 15 people,[80] and an attack on an African Union (AU) base in Somalia that killed dozens of soldiers.[81] The unrest extended beyond Somalia's borders and notably into Kenya, where Al-Shabaab carried out several attacks. For instance, in April, Al-Shabaab militants carried out an attack at the University of Garissa, killing up to 150 people.[82] In response, Kenya launched airstrikes against Al-Shabaab camps in Somalia.[83]

Meanwhile, the US continued to carry out drone strikes targeted at Al-Shabaab militants, reportedly killing several senior commanders of the group, including Abdi Nur Mahdi, who was the group's chief of external operations, and Adnan Garaar, who was believed to be the mastermind of the 2013 attack on a Kenyan shopping mall that killed 67 people.[84]

Finally, AMISOM troops have been accused of indiscriminate shooting at civilians.[85]

9.1.13 South Sudan

The conflict that started at the end of 2013 between government forces supporting President Salva Kiir and rebels led by Riek Machar continued throughout 2015. Violence escalated in April, when governmental forces launched a large offensive

---

[80] BBC (2015) Somalia: Al-Shabab attack kills 15 in Mogadishu hotel. http://www.bbc.com/news/world-asia-34691602. Accessed 12 May 2016.

[81] France 24 (2015) Al Shabaab militants attack African Union base in Somalia. http://www.france24.com/en/20150901-al-shabaab-militants-attack-african-union-base-somalia. Accessed 12 May 2016.

[82] The Guardian (2015) Death toll from Kenyan university massacre expected to rise. http://www.theguardian.com/world/2015/apr/04/death-toll-from-kenyan-university-massacre-expected-to-rise. Accessed 12 May 2016.

[83] Mutiga M (2015) Kenya launches air strikes against al-Shabaab camps in Somalia. http://www.theguardian.com/world/2015/apr/06/kenya-launches-air-strikes-against-al-shabaab-camps-in-somalia. Accessed 16 June 2016; Jorgic D and Honan E (2015) Kenya says it destroys two al Shabaab camps in Somalia. http://www.reuters.com/article/us-kenya-security-military-idUSKBN0MX0EA20150406. Accessed 12 May 2016.

[84] Al Jazeera (2015) Somalia: US drone strike killed top Al-Shabab figure. http://www.aljazeera.com/news/2015/02/somalia-drone-strike-killed-top-al-shabab-figure-150206111810686.html. Accessed 16 June 2016; Reuters (2015) U.S. drone strike killed al Shabaab leader Garaar in Somalia: Pentagon. http://www.reuters.com/article/us-somalia-security-usa-idUSKBN0ME2QI20150318. Accessed 16 June 2016; BBC (2015) Somali al-Shabab commanders 'killed in drone strike'. http://www.bbc.com/news/world-africa-33550390. Accessed 16 June 2016; Reuters (2015) Suspected drone strike kills al Shabaab fighters in Somalia: police. http://www.reuters.com/article/us-somalia-security-idUSKBN0TB0LO20151122. Accessed 12 May 2016.

[85] Kaplan M (2015) In Somalia, African Union Troops Accused of Killing Dozens of Civilians Following Grenade Attack. http://www.ibtimes.com/somalia-african-union-troops-accused-killing-dozens-civilians-following-grenade-2018439. Accessed 12 May 2016.

in the course of which hundreds of civilians were killed, and more than 100,000 forced to flee their homes.[86] Both sides of the conflict have reportedly committed violations of humanitarian law, including deliberate attacks on civilians, sexual abuses, abductions, and the recruitment of child soldiers.[87] A peace agreement was signed in August,[88] but fighting persisted.[89]

9.1.14 Sudan

Hostilities between the Government and armed rebel groups have been continuing in the areas of Darfur, South Kordofan, and Blue Nile. In Darfur, governmental forces conducted a military campaign against rebel groups during which serious abuses were committed, including killings, rape, torture, and mass displacements.[90] The United Nations–African Union Mission in Darfur (UNAMID) has been unable to protect civilians from violence, in part because the Government prevented its troops from accessing areas affected by conflict.[91] Similarly, in the

[86] Intergovernmental Authority on Development (2015) IGAD Mediators profoundly deplore the escalation of fighting in south Sudan and urge the warring Parties to immediately cease all hostilities. http://igad.int/index.php?option=com_content&view=article&id=1134:igad-mediators-profoundly-deplore-the-escalation-of-fighting-in-south-sudan-and-urge-the-warring-parties-to-immediately-cease-all-hostilities&catid=61:statements&Itemid=150. Accessed 16 June 2016; Doctors Without Borders (2015) South Sudan: Rape and killing in Unity state. http://www.msf.org.uk/article/south-sudan-rape-and-killing-in-unity-state. Accessed 17 May 2016.

[87] Amnesty International, above n 16, p. 332; Human Rights Watch, above n 2, p. 520.

[88] Anderson M (2015) South Sudan peace deal greeted with quiet optimism by humanitarian world. http://www.theguardian.com/global-development/2015/aug/27/south-sudan-peace-deal-greeted-with-quiet-optimism-by-humanitarian-world. Accessed 17 May 2016.

[89] Al Jazeera (2015) Scores of civilians, including children, killed in South Sudan in October. http://america.aljazeera.com/articles/2015/10/24/scores-of-civilians-including-children-killed-in-south-sudan-in-october.html. Accessed 17 May 2016.

[90] Al Jazeera (2015) UN warns of worsening situation in Sudan's Darfur. http://www.aljazeera.com/news/2015/06/sudan-darfur-security-council-150610235631458.html. Accessed 16 June 2016; Human Rights Watch (2015) Sudan: Mass Rape by Army in Darfur. https://www.hrw.org/news/2015/02/11/sudan-mass-rape-army-darfur. Accessed 16 May 2016.

[91] Al Jazeera (2015) UN warns of worsening situation in Sudan's Darfur. http://www.aljazeera.com/news/2015/06/sudan-darfur-security-council-150610235631458.html. Accessed 16 June 2016; Gatten E (2015) UN peacekeeping force turns blind eye to mass rape in Darfur, victims say. http://www.independent.co.uk/news/world/africa/un-peacekeepers-turn-blind-eye-to-mass-rape-in-darfur-victims-say-a6725756.html. Accessed 16 May 2016.

South Kordofan and Blue Nile regions, governmental forces committed numerous abuses arguably amounting to war crimes, including indiscriminate killings[92] and the bombing of a hospital operated by MSF.[93]

In April 2015, Omar al-Bashir was re-elected President[94] in what was described as "a poll that did not meet international standards for free and fair elections".[95] In June, as he was in South Africa for an African Union summit, civil society organisations pushed for the execution by South Africa of the ICC arrest warrant of which he is the subject, but al-Bashir was able to leave the country while South African courts were examining the case.[96]

9.1.15 Syria

The situation in Syria, where a conflict has been raging since 2011, remained dire in 2015.[97] Forces involved in the conflict in Syria include governmental forces loyal to President Bashar al-Assad, opposition groups such as the Free Syrian Army (FSA), Islamist groups such as IS and the Al-Nusra Front (ANF), and Kurdish forces (Kurdish People's Protection Unit, YPG).[98] In addition, Western forces have been undertaking an aerial anti-IS campaign without Syria's consent, while Russia has been involved in hostilities against IS in support of the Assad regime.[99]

---

[92] Amnesty International (2015) Sudan: Attacks in South Kordofan 'constitute war crimes'. https://www.amnesty.org/en/latest/news/2015/08/sudan-attacks-in-south-kordofan-constitute-war-crimes/. Accessed 16 June 2016; Amnesty International (2015) Sudan: Don't We Matter?: Four Years of Unrelenting Attacks Against Civilians in Sudan's South Kordofan State. https://www.amnesty.org/en/documents/afr54/2162/2015/en/. Accessed 16 May 2016.

[93] Doctors Without Borders (2015) Sudan: MSF Hospital Bombed in South Kordofan. http://www.doctorswithoutborders.org/article/sudan-msf-hospital-bombed-south-kordofan. Accessed 16 May 2016.

[94] Smith D (2015) Sudan's Omar al-Bashir extends 26-year presidency with 94.5 % of the vote. http://www.theguardian.com/world/2015/apr/27/sudan-bashir-elected-majority-vote. Accessed 16 May 2016.

[95] Human Rights Watch, above n 2, p. 535.

[96] Onishi N (2015) Omar al-Bashir, Leaving South Africa, Eludes Arrest Again. http://www.nytimes.com/2015/06/16/world/africa/omar-hassan-al-bashir-sudan-south-africa.html. Accessed 16 May 2016; See below, Sect. 9.2.1.4, p. 26, at footnote 208.

[97] Amnesty International, above n 16, p. 350; Human Rights Watch, above n 2, p. 547.

[98] Sary G (2015) Syria conflict: Who are the groups fighting Assad? http://www.bbc.com/news/world-middle-east-34710635. Accessed 24 May 2016.

[99] BBC (2015) Syria crisis: Where key countries stand. http://www.bbc.com/news/world-middle-east-23849587. Accessed 16 June 2016; Fantz A (2015) War on ISIS: Who's doing what? http://edition.cnn.com/2015/11/20/world/war-on-isis-whos-doing-what/. Accessed 24 May 2016.

Throughout 2015, Assad's forces have continued to carry out deliberate and indiscriminate attacks on civilians, Islamist groups "were responsible for systematic and widespread violations",[100] and opposition groups also carried out serious abuses.[101] Amongst others abuses, Governmental forces have been accused of using chemical weapons against the population on numerous occasions, by launching barrel bombs with chlorine gas in civilian areas,[102] while IS and ANF have reportedly engaged in mass executions, torture, sexual slavery, and other inhumane acts.[103] At the end of the year, it was estimated that more than 250,000 people had died since the beginning of the conflict, including over 100,000 civilians.[104] In its 10th Report published in September, the Independent International Commission of Inquiry on the Syrian Arab Republic stated that "[t]he violence is endemic, regrettably proliferating in its scope and extent"[105] and reiterated its call for all parties to end violence and to ensure the effective protection of civilians.[106] In December, the UN Security Council unanimously adopted a resolution attempting to pave the way towards peace negotiations under UN auspices.[107]

9.1.16 Ukraine

The conflict between the Ukrainian government and pro-Russian separatist forces that erupted in eastern Ukraine in mid-2014 continued in 2015.[108] In January, fighting intensified, despite the signing of a ceasefire—the Minsk Protocol—in

---

[100] Human Rights Watch, above n 2, p. 547.

[101] Ibid.

[102] Taylor G (2015) Assad steps up chemical attacks despite Obama pledge he rid Syria of weapons. http://www.washingtontimes.com/news/2015/jun/17/bashar-assad-steps-chemical-attacks-despite-obama-/. Accessed 16 June 2016; Pannell I (2015) Syria civilians still under chemical attack. http://www.bbc.com/news/world-middle-east-34212324. Accessed 16 June 2016; Barnard A and Senguptamay S (2015) Syria Is Using Chemical Weapons Again, Rescue Workers Say. http://www.nytimes.com/2015/05/07/world/middleeast/syria-chemical-weapons.html. Accessed 18 May 2016. See below Sect. 9.3.2

[103] UN General Assembly (2015) Human Rights Council: Report of the Independent International Commission of Inquiry on the Syrian Arab Republic, UN Doc. A/HRC/30/48. http://www.ohchr.org/EN/HRBodies/HRC/RegularSessions/Session30/Documents/A_HRC_30_48_ENG.doc. Accessed 18 May 2016; Human Rights Watch, above n 2, p. 550.

[104] Human Rights Watch, above n 2, p. 547.

[105] UN General Assembly, above n 103, p. 21.

[106] Ibid., pp. 21–22.

[107] UN Security Council (2015) Resolution 2254 (2015), UN Doc. S/RES/2254; Sengupta S and Sanger DE (2015) After Years of War in Syria, U.N. Passes Resolution on Talks. http://www.nytimes.com/2015/12/19/world/middleeast/syria-talks-isis.html. Accessed 18 May 2016.

[108] Amnesty International, above n 16, p. 597.

September 2014.[109] Another agreement was reached in February,[110] but again failed to put an end to the conflict.[111] At the end of 2015, the conflict remained unresolved but involved a relatively low level of hostilities, leading some to describe it as a "frozen conflict".[112] According to the OHCHR, more than 9000 people have died from the conflict since mid-2014.[113]

9.1.17 Yemen

Yemen entered into a conflict in March 2015, after rebel Houthi fighters took control of the capital Sanaa and forced President Abd Rabbuh Mansur Hadi to flee.[114] Since then, the two opposing factions, Houthi and pro-Hadi, have been fighting to gain control of the territory.[115] In response, Saudi Arabia together with allies launched a military air campaign aiming at restoring the Hadi government.[116] The coalition, led by Saudi Arabia, was joined by Bahrain, Egypt, Jordan, Kuwait, Morocco, Qatar, Sudan, and the United Arab Emirates and operated with logistical support from the USA.[117] At the same time, Al-Qaeda in the Arabian Peninsula (AQAP) and other extremist groups gained control of part of the territory and carried out deadly attacks

---

[109] BBC (2015) Ukraine crisis: Fierce fighting after Minsk peace deal. http://www.bbc.com/news/world-europe-31449981. Accessed 18 May 2016.

[110] BBC (2015) Ukraine crisis: Leaders agree peace roadmap. http://www.bbc.com/news/world-europe-31435812. Accessed 18 May 2016.

[111] Reuters (2015) Killings of soldiers and civilians fray Ukraine's ceasefire. http://www.reuters.com/article/us-ukraine-crisis-casualties-idUSKBN0OR15U20150611. Accessed 16 June 2016; The Economist (2015) The war in Ukraine's east has come back to Kiev. http://www.economist.com/news/europe/21663138-soldiers-riot-over-terms-peace-deal-and-post-maidan-government-may-crack-apart-war. Accessed 18 May 2016.

[112] Kramer (2015) A Bleak Future in Eastern Ukraine's Frozen Zone. http://www.nytimes.com/2015/11/11/world/europe/ukraine-frozen-zone-virtual-reality.html. Accessed 18 May 2016.

[113] Office of the High Commissioner for Human Rights (OHCHR) (2015) Report on the human rights situation in Ukraine: 16 August to 15 November 2015. http://www.ohchr.org/Documents/Countries/UA/12thOHCHRreportUkraine.pdf. Accessed 18 May 2016, p. 2.

[114] Bayoumy Y and Ghobari M (2015) Yemen president quits, throwing country deeper into chaos. http://www.reuters.com/article/us-yemen-security-houthis-idUSKBN0KV0HT20150122. Accessed 24 May 2016.

[115] See, e.g., Al Jazeera (2015) Houthis and Hadi loyalists battle for control of Aden. http://www.aljazeera.com/news/2015/04/yemen-aden-150404090350157.html. Accessed 24 May 2016.

[116] Al Jazeera (2015) Saudi and Arab allies bomb Houthi positions in Yemen. http://www.aljazeera.com/news/middleeast/2015/03/saudi-ambassador-announces-military-operation-yemen-150325234138956.html. Accessed 24 May 2016.

[117] Thompson N and Torre I (2015) Yemen: Who's joining Saudi Arabia's fight against the Houthis? http://edition.cnn.com/2015/03/27/world/yemen-saudi-coalition-map/. Accessed 24 May 2016.

throughout the year.[118] Finally, the US reportedly continued to carry out drone strikes targeting suspected members of extremist groups.[119]

In the course of the hostilities, numerous alleged violations of humanitarian law have been reported. Notably, coalition forces have been accused of conducting several indiscriminate airstrikes, including the bombing of a refugee camp that killed at least 29 civilians,[120] the targeting of a dairy factory killing more than 30 civilians,[121] and the bombing of a residential area that killed at least 65 civilians,[122] as well as of using cluster bombs.[123] Houthi fighters have also been accused of violations, including the use of landmines.[124] The conflict has had a heavy impact on civilians, with 2795 people killed and 5324 wounded between 26 March and 31 December 2015 alone.[125]

9.2 Tribunal and Courts

9.2.1 International Tribunals

9.2.1.1 International Criminal Tribunal for the Former Yugoslavia

The International Criminal Tribunal for the former Yugoslavia (ICTY) is expected to complete its judicial work by the end of 2017[126] and, at the beginning of 2016,

---

[118] Al-Batati S and Fahimapril K (2015) War in Yemen Is Allowing Qaeda Group to Expand. http://www.nytimes.com/2015/04/17/world/middleeast/khaled-bahah-houthi-rebel-yemen-fighting.html. Accessed 24 May 2016.

[119] Shaheen K (2015) US drone strike kills Yemen al-Qaida leader Nasir al-Wuhayshi. http://www.theguardian.com/world/2015/jun/16/yemen-al-qaida-leader-nasir-al-wuhayshi-killed-us-drone-strike. Accessed 24 May 2016.

[120] Human Rights Watch (2015) Yemen: Airstrike on Camp Raises Grave Concerns. https://www.hrw.org/news/2015/04/01/yemen-airstrike-camp-raises-grave-concerns. Accessed 24 May 2016.

[121] Human Rights Watch (2015) Yemen: Factory Airstrike Killed 31 Civilians. https://www.hrw.org/news/2015/04/15/yemen-factory-airstrike-killed-31-civilians-0. Accessed 24 May 2016.

[122] Human Rights Watch (2015) Yemen: Coalition Strikes on Residence Apparent War Crime. https://www.hrw.org/news/2015/07/27/yemen-coalition-strikes-residence-apparent-war-crime. Accessed 24 May 2016.

[123] Brumfield B and Shelbayah S (2015) Report: Saudi Arabia used U.S.-supplied cluster bombs in Yemen. http://edition.cnn.com/2015/05/03/middleeast/yemen-hrw-cluster-munitions-saudi-arabia/index.html. Accessed 24 May 2016.

[124] Human Rights Watch (2015) Yemen: Houthis Used Landmines in Aden. https://www.hrw.org/news/2015/09/05/yemen-houthis-used-landmines-aden. Accessed 24 May 2016.

[125] OHCHR (2016) Press briefing notes on Yemen. http://www.ohchr.org/EN/NewsEvents/Pages/DisplayNews.aspx?NewsID=16923&LangID=E. Accessed 24 May 2016.

[126] UN Security Council (2015) Letter dated 16 November 2015 from the President of the International Tribunal for the Prosecution of Persons Responsible for Serious Violations of International Humanitarian Law Committed in the Territory of the Former Yugoslavia since 1991, addressed to the President of the Security Council, UN Doc. S/2015/874. http://www.icty.org/x/file/About/Reports%20and%20Publications/CompletionStrategy/151116_icty_progress_report_en.pdf. Accessed 3 May 2016, Annex 1, para 5.

only four trial cases and two appeals cases remained. Of the ongoing trials at the end of 2015, the *Hadžić* case remained adjourned due to the accused's ill health,[127] the two trial judgments in the *Karadžić* case and the *Šešelj* case were scheduled for early 2016,[128] and the judgment in the *Mladić* case was expected to be delivered by November 2017.[129] Appeals proceedings emanating from these judgments will be handled by the Mechanism for International Criminal Tribunals (MICT). At the appeals level, the judgment in the case of *Jadranko Prlić* et al. was expected in November 2017 and the judgment in the case of *Stanišić and Župljanin* was anticipated in mid-2016.[130] The year 2015 also marked the 20th anniversary of the genocide in Srebrenica, with both Prosecutor Brammertz and President Meron of the ICTY attending commemorative services held in Potočari on 11 July.[131] Furthermore, on 1 December, the ICTY announced that Petar Jojić, Jovo Ostojić, and Vjerica Radeta had been charged with contempt of the Tribunal in relation to alleged witness tampering.[132]

Appeals Judgments

In 2015, the Appeals Chamber delivered three judgments. First, on 30 January 2015, the Appeals Chamber issued its judgment in the *Popović* et al. case,[133] which concerned five senior Bosnian Serbian military officials and crimes committed in 1995 after the takeover of the protected areas of Srebrenica and Žepa.[134] In the ICTY's largest completed case to date, the Appeals Chamber dismissed, either unanimously or by majority, the greater part of the appellants' grounds of

---

[127] Ibid, paras 12–13.

[128] Ibid, paras 14 and 17.

[129] Ibid, para 16.

[130] Ibid, paras 18 and 20.

[131] International Criminal Tribunal for the Former Yugoslavia (ICTY) (2015) 20th anniversary of the Srebrenica genocide: Prosecutor Serge Brammertz pays tribute to the victims. http://www.icty.org/en/press/20th-anniversary-srebrenica-genocide-prosecutor-serge-brammertz-pays-tribute-victims. Accessed 3 May 2016; and ICTY (2015) President Meron addresses Srebrenica Genocide 20th Anniversary Commemoration at Potočari Memorial. http://www.icty.org/en/press/president-meron-addresses-srebrenica-genocide-20th-anniversary-commemoration-poto%C4%8Dari-memorial. Accessed 3 May 2016.

[132] ICTY (2015) Petar Jojić, Jovo Ostojić, and Vjerica Radeta charged with Contempt of Court. http://www.icty.org/en/press/petar-joji%C4%87-jovo-ostoji%C4%87-and-vjerica-radeta-charged-contempt-court. Accessed 30 May 2016.

[133] ICTY, *Prosecutor v Vujadin Popović, Ljubiša Beara, Drago Nikolić, Radivoje Miletić & Vinko Pandurević*, Judgement, 30 January 2015, Case No. IT-05-88-A (*Popović*).

[134] ICTY (2015) Appeals Chamber upholds convictions of five senior Bosnian Serb officials for Srebrenica and Žepa crimes. http://www.icty.org/en/press/appeals-chamber-upholds-convictions-five-senior-bosnian-serb-officials-srebrenica-and-%C5%BEepa. Accessed 3 May 2016.

appeal and each of the five appellants had most of their convictions upheld, albeit with some small alterations.[135] Several examples include: first, in relation to Mr. Popović and Mr. Beara, the Appeals Chamber entered new convictions concerning their responsibility for conspiracy to commit genocide;[136] second, the Appeals Chamber entered a new conviction for Mr. Miletić for murder as a war crime in relation to the "opportunistic" killings in Potočari;[137] and third, new convictions were entered against Mr. Pandurević in relation to aiding and abetting persecution through murder as a crime against humanity with regard to the Milići Prisoners, and for failing to punish crimes and persecution perpetrated by his subordinates that occurred between 13 and 16 July 1995.[138] In addition, Mr. Miletić's conviction surrounding forcible transfer as a crime against humanity in relation to the departure of men from Žepa across the Drina River was reversed as the nexus requirement was not met.[139] The convictions of Mr. Beara, Mr. Nikolić, and Mr. Popović concerning the Trnovo killings by the Scorpions Unit were likewise reversed as members of the Unit were not found to be members of the joint criminal enterprise nor was there a link between the Unit and a member of the joint criminal enterprise.[140] Despite these changes, only Mr. Miletić's sentence was altered with the Appeals Chamber reducing it from 19 to 18 years of imprisonment.[141] Notably, the Appeals Chamber reaffirmed that the existence of a State policy is not a requirement for proving the crime of genocide[142] and that specific direction is neither part of the *mens rea* nor *actus reus* of aiding and abetting.[143] Judges Robinson and Pocar added partially dissenting opinions and Judge Niang provided a dissenting opinion.

On 8 April 2015, the Appeals Chamber issued its second decision of 2015 in the case of *Tolimir*,[144] who had been Assistant Commander and Chief of the Sector for Intelligence and Security Affairs of the Main Staff of the Army of the Republika Srpska.[145] Mr. Tolimir was convicted of crimes, including crimes

---

135 Ibid.

136 *Popović*, above n 133, para 557.

137 Ibid, paras 1710–1719.

138 Ibid, paras 1836 and 1947.

139 Ibid, paras 772–775.

140 Ibid, paras 1059–1070.

141 Ibid, para 2113.

142 Ibid, paras 430–443.

143 Ibid, paras 1755–1759.

144 ICTY, *Prosecutor v Zdravko Tolimir*, Judgement, 8 April 2015, Case No. IT-05-88/2-A (*Tolimir*).

145 ICTY (2015) Appeals Chamber upholds Tolimir's convictions for genocide and unanimously upholds life sentence. http://www.icty.org/en/press/appeals-chamber-upholds-tolimirs-convictions-genocide-and-unanimously-upholds-life-sentence. Accessed 3 May 2016.

against humanity and genocide, committed in Srebrenica and Žepa in 1995 and, as a result of the appeal, several convictions were overturned, including the convictions for extermination as a crime against humanity and for genocide pertaining to the killing of the three Žepa leaders;[146] the conviction for genocide through causing serious mental harm relating to the forcible transfer of Bosnian Muslims from Žepa;[147] the conviction for genocide pertaining to the forcible transfer operations in Srebrenica and Žepa as the Appeals Chamber found it had not been established beyond a reasonable doubt that the policy was designed to cause the physical destruction of these peoples;[148] and the convictions for genocide, extermination as a crime against humanity and murder as a violation of the laws of war that related to the killings of six men by the Scorpions Unit near Trnovo.[149] The Appeals Chamber clarified that its findings do "not mean that the Muslim civilians of Žepa were not the victims of genocide" nor does it "diminish the status of Žepa's Muslim populations as victims of the genocide".[150] Furthermore, despite the reversals, the Appeals Chamber did not reduce Mr. Tolimir's sentence as, "in light of [the] [...] genocide convictions alone", it felt life imprisonment was still appropriate.[151]

Thirdly, on 15 December 2015, the Appeals Chamber quashed the acquittals of Jovica Stanišić and Franko Simatović[152] and ordered a retrial on all counts of the indictment.[153] Mr. Stanišić and Mr. Simatović had been accused of participating in a joint criminal enterprise between April 1991 and December 1995 that aimed to forcibly and permanently remove the majority of the non-Serb population from parts of Bosnia and Herzegovina and Croatia.[154] Mr. Stanišić had been the deputy chief and then chief of the Serbian State Security Service and Mr. Simatović had also been working within the Second Administration of the Serbian State Security Service and the Ministry of Interior.[155] Although the Trial Chamber had found that many of the crimes within the indictment had been perpetrated, it did not find either accused liable under the joint criminal enterprise due to a lack of *mens rea*, it held it was not proven beyond a reasonable doubt that the accused had planned or ordered the crimes, and it found that the *actus reus* for aiding and abetting had

---

146 *Tolimir*, above n 144, paras 150 and 269–270.

147 Ibid, para 221.

148 Ibid, paras 229, 230 and 233–235.

149 Ibid, paras 434–435 and 649.

150 Ibid, para 236.

151 Ibid, para 648.

152 ICTY, *Prosecutor v Jovica Stanišić & Franko Simatović*, Judgement, 9 December 2015, Case No. IT-03-69-A (*Stanišić & Simatović*).

153 ICTY (2015) Appeals Chamber Orders Retrial of Jovica Stanišić and Franko Simatović. http://www.icty.org/en/press/appeals-chamber-orders-retrial-jovica-stani%C5%A1i%C4%87-and-franko-simatovi%C4%87. Accessed 3 May 2016.

154 *Stanišić & Simatović*, above n 152, para 4.

155 Ibid, paras 2–3.

not been established.[156] The Appeals Chamber found that the Trial Chamber had failed to first determine whether the *actus reus* for a joint criminal enterprise existed which constituted an error in law.[157] Without having done this and without having determined the existence and extent of the common criminal purpose of the group, "the Trial Chamber could not have properly adjudicated Mr. Stanišić and Mr. Simatović's *mens rea*".[158] This led the Appeals Chamber to conclude that the Trial Chamber failed to adjudicate upon and provide a reasoned opinion in relation to elements essential to proving a joint criminal enterprise.[159] In addition, it reaffirmed that specific direction is not an element of aiding and abetting neither in the jurisprudence of the international criminal tribunals nor under customary international law, constituting a second error in law by the Trial Chamber.[160] Accordingly, and given the composition of the original Trial Chamber had altered, the Appeals Chamber used its discretion to remit the case to a retrial.[161]

9.2.1.2 International Criminal Tribunal for Rwanda

The International Criminal Tribunal for Rwanda (ICTR) officially closed on 31 December 2015 with members of the UN Security Council acknowledging "the substantial contribution of the ICTR to the process of national reconciliation and the restoration of peace and security, and to the fight against impunity and the development of international criminal justice, especially in relation to the crime of genocide".[162] At the start of 2015, the ICTR only had one case remaining, the *Nyiramasuhuko* et al. (*Butare*) case, and its closure was slated for the end of 2015.

Following oral hearings that took place in April 2015,[163] the ICTR delivered its final verdict in the *Butare* case[164] on 14 December 2015.[165] This case concerned

---

156 Ibid, para 6.

157 Ibid, paras 79–80.

158 Ibid, paras 87–88.

159 Ibid, paras 88 and 90.

160 Ibid, paras 104–108.

161 Ibid, paras 126–129.

162 UN Security Council (2015) Security Council Press Statement on Closure of International Criminal Tribunal for Rwanda. http://www.un.org/press/en/2015/sc12188.doc.htm. Accessed 3 May 2016.

163 International Criminal Tribunal for Rwanda (ICTR) (2015) The Appeals Chamber Hears Oral Arguments in the Nyiramasuhuko et al. Case. http://unictr.unmict.org/en/news/appeals-chamber-hears-oral-arguments-nyiramasuhuko-etal-case. Accessed 3 May 2016.

164 ICTR, *The Prosecutor v Pauline Nyiramasuhuko, Arsène Shalom Ntahobali, Sylvain Nsabimana, Alphonse Nteziryayo, Joseph Kanyabashi and Élie Ndayambaje*, Judgement, 14 December 2015, Case No. ICTR-98-42-A (*Butare*).

165 ICTR (2015) Appeals Chamber Delivers Judgement in the Nyiramasuhuko et al. Case. http://unictr.unmict.org/en/news/appeals-chamber-delivers-judgement-nyiramasuhuko-etal-case. Accessed 9 May 2016.

six individuals, including Pauline Nyiramasuhuko, previously the Minister of Family and Women's Development and member for Butare Prefecture; Arsène Shalom Ntahobali, son of Ms. Nyiramasuhuko, student and part-time manager of a hotel in Butare Prefecture; Sylvain Nsabimana, prefect of Butare for part of 1994; Alphonse Nteziryayo, prefect of Butare for part of 1994; Joseph Kanyabashi, *bourgmestre* of Ngoma Commune in Butare Prefecture; and Élie Ndayambaje, *bourgmestre* of Muganza Commune in Butare Prefecture.[166] They had been initially convicted of a variety of charges, including conspiracy to commit genocide, genocide, crimes against humanity, serious violations of Article 3 common to the Geneva Conventions, and incitement to genocide.[167] In addition to the Prosecution, all the individuals involved in the case lodged appeals.[168]

The majority of the appeals were dismissed by the Appeals Chamber with some notable exceptions.[169] These include the following: the Appeals Chamber's finding that there had been a violation of the right to be tried without undue delay for all of the accused that caused prejudice due to "the Prosecution's conduct and delays resulting from the Trial Chamber judges' simultaneous assignment to multiple cases";[170] the reversal of convictions for Ms. Nyiramasuhuko, Mr. Ntahobali, Mr. Nsabimana, Mr. Kanyabashi and Mr. Ndayambaje in relation to persecution on "ethnic grounds" as a crime against humanity as "ethnic grounds" are not an enumerated discriminatory ground of persecution within the ICTR's statute;[171] and the decrease of all the sentences of all the accused, reducing their sentences to 47 years for Ms. Nyiramasuhuko, Mr. Ntahobali, and Mr. Ndayambaje;[172] 25 years for Mr. Nteziryayo;[173] 20 years for Mr. Kanyabashi;[174] and 18 years for Mr. Nsabimana.[175]

9.2.1.3 Mechanism for International Criminal Tribunals

The Mechanism for International Criminal Tribunals (MICT) continued its work in the light of the ongoing winding down at the ICTY and the closure of the ICTR. The MICT's workload increased at the Arusha branch as it took over the

[166] *Butare*, above n 164, paras 2–7.
[167] Ibid, paras 13–18.
[168] Ibid, paras 19–27.
[169] See Ibid, para 3539.
[170] Ibid, paras 378 and 397–398.
[171] Ibid, paras 2136 and 2139–2141.
[172] Ibid, paras 3523, 3526 and 3538.
[173] Ibid, para 3532.
[174] Ibid, para 3535.
[175] Ibid, para 3529.

remaining ICTR functions, including the management of the UN Detention Facility.[176] It anticipates taking over the ICTY's functions at its planned closure in 2017.[177] From an administrative standpoint, the takeover included the transfer of files from the ICTY to the MICT, which began at the start of 2015[178] and, by July, the transfer of closed cases' records was complete.[179] Moreover, the UN and the Netherlands signed the headquarters agreement concerning The Hague branch for the MICT in February.[180]

In his report to the UN Security Council, MICT's President Meron noted that the main challenges facing the MICT continue to be arresting the remaining fugitives of the ICTR, and facilitating the resettlement of individuals acquitted by the ICTR and those who have served their sentences.[181] To this end, 2015 saw some success with the arrest of Mr. Ladislas Ntaganzwa in the Democratic Republic of Congo in December.[182] Mr. Ntaganzwa's case is one of the six remaining cases that was referred to Rwanda under Rule 11*bis* of the ICTR's Rules of Procedure and Evidence and his arrest leaves eight other fugitives still at large.[183]

The MICT also dealt with several requests for review in 2015. This included the application of Milan Lukić, who requested a review of his convictions and sentence in the light of new evidence.[184] This was dismissed by the Appeals Chamber due to a failure to show any new facts as per Rule 146 of the MICT's Rules of Procedure and Evidence (MRPE).[185] Mr. Lukić attempted to appeal this decision, but the Appeals Chamber found that Article 23 of the Statute of the MICT and Rule 133 of the MRPE were "not applicable in the [...] circumstances where the

176 Mechanism for International Criminal Tribunals (MICT) (2015) President Meron addresses the UN Security Council. http://www.unmict.org/en/news/president-meron-addresses-un-security-council-0. Accessed 12 May 2016.

177 MICT (2015) President Meron Presents Third Annual Report to the United Nations General Assembly. http://www.unmict.org/en/news/president-meron-presents-third-annual-report-united-nations-general-assembly. Accessed 12 May 2016.

178 ICTY (2015) Tribunal Begins Transfer of Judicial Records to MICT. http://www.icty.org/en/press/tribunal-begins-transfer-judicial-records-mict. Accessed 3 May 2016.

179 MICT (2015) Transfer of all closed cases' records from the ICTY to the MICT is finalised. http://www.unmict.org/en/news/transfer-all-closed-cases%E2%80%99-records-icty-mict-finalised. Accessed 12 May 2016.

180 MICT (2015) United Nations and the Netherlands sign agreement on Mechanism headquarters. http://www.unmict.org/en/news/united-nations-and-netherlands-sign-agreement-mechanism-headquarters. Accessed 12 May 2016.

181 MICT (2015) President Meron addresses the UN Security Council. http://www.unmict.org/en/news/president-meron-addresses-un-security-council-0. Accessed 12 May 2016.

182 MICT (2015) Rwandan Genocide Fugitive Arrested in the DRC. http://www.unmict.org/en/news/rwandan-genocide-fugitive-arrested-drc. Accessed 12 May 2016.

183 Ibid.

184 MICT, *Prosecutor v Milan Lukić*, Decision on Milan Lukić's Application for Review, 7 July 2015, Case No. MICT-13-52-R.1, para 2.

185 Ibid, paras 17, 23, 31 and 37.

impugned decision was rendered by the Appeals Chamber".[186] In a similar motion, Sreten Lukić requested that his convictions and sentence be reviewed due to new facts, evidence and jurisprudence.[187] In dismissing the motion for a lack of new facts,[188] the Appeals Chamber reaffirmed that "review of a final judgment is an exceptional procedure and not an additional opportunity for a party to re-litigate arguments that failed on trial or on appeal".[189] Moreover, it reiterated that a "'new fact' [...] consists of 'new information of an evidentiary nature of a fact that was not in issue during the trial or appeal proceedings'".[190]

In addition, the Trial Chamber of the MICT issued a decision in the case of Jean Uwinkindi concerning the referral of his case to Rwanda.[191] Under Rule 11*bis* of the ICTR Rules, Trial Chambers may refer cases to national jurisdictions where they are satisfied that the accused's fair trial rights will be guaranteed and that the death penalty will not be imposed.[192] Referred cases are to be monitored by the MICT under Article 6(5) of the MICT's Statute.[193] The case was ultimately dismissed as the Trial Chamber did not find that any of Uwinkindi's complaints, relating predominantly to fair trial issues, demonstrated that the situation no longer complied with the conditions of referral.[194] Furthermore, following the Appeals judgment at the ICTY discussed above,[195] Mr. Stanišić and Mr. Simatović made their first appearance for their retrial before the Trial Chamber of the MICT on 18 December.[196] Both pleaded not guilty to the charges in what shall be the first retrial held at the MICT.[197]

---

[186] MICT, *Prosecutor v Milan Lukić*, Decision on Prosecutor's Motion to Strike Milan Lukić's Notice of Appeal of Decision on Application for Review, 13 November 2015, Case No. MICT-13-52-R.1, p. 2.

[187] MICT, *Prosecutor v Sreten Lukić*, Decision on Sreten Lukić's Application for Review, 8 July 2015, Case No. MICT-14-67-R.1, para 3.

[188] Ibid, paras 11, 18 and 22.

[189] Ibid, paras 6 and 24.

[190] Ibid, para 6.

[191] MICT, *Prosecutor v Jean Uwinkindi*, Decision on Uwinkindi's Request for Revocation, 22 October 2015, Case No. MICT-12-25-R14.1.

[192] *Prosecutor v Jean Uwinkindi*, Decision on Uwinkindi's Request for Revocation, 22 October 2015, Case No. MICT-12-25-R14.1, para 7.

[193] Ibid.

[194] Ibid, para 41.

[195] See, above, Sect. 9.2.1.1.

[196] MICT (2015) Initial Appearance of Stanišić and Simatović before the Mechanism. http://www.unmict.org/en/news/initial-appearance-stani%C5%A1i%C4%87-and-simatovi%C4%87-mechanism. Accessed 12 May 2016.

[197] Ibid.

9.2.1.4 International Criminal Court

The ICC had a relatively busy year in 2015, which included the 14th Session of the Assembly of States Parties.[198]

New States Parties and Preliminary Examinations

Early on, the number of situations before the Court showed signs of expansion as the ICC gained a new State Party when Palestine acceded to the Rome Statute on 7 January.[199] The Prosecutor subsequently opened a Preliminary Examination into the situation in Palestine on 16 January.[200] The Prosecutor likewise extended the Preliminary Examination into the situation in Ukraine on 29 September, following Ukraine's second Article 12(3) declaration through which it accepted the Court's jurisdiction from 20 February 2014 onwards.[201] On 13 October, the Prosecutor requested permission to initiate an investigation into the situation in Georgia, marking the conclusion of the Prosecutor's Preliminary Examination into the August 2008 armed conflict.[202] Finally, in October, the Prosecutor formally announced the closure of the Preliminary Examination into the situation in Honduras as it found "no reasonable basis to proceed with an investigation".[203]

---

198 For further information, see International Criminal Court (ICC) (2015) Assembly of States Parties to the Rome Statute of the International Criminal Court Official Records—Official Records: Volume I. https://asp.icc-cpi.int/iccdocs/asp_docs/ASP14/OR/ICC-ASP-14-20-OR-vol-I-ENG.pdf. Accessed 30 May 2016; and ICC (2015) Assembly of States Parties to the Rome Statute of the International Criminal Court Official Records—Official Records: Volume II. https://asp.icc-cpi.int/iccdocs/asp_docs/ASP14/OR/ICC-ASP-14-20-ENG-OR-vol-II.pdf. Accessed 30 May 2016.

199 ICC (2015) The State of Palestine accedes to the Rome Statute. https://www.icc-cpi.int/Pages/item.aspx?name=pr1082_2. Accessed 11 May 2016.

200 ICC (2015) The Prosecutor of the International Criminal Court, Fatou Bensouda, opens a preliminary examination of the situation in Palestine. https://www.icc-cpi.int/Pages/item.aspx?name=pr1083. Accessed 11 May 2016.

201 ICC (2015) ICC Prosecutor extends preliminary examination of the situation in Ukraine following second article 12(3) declaration. https://www.icc-cpi.int/Pages/item.aspx?name=pr1156. Accessed 11 May 2016.

202 ICC (2015) The Prosecutor of the International Criminal Court, Fatou Bensouda, requests judges for authorisation to open an investigation into the situation in Georgia. https://www.icc-cpi.int/Pages/item.aspx?name=pr1159. Accessed 11 May 2016.

203 The Office of the Prosecutor (2015) Situation in Honduras—Article 5 Report. https://www.icc-cpi.int/iccdocs/otp/SAS-HON-Article_5_Report-Oct2015-ENG.PDF. Accessed 30 May 2016, paras 141–143.

Arrest Warrants and Cases in the Pre-trial Phase

The ICC had a mixed year with its arrest warrants. Positively, the Court gained custody of two individuals subject to its arrest warrants: first, Dominic Ongwen was transferred to the ICC's custody on 17 January in accordance with an arrest warrant issued on 8 July 2005;[204] and second, Ahmad Al Faqi Al Mahdi was surrendered to the Court on 26 September following the issuance of an arrest warrant on 18 September 2015.[205] As to the former accused, Mr. Ongwen's case was formally separated from that of *Kony* et al. in order prevent a delay in his proceedings.[206] In the latter case, it marked the first time an individual has been brought before the ICC to face war crimes charges that relate to the destruction of religious or historical monuments.[207] Despite this, the Court still faced struggles with securing the arrest of high-profile individuals and referred several instances of non-cooperation in this regard to the UN Security Council.[208] Additionally, Pre-Trial Chamber II terminated proceedings against Okot Odhiambo following the confirmation of his death.[209]

Cases in the Trial Phase

There were several notable developments in cases at the trial stage in 2015. Two new trials began at the ICC in 2015: first, the case concerning *Ntaganda*[210]

---

204 ICC (2015) Dominic Ongwen transferred to The Hague. https://www.icc-cpi.int/Pages/item.aspx?name=pr1084. Accessed 11 May 2016.

205 ICC (2015) Situation in Mali: Ahmad Al Faqi Al Mahdi surrendered to the ICC on charges of war crimes regarding the destruction of historical and religious monuments in Timbuktu. https://www.icc-cpi.int/Pages/item.aspx?name=pr1154. Accessed 11 May 2016.

206 ICC (2015) ICC Pre-Trial Chamber II separates Dominic Ongwen case from Kony et al. case. https://www.icc-cpi.int/Pages/item.aspx?name=pr1088&ln=en. Accessed 12 May 2016.

207 ICC, above n 205.

208 See, for example, South Africa's failure to arrest Omar Hassan Ahmad Al Bashir which is discussed in: ICC, *The Prosecutor v Omar Hassan Ahmad Al Bashir*, Decision following the Prosecutor's request for an order further clarifying that the Republic of South Africa is under the obligation to immediately arrest and surrender Omar Al Bashir, 13 June 2015, Case No. ICC-02/05-01/09-242; and ICC, *The Prosecutor v Omar Hassan Ahmad Al Bashir*, Decision on the request of the Republic of South Africa for an extension of the time limit for submitting their views for the purposes of proceedings under article 87(7) of the Rome Statute, 15 October 2015, Case No. ICC-02/05-01/09-249. See also: ICC (2015) Pre-Trial Chamber II informs the United Nations Security Council about Sudan's non-cooperation in the arrest and surrender of Omar Al Bashir. https://www.icc-cpi.int/Pages/item.aspx?name=pr1094. Accessed 11 May 2016; ICC (2015) The President of the Assembly calls on States Parties to fulfil their obligations to execute the Arrest warrants against Mr. Al Bashir. https://www.icc-cpi.int/Pages/item.aspx?name=pr1117. Accessed 11 May 2016; and ICC (2015) ICC Pre-Trial Chamber II refers the UNSC Sudan's non-cooperation and failure to arrest Mr Abdel Raheem Hussein. https://www.icc-cpi.int/Pages/item.aspx?name=pr1123. Accessed 11 May 2016.

209 ICC (2015) ICC terminates proceedings against Okot Odhiambo following forensic confirmation of his passing. https://www.icc-cpi.int/Pages/item.aspx?name=pr1147&ln=en. Accessed 30 May 2015.

210 ICC, *The Prosecutor v Bosco Ntaganda*, Case No. ICC-01/04-02/06.

commenced on 2 September;[211] and second, the Article 70 case concerning *Bemba* et al.[212] started on 29 September.[213] Mr. Ntaganda, the former deputy chief of the General Staff of the *Force Patriotiques pour la Libération du Congo*, is accused of 13 counts of war crimes and five counts of crimes against humanity that were allegedly committed in Ituri, in the Democratic Republic of Congo (DRC) in 2002–2003.[214] The trial commenced in The Hague following a decision by the Presidency under Articles 3 and 62 of the Rome Statute not to hold the opening statements in Bunia, in DRC.[215] The *Bemba* et al. case has five co-accused who are facing charges relating to offences against the administration of justice and witnesses' testimony under Article 70 of the Rome Statute in the *Bemba* case.[216]

In the Kenya situation, on 13 March, Trial Chamber V(b) formally terminated the case and the summons to appear against Mr. Kenyatta.[217] This was done in the light of the Prosecutor's decision to withdraw charges following the Chamber's decision of 3 December 2014 in which it "directed the Prosecution to file, within one week, a notice of its withdrawal of charges, or an indication that the evidentiary base had improved to a degree which would justify proceeding to trial".[218] In the *Ruto and Sang* case, Trial Chamber V(a) issued its decision on the use of prior recorded testimony on 19 August,[219] and the Defence teams filed "No Case to Answer" Motions on 26 October 2015.[220] The latter motions requested that Trial Chamber V(a) enter a judgment of acquittal and to dismiss the case on the basis that the Prosecutor had not provided sufficient evidence to link the co-accused to a

[211] ICC (2015) Ntaganda trial opens at International Criminal Court. https://www.icc-cpi.int/Pages/item.aspx?name=pr1143&ln=en. Accessed 12 May 2016.

[212] ICC, *The Prosecutor v Jean-Pierre Bemba Gombo, Aimé Kilolo Musamba, Jean-Jacques Mangenda Kabongo, Fidèle Babala Wandu & Narcisse Arido*, Case No. ICC-01/05-01/13.

[213] ICC (2015) Bemba, Kilolo et al. trial opens at International Criminal Court. https://www.icc-cpi.int/Pages/item.aspx?name=pr1155&ln=en. Accessed 12 May 2016.

[214] ICC (2015) Ntaganda trial opens at International Criminal Court. https://www.icc-cpi.int/Pages/item.aspx?name=pr1143&ln=en. Accessed 12 May 2016.

[215] ICC, *The Prosecutor v Bosco Ntaganda*, Decision on the recommendation to the Presidency on holding part of the trial in the State concerned, 15 June 2015, Case No. ICC-01/04-02/06-645-Red, paras 3 and 27.

[216] ICC, above n 213; ICC, *The Prosecutor v Jean-Pierre Bemba Gombo*, Case No. ICC-01/05-01/08.

[217] ICC, *The Prosecutor v Uhuru Muigai Kenyatta*, Decision on the withdrawal of charges against Mr Kenyatta, 13 March 2015, Case No. ICC-01/09-02/11-1005, para 10.

[218] Ibid, para 8.

[219] ICC, *The Prosecutor v William Samoei Ruto & Joshua Arap Sang*, Public redacted version of: Decision on Prosecution Request for Admission of Prior Recorded Testimony, 19 August 2015, Case No. ICC-01/09-01/11-1938-Red-Corr.

[220] ICC, *The Prosecutor v William Samoei Ruto & Joshua Arap Sang*, Public redacted version of: Decision on Defence Applications for Judgments of Acquittal, 5 April 2016, Case No. ICC-01/09-01/11-2027-Red (*Ruto* 2016), paras 8–9.

crime or to prove their criminal liability beyond a reasonable doubt.[221] The Prosecution filed its response on 20 November and the case is expected to continue in 2016.[222]

In the situation concerning Côte d'Ivoire, Trial Chamber I decided to join the *Gbagbo* and *Blé Goudé* cases on 11 March.[223] This marked the first time the Prosecution has requested a joinder of trials before a Trial Chamber, and it allowed the Chamber to consider its discretionary powers under Article 64(5) of its Statute and Rule 136 of the ICC's Rules of Procedure and Evidence (RPE).[224] In so doing, it determined that it has the power to "join charges against more than one accused, even when those charges are not identical".[225] In arriving at its decision, Trial Chamber I considered that: Mr. Gbagbo and Mr. Blé Goudé's charges arise largely from the same circumstances, involving the same crimes, the same perpetrators and the same victims; they were both alleged to be part of the same "inner circle"; their contributions to the crimes are linked; the factual background established in the separate Confirmation of Charges decisions shall not be amended; "serious prejudice" will not be caused to either accused; and separate trials are not necessary in the "interests of justice".[226] The Chamber subsequently refused a Defence request for leave to appeal the joinder decision.[227]

Notable Appeals Judgments

In the DRC situation, the Appeals Chamber issued its 117 page judgment in the case of *Ngudjolo* on 27 February, confirming his acquittal.[228] The judgment arose from the Prosecutor's appeal of Mr. Ngudjolo's initial acquittal in December 2012.[229] The

221 Ibid.

222 ICC, *The Prosecutor v William Samoei Ruto & Joshua Arap Sang*, Decision on Page and Time Limits for the 'No Case to Answer' Motion, 18 September 2015, Case No. ICC-01/09-01/11-1970, p. 9; *Ruto* 2016, above n 220, para 10.

223 ICC, *The Prosecutor v Laurent Gbagbo* and *The Prosecutor v Charles Blé Goudé*, Decision on Prosecution requests to join the cases of *The Prosecutor v Laurent Gbagbo* and *The Prosecutor v Charles Blé Goudé* and related matters, 11 March 2015, Case No. ICC-01/11-01/11-1, para 68.

224 Ibid, paras 42 and 44.

225 Ibid, para 48.

226 Ibid, paras 52–67.

227 ICC, *The Prosecutor v Laurent Gbagbo and Charles Blé Goudé*, Decision on Defence requests for leave to appeal the 'Decision on Prosecution requests to join the cases of *The Prosecutor v Laurent Gbagbo* and *The Prosecutor v Charles Blé Goudé* and related matters', 22 April 2015, Case No. ICC-02/11-01/15-42, paras 17–19.

228 ICC, *The Prosecutor v Mathieu Ngudjolo Chui*, Judgment on the Prosecutor's appeal against the decision of Trial Chamber II entitled "Judgment pursuant to article 74 of the Statute", 27 February 2015, Case No. ICC-01/04-02/12 A, p. 6.

229 Ibid, paras 4–5.

Prosecutor advanced three grounds of appeal: first, an alleged misapplication of the standard of proof; second, an alleged failure to consider the totality of the evidence; and third, the Prosecutor's right to have an adequate opportunity to present her case.[230] The Appeals Chamber rejected the Prosecutor's first ground, holding that the Trial Chamber's conclusions were not unreasonable and that it had not applied an overly stringent standard in assessing the evidence presented to it.[231] In relation to the second ground, the Prosecution alleged a number of failures to consider evidence, which in turn impacted upon the Trial Chamber's factual findings.[232] The Appeals Chamber addressed each alleged instance identified by the Prosecutor but ultimately also rejected this ground.[233]

The third ground of appeal concerned allegations that Mr. Ngudjolo interfered with witnesses while he was detained and the Prosecution argued that the Trial Chamber's procedural errors had violated its right to a fair trial.[234] Namely, the Prosecutor alleged that the Trial Chamber had erred in failing to give it access to recorded conversations and parts of Registry reports as well as by preventing its attempts to obtain explanations from witnesses regarding inconsistent testimony.[235] First, the Appeals Chamber held, contrary to Mr. Ngudjolo's submissions, that this issue concerned "the objective of establishing the truth" as per Articles 54(1) and 69(3), which is required of both the Prosecutor and the Trial Chamber.[236] Accordingly, grounds of appeal that relate to the Prosecutor's ability to present a case may be raised under Article 81(1)(a)(i) of the Statute.[237] In turning to the substance of the Prosecutor's complaint, the Appeals Chamber held that in two instances the Trial Chamber had exercised its discretion unreasonably but that these errors "had no material impact on the Acquittal Decision".[238] Accordingly, the Appeals Chamber upheld the original decision, with Judge Tarfusser and Judge Trendafilova providing a joint dissenting opinion.[239]

In the *Lubanga* case, the Appeals Chamber delivered a judgment on reparations on 3 March that amended an earlier Trial Chamber order.[240] The Appeals

230 Ibid, paras 42, 127 and 227.

231 Ibid, paras 117–118 and 126.

232 Ibid, para 227.

233 Ibid, paras 228–229.

234 Ibid, paras 230 and 252.

235 Ibid, para 252.

236 Ibid, paras 256–257.

237 Ibid, para 257.

238 Ibid, paras 276, 283 and 294.

239 Ibid, paras 295–296.

240 ICC (2015) Lubanga case: ICC Appeals Chamber amends the Trial Chamber's order for reparations for victims. https://www.icc-cpi.int/Pages/item.aspx?name=pr1092. Accessed 12 May 2016.

Chamber, *inter alia*, provided clarification on the procedural elements required for an order of reparations, noting that: it must be directed against the convicted person; it must "establish and inform" the convicted person of their liability; it must specify whether collective, individual or both forms of reparations are ordered and why; it must clarify the harm caused to both direct and indirect victims; and it must highlight the criteria that determine which victims may be eligible for reparations.[241] It ordered the Trust Fund for Victims to file a new implementation plan for reparations within 6 months of the delivery of the judgment.[242]

The *Simone Gbagbo* case in the situation in Côte d'Ivoire was also the subject of an appeals decision concerning admissibility on 27 May.[243] This was an appeal by Côte d'Ivoire against a Pre-Trial Chamber decision that rejected its initial admissibility challenge, which relied on Articles 17, 19, and 95 of the Statute.[244] The initial challenge argued that the case against Mrs. Gbagbo was inadmissible as Côte d'Ivoire had commenced domestic proceedings in which similar allegations had been made, demonstrating that Côte d'Ivoire was both willing and able to try Mrs. Gbagbo for these crimes.[245] On appeal, Côte d'Ivoire argued that the Pre-Trial Chamber had erred in law through the legal tests used for determining admissibility under Article 17 and had also erred in its factual findings.[246]

In relation to the first ground of appeal, while the Appeals Chamber found that a presumption in favour of domestic jurisdictions exists, it held that it "only applies where it has been shown that there are (or have been) investigations and/or prosecutions at the national level" and found that the Pre-Trial Chamber had not erred in relying upon this.[247] In relation to the issues of fact, the Appeals Chamber held that the Pre-Trial Chamber had not erred in its findings and that, under Article 17(1)(a), "[i]t does not suffice that some or any case is being investigated domestically; it must be the same case (substantially the same conduct) that is being investigated domestically".[248] Moreover, when examining whether a case is "being

[241] ICC, *The Prosecutor v Thomas Lubanga Dyilo*, Judgement on the appeals against the "Decision establishing the principles and procedures to be applied to reparations" of 7 August 2012 with AMENDED order for reparations (Annex A) and public annexes 1 and 2, 3 March 2015, Case No. ICC-01/04-01/06-3129, p. 7.

[242] ICC (2015) Lubanga case: ICC Appeals Chamber amends the Trial Chamber's order for reparations for victims. https://www.icc-cpi.int/Pages/item.aspx?name=pr1092. Accessed 12 May 2016.

[243] ICC, *The Prosecutor v Simone Gbagbo*, Judgment on the appeal of Côte d'Ivoire against the decision of Pre-Trial Chamber I of 11 December 2014 entitled "Decision on Côte d'Ivoire's challenge to the admissibility of the case against Simone Gbagbo", 27 May 2015, Case No. ICC-02/11-01/12-75-Red.

[244] Ibid, paras 7 and 14.

[245] Ibid, para 7.

[246] Ibid, paras 47–48 and 81.

[247] Ibid, paras 58–59.

[248] Ibid, paras 92, 98 and 140.

investigated" in accordance with Article 17(1)(a), the burden of proof is upon the State to show that its investigations are genuine and to provide the Court with "'evidence of a sufficient degree of specificity and probative value' that demonstrates that it is indeed investigating the case".[249] In Mrs. Gbagbo's domestic proceedings, steps, such as obtaining witness testimony or forensic evidence, had not yet been ordered by the investigating Judge or Prosecutor.[250] Accordingly, the Appeals Chamber declined to overturn the Pre-Trial Chamber decision and affirmed that the case is admissible at the ICC.[251]

On 6 November 2015, the Appeals Chamber dismissed the Prosecutor's appeal against a decision from July by Pre-Trial Chamber I in which it requested that the Prosecutor "reconsider the decision not to initiate an investigation" into the 31 May 2010 Israeli raid on the Humanitarian Aid Flotilla bound for the Gaza Strip.[252] The Pre-Trial Chamber had held that the Prosecutor's conclusions concerning "gravity" under Article 17(1)(d) of the Statute had, through a combination of five errors, affected her conclusions.[253] Upon Appeal, the Chamber found it was first necessary to determine whether the appeal was admissible before considering the merits of the Prosecutor's appeal.[254] After a review of Article 53 and the relevant jurisprudence relating to admissibility challenges, the Appeals Chamber held that the Pre-Trial Chamber decision was not an admissibility decision as per Article 82(1)(a) of the Statute and that, consequently, the Prosecutor's appeal was inadmissible and the merits were not considered.[255]

Reviews of Sentence

Two previously handed down sentences were reviewed in accordance with Article 110(3) in late 2015. The first decision concerned the *Lubanga* case.[256] Mr. Lubanga was sentenced to 14 years' imprisonment on 10 July 2012 for conscripting and enlisting children under the age of fifteen years and for using them to participate actively in hostilities.[257] Although the Panel found that "there is a prospect for the resocialisation and successful resettlement" for Mr. Lubanga, there were no

---

[249] Ibid, para 128.

[250] Ibid, para 130.

[251] Ibid, para 141.

[252] ICC, *Situation on Registered Vessels of the Union of the Comoros, the Hellenic Republic and the Kingdom of Cambodia*, Decision on the admissibility of the Prosecutor's appeal against the "Decision on the request of the Union of the Comoros to review the Prosecutor's decision not to initiate an investigation", 6 November 2015, Case No. ICC-01/13-51, paras 1–3.

[253] Ibid, para 16.

[254] Ibid, para 7.

[255] Ibid, paras 66–67.

[256] ICC, *The Prosecutor v Thomas Lubanga Dyilo*, Decision on the review concerning reduction of sentence of Mr Thomas Lubanga Dyilo, 22 September 2015, Case No. ICC-01/04-01/06-3173.

[257] Ibid, paras 1–2.

other reasons in favour of the sentence reduction.[258] Mr. Lubanga will be eligible for a further review of sentence on 22 September 2017.[259] The second decision concerned Mr. Germain Katanga who was sentenced to 12 years' imprisonment following his conviction for crimes against humanity and war crimes in 2014.[260] In contrast to the *Lubanga* decision, the Panel found that Mr. Katanga had been willing to cooperate with the Court, that he had disassociated himself from his crimes while detained, that he has a good prospect of reintegration, and that there were particular individual circumstances—all of which weighed in favour of Mr. Katanga's release.[261] Accordingly, the Panel reduced his sentence by three years and eight months, scheduling his release for 18 January 2016.[262]

9.2.2 *Hybrid Tribunals*

9.2.2.1 Kosovo

EULEX

EULEX continued its work in Kosovo in 2015. On 25 May 2015, the Judicial Panel at the Mitrovica Basic Court delivered its verdict pertaining to the Drenica 1 Case.[263] This case concerned alleged war crimes committed between June and September 1998 against the civilian population that occurred at the Kosovo Liberation Army (KLA) Detention Centre in Likoc/Likovac.[264] In the verdict, Mr. Sami Lushtaku was found guilty of murder and Mr. Sylejman Selimi was found guilty of war crimes relating to the violation of Article 3 common to the Geneva Conventions.[265] They received sentences, respectively, of 12 and six years. The other accused were acquitted.[266]

Later in the same week, the Mitrovica Basic Court rendered its judgment in the Drenica 2 Case.[267] This case also concerned the same KLA Detention Centre and focused on claims that KLA members had committed war crimes, including

---

[258] Ibid, paras 77–78.

[259] Ibid, para 79.

[260] ICC, *The Prosecutor v Germain Katanga*, Decision on the review concerning reduction of sentence of Mr Germain Katanga, 13 November 2015, Case No. ICC-01/04-01/07-3615, paras 1–2.

[261] Ibid, para 111.

[262] Ibid, para 116.

[263] EULEX Kosovo (2015) Drenica 1 Verdict. http://www.eulex-kosovo.eu/?page=2,10,228. Accessed 9 May 2016.

[264] Ibid.

[265] Ibid.

[266] Ibid.

[267] EULEX Kosovo (2015) Drenica 2 Verdict. http://www.eulex-kosovo.eu/?page=2,10,229. Accessed 9 May 2016.

torture and humiliating or degrading treatment, against the civilian population of Albanian Kosovars between August and September 1998.[268] Four individuals, namely Mr. Sylejman Selimi, Mr. Jahir Demaku, Mr. Zeqir Demaku, and Mr. Isni Thaci, were found guilty of offences relating to violence, cruel treatment, torture, and humiliating and degrading treatment against citizens.[269] In addition, Mr. Agim Demaj, Mr. Bashkim Demaj, Mr. Driton Demaj, Mr. Selman Demaj, Mr. Fadil Demaku, and Mr. Nexhat Demaku were found guilty of maltreating detainees.[270] All ten convicted accused received sentences between five and eight years.[271]

Special Tribunal

On 3 August 2015, the Kosovar Parliament voted in favour of establishing a special tribunal to address war crimes allegations against former members of the KLA that occurred during the war with Serbia in the 1990s.[272] This law, known as the *Law on Specialist Chambers and Specialist Prosecutor's Office*,[273] amended the Kosovar Constitution[274] and came into being after a failed vote in June,[275] despite ongoing opposition to any court or tribunal.[276] Its jurisdiction is limited to crimes committed by former KLA members between 1 January 1998 and 31 December 2000, and it will address, *inter alia*, alleged instances of crimes against humanity, war crimes, and organ harvesting.[277] The special tribunal is expected to be set up in the Netherlands in 2016 to allay concerns relating to witness intimidation and judicial corruption in Kosovo.[278] It will consist of international judges who will exclusively apply Kosovar law.[279]

---

268 Ibid.

269 Ibid.

270 Ibid.

271 Ibid.

272 Sander A (2015) Kosovo agrees to war crimes tribunal. http://www.politico.eu/article/kosovo-agrees-to-war-crimes-tribunal-serbia/. Accessed 10 May 2016; International Justice Resource Centre (2015) Kosovo to Create Special War Crimes Court but Faces Challenges. http://www.ijrcenter.org/2015/08/25/kosovo-to-create-special-war-crimes-court-but-faces-challenges/. Accessed 10 May 2016.

273 International Justice Resource Centre (2015) Kosovo to Create Special War Crimes Court but Faces Challenges. http://www.ijrcenter.org/2015/08/25/kosovo-to-create-special-war-crimes-court-but-faces-challenges/. Accessed 10 May 2016.

274 Ibid.

275 Bytyci F (2015) Under Western pressure, Kosovo to put war crimes court to new vote. http://www.reuters.com/article/us-kosovo-warcrimes-idUSKCN0Q515P20150731?feedType=RSS&feedName=worldNews&rpc=69. Accessed 10 May 2016.

276 Sander A (2015) Kosovo agrees to war crimes tribunal. http://www.politico.eu/article/kosovo-agrees-to-war-crimes-tribunal-serbia/. Accessed 10 May 2016.

277 International Justice Resource Centre, above n 273.

278 Sander, above n 276.

279 Ibid.

9.2.2.2 Extraordinary Chambers in the Courts of Cambodia

In 2015, hearings at the Extraordinary Chambers in the Courts of Cambodia (ECCC) were ongoing and, in addition, a number of accused individuals were charged. It also included the conclusion of a judicial investigation.

Case 002/02, which is the second case against Nuon Chea and Khieu Samphan, continued in January with witness testimony.[280] Mr. Chea and Mr. Samphan are accused of crimes against humanity, genocide, and grave breaches of the Geneva Conventions and have previously been convicted in Case 002/01 which is subject to ongoing appeals proceedings.[281] The case has been prolonged due to the illness of the accused as well as issues pertaining to the presence of defence counsel.[282] Witness testimony continued throughout the year,[283] and the submissions and evidence relating to the genocide charges commenced on 7 September.[284]

The first hearing in the appeals proceedings in Case 002/01 was held on 2 July, with three witnesses providing their evidence.[285] As mentioned, this case also concerns Mr. Chea and Mr. Samphan and, in addition to an appeal by the co-prosecutors, they have, respectively, put forward 223 and 148 grounds of appeal.[286] Although additional hearings were scheduled for November, the proceedings were adjourned following Mr. Chea's announcement that he has instructed "his international and national lawyers [... to] not participate in the proceedings" and that he would instead rely on his written briefs.[287] As such, the Supreme Court Chamber

280 The Extraordinary Chambers in the Courts of Cambodia (ECCC) (2015) The Court Report—January. http://www.eccc.gov.kh/en/publication/court-report-january-2015. Accessed 13 May 2016 (January Report), p. 1; ECCC (2005–2015) Case 002/02. http://www.eccc.gov.kh/en/case/topic/1299. Accessed 13 May 2016.

281 ECCC (2006–2015) Case 002. http://www.eccc.gov.kh/en/case/topic/2. Accessed 13 May 2016.

282 January Report, above n 280, pp. 1–2.

283 See, for example, ECCC (2015) The Court Report—March. http://www.eccc.gov.kh/en/publication/court-report-march-2015. Accessed 13 May 2016, p. 3; ECCC (2015) The Court Report—April. http://www.eccc.gov.kh/en/publication/court-report-april-2015. Accessed 13 May 2016, p. 3; ECCC (2015) The Court Report—July. http://www.eccc.gov.kh/en/publication/court-report-july-2015. Accessed 13 May 2016 (July Report), p. 9; ECCC (2015) The Court Report—August. http://www.eccc.gov.kh/en/publication/court-report-august-2015. Accessed 13 May 2016, p. 9; ECCC (2015) The Court Report—September. http://www.eccc.gov.kh/en/publication/court-report-september-2015. Accessed 13 May 2016, p. 1; and ECCC (2015) The Court Report—December. http://www.eccc.gov.kh/en/publication/court-report-december-2015. Accessed 13 May 2016 (December Report), pp. 1–2.

284 ECCC (2015) Press Release: First genocide charges to be heard at the ECCC. http://www.eccc.gov.kh/sites/default/files/media/ECCC%20PR%204%20Sep%202015%20Eng.pdf. Accessed 13 May 2016.

285 July Report, above n 283, pp. 1–2.

286 Ibid, p. 1.

287 ECCC (2015) The Court Report—November. http://www.eccc.gov.kh/en/publication/court-report-november-2015. Accessed 13 May 2016, pp. 1–2.

decided to appoint standby counsel for Mr. Chea to assist in future hearings if necessary.[288]

In addition to these hearings, the ECCC presented charges against a number of new individuals in 2015. These include the following: Im Chaem, who was charged *in absentia* with homicide and crimes against humanity in Case 004;[289] Ao An, who was charged with premeditated homicide and crimes against humanity in Case 004;[290] Yim Tith, who was charged with genocide, crimes against humanity, grave breaches of the Geneva Conventions and premeditated homicide in Case 004;[291] and Meas Muth, who was initially charged *in absentia* in Case 003 in March, but this was overruled by later charges relating to genocide, crimes against humanity, grave breaches of the Geneva Conventions and premediated homicide when he appeared voluntarily in person in December.[292] Following her charges, the investigation into Im Chaem was formally concluded by the co-investigating judges on 18 December.[293]

9.2.2.3 Special Tribunal for Lebanon

During 2015, the Special Tribunal for Lebanon (STL) continued its work, focusing on the ongoing trial in the case of *Ayyash* et al.[294] and several related contempt proceedings.[295] Early in 2015, President Ivana Hrdličková was elected to office[296]

[288] December Report, above n 283, p. 3.

[289] ECCC (2015) The International Co-Investigating Judge Charges Im Chaem in absentia in Case 004. http://www.eccc.gov.kh/en/articles/international-co-investigating-judge-charges-im-chaem-absentia-case-004. Accessed 13 May 2016.

[290] ECCC (2015) The International Co-Investigating Judge Charges Ao An in Case 004. http://www.eccc.gov.kh/en/articles/international-co-investigating-judge-charges-ao-case-004. Accessed 13 May 2016.

[291] ECCC (2015) Mr Yim Tith charged in Case 004. http://www.eccc.gov.kh/en/articles/mr-yim-tith-charged-case-004. Accessed 13 May 2016.

[292] ECCC (2015) The International Co-Investigating Judge Charges Meas Muth in absentia in Case 003. http://www.eccc.gov.kh/en/articles/international-co-investigating-judge-charges-meas-muth-absentia-case-003. Accessed 13 May 2016; and ECCC (2015) Mr Meas Muth charged in Case 003. http://www.eccc.gov.kh/en/articles/mr-meas-muth-charged-case-003. Accessed 13 May 2016.

[293] ECCC (2015) Conclusion of Judicial Investigation Against Im Chaem in Case 004/20-11-2008/ECCC/OCIJ. http://www.eccc.gov.kh/sites/default/files/media/ECCC%20OCIJ%2018%20Dec%202015%20En.pdf. Accessed 13 May 2016.

[294] STL, *The Prosecutor v Salim Jamil Ayyash, Mustafa Amine Badreddine, Hassan Habib Mehri, Hussein Hassan Oneissi & Assad Hassan Sabra*, Case No. STL-11-01 (*Ayyash*).

[295] STL, *In the Case against Al Jadeed [CO.] S.A.L./NEW T.V. S.A.L (N.T.V.) and Karma Mohamed Tahsin Al Khayat*, Case No. STL-14-05; and *In the Case against Akhbar Beirut S.A.L. and Ibrahim Mohamed Al Amin*, Case No. STL-14-06.

[296] Special Tribunal for Lebanon (STL) (2015) Election of Judge Ivana Hrdličková as new STL President. http://www.stl-tsl.org/en/news-and-press/press-releases/3814-election-of-judge-ivana-hrdlickova-as-new-stl-president. Accessed 11 May 2016.

and, not long afterwards, the judges amended the Rules of Procedure and Evidence concerning the disqualification or excusal of judges and in order to better harmonise them with the Host State Agreement.[297]

In the *Ayyash* et al. case, which focuses on the 14 February 2005 attack that killed former Lebanese Prime Minister Rafik Hariri and 21 others, the Prosecution's evidence in chief continued throughout 2015.[298] The Prosecution expects to finish presenting its evidence in 2016.[299] This case continues *in absentia* as provided for by the STL's Statute.[300] The two contempt cases discussed below relate to the primary proceedings in this case.[301]

On 23 January 2015, the Appeals Panel delivered a decision in the case of *Akhbar Beirut S.A.L. and Al Amin*.[302] This interlocutory appeal concerned whether the STL has jurisdiction *rationae personae* to hold contempt proceedings pursuant to Rule 60 *bis* against legal persons, namely news corporation *Akhbar Beirut S.A.L.* in the present case.[303] In deciding this case, the Appeals Panel followed its past jurisprudence and held that the Contempt Judge had erred in finding that "Rule 60 *bis* is a clear and unambiguous provision that provides for criminal responsibility for contempt of natural persons only".[304] In determining that the word "person" in Rule 60 *bis* is ambiguous, the Appeals Panel held that "person" applies to both legal and natural persons, and that this finding does not violate *nullum crimen sine lege*.[305] As such, the contempt charges against *Akhbar Beirut S.A.L.* were reinstated[306] and the opening of the trial is set for early 2016.[307]

In the case of Al Jadeed S.A.L. and Al Khayat, 2015 saw the trial finish and the judgment relating to the contempt proceedings delivered.[308] This case considered

---

297 STL (2015) STL Judges amend the Rules of the Tribunal. http://www.stl-tsl.org/en/news-and-press/press-releases/3818-23-02-2015-stl-judges-amend-the-rules-of-the-tribunal. Accessed 11 May 2016.

298 STL (2015–2016) Special Tribunal for Lebanon: Seventh Annual Report (2015–2016), p. 6.

299 Ibid.

300 Ibid.

301 Ibid, pp. 6–7.

302 STL, *In the Case against Akhbar Beirut S.A.L. and Ibrahim Mohamed Al Amin*, Decision on Interlocutory Appeal Concerning Personal Jurisdiction in Contempt Proceedings, 23 January 2015, Case No. STL-14-06/PT/AP/AR126.1.

303 Ibid, paras 7–9.

304 Ibid, para 73.

305 Ibid, paras 72–75.

306 Ibid, para 75.

307 STL (2015) New date for the start of trial in the contempt case against Akhbar and Mr Ibrahim Al Amin (STL-14-06). http://www.stl-tsl.org/en/news-and-press/press-releases/4671-21-12-2015-new-date-for-the-start-of-trial-in-the-contempt-case-against-akhbar-and-mr-ibrahim-al-amin-stl-14-06. Accessed 12 May 2016.

308 STL, In the Case against Al Jadeed [CO.] S.A.L./NEW T.V. S.A.L (N.T.V.) and Karma Mohamed Tahsin Al Khayat, Public Redacted Version of Judgment, 18 September 2015, Case No. STL-14-05/T/CJ.

whether the broadcast in Lebanon of television episodes concerning alleged confidential STL witnesses, which were subsequently made available online, constituted an interference with the administration of justice.[309] Following the publication of the online content, the Pre-Trial Judge in the *Ayyash* et al. case ordered it removed from the website which did not occur.[310] These contempt proceedings were particularly "unconventional" as one of the accused was a legal person, making it international criminal law's first case with an accused who is not a natural person.[311] Although acquitted of one charge, Ms. Khayat, the Deputy Head of News and Political Programs of the company, was found to have deliberately violated the Court's order.[312] Judge Lettieri found the company not guilty of both charges as neither Ms. Khayat's conduct nor that of Ms Al Bassam, Head of News and Political Programs, could be attributed to the company.[313] Ms. Khayat was fined 10,000 euros in the sentencing judgment[314] and the decision is subject to an appeal by the Amicus Curiae Prosecutor.[315]

9.2.3 National Courts[316]

9.2.3.1 Bangladesh

The Bangladesh International Crimes Tribunal (BICT) continued functioning throughout 2015. Due to a decline in the number of pending cases, this year saw the reconstitution of Tribunal-1 and the status of Tribunal-2 changed to "inactive" on 15 September.[317] The BICT, which "is trying persons who allegedly collabo-

---

309 Ibid, para 1.

310 Ibid, paras 5 and 51.

311 Ibid, paras 1 and 55.

312 Ibid, paras 4 and 176.

313 Ibid, paras 179 and 190.

314 STL (2015) Sentencing judgment in the case against Ms Karma Al Khayat. http://www.stl-tsl.org/en/news-and-press/press-releases/4396-28-09-2015-sentencing-judgment-in-the-case-against-ms-karma-al-khayat. Accessed 12 May 2016.

315 STL (2015) Amicus Curiae Prosecutor Press Release. http://www.stl-tsl.org/en/news-and-press/press-releases/4398-29-09-2015-amicus-curiae-prosecutor-press-release. Accessed 12 May 2016.

316 Although it was already mentioned in the abstract of this article that this *Year in Review* cannot be comprehensive in scope, this goes *a fortiori* for the domestic context, where more and more cases on international humanitarian law and international criminal law are adjudicated. The current (domestic) section will therefore only select a few cases. Further analysis of national cases can be found at the T.M.C. Asser Instituut's International Crimes Database (http://www.internationalcrimesdatabase.org), where one will also find analysis of cases adjudicated by hybrid and international tribunals.

317 International Crimes Tribunal-1, Bangladesh (2015) About ICT-BD. http://www.ict-bd.org/ict1/indexdetails.php. Accessed 23 May 2016; The Daily Star (2015) One war crimes tribunal to be inactive from Sunday. http://www.thedailystar.net/country/icts-merge-sunday-137200. Accessed 23 May 2016.

rated with Pakistani forces who tried to prevent Bangladesh (then East Pakistan) from becoming an independent state",[318] has been criticised by groups such as Amnesty International.[319]

The Tribunal handed down several trial judgments throughout 2015, including convictions for the following: crimes against humanity for Mr. Moulana Abdus Sobhan,[320] Mr. Md. Mahidur Rahman,[321] Mr. Md. Asaf Hossain Chutu,[322] Mr. Syed Md. Hachhan,[323] Mr. Md. Forkan Mallik,[324] and Mr. Khan Akram Hossain;[325] and crimes against humanity and genocide for Mr. Md. Abdul Jabbar Engineer[326] and Mr. Sheikh Sirajul Haque.[327] On appeal, the Supreme Court upheld the death sentences of Mr. Ali Ahsan Mohammad Mojaheed, Mr. Muhammad Kamaruzzaman, and Mr. Salahuddin Quader Chowdhury.[328]

In addition to these convictions, the BICT also sentenced and carried out the sentences of a number of persons. Of those convicted in 2015, Mr. Sobhan, Mr. Hachhan, Mr. Haque, and Mr. Mallik were sentenced to death, although Mr. Hachhan remains a fugitive.[329] This year also saw the execution of three men.

---

[318] Paulussen et al. 2015, p. 194.

[319] Amnesty International (2015) Bangladesh: Two opposition leaders face imminent execution. https://www.amnesty.org.uk/press-releases/bangladesh-two-opposition-leaders-face-imminent-execution. Accessed 16 June 2016.

[320] BICT, *The Chief Prosecutor v Moulana Abdus Sobhan*, Judgment, 18 February 2015, Case No. 01 of 2014 (*Sobhan*), para 570.

[321] BICT, *The Chief Prosecutor v Md. Mahidur Rahman and Md. Afsar Hossain Chutu*, Judgment, 20 May 2015, Case No. 02 of 2014, p. 132.

[322] Ibid.

[323] BICT, *The Chief Prosecutor v Syed Md. Hachhan alias Syed Md. Hasan alias Hachhen Ali*, Judgment, 9 June 2015, Case No. 02 of 2014 (*Hachhan*), para 246.

[324] BICT, *The Chief Prosecutor v Md. Forkan Mallik Forkan*, Judgment, 16 July 2015, Case No. 03 of 2014 (*Mallik*), para 277.

[325] BICT, *The Chief Prosecutor v Sheikh Sirajul Haque alias Siraj Master, Khan Akram Hossain and Abdul Latif Talukder [now dead]*, Judgment, 11 August 2015, Case No. 03 of 2014 (*Haque and Hossain*), pp. 124–125.

[326] BICT, *The Chief Prosecutor v Md. Abdul Jabbar Engineer*, Judgment, 24 February 2015, Case No. 01 of 2014, paras 292–296.

[327] *Haque and Hossain*, above n 325, pp. 124–125.

[328] Sarkar A (2015) Bangladesh's apex court upholds capital punishment for Jamaat leader. http://www.thedailystar.net/frontpage/sc-upholds-verdict-98266. Accessed 23 May 2016; Felder B (2015) Bangladesh appeals court upholds death sentence for convicted war criminal. http://www.jurist.org/paperchase/2015/04/bangladesh-appeals-court-upholds-death-sentence-for-convicted-war-criminal.php. Accessed 23 May 2016; AFP (2015) Bangladesh upholds opposition politician's death sentence. http://tribune.com.pk/story/928471/bangladesh-upholds-opposition-politicians-death-sentence/. Accessed 23 May 2016.

[329] *Sobhan*, above n 320, p. 164; *Hachhan*, above n 323, pp. 123–124; *Haque and Hossain*, above n 325, p. 131; *Mallik*, above n 324, p. 98.

Mr. Kamaruzzaman, who had been a high ranking official in the Jamaat-e-Islami party that had been found guilty of war crimes, was executed on 11 April 2015.[330] Similarly, following the rejection of mercy petitions, Mr. Mojaheed and Mr. Chowdhury, who were, respectively, members of the Jammat-e-Islami and Bangladesh Nationalist Party, were also executed in November.[331]

9.2.3.2 Bosnia and Herzegovina

The War Crimes Section of the Court of Bosnia and Herzegovina was very busy in 2015, confirming a significant number of indictments and issuing many decisions both at the trial and appeal levels.[332]

As reported in early January 2015, the War Crimes Section of the Court confirmed genocide charges, relating to the events in Srebrenica, against Dragomir Vasic.[333] Mr. Vasic is currently a member of parliament in Republika Srpska and was a police commander in the 1990s.[334] In June, the Court handed down a decision in which it awarded compensation to a victim of war time rape for the first time.[335] The compensation was awarded as part of the verdict in criminal proceedings against Bosiljko Marković and Ostoja Marković who were also jailed for ten years.[336]

Following his arrest pursuant to a Serbian arrest warrant in Switzerland, Naser Orić was instead extradited to his native Bosnia and Herzegovina to face war crimes charges in July.[337] Mr. Orić, who was the former Bosnian Muslim commander at Srebrenica, had previously been tried and acquitted by the ICTY.[338]

---

330 Perez, E (2015) Bangladesh executed Islamist leader for war crimes. http://www.jurist.org/paperchase/2015/04/bangladesh-executes-islamist-leader-for-war-crimes.php. Accessed 23 May 2016.

331 Asia Times (2015) Bangladesh executes two opposition leaders for 1971 war crimes. http://atimes.com/2015/11/decks-cleared-for-execution-of-2-war-criminals-in-bangladesh/. Accessed 23 May 2016.

332 For further information, see the Court of Bosnia and Herzegovina (2015) News. http://www.sudbih.gov.ba/kategorija/vijesti-1/1. Accessed 23 May 2016.

333 Howell V (2015) Bosnia court indicts Serb politician for genocide. http://www.jurist.org/paperchase/2015/01/bosnia-court-indicts-serb-politician-for-genocide.php. Accessed 26 May 2016.

334 Ibid.

335 Zuvela M (2015) Bosnian court grants first ever compensation to wartime rape victim. http://www.reuters.com/article/us-bosnia-warcrimes-rape-idUSKBN0P427I20150624. Accessed 26 May 2016.

336 Ibid.

337 AFP (2015) Srebrenica Muslim commander charged with war crimes. https://www.yahoo.com/news/srebenica-muslim-commander-charged-war-crimes-233132762.html?ref=gs. Accessed 26 May 2016.

338 ICTY, *Prosecutor v Naser Orić*, Judgement, 3 July 2008, Case No. IT-03-68-A, p. 64.

He pleaded not guilty to the Bosnian charges in August, which concern the alleged mistreatment and killing of Serbian prisoners of war.[339]

9.2.3.3 Central African Republic

In April 2015, the government of the CAR voted to establish a Special Criminal Court.[340] This Court is expected to deal with "the atrocities committed during recent unrest in the country which has left thousands dead and many more displaced".[341] It will consist of 27 judges, 13 of whom shall be international and 14 shall come from the CAR.[342] Human Rights Watch advocated for this Court, arguing that it would help fight impunity in the CAR, that its maximum sentence of life imprisonment would be a positive move away from the death penalty, and that it would assist victims.[343]

9.2.3.4 Croatia

In May, a law that compensates war time rape victims was passed in Croatia.[344] Victims from the 1991–1995 war will receive a one-off payment as well as a monthly allowance, medical aid, legal assistance, and counselling.[345] The law will take effect from January 2016.[346]

9.2.3.5 Germany

In September, two Rwandans, who were charged with 26 counts of crimes against humanity and 39 counts of war crimes, were sentenced to 13 years' and eight

[339] Helbling W (2015) Former Bosnian general pleads not guilty of war crimes. http://www.jurist.org/paperchase/2015/10/former-bosnia-general-pleads-not-guilty-for-war-crimes.php. Accessed 26 May 2016.

[340] Snyder P (2015) Central African Republic government establishes special criminal court. http://www.jurist.org/paperchase/2015/04/central-african-republic-government-establishes-special-criminal-court.php. Accessed 23 May 2016.

[341] Ibid.

[342] Ibid.

[343] Human Rights Watch (2015) Why a Special Criminal Court for the Central African Republic Deserves Your Support. https://www.hrw.org/news/2015/02/20/why-special-criminal-court-central-african-republic-deserves-your-support. Accessed 24 May 2016.

[344] Gillan T (2015) Croatia approves law to compensate war rape victims. http://www.jurist.org/paperchase/2015/05/croatia-approves-law-to-compensate-war-rape-victims.php. Accessed 26 May 2016.

[345] Radosavljevic Z (2015) Croatia passes law to compensate war rape victims. http://uk.reuters.com/article/uk-croatia-rape-idUKKBN0OE1M820150529. Accessed 26 May 2016.

[346] Gillan, above n 344.

years' imprisonment respectively.[347] The men, Ignance Murwanashyaka and Straton Musoni, are the leader and deputy leader of the Democratic Forces for the Liberation of Rwanda and were accused of "masterminding massacres in eastern Democratic Republic of the Congo from their homes in Germany" where they had lived for over 20 years.[348] The convictions were the first under a German law that permits the investigation and prosecution of war crimes, crimes against humanity, and genocide regardless of where the acts occur.[349]

9.2.3.6 Guatemala

The retrial of General Efraín Ríos Montt, Guatemala's former head of State, commenced in January 2015 but encountered a series of hurdles due to missing records and the poor health of the accused.[350] Mr. Montt and his co-accused, Mr. José Mauricio Rodríguez Sánchez, are charged with genocide and crimes against humanity that were allegedly committed in 1982 and 1983.[351] Mr. Montt's health and his fitness to stand trial were ongoing issues in 2015,[352] and the Court

[347] Millar L (2015) German court convicts Rwandan rebel leaders over mass murder, rape in landmark trial. http://www.abc.net.au/news/2015-09-29/german-court-convicts-rwandan-rebel-leaders-in-landmark-trial/6811798. Accessed 26 May 2016.

[348] AFP (2015) Rwandan rebel leaders jailed in Germany for war crimes. http://www.theguardian.com/global-development/2015/sep/28/rwandan-rebel-leaders-jailed-in-germany-for-war-crimes. Accessed 26 May 2016.

[349] Ibid.

[350] TeleSUR (2015) Guatemalan Genocide Retrial Begins, Then Suspended. http://www.telesurtv.net/english/news/Guatemalan-Genocide-Retrial-Begins-Then-Suspended-20150105-0010.html. Accessed 24 May 2016; MacLean E & Beaudoin S (2015) Eighteen Months After Initial Conviction, Historic Guatemalan Genocide Trial Reopens but is Ultimately Suspended. http://www.ijmonitor.org/2015/01/eighteen-months-after-initial-conviction-historic-guatemalan-genocide-trial-reopens-but-is-ultimately-suspended/. Accessed 24 May 2016.

[351] MacLean E and Beaudoin S (2015) Eighteen Months After Initial Conviction, Historic Guatemalan Genocide Trial Reopens but is Ultimately Suspended. http://www.ijmonitor.org/2015/01/eighteen-months-after-initial-conviction-historic-guatemalan-genocide-trial-reopens-but-is-ultimately-suspended/. Accessed 24 May 2016.

[352] See for example: Reuters (2015) Ex-dictator found mentally unfit for new Guatemala genocide trial. http://www.dailymail.co.uk/wires/reuters/article-3152883/Ex-dictator-mentally-unfit-new-Guatemala-genocide-trial.html. Accessed 24 May 2016; Beaudoin S (2015) Guatemalan Genocide Trial Scheduled to Reopen this Week Amid Growing Corruption Crisis. http://www.ijmonitor.org/2015/07/guatemalan-genocide-trial-scheduled-to-reopen-this-week-amid-growing-corruption-crisis/. Accessed 24 May 2016; Brailey T (2015) Guatemala court orders Rios Montt competency evaluation. http://www.jurist.org/paperchase/2015/08/guatemala-court-orders-rios-montt-competency-evaluation.php. Accessed 24 May 2016; and TeleSUR (2015) Guatemala: Court Suspends Dictator Rios Montt's Genocide Trial. http://www.telesurtv.net/english/news/Guatemala-Court-Suspends-Dictator-Rios-Montts-Genocide-Trial--20150818-0041.html. Accessed 24 May 2016.

ultimately heard evidence that he suffered from dementia.[353] On 25 August, the Court ruled that Mr. Montt's trial will go forward in January 2016 but that hearings will be behind closed doors due to his dementia.[354] Mr. Montt was determined to be fit to stand trial "but cannot be sentenced because he suffers from dementia".[355]

In another case, Pedro García Arredondo was found guilty of murder, attempted murder and crimes against humanity on 19 January 2015.[356] His convictions relate to the deaths of 37 people who passed away in a fire at the Spanish Embassy in Guatemala on 31 January 1980.[357] The individuals inside the Embassy had been indigenous rights and rural activists, and Mr. Arredondo "was found guilty of ordering officers to keep anyone from leaving the building as it burned".[358] He was sentenced to 90 years' imprisonment: 40 years for the siege at the Embassy and 50 years for the murder of two students.[359]

9.2.3.7 Nepal

In February 2015, Nepal established two commissions to address alleged crimes committed during the civil war that ended in 2006.[360] The Commission on Enforced Disappearances is designed to focus on the disappearances of over 1300 people who remain missing today and the Truth and Reconciliation Commission will focus on alleged crimes that occurred during the conflict.[361] Both Maoists and

---

[353] TeleSUR (2015) Guatemala: Court Suspends Dictator Rios Montt's Genocide Trial. http://www.telesurtv.net/english/news/Guatemala-Court-Suspends-Dictator-Rios-Montts-Genocide-Trial--20150818-0041.html. Accessed 24 May 2016.

[354] Malkin E (2015) Genocide Retrial Is Set for Guatemalan Former Dictator. http://www.nytimes.com/2015/08/26/world/americas/genocide-retrial-is-set-for-guatemalan-former-dictator.html?_r=2. Accessed 24 May 2016.

[355] Felder B (2015) Guatemala court: Former dictator can be tried, not sentenced. http://www.jurist.org/paperchase/2015/08/guatemala-court-former-dictator-can-be-tried-not-sentenced.php. Accessed 24 May 2016.

[356] TeleSUR (2015) Guatemalan Court Sentences Ex-Police Chief for Murdering 37. http://www.telesurtv.net/english/news/Guatemalan-Court-Sentences-Ex-Police-Chief-for-Murdering-37-20150119-0043.html. Accessed 24 May 2016.

[357] Ibid.

[358] BBC (2015) Guatemala ex-police chief sentenced over embassy attack. http://www.bbc.com/news/world-latin-america-30895524. Accessed 24 May 2016.

[359] TeleSUR (2015) World Responds to 90-Year Sentence of Guatemalan Police Chief. http://www.telesurtv.net/english/news/World-Responds-to-90-Year-Sentence-of-Guatemalan-Police-Chief---20150120-0019.html. Accessed 24 May 2016; BBC (2015) Guatemala ex-police chief sentenced over embassy attack. http://www.bbc.com/news/world-latin-america-30895524. Accessed 24 May 2016.

[360] Farone A (2015) Nepal forms commissions to probe war crimes. http://www.jurist.org/paperchase/2015/02/nepal-forms-commissions-to-probe-war-crimes.php. Accessed 24 May 2016.

[361] Ibid.

State forces have been accused of a variety of abuses, and both Commissions will have two years in which to finish their work.[362] In addition to the new Commissions, Nepal's Supreme Court struck down amnesty provisions in the law, the inclusion of which had been "widely condemned as a move to protect alleged perpetrators [… as] many […] still occupy positions of influence in the military and political parties".[363]

9.2.3.8 Norway

Sadi Bugingo, who was the first person to be convicted of genocide in Norway, had his conviction upheld in late 2014[364] and his sentence of 21 years' imprisonment confirmed in January 2015.[365] Mr. Bugingo was originally charged with, *inter alia*, genocide, complicity in genocide, conspiracy to commit genocide, and crimes against humanity, and he was convicted of genocide, being found "guilty of the killing of 2000 persons during three different attacks".[366]

9.2.3.9 Senegal

The trial of former Chadian dictator Hissène Habré commenced at the Extraordinary African Chambers in Senegal on 20 July.[367] Mr. Habré has denied charges, which concern his presidency from 1982 to 1990 in Chad, and does not recognise the Court, which was established by Senegal and the African Union.[368] He is accused of torture, war crimes, and crimes against humanity[369] but shortly

362 Sharma G (2015) Nepal sets up panel to probe war crimes amid cries for justice. http://www.reuters.com/article/us-nepal-human-rights-idUSKBN0LE18Y20150210. Accessed 24 May 2016.

363 Adkin R (2015) Nepal Supreme Court rejects amnesty for war crimes. http://uk.reuters.com/article/uk-nepal-rights-idUKKBN0LV0CE20150227. Accessed 24 May 2016.

364 AFP (2014) Rwandan loses genocide appeal in Norway. http://www.dailymail.co.uk/wires/afp/article-2876476/Rwandan-loses-genocide-appeal-Norway.html. Accessed 26 May 2016.

365 AFP (2015) Norwegian court upholds Rwandan genocide sentence. https://www.yahoo.com/news/norwegian-court-upholds-rwandan-genocide-sentence-111322260.html?ref=gs. Accessed 26 May 2016.

366 TRIAL (2016) Sadi Bugingo. http://www.trial-ch.org/en/resources/trial-watch/trial-watch/profiles/profile/1059/action/show/controller/Profile/tab/legal-procedure.html. Accessed 26 May 2016.

367 Brody R (2015) Hissène Habré's Day of Reckoning. https://www.hrw.org/blog-feed/trial-hissene-habre. Accessed 24 May 2016; Brody R (2015) Hissène Habré Set to Begin. https://www.hrw.org/blog-feed/trial-hissene-habre. Accessed 24 May 2016.

368 BBC (2015) Chad ex-leader Hissene Habre to be tried in Senegal. http://www.bbc.com/news/world-africa-31465670. Accessed 25 May 2016.

369 Cruvellier T (2015) For Hissène Habré, a Trial by Refusal. http://www.nytimes.com/2015/07/28/opinion/for-hissene-habre-a-trial-by-refusal.html. Accessed 25 May 2016.

after commencing, the trial was delayed until September 2015 as Mr. Habré's newly appointed defence counsel required time to prepare.[370] The trial resumed in September and continued with evidence from both experts, victims and witnesses.[371] It remains ongoing and is expected to conclude in 2016, following the final depositions from witnesses in December 2015.[372]

9.2.3.10 Serbia

Early in 2015, Serbia arrested eight former policemen who were accused of participating in the Srebrenica massacre in 1995.[373] These are the first arrests in Serbia in relation to individuals suspected of directly taking part in the events in Srebrenica in 1995 and the men allegedly killed over 1000 Muslim Bosniaks.[374] The suspects were indicted in September and have been charged with war crimes.[375]

Not long afterwards, the Organization for Security and Co-operation in Europe (OSCE) released a report in which it highlighted concerns with the Serbian approach to war crimes prosecutions.[376] The report suggests that factors such as the lack of access to evidence and witnesses as well as judicial errors have impacted upon the investigations and prosecutions of war crimes.[377] In December, the first ever draft National War Crimes Strategy was published by Serbia's Justice

---

[370] Brody R (2015) An Unexpected Delay for Habré Victims. https://www.hrw.org/blog-feed/trial-hissene-habre. Accessed 24 May 2016.

[371] Body R (2015) The Victims Testify. https://www.hrw.org/blog-feed/trial-hissene-habre. Accessed 25 May 2016; Brody R (2015) Sexual Slavery and Insults. https://www.hrw.org/blog-feed/trial-hissene-habre. Accessed 25 May 2016; Brody R (2015) Souleymane Guengueng Fulfills his Oath. https://www.hrw.org/blog-feed/trial-hissene-habre. Accessed 25 May 2016; and Brody R (2015) A Senegalese Merchant Testifies. https://www.hrw.org/blog-feed/trial-hissene-habre. Accessed 25 May 2016.

[372] Trust Africa (2016) Hissène Habré Trial before the Extraordinary African Chambers: December Hearings. http://www.ijmonitor.org/2016/02/hissene-habre-trial-before-the-extraordinary-african-chambers-december-hearings/. Accessed 25 May 2016; Sall F (2016) Hissène Habré Trial—Criminal phase to End in February. http://www.trustafrica.org/en/resource/news/item/3244-hissane-habre-trial-criminal-phase-set-to-end-in-february. Accessed 25 May 2016.

[373] Vasovic A (2015) Serbia makes first arrests of suspected Srebrenica gunmen. http://www.reuters.com/article/us-serbia-warcrimes-idUSKBN0ME0R120150318. Accessed 26 May 2016.

[374] Ibid.

[375] Farone A (2015) Serbia prosecutors bring charges against Srebrenica massacre suspects. http://www.jurist.org/paperchase/2015/09/serbia-prosecutors-bring-charges-against-srebrenica-massacre-suspects.php. Accessed 26 May 2016.

[376] Jones M (2015) OSCE: Serbia war crimes prosecution inadequate, incomplete. http://www.jurist.org/paperchase/2015/10/report-details-serbia-war-crimes-prosecutions-inadequate.php. Accessed 26 May 2016.

[377] Ibid.

Ministry.[378] The three main goals to be addressed include the following: "adequate punishment for those responsible for war crimes, justice for victims, and location of the bodies of the missing".[379]

9.2.3.11 Spain

On 9 April, Judge Pablo Ruz ruled that there was sufficient evidence to put 11 former officials of Morocco on trial for genocide.[380] The allegations concern the treatment of the Sahrawai people after the annexation of Western Sahara by Morocco, which occurred in 1976. Western Sahara is a former Spanish protectorate and the case was made possible through universal jurisdiction laws in Spain.[381] Judge Ruz requested the arrest and extradition of seven former Moroccan military and political officials in connection with an alleged "campaign of bombings, killings, disappearances and torture from the period of the war".[382]

In contrast, in October, the Spanish Supreme Court dismissed another universal jurisdiction case that focused on the aftermath of the genocide in Rwanda.[383] The Spanish universal jurisdictions laws had been altered to only permit cases to be heard in which there are Spanish victims or where the crime is committed on Spanish territory.[384] The case had accused 40 Rwandan officials of revenge killings after the genocide, and arrest warrants, charging the officials with crimes against humanity, genocide, and terrorism, had been issued in 2008.[385] While the October ruling terminates the arrest warrants against the 40 officials, 29 individuals may still be pursued if they travel to Spanish territory.[386]

---

378 Nikolic I (2015) Serbia to Adopt National War Crimes Strategy. http://www.balkaninsight.com/en/article/serbia-awaits-war-srimes-strategy-11-26-2015. Accessed 26 May 2016; Ristic M (2015) Serbia Unveils First-Ever War Crimes Strategy. http://www.balkaninsight.com/en/article/serbia-publishes-war-crimes-strategy-12-13-2015. Accessed 26 May 2016.

379 Ristic M (2015) Serbia Unveils First-Ever War Crimes Strategy. http://www.balkaninsight.com/en/article/serbia-publishes-war-crimes-strategy-12-13-2015. Accessed 26 May 2016.

380 Gall C (2015) Spanish Judge Accuses Moroccan Former Officials of Genocide in Western Sahara. http://www.nytimes.com/2015/04/11/world/europe/spanish-judge-accuses-moroccan-former-officials-of-genocide-in-western-sahara.html?_r=0. Accessed 25 May 2016.

381 Ibid.

382 Ibid.

383 BBC (2015) Spain dismisses Rwanda war crimes case against 40 officials. http://www.bbc.com/news/world-africa-34477883. Accessed 26 May 2016.

384 Farone A (2015) Spain top court dismisses Rwanda war crimes case. http://www.jurist.org/paperchase/2015/10/spain-high-court-dismisses-rwanda-war-crimes-case.php. Accessed 26 May 2016.

385 BBC, above n 383.

386 Ibid.

9.2.3.12 Sri Lanka

In December, the Sri Lankan government announced that a new court will be established to investigate alleged war crimes that were committed during the last stages of the civil war.[387] Chandrika Kumaratunga, the head of the Sri Lankan Reconciliation Unit, said that the court will not be internationalised but may receive "technical assistance" from the international community, and it is anticipated to be up and running in early 2016.[388]

9.2.3.13 Uruguay

On 19 May, President Tabare Vazquez signed a decree that established the Truth and Justice Working Group.[389] This commission will "probe human rights violations perpetrated from 1968 to 1985 as the government cracked down brutally on a leftist rebellion" and will investigate crimes against humanity.[390]

9.3 Arms Control and Disarmament

9.3.1 Conventional Weapons

Following the entry into force of the Arms Trade Treaty[391] (ATT) in December 2014, the ATT's geographical scope expanded in 2015, with the accession of the CAR and Mauritius, and through ratification by Barbados, Belize, Chad, Côte d'Ivoire, Dominica, Ghana, Liberia, Mauritania, Moldova, Niger, Paraguay, San Marino, Seychelles, Switzerland, Togo, and Tuvalu.[392] States Parties arranged two Preparatory Meetings (on 23–24 February 2015 in Port-of-Spain, Trinidad and Tobago; and on 6–8 July 2015 in Geneva, Switzerland) and the Third Informal

---

387 Reuters (2015) Sri Lanka to start up special court on alleged war crimes. http://www.reuters.com/article/us-sri-lanka-rights-idUSKBN0TK5E120151201#oMoXuYRtwrCrFbXz.97. Accessed 26 May 2016.

388 Ibid.

389 International Centre for Transitional Justice (2015) Uruguay to probe dictatorship crimes. https://www.ictj.org/news/uruguay-probe-dictatorship-crimes. Accessed 25 May 2016.

390 Lessa F (2015) Justice at a crossroads in Uruguay. http://www.aljazeera.com/indepth/opinion/2015/03/justice-crossroads-uruguay-150304101945537.html. Accessed 16 June 2016.

391 Arms Trade Treaty, opened for signature 2 April 2013, No. 52373 (entered into force 24 December 2014).

392 UN Treaty Collection (2016) Status of the Arms Trade Treaty. https://treaties.un.org/pages/ViewDetails.aspx?src=TREATY&mtdsg_no=XXVI-8&chapter=26&lang=en. Accessed 10 June 2016.

Consultation (on 20–21 April 2015 in Vienna, Austria) before convening for the first Conference of States Parties (CSP) on 24–27 August 2015 in Cancún, Mexico.[393] The CSP adopted various decisions aiming at operationalising the ATT, including the selection of Geneva as the seat of the ATT's Permanent Secretariat, the adoption of the rules of procedure for future CSPs, and the development of the reporting templates for the ATT's implementation and for arms transfers.[394] As reported by the Stockholm International Peace Research Institute (SIPRI), the volume of international transfers of major weapons increased by 16 % between the periods of 2005–2009 and 2010–2014, with the US, Russia, China, Germany, and France accounting for 74% of the total global volume of arms exports.[395]

From 13 to 17 April 2015, the Meeting of Experts on Lethal Autonomous Weapons Systems (LAWS), which is part of the meetings on the operation of the Convention on Certain Conventional Weapons (CCW), was held. Recognising the need for a clearer understanding of the defining elements of autonomous weapons, experts discussed various topics, including the state of play on autonomous weapons, the military rationale for autonomous functions in weapons systems, what constitutes meaningful human control, dual use characteristics of technology, legal responsibility for actions of autonomous systems, regulations regarding civilian autonomous technology, and implications of autonomous weapons for international humanitarian law.[396]

In September 2015, Human Rights Watch released its Cluster Munition Monitor 2015, reviewing the status and operation of the Convention on Cluster Munitions and the use of cluster munitions during the last five years (2010–2014).[397] It reported that cluster munitions had been used during 2015 in Libya, Sudan, Syria, Ukraine, and Yemen (in the latter by forces of the Saudi Arabia-led coalition), causing harm to civilians.[398] None of the aforementioned States are signatory to the Convention on Cluster Munitions. Similarly, in November 2015, the Landmine Monitor 2015 was published, which reviewed the practice in the last five years (2010–2014) on the status and operation of the Ottawa Convention on

---

393 UN Office for Disarmament Affairs (2015) First Conference of States Parties to the Arms Trade Treaty. https://www.un.org/disarmament/convarms/att/csp1/. Accessed 2 June 2016.

394 Bauer S and Mark Bromley M (2015) 'Rules of the Road' for the Arms Trade Treaty agreed in Cancun but stiffer tests lie ahead. http://www.sipri.org/media/expert-comments/bromley-aug-2015. Accessed 2 June 2016.

395 Stockholm International Peace Research Institute (2015) Yearbook. http://www.sipri.org/yearbook/2015. Accessed 2 June 2016.

396 UN Office at Geneva (2015) Meeting of Experts on LAWS. http://www.unog.ch/80256EE600585943/(httpPages)/6CE049BE22EC75A2C1257C8D00513E26?OpenDocument. Accessed 2 June 2016.

397 The Monitor (2015) Cluster Munition Monitor 2015. http://the-monitor.org/media/2135498/2015_ClusterMunitionMonitor.pdf. Accessed 2 June 2016.

398 Ibid., p. 1.

Anti-Personnel Landmines.[399] Amongst the various developments, the Monitor reports that Oman, Poland, and Somalia made recent commitments on destroying their stockpiles of anti-personnel landmines, while Belarus, Greece, and Ukraine remain in violation of Article 4 of the Convention after failing to complete the destruction of their stockpiles within their four-year deadline.[400]

At the 70th Session of the General Assembly in December 2015, during the general debate on all disarmament and international security agenda items, the International Committee of the Red Cross (ICRC) made a statement that reflected upon progress made in advancing disarmament and the regulation of armaments. It addressed various developments and questions, including the need for States to make known their policy and practice on the use of explosive weapons in populated areas, and the need for States to consider respect for international humanitarian law and human rights law in their arms transfer decisions and to prevent the diversion of weapons as aimed by the ATT.[401]

During the Session, the UN General Assembly adopted numerous resolutions on matters concerning arms control and disarmament. On conventional weapons, it adopted Resolution A/RES/70/21 in which it reiterated its call upon UN Member States "to provide the Secretary-General, by 30 April annually, with a report on their military expenditures".[402] In another Resolution, the General Assembly encouraged the Secretary-General to pursue his efforts aimed at curbing the illicit circulation of small arms and light weapons (SALW),[403] encouraged countries of the Sahelo-Saharan subregion to facilitate the effective functioning of national commissions to combat the illicit proliferation of SALW,[404] and encouraged the collaboration of civil society organisations and associations in efforts to combat the illicit proliferation of SALW.[405] Furthermore, the General Assembly called upon all States to implement the International Tracing Instrument[406] by, *inter alia*,

399 The Monitor (2015) Landmine Monitor 2015. http://www.the-monitor.org/media/2152583/Landmine-Monitor-2015_finalpdf.pdf. Accessed 2 June 2016.

400 Ibid, p. 13.

401 International Committee of the Red Cross (2015) Weapons: ICRC statement to the United Nations. https://www.icrc.org/en/document/weapons-icrc-statement-united-nations-2015. Accessed 2 June 2016.

402 UN General Assembly (2015) Resolution adopted by the General Assembly on 7 December 2015: Objective information on military matters, including transparency of military expenditures, UN Doc. A/RES/70/21, para 1.

403 UN General Assembly (2015) Resolution adopted by the General Assembly on 7 December 2015: Assistance to States for curbing the illicit traffic in small arms and light weapons and collecting them, UN Doc. A/RES/70/29, para 2.

404 Ibid, para 4.

405 Ibid, para 5.

406 UN General Assembly (2005) International Instrument to Enable States to Identify and Trace, in a Timely and Reliable Manner, Illicit Small Arms and Light Weapons, UN Doc. A/CONF.192/15. http://www.un.org/events/smallarms2006/pdf/international_instrument.pdf. Accessed 10 June 2016.

including in their national reports the details of the national contact points and information on national marking practices used to indicate the country of manufacture and/or country of import.[407]

Concerning problems arising from the accumulation of conventional ammunition stockpiles in surplus, the General Assembly encouraged all interested States to assess whether parts of their ammunition stockpiles should be considered to be in surplus and appealed to all States to determine the size and nature of their surplus stockpiles of conventional ammunition, whether they pose a security risk, what their means of destruction are, and whether external assistance is needed to eliminate this risk.[408]

Turning to improvised explosive devices (IEDs), the General Assembly strongly urged States to develop and implement all necessary national measures to promote the exercise of vigilance by natural and legal persons in their territory or subject to their jurisdiction and that are involved in the production, sale, supply, and storage of precursor components and materials that could be used to make IEDs.[409] Furthermore, States were urged to fully comply with UN Resolutions, including those related to the prevention of the use and access by terrorist groups of materials that can be used in the making of IEDs.[410] The General Assembly also stressed the need for States to take appropriate measures to strengthen their own national ammunition stockpile management in order to prevent the diversion of materials for making IED to illicit markets and it encouraged the application of the International Ammunition Technical Guidelines.[411]

On the implementation of the Cluster Munitions Convention, the General Assembly urged all States outside the Convention to join as soon as possible, and to provide the Secretary-General with complete and timely information as required under Article 7 of the Cluster Munitions Convention.[412] Similarly, on the implementation of the Ottawa Convention, the General Assembly invited all States outside the Convention to ratify it or to accede it without delay and urged States Parties to provide the Secretary-General with complete and timely information as required under Article 7 of the Ottawa Convention.[413]

---

[407] UN General Assembly (2015) Resolution adopted by the General Assembly on 7 December 2015: The illicit trade in small arms and light weapons in all its aspects, UN Doc. A/RES/70/49, para 17.

[408] UN General Assembly (2015) Resolution adopted by the General Assembly on 7 December 2015: Problems arising from the accumulation of conventional ammunition stockpiles in surplus, UN Doc. A/RES/70/35, paras 1 and 2.

[409] UN General Assembly (2015) Resolution adopted by the General Assembly on 7 December 2015: Countering the threat posed by improvised explosive devices, UN Doc. A/RES/70/46, para 1.

[410] Ibid, para 10.

[411] Ibid, para 11.

[412] UN General Assembly (2015) Resolution adopted by the General Assembly on 7 December 2015: Implementation of the Convention on Cluster Munitions, UN Doc. A/RES/70/54, paras 1 and 4.

[413] UN General Assembly (2015) Resolution adopted by the General Assembly on 7 December 2015: Implementation of the Convention on the Prohibition of the Use, Stockpiling, Production and Transfer of Anti-Personnel Mines and on Their Destruction, UN Doc. A/RES/70/55, paras 1 and 5.

9.3.2 *Chemical, Biological and Nuclear Weapons and Their Delivery Systems*

In 2015, the question of chemical weapons disarmament remained in the foreground. After Syria's accession to the Chemical Weapons Convention[414] in 2013, there were still allegations concerning the weaponised use of chlorine in Syria. Furthermore, inconsistencies were found by the Technical Secretariat's Declaration Assessment Team of the Organisation for the Prohibition of Chemical Weapons (OPCW) in the declarations submitted by Syria, necessitating further consultation and fact finding.[415] The OPCW Director-General established the fact-finding mission (FFM) in mid-2014.

In February 2015, based on the early report of the FFM, the OPCW's Executive Council (OPCW EC) expressed serious concern[416] about the FFM's finding with a high degree of confidence that chlorine had been used repeatedly and systematically as a weapon.[417] These findings prompted the UN Security Council to adopt Resolution 2235 (2015), which established the OPCW-UN Joint Investigative Mechanism in Syria.[418] In this Resolution, the Security Council furthermore reiterated its condemnation in the strongest terms of any use of toxic chemicals, such as chlorine, as a weapon in Syria.[419] To ensure the success of the Joint Investigative Mechanism, the Security Council also called upon all States to fully cooperate with the Mechanism, and to provide it and the OPCW FFM with any relevant information.[420] The Resolution was welcomed by the OPCW EC, which also expressed its grave concern about the allegations.[421]

---

414 Convention on the Prohibition of the Development, Production, Stockpiling and Use of Chemical Weapons and on their Destruction, opened for signature 3 September 1992, 1974 UNTS 45 (entered into force 29 April 1997).

415 See for example, UN Security Council (2015) Letter dated 25 March 2015 from the Secretary-General addressed to the President of the Security Council, UN Doc. S/2015/211. http://www.securitycouncilreport.org/atf/cf/%7B65BFCF9B-6D27-4E9C-8CD3-CF6E4FF96FF9%7D/s_2015_211.pdf. Accessed 2 June 2016; and UN Security Council (2015) Letter dated 28 July from the Secretary-General addressed to the President of the Security Council, UN Doc. S/2015/572, http://www.securitycouncilreport.org/atf/cf/%7B65BFCF9B-6D27-4E9C-8CD3-CF6E4FF96FF9%7D/s_2015_572.pdf. Accessed 2 June 2016.

416 OPCW Executive Council (2015) Decision: Reports of the OPCW Fact-Finding Mission in Syria. https://www.opcw.org/fileadmin/OPCW/EC/M-48/ecm48dec01_e_.pdf. Accessed 2 June 2016.

417 UN Press (2015) Joint Investigative Mechanism Panel Visits Syria. http://www.un.org/press/en/2015/dc3597.doc.htm. Accessed 2 June 2016.

418 UN Press (2015) Security Council Unanimously Adopts Resolution 2235 (2015), Establishing Mechanism to Identify Perpetrators Using Chemical Weapons in Syria. http://www.un.org/press/en/2015/sc12001.doc.htm. Accessed 2 June 2016.

419 UN Security Council (2015) Resolution 2235 (2015), UN Doc. S/RES/2235 (Resolution 2235), para 1.

420 Ibid., para 8.

421 OPCW Executive Council (2015) Decision: Further Reports of the OPCW Fact-Finding Mission in Syria. https://www.opcw.org/fileadmin/OPCW/EC/M-50/en/ecm50dec01_e_.pdf. Accessed 2 June 2016.

In December 2015, as part of the operationalisation of the OPCW-UN Joint Investigative Mechanism, the UN and Syria signed a Status of Mission Agreement in which Syria agreed to provide support to the Mechanism to conduct its activities in accordance with UN Security Council Resolution 2235 (2015).[422] The Mechanism's mandate was to investigate the allegations of chemical weapon attacks in Syria and to identify the individuals, entities, groups, or governments who were perpetrators, organisers, sponsors or otherwise involved in the use of the chemicals as weapons in Syria.[423] Also in December 2015, the FFM submitted its full report of the facts regarding 26 incidents of alleged use of toxic chemicals, particularly chlorine, as a weapon between 2013 and 2015.[424]

At its 70th Session, the General Assembly stressed, in view of the allegations on Syria, the importance of fully verifying the Syrian submissions for their accuracy and completeness and urged all to the Chemical Weapons Convention to meet in full and on time their obligations under the Convention.[425] There were also allegations about the use of chemical weapons by non-State actors in the (civil) war in Iraq. In the summer of 2015, reports arose about IS fighters using mortar shells and rockets filled with chemical substances (confirmed as mustard agent in some reports)[426] in various clashes with Iraqi-Kurdish forces.[427] Furthermore, the OPCW revisited the agenda item concerning the destruction of declared chemical weapons by the possessor States at OPCW EC Sessions in March, July, and October 2015.[428] During these Sessions, the US, Russia, and Libya briefed the OPCW about the destruction of their declared chemical weapons, and Japan and

---

422 UN Press, above n 417.

423 Resolution 2235, above n 419, paras 5 and 6.

424 OPCW (2015) Note by the Technical Secretariat, Report of the OPCW Fact-Finding Mission in Syria regarding the incidents described in communications from the Deputy Minister for Foreign Affairs and Expatriates and Head of the National Authority of the Syrian Arab Republic, UN Doc. S/1318/2015/Rev.1. http://www.the-trench.org/wp-content/uploads/2016/01/OPCW-FFM-20151217-Syria-request-Rev1.pdf. Accessed 2 June 2016.

425 UN General Assembly (2015) Resolution adopted by the General Assembly on 7 December 2015: Implementation of the Convention on the Prohibition of the Development, Production, Stockpiling and Use of Chemical Weapons and on Their Destruction, UN Doc. Resolution A/RES/70/41, para 10.

426 BBC (2015) 'Chemical agent' traced in IS mortar fire, says US general. http://www.bbc.com/news/world-middle-east-34020268. Accessed 2 June 2016.

427 Vice News (2015) US Says Evidence Suggests the Islamic State Used Mustard Gas on Kurds in Iraq, 24 August 2015. https://news.vice.com/article/us-says-evidence-suggests-the-islamic-state-used-mustard-gas-on-kurds-in-iraq.

428 OPCW (2015) Report of the Seventy-Eighth Session of the Executive Council, Doc. EC-78/2. https://www.opcw.org/fileadmin/OPCW/EC/78/en/ec7802_e_.pdf. Accessed 17 June 2016 (Seventy-Eighth Session); Report of the Seventy-Ninth Session of the Executive Council, Doc. EC-79/6. https://www.opcw.org/fileadmin/OPCW/EC/79/en/ec7906_e_.pdf. Accessed 17 June 2016 (Seventy-Ninth Session); and Report of the Eightieth Session of the Executive Council, Doc. EC-80/4. https://www.opcw.org/fileadmin/OPCW/EC/80/en/ec8004_e_.pdf. Accessed 2 June 2016 (Eightieth Session).

China briefed the OPCW about the destruction of chemical weapons abandoned by Japan on the territory of China.[429]

In May 2014, Russia sent questionnaires to numerous States party to the Biological and Toxin Weapons Convention (BTWC) in order to enquire about their views on resuming negotiations on a legally binding verification protocol to the BTWC.[430] Consequently, questions surrounding the development and adoption of a verification protocol returned to the BTWC fora, including in 2015 at the Meeting of Experts and the Meeting of States Parties. Questions on this topic concerned, *inter alia*, whether such efforts should be pursued, especially in view of the need to also develop other instruments, and what could be potential alternatives.[431] Moreover, natural disease outbreaks and the security implications of scientific and technological developments remained important agenda items. Furthermore, the Report of the 2015 Meeting of States Parties established the arrangements for the Preparatory Meetings and the Review Conference to be held in Geneva in 2016.[432]

In 2015, the Review Conference of the Parties to the Treaty on the Non-Proliferation of Nuclear Weapons[433] (NPT) also took place. From 27 April to 22 May 2015, the delegates of NPT States Parties convened at the UN Headquarters in New York to review the operation of the NPT and the implementation of its provisions. Various Working Papers were submitted by States Parties.[434] States Parties, however, were not able to reach an agreement on a final document of the Review Conference, highlighting the increasingly diverging views between various States Parties. Furthermore, the US, Russia, France and China embarked on a process of modernising their nuclear warheads and delivery systems.[435]

---

429 Seventy-Eighth Session, above n 428, para 6.5; Seventy-Ninth Session, above n 428, para 6.4; and Eightieth Session, above n 428, para 7.5.

430 Lentzos F (2014) Workshop Report, Confidence & Compliance with the Biological Weapons Convention, Department of Social Science, Health & Medicine, King's College London & Geneva Centre for Security Policy. http://www.filippalentzos.com/wp-content/uploads/2014/11/BWC-workshop-report-NEW-web.pdf. Accessed 2 June 2016.

431 Guthrie R (2015) MX report 6, BioWeapons Prevention Project & CBW-Events. http://www.cbw-events.org.uk/MX15-combined.pdf. Accessed 2 June 2016; and Guthrie R (2015) MSP reports 1, 2 and 4, BioWeapons Prevention Project & CBW-Events, http://www.cbw-events.org.uk/MSP15-combined.pdf. Accessed 2 June 2016.

432 UN Office at Geneva (2015) Report of the Meeting of States Parties to the BTWC, BWC/MSP/2015/6. http://www.unog.ch/80256EDD006B8954/(httpAssets)/88768BCA419C9EF2C1257F8B004DBFB7/$file/BWC_MSP_2015_6_English.pdf. Accessed 2 June 2016, para 56.

433 Treaty on the Non-Proliferation of Nuclear Weapons, opened for signature 1 July 1968, 7 UNTS 161 (entered into force 5 March 1970).

434 UN (2015) Review Conference of States Parties to the Treaty on the Non-Proliferation of Nuclear Weapons (NPT): Working Papers. http://www.un.org/en/conf/npt/2015/working-papers.shtml. Accessed 2 June 2016.

435 Mecklin J (2015) Disarm and Modernize. http://foreignpolicy.com/2015/03/24/disarm-and-modernize-nuclear-weapons-warheads/. Accessed 2 June 2016.

In 2014, the US and Russia accused each other of violating the Intermediate-Range and Shorter-Range Nuclear Forces (INF) Treaty,[436] a treaty which bilaterally bans all ground-launched ballistic and cruise missiles with ranges between 500 and 5500 km. The allegations continued in 2015, with the US issuing a report stating that Russia continued to be in violation of the INF Treaty by testing cruise missiles.[437] The claim furthermore asserted that Russia was also violating the Open Skies Treaty by imposing new restrictions for unarmed observation flights over Kaliningrad.[438] In bilateral meetings, Russia made its counterclaim that the US Aegis Ashore Missile Defense System launcher is capable of launching offensive ground-launched ballistic or cruise missiles and is inconsistent with the obligations under the INF Treaty.[439]

Moreover, the date of 6 August 2015 marked the 70th anniversary of the atomic bombings of Hiroshima and Nagasaki. The events were commemorated in Japan with the annual vigil, attended also by international visitors (including the Executive Secretary of the Preparatory Commission for the Comprehensive Nuclear-Test-Ban Treaty Organization).[440]

In October, Iran launched a ballistic missile for testing purposes. It was a medium-range missile, capable of carrying a nuclear warhead. US officials responded by stating that the launch violated UN Security Council Resolution 1929 (2010).[441]

In December, Kim Jong-Un, leader of the Democratic People's Republic of Korea (DPRK), claimed that the DPRK had developed a hydrogen bomb and that it was ready to detonate one to demonstrate the country's capabilities. Internationally, the claim was received with scepticism from government officials and other experts.[442]

At its 70th Session, recalling earlier resolutions on taking forward multilateral nuclear disarmament negotiations and in view of the concerns about the catastrophic humanitarian consequences of any use of nuclear weapons,[443] the UN

[436] Treaty on the elimination of their intermediate-range and shorter-range missiles (Union of Soviet Socialist Republics and United States of America), opened for signature 8 December 1987, 1657 UNTS 2 (entered into force 1 June 1988).

[437] US Department of State (2015) 2015 Report on Adherence to and Compliance With Arms Control, Nonproliferation, and Disarmament Agreements and Commitments. http://www.state.gov/t/avc/rls/rpt/2015/243224.htm#Adherence. Accessed 2 June 2016.

[438] Ibid.

[439] Ibid.

[440] CTBTO Preparatory Commission Information Centre (2015) 70 Years After the Bombings of Nagasaki and Hiroshima. https://www.ctbto.org/press-centre/highlights/2015/70-years-after-the-bombing-of-hiroshima-and-nagasaki/. Accessed 2 June 2016.

[441] Reuters (2015) U.S. confirms Iran tested nuclear-capable ballistic missile. http://www.reuters.com/article/us-iran-missiles-usa-idUSKCN0SA20Z20151016. Accessed 2 June 2016.

[442] The New York Times (2015) Kim Jong-Un's Claim of North Korea Hydrogen Bomb Draws Skepticism. http://www.nytimes.com/2015/12/11/world/asia/north-korea-kim-hydrogen-bomb.html?_r=0. Accessed 2 June 2016.

[443] Vienna Conference on the Humanitarian Impact of Nuclear Weapons, 8–9 December 2014.

General Assembly decided to convene an Open-Ended Working Group (OEWG) in Geneva in 2016 to substantively address concrete legal measures that would need to be concluded to attain and maintain a world without nuclear weapons.[444] The OEWG will submit a report on its substantive work and agreed recommendations at the 71st Session of the General Assembly.[445] Furthermore, in follow-up to the 2013 high-level meeting of the General Assembly on nuclear disarmament, it also called for the urgent commencement of negotiations to conclude a comprehensive convention on the prohibition of nuclear weapons.[446]

In Resolution A/RES/70/24, the General Assembly urged all parties directly concerned to consider taking the practical and urged steps required for the implementation of the proposal to establish a nuclear-weapon-free zone in the region of the Middle East in accordance with the relevant resolutions of the UN General Assembly, and, as a means of promoting this objective, invited the countries concerned to adhere to NPT.[447] Pending the establishment of a nuclear-weapon-free zone, the General Assembly also invited all countries of the region to declare their support for establishing such a zone and to deposit their declarations with the Security Council.[448] Furthermore, all parties were invited to consider the appropriate means that may contribute towards the goal of general and complete disarmament and the establishment of a zone free of weapons of mass destruction in the Middle East.[449]

In order to renew determination towards the total elimination of nuclear weapons, the General Assembly reaffirmed the unequivocal undertaking of the nuclear-weapon States to accomplish the total elimination of their nuclear arsenals, leading to nuclear disarmament as enshrined in Article VI of the NPT.[450] To this end, and bearing in mind that the Chemical Weapons Convention (CWC) and BTWC have already established complete prohibitions on chemical and biological weapons, the General Assembly urged the nuclear-weapon States to immediately stop the qualitative improvement, development, production and stockpiling of nuclear warheads

---

444 UN General Assembly (2015) Resolution adopted by the General Assembly on 7 December 2015: Taking forward multilateral nuclear disarmament negotiations, UN Doc. A/RES/70/33, paras 2 and 5.

445 Ibid, para 7.

446 UN General Assembly (2015) Resolution adopted by the General Assembly on 7 December 2015: Follow-up to the 2013 high-level meeting of the General Assembly on nuclear disarmament, UN Doc. A/RES/70/34, para 4.

447 UN General Assembly (2015) Resolution adopted by the General Assembly on 7 December 2015: Establishment of a nuclear-weapon-free zone in the region of the Middle East, UN Doc. A/RES/70/24, para 3.

448 Ibid, para 5.

449 Ibid, para 9.

450 UN General Assembly (2015) Resolution adopted by the General Assembly on 7 December 2015: United action with renewed determination towards the total elimination of nuclear weapons, UN Doc. A/RES/70/40, para 2.

and their delivery systems, and, as an interim measure, to de-alert and deactivate immediately their nuclear weapons and to take other concrete measures to reduce the operational status of their nuclear-weapon systems.[451] Furthermore, the General Assembly urged the nuclear-weapon States to carry out further reductions of non-strategic nuclear weapons, including on unilateral initiatives and as an integral part of the nuclear arms reduction and disarmament process, and called for the conclusion of an international legal instrument on unconditional security assurances to non-nuclear-weapon States against the threat or use of nuclear weapons under any circumstances.[452]

Welcoming the discussions on the effects of a nuclear-weapon detonation that were held at the conferences in 2013 and 2014 in Norway, Mexico, and Austria, the General Assembly called upon all States, in their shared responsibility, to prevent the use of nuclear weapons, to prevent their vertical and horizontal proliferation, and to achieve nuclear disarmament. Furthermore, it urged States to exert all efforts to totally eliminate the threat of these weapons of mass destruction.[453] Additionally, in view of the humanitarian pledge for the prohibition and elimination of nuclear weapons that was endorsed by 120 States, the General Assembly urged all NPT States Parties to renew their commitment to the urgent and full implementation of their existing obligations under Article VI of the NPT and called upon all States to identify and pursue effective measures to fill the legal gap for the prohibition and elimination of nuclear weapons.[454]

On the question of non-state actors, the General Assembly urged all Member States to take and strengthen national measures to prevent terrorists from acquiring weapons of mass destruction, their means of delivery, and materials and technologies related to their manufacture.[455] Regarding existing nuclear weapons, the General Assembly called for a review of the nuclear doctrines, and for States to take urgent steps in reducing the risks of unintentional and accidental use of nuclear weapons, and requested the five nuclear-weapon States to take measures to implement this call.[456]

---

[451] UN General Assembly (2015) Resolution adopted by the General Assembly on 7 December 2015: Nuclear disarmament, UN Doc. A/RES/70/52, paras 6 and 7.

[452] Ibid, paras 9, 15 and 18.

[453] UN General Assembly (2015) Resolution adopted by the General Assembly on 7 December 2015: Humanitarian consequences of nuclear weapons, UN Doc. A/RES/70/47, paras 5 and 6.

[454] UN General Assembly (2015) Resolution adopted by the General Assembly on 7 December 2015: Humanitarian pledge for the prohibition and elimination of nuclear weapons, UN Doc. A/RES/70/48, para 3.

[455] UN General Assembly (2015) Resolution adopted by the General Assembly on 7 December 2015: Measures to prevent terrorists from acquiring weapons of mass destruction, UN Doc. A/RES/70/36, para 3.

[456] UN General Assembly (2015) Resolution adopted by the General Assembly on 7 December 2015: No first placement of weapons in outer space, UN Doc. A/RES/70/27 (Resolution 70/27), paras 1 and 2.

9.3.3 *Outer Space*

In August 2015 in Geneva, with support from China and the US, the UN Institute for Disarmament Research organised the 2015 Space Security Conference. Panels were held on topics such as national approaches to space security; space security in general international law, military, and civilian perspectives; and legal and diplomatic aspects.[457] In Resolution A/RES/70/27, the General Assembly reaffirmed the importance and urgency of the objective to prevent an arms race in outer space,[458] urging an early commencement of substantive work based on the updated draft Treaty on the Prevention of the Placement of Weapons in Outer Space and of the Threat or Use of Force against Outer Space Objects (as introduced by China and Russia at the Conference on Disarmament in 2008).[459] Additionally, the General Assembly called upon its Member States and relevant entities and organisations of the UN system to support the implementation of the full range of conclusions and recommendations contained in the report of the Group of Governmental Experts on Transparency and Confidence-building Measures in Outer Space Activities.[460]

9.4 Miscellaneous

9.4.1 *Initiative on Strengthening Compliance with International Humanitarian Law*

The initiative on strengthening compliance with international humanitarian law launched by the Swiss Government and the ICRC in 2011[461] drew to an end after States failed to agree on the new mechanism proposed to strengthen compliance with international humanitarian law.[462] The four-year process involved extensive consultations with States and resulted in a concluding report that included options and recommendations submitted by the ICRC and Switzerland at the 32nd International Conference of the Red Cross and Red Crescent of December

[457] UNIDIR (2015) Space Security Conference. http://www.unidir.org/files/publications/pdfs/space-security-2015-en-640.pdf. Accessed 2 June 2016.

[458] Resolution 70/27, above n 456, para 1.

[459] Ibid, para 3.

[460] UN General Assembly (2015) Resolution adopted by the General Assembly on 7 December 2015: Transparency and confidence-building measures in outer space activities, UN Doc. A/RES/70/53, para 7.

[461] See Paulussen et al. 2015, p. 214.

[462] ICRC (2015) No agreement by States on mechanism to strengthen compliance with rules of war. https://www.icrc.org/en/document/no-agreement-states-mechanism-strengthen-compliance-rules-war. Accessed 12 May 2016.

2015.[463] The proposal notably suggested the establishment of an annual Meeting of States Parties to the Geneva Conventions to serve as a forum for dialogue and cooperation, and a framework for periodic reporting.[464] Instead, an intergovernmental process was launched, to find an agreement amongst States on ways to enhance the implementation of IHL, the outcome of which is to be presented at the 33rd International Conference in 2019.[465]

9.4.2 The "Drone Papers"

In October, online newspaper The Intercept leaked national security documents on the US's use of drones for targeted killings.[466] The leaked documents revealed that, despite claims by the US administration that its drone strikes are precise, the methods used to identify and track targets are often flawed and lead to the killing of innocent civilians.[467] According to The Intercept, "nearly 90 percent of the people killed in airstrikes were not the intended targets".[468] Besides, the documents provided details on the approval process for drone strikes and showed that it might differ from official US policies; while the 2013 policy states that drone strikes can be authorised when there is near-certainty that no civilians will be killed or injured,[469] the leaked documents only refer to a low collateral damage environment.[470]

References

Books, Articles and Other Documents

Paulussen C, Dorsey J, Koulen S-J (2015) Year in Review 2013. In: Gill T et al (eds) Yearbook of International Humanitarian Law. T.M.C. Asser Press, The Hague, pp 147–216

[463] ICRC (2015) Strengthening Compliance with International Humanitarian Law: Concluding Report. https://www.icrc.org/en/download/file/10645/concluding-report-strengthening-compliance-ihl-icrc-06-2015-.pdf. Accessed 12 May 2016.

[464] Ibid.

[465] ICRC, above n 462.

[466] The Intercept (2015) The Drone Papers. https://theintercept.com/drone-papers/. Accessed 6 June 2016.

[467] Scahill J (2015) The Assassination Complex. https://theintercept.com/drone-papers/the-assassination-complex/. Accessed 6 June 2016.

[468] Ibid.

[469] US (2013) Policy Standards and Procedures for the Use of Force in Counterterrorism Operations Outside the United States and Areas of Active Hostilities. https://www.whitehouse.gov/sites/default/files/uploads/2013.05.23_fact_sheet_on_ppg.pdf. Accessed 6 June 2016.

[470] Currier C (2015) The Kill Chain. https://theintercept.com/drone-papers/the-kill-chain/. Accessed 6 June 2016.

UN General Assembly (2015) Resolution adopted by the General Assembly on 7 December 2015: Assistance to States for curbing the illicit traffic in small arms and light weapons and collecting them, UN Doc. A/RES/70/29
UN General Assembly (2015) Resolution adopted by the General Assembly on 7 December 2015: Countering the threat posed by improvised explosive devices, UN Doc. A/RES/70/46
UN General Assembly (2015) Resolution adopted by the General Assembly on 7 December 2015: Establishment of a nuclear-weapon-free zone in the region of the Middle East, UN Doc. A/RES/70/24
UN General Assembly (2015) Resolution adopted by the General Assembly on 7 December 2015: Follow-up to the 2013 high-level meeting of the General Assembly on nuclear disarmament, UN Doc. A/RES/70/34
UN General Assembly (2015) Resolution adopted by the General Assembly on 7 December 2015: Humanitarian consequences of nuclear weapons, UN Doc. A/RES/70/47
UN General Assembly (2015) Resolution adopted by the General Assembly on 7 December 2015: Humanitarian pledge for the prohibition and elimination of nuclear weapons, UN Doc. A/RES/70/48
UN General Assembly (2015) Resolution adopted by the General Assembly on 7 December 2015: Implementation of the Convention on Cluster Munitions, UN Doc. A/RES/70/54
UN General Assembly (2015) Resolution adopted by the General Assembly on 7 December 2015: Implementation of the Convention on the Prohibition of the Development, Production, Stockpiling and Use of Chemical Weapons and on Their Destruction, UN Doc. Resolution A/RES/70/41
UN General Assembly (2015) Resolution adopted by the General Assembly on 7 December 2015: Implementation of the Convention on the Prohibition of the Use, Stockpiling, Production and Transfer of Anti-Personnel Mines and on Their Destruction, UN Doc. A/RES/70/55
UN General Assembly (2015) Resolution adopted by the General Assembly on 7 December 2015: Measures to prevent terrorists from acquiring weapons of mass destruction, UN Doc. A/RES/70/36
UN General Assembly (2015) Resolution adopted by the General Assembly on 7 December 2015: No first placement of weapons in outer space, UN Doc. A/RES/70/27
UN General Assembly (2015) Resolution adopted by the General Assembly on 7 December 2015: Nuclear disarmament, UN Doc. A/RES/70/52
UN General Assembly (2015) Resolution adopted by the General Assembly on 7 December 2015: Objective information on military matters, including transparency of military expenditures, UN Doc. A/RES/70/21
UN General Assembly (2015) Resolution adopted by the General Assembly on 7 December 2015: Problems arising from the accumulation of conventional ammunition stockpiles in surplus, UN Doc. A/RES/70/35
UN General Assembly (2015) Resolution adopted by the General Assembly on 7 December 2015: Taking forward multilateral nuclear disarmament negotiations, UN Doc. A/RES/70/33
UN General Assembly (2015) Resolution adopted by the General Assembly on 7 December 2015: The illicit trade in small arms and light weapons in all its aspects, UN Doc. A/RES/70/49
UN General Assembly (2015) Resolution adopted by the General Assembly on 7 December 2015: Transparency and confidence-building measures in outer space activities, UN Doc. A/RES/70/53
UN General Assembly (2015) Resolution adopted by the General Assembly on 7 December 2015: United action with renewed determination towards the total elimination of nuclear weapons, UN Doc. A/RES/70/40
UN Security Council (2015) Letter dated 16 November 2015 from the President of the International Tribunal for the Prosecution of Persons Responsible for Serious Violations of International Humanitarian Law Committed in the Territory of the Former Yugoslavia since 1991, addressed to the President of the Security Council, UN Doc. S/2015/874

UN Security Council (2015) Resolution 2217 (2015), UN Doc. S/RES/2217
UN Security Council (2015) Resolution 2235 (2015), UN Doc. S/RES/2235
UN Security Council (2015) Resolution 2254 (2015), UN Doc. S/RES/2254
van Oijen F, Dorsey J (2016) Year in Review 2014. In: Gill T et al (eds) Yearbook of International Humanitarian Law. T.M.C. Asser Press, The Hague, pp 215–276

Case Law

BICT, *The Chief Prosecutor v Md. Abdul Jabbar Engineer*, Judgment, 24 February 2015, Case No. 01 of 2014
BICT, *The Chief Prosecutor v Md. Forkan Mallik Forkan*, Judgment, 16 July 2015, Case No. 03 of 2014
BICT, *The Chief Prosecutor v Md. Mahidur Rahman and Md. Afsar Hossain Chutu,* Judgment, 20 May 2015, Case No. 02 of 2014
BICT, *The Chief Prosecutor v Moulana Abdus Sobhan*, Judgment, 18 February 2015, Case No. 01 of 2014
BICT, *The Chief Prosecutor v Sheikh Sirajul Haque alias Siraj Master, Khan Akram Hossain and Abdul Latif Talukder [now dead]*, Judgment, 11 August 2015, Case No. 03 of 2014
BICT, *The Chief Prosecutor v Syed Md. Hachhan alias Syed Md. Hasan alias Hachhen Ali*, Judgment, 9 June 2015, Case No. 02 of 2014
ICC, *Situation on Registered Vessels of the Union of the Comoros, the Hellenic Republic and the Kingdom of Cambodia*, Decision on the admissibility of the Prosecutor's appeal against the "Decision on the request of the Union of the Comoros to review the Prosecutor's decision not to initiate an investigation", 6 November 2015, Case No. ICC-01/13-51
ICC, *The Prosecutor v Bosco Ntaganda*, Case No. ICC-01/04-02/06
ICC, *The Prosecutor v Bosco Ntaganda*, Decision on the recommendation to the Presidency on holding part of the trial in the State concerned, 15 June 2015, Case No. ICC-01/04-02/06-645-Red
ICC, *The Prosecutor v Germain Katanga*, Decision on the review concerning reduction of sentence of Mr Germain Katanga, 13 November 2015, Case No. ICC-01/04-01/07-3615
ICC, *The Prosecutor v Jean-Pierre Bemba Gombo, Aimé Kilolo Musamba, Jean-Jacques Mangenda Kabongo, Fidèle Babala Wandu & Narcisse Arido*, Case No. ICC-01/05-01/13
ICC, *The Prosecutor v Jean-Pierre Bemba Gombo*, Case No. ICC-01/05-01/08
ICC, *The Prosecutor v Laurent Gbagbo and Charles Blé Goudé*, Decision on Defence requests for leave to appeal the 'Decision on Prosecution requests to join the cases of *The Prosecutor v Laurent Gbagbo* and *The Prosecutor v Charles Blé Goudé* and related matters', 22 April 2015, Case No. ICC-02/11-01/15-42
ICC, *The Prosecutor v Laurent Gbagbo* and *The Prosecutor v Charles Blé Goudé*, Decision on Prosecution requests to join the cases of *The Prosecutor v Laurent Gbagbo* and *The Prosecutor v Charles Blé Goudé* and related matters, 11 March 2015, Case No. ICC-01/11-01/11-1
ICC, *The Prosecutor v Mathieu Ngudjolo Chui*, Judgment on the Prosecutor's appeal against the decision of Trial Chamber II entitled "Judgment pursuant to article 74 of the Statute", 27 February 2015, Case No. ICC-01/04-02/12 A
ICC, *The Prosecutor v Omar Hassan Ahmad Al Bashir*, Decision following the Prosecutor's request for an order further clarifying that the Republic of South Africa is under the obligation to immediately arrest and surrender Omar Al Bashir, 13 June 2015, Case No. ICC-02/05-01/09-242
ICC, *The Prosecutor v Omar Hassan Ahmad Al Bashir*, Decision on the request of the Republic of South Africa for an extension of the time limit for submitting their views for the purposes of proceedings under article 87(7) of the Rome Statute, 15 October 2015, Case No. ICC-02/05-01/09-249

ICC, *The Prosecutor v Simone Gbagbo*, Judgment on the appeal of Côte d'Ivoire against the decision of Pre-Trial Chamber I of 11 December 2014 entitled "Decision on Côte d'Ivoire's challenge to the admissibility of the case against Simone Gbagbo", 27 May 2015, Case No. ICC-02/11-01/12-75-Red

ICC, *The Prosecutor v Thomas Lubanga Dyilo*, Decision on the review concerning reduction of sentence of Mr Thomas Lubanga Dyilo, 22 September 2015, Case No. ICC-01/04-01/06-3173

ICC, *The Prosecutor v Thomas Lubanga Dyilo*, Judgement on the appeals against the "Decision establishing the principles and procedures to be applied to reparations" of 7 August 2012 with AMENDED order for reparations (Annex A) and public annexes 1 and 2, 3 March 2015, Case No. ICC-01/04-01/06-3129

ICC, *The Prosecutor v Uhuru Muigai Kenyatta*, Decision on the withdrawal of charges against Mr Kenyatta, 13 March 2015, Case No. ICC-01/09-02/11-1005

ICC, *The Prosecutor v William Samoei Ruto & Joshua Arap Sang*, Decision on Page and Time Limits for the 'No Case to Answer' Motion, 18 September 2015, Case No. ICC-01/09-01/11-1970

ICC, *The Prosecutor v William Samoei Ruto & Joshua Arap Sang*, Public redacted version of: Decision on Defence Applications for Judgments of Acquittal, 5 April 2016, Case No. ICC-01/09-01/11-2027-Red

ICC, *The Prosecutor v William Samoei Ruto & Joshua Arap Sang*, Public redacted version of: Decision on Prosecution Request for Admission of Prior Recorded Testimony, 19 August 2015, Case No. ICC-01/09-01/11-1938-Red-Corr

ICTR, *The Prosecutor v Pauline Nyiramasuhuko, Arsène Shalom Ntahobali, Sylvain Nsabimana, Alphonse Nteziryayo, Joseph Kanyabashi and Élie Ndayambaje*, Judgement, 14 December 2015, Case No. ICTR-98-42-A

ICTY, *Prosecutor v Jovica Stanišić & Franko Simatović*, Judgement, 9 December 2015, Case No. IT-03-69-A

ICTY, *Prosecutor v Naser Orić*, Judgement, 3 July 2008, Case No. IT-03-68-A

ICTY, *Prosecutor v Vujadin Popović, Ljubiša Beara, Drago Nikolić, Radivoje Miletić & Vinko Pandurević*, Judgement, 30 January 2015, Case No. IT-05-88-A

ICTY, *Prosecutor v Zdravko Tolimir*, Judgement, 8 April 2015, Case No. IT-05-88/2-A

MICT, *Prosecutor v Jean Uwinkindi*, Decision on Uwinkindi's Request for Revocation, 22 October 2015, Case No. MICT-12-25-R14.1

MICT, *Prosecutor v Milan Lukić*, Decision on Milan Lukić's Application for Review, 7 July 2015, Case No. MICT-13-52-R.1

MICT, *Prosecutor v Milan Lukić*, Decision on Prosecutor's Motion to Strike Milan Lukić's Notice of Appeal of Decision on Application for Review, 13 November 2015, Case No. MICT-13-52-R.1

MICT, *Prosecutor v Sreten Lukić*, Decision on Sreten Lukić's Application for Review, 8 July 2015, Case No. MICT-14-67-R.1

STL, *In the Case against Akhbar Beirut S.A.L. and Ibrahim Mohamed Al Amin*, Case No. STL-14-06

STL, *In the Case against Akhbar Beirut S.A.L. and Ibrahim Mohamed Al Amin*, Decision on Interlocutory Appeal Concerning Personal Jurisdiction in Contempt Proceedings, 23 January 2015, Case No. STL-14-06/PT/AP/AR126.1

STL, *In the Case against Al Jadeed [CO.] S.A.L./NEW T.V. S.A.L (N.T.V.) and Karma Mohamed Tahsin Al Khayat*, Case No. STL-14-05

STL, *In the Case against Al Jadeed [CO.] S.A.L./NEW T.V. S.A.L (N.T.V.) and Karma Mohamed Tahsin Al Khayat*, Public Redacted Version of Judgment, 18 September 2015, Case No. STL-14-05/T/CJ

STL, *The Prosecutor v Salim Jamil Ayyash, Mustafa Amine Badreddine, Hassan Habib Mehri, Hussein Hassan Oneissi & Assad Hassan Sabra*, Case No. STL-11-01

Treaties

Arms Trade Treaty, opened for signature 2 April 2013, No. 52373 (entered into force 24 December 2014)

Convention on the Prohibition of the Development, Production, Stockpiling and Use of Chemical Weapons and on their Destruction, opened for signature 3 September 1992, 1974 UNTS 45 (entered into force 29 April 1997)

Treaty on the elimination of their intermediate-range and shorter-range missiles (Union of Soviet Socialist Republics and United States of America), opened for signature 8 December 1987, 1657 UNTS 2 (entered into force 1 June 1988)

Treaty on the Non-Proliferation of Nuclear Weapons, opened for signature 1 July 1968, 7 UNTS 161 (entered into force 5 March 1970)

Table of Cases

INTERNATIONAL

Ad Hoc Arbitration

European Court of Human Rights

Inter-American Commission on Human Rights

International Court of Justice

T.D. Gill et al. (eds.), *Yearbook of International Humanitarian Law 2015*,
Yearbook of International Humanitarian Law 18,
DOI 10.1007/978-94-6265-141-8

International Criminal Court

International Criminal Tribunal for the Former Yugoslavia

International Criminal Tribunal for Rwanda

Mechanism for International Criminal Tribunals

Nuremberg Military Tribunal

Permanent Court of International Justice

Special Court for Sierra Leone

Special Tribunal for Lebanon

NATIONAL

Bangladesh

International Crimes Tribunal

Bosnia and Herzegovina

War Crimes Section of the Court of Bosnia and Herzegovina

Cambodia

Canada

Congo Democratic Republic

Germany

Guatemala

Israel

Italy

Kosovo

Norway

Rwanda

Senegal

Spain

United Kingdom

United States

Index

T.D. Gill et al. (eds.), *Yearbook of International Humanitarian Law 2015*,
Yearbook of International Humanitarian Law 18,
DOI 10.1007/978-94-6265-141-8

T

U

V

FSC
www.fsc.org
MIX
Papier | Fördert gute Waldnutzung
FSC® C083411

Kolibri 360 GmbH
Ferdinand-Jühlke-Straße 7
99095 Erfurt, Deutschland
produktsicherheit@kolibri360.de